Nourishing Meals

Nourishing Meals

*Healthy Gluten-Free Recipes
for the Whole Family*

Alissa Segersten
Tom Malterre, MS, CN

WHOLE LIFE PRESS

First Printing, August 2012

Published by Whole Life Press
Printed in the United States of America

Wholesale ordering:
Phone: **360-676-2297**
Fax: **360-671-5372**
Email: **orders@wholelifepress.com**

ISBN: 0-9798859-2-2   *11/12 4975 5852*

ISBN-13: 978-0-9798859-2-1

Library of Congress Control Number: 2012942682

Cover Design & Interior Layout: Jessica Renner, Studiohatch **www.studiohatch.com**

Cover Photographs by Alissa Segersten

DISCLAIMER: This book is for educational purposes only and is not intended to treat or diagnose any health condition. Please seek professional help regarding any health conditions. The authors are not responsible for any adverse food or health reactions from any of the information and recipes contained herein.

This book is dedicated to
my Grandmother Marie
for nourishing my mother
so she could nourish me.

Alissa

This book is dedicated to
all parents who
relentlessly seek out
what is best for their children,
and to all children
who deserve an opportunity
to experience life to the fullest.

Tom

Table of Contents

Acknowledgements

Most importantly, I'd like to thank my five children for putting up with all of the recipe testing and computer work that went into this book. They helped taste test each and every recipe, clean the kitchen when it was a big mess, and sometimes helped with more than their fair share of house duties. I'd also like to put in a special mention to my oldest daughter, Lily, who prepared breakfast, lunch, and dinner many times when I was too busy writing.

Thank you to all of my recipe testers; your honest feedback was much appreciated. I'd also like to give special mention to a few people who tested nearly every recipe in this book: Mary Jensen, Linda Stiles, and my mom, Deb Segersten.

I'd like to thank my designer, Jessica Renner, for turning this massive manuscript into something beautiful and user-friendly; and my editor, Teresa Halfacre, for correcting my grammar, making sure all of my recipes were organized, and for helping me get my points across.

Finally, I'd like to thank my parents for being my constant cheerleaders; my mom for flying halfway across the country to help out so many times; my friend Jenna Anderson for her honest feedback in previewing some of the chapters; our personal assistant, Dot, for her constant work keeping our business and house organized; and Tom for collaborating with me on this project.

Alissa

First and foremost, I find it imperative to acknowledge Ali for her intuitive genius in creating and preparing new recipes faster than any human I have ever witnessed. Our children Lily, Grace, Sam, Ben, and Camille deserve medals for their patience while we worked through crazy schedules. HUGE kudos and thanks to our parents—you are our lifeboats! Thank you for coming out to help so many times while I traveled to medical conferences.

There are many researchers and clinicians that I would love to thank for inspiring me along the way but I'd like to give a special mention to a few. Bruce Ames for his eloquent theories on nutritional deficiencies. Dr. Don Huber and Jeffrey Smith for their diligence, intelligence, and wit in informing us all about the negative effects of GMOs. Dr. Stephen Genuis for bringing awareness to how environmental exposures and nutrient deficiencies are partnering to change our immune systems. The Autism Research Institute faculty, clinicians, and staff who are putting together the pieces of environment, genetics, and nutrition into the puzzle of neurological decline in our children. I would also like to thank the Institute for Functional Medicine for their thorough training in evidence-based medicine that looks at all facets of life to find nourishment.

Tom

Preface

When we began our nutritional counseling practice, Whole Life Nutrition, there were fewer cases of food sensitivities, allergies, and other childhood disorders. In recent years, we started to see more cases of ADHD, autism, eczema, nut and soy allergies, digestive disorders, gluten sensitivities, and seasonal allergies. We wanted to know why these conditions were rising so quickly, so we looked to science for answers.

We found many connections between our immune system and our environment. Toxins from our food, water, and air are damaging our body's ability to recognize food. We kept coming back to the need to eat a gluten-free diet rich in plants, especially cruciferous vegetables, for maintaining optimal health, preventing disease, and healing food allergies.

After a few years of recommending gluten-free diets, we noticed that many people were beginning to consume more processed foods, thinking that because it was gluten-free, it was healthy. This helped us to refine our education and cooking skills even further to help others remember that it is optimal to maintain a diet based off of organic whole foods and to leave the processed gluten-free products lining the grocery store shelves out of the diet.

Childhood is fleeting, and having the whole family in good health makes life more fun and enjoyable for everyone. We wrote this book to offer parents and caregivers a tool—useful recipes that are both healing and nourishing. Filled with over 300 whole foods recipes, this book sets a foundation for raising healthy, resilient children.

There is no one right way when it comes to diet. We all face unique health issues, requiring different diets at different times in our lives. The key is to remain open and evolve your current diet when you see fit. With this book, our hope was to offer a wide variety of recipes, from plant-based main-dishes to nourishing grain-free desserts, so that no matter what your current diet is, there is room for growth. Remember that implementing new dietary changes can be a process. It can take time for the brain and the body to adjust. This is okay; just going gluten-free can be a huge transition! It is important to set your own pace so you don't get overwhelmed.

We hope that this cookbook will provide an invaluable resource to support your family in health for years to come.

Introduction

We all want the best for our children. We want them to grow up into strong, healthy, capable adults, but our children face more obstacles to this than ever before, As of 2008, 1 in 88 children—1 in 54 boys—are afflicted with autism. With the current diet trends, by the year 2050, 1 in 3 adults born after the year 2000 will develop type II diabetes! ADHD rates are at an all-time high; childhood cancers are increasing; obesity rates continue to climb; and more and more adults and children are being diagnosed with food allergies and food sensitivities.

Many of us are looking for ways to nurture our children so they not only survive, but thrive in this world. Nourishing our children with real food—meals that are whole foods based and gluten-free—may offer them the best chance to thrive.

Humans are amazingly adaptable creatures that should be able to eat and flourish from what is in their environment—from high-starch diets to meat-based diets. But what if our environment is so out of balance that it can no longer support the healthy development of life? What if the majority of our food is so denatured that it no longer does what it is supposed to in the body? This is the time we live in right now—a time when corporate goals take precedence over human health and the health of our planet. Humans have, for tens of thousands of years, lived in small tribes or clans that worked with the land— honored it—because they knew that by supporting the land, they supported themselves. When we don't support and cultivate what gives us life, we contribute to our own demise and the degeneration of our species.

Consuming denatured, highly processed food full of chemical residues is the cultural norm these days, but realize that it is only very recently since this food system has been in place. It wasn't until the 1930's that we began getting heavily exposed to processed foods, so only a few generations have been around to experience the results of this radical shift. Our great grandparents ate seasonal whole foods—not altered in any way—and did not have the pollution we see today. With each generation, our diets became further and further from nature. Chemical agriculture became widespread after World War II. Natural and organic farming methods were replaced with the use of chemical fertilizers and pesticides. The 1950's saw a boom in processed foods mainly due to the invention of the supermarket. No longer did people go to the butcher for meat, the baker for bread, or the market for vegetables. Canned and packaged food was in! Our grandparents and parents got to ride the wave of resilience passed down to them from previous generations. They could handle a certain amount of processed foods and environmental toxicity without seeing as much of an effect on health as we see today.

Now our bodies are being subjected to more environmental chemicals than ever before, the consumption of highly processed foods continues to climb, and eating genetically engineered foods has become commonplace. This environment is changing the way our genes are being expressed, causing damage to our guts, creating chronic inflammation, and contributing to a rise in food and environmental allergies like we have never seen before.

True nourishment is possible when we educate ourselves about foods that heal and prevent disease. For many people, eliminating gluten from the diet can help heal the body by lowering inflammation, healing the intestines, and allowing for proper nutrient absorption—especially important for growing children and women who are pregnant or trying to conceive. An estimated 1 in every 133 people has celiac disease, though the total number of people reacting to gluten is much higher when you include the incidences of gluten sensitivities and intolerances. Gluten is ubiquitous in our food supply, and only by removing it 100 percent from the diet do we begin to heal from its adverse effects. It is easy to get on the gluten-free bandwagon and begin relying on processed gluten-free versions of old favorites, but this isn't what will bring about healing and long-term health, and can often perpetuate the cycle of being malnourished. It is important to work towards a diet that is full of healing whole foods.

By eating foods in their whole natural state, organic and GMO-free, we retrain our bodies to act in a way they are supposed to. Phytochemicals from fruits and vegetables signal our cells to produce more natural antioxidants. Healthy fats provide our cell membranes compounds to communicate with each other and keep inflammation in check. Complex carbohydrates from starchy vegetables and whole grains give us clean burning energy that won't raise blood sugar too quickly. Protein from grass-fed animals, beans, nuts and seeds gives us the building blocks to repair and build new cells—critical for someone healing from celiac disease and other nutrient-deficiency disorders.

Let us be grateful for the rise in food sensitivities because they remind us to get back to basics, to eat whole foods, to eat locally, and to eat a LOT of vegetables. They are reminding us to look towards the environment and realize that our immune system is working overtime to rid the body of toxins. They remind us that we are as much a part of the solution as we are part of the problem.

Foundations of Health

Why Whole Foods?

The definition of the word **whole** is a thing that is complete in itself. When we eat foods in their whole form we get all nutrients, carbohydrates, proteins, and fats in perfect balance. These compounds act synergistically to orchestrate all reactions in our bodies. When some nutrients are missing, the body cannot function properly, and when many nutrients are missing for an extended period of time, the body can become diseased. Obesity, chronic inflammation, food allergies, infertility, and many other diseases stem from the body being starved of essential nutrients lacking in a processed foods diet.

Food is a Signaling Substance

It is easy to lose sight of the reasons why we eat. We feel hungry and immediately think of calories—eating to fill up. The real reasons our bodies need food goes beyond the ingestion of calories. Food by nature, is a signaling substance.

The chemical composition of food, its vitamins and phytochemicals, send signals to our cells designating how the genes will express themselves; this means that every time we eat we tell our bodies which genes to turn on, and which genes to turn off. Did you know that there is more gene expression within two hours after eating than any other time of the day? This is the fascinating world of nutrigenomics, the idea that food is information not merely calories.

Processed Foods and Gene Expression

With this understanding of gene expression, it's not a leap to see that when you eat a diet of processed foods full of chemicals and devoid of nutrients, you may be telling your genes to turn on for certain diseases you are predisposed to. On the other hand, when you eat a whole foods diet rich in plants the opposite is possible.

Research has indicated that a plant-rich whole foods diet can communicate to your genes in such a way that can prevent and alter disease progression. For example, a child could have the genetics that would predispose him to type I diabetes. With a processed foods diet devoid in nutrients and high in gluten, dairy, sugar, and other non-food constituents, he could develop this disease in childhood. If this child was fed a gluten-free, dairy-free whole foods diet from the time he was in the womb, he would be more likely to never develop diabetes.

If you want to lower the risk of developing allergies and disease, then you can change the way your genes are being expressed by eliminating all processed foods and begin to consume a nutrient-dense, whole foods diet.

What Constitutes a Processed Food?

There is a lot of debate on what actually constitutes a processed food. In reality there is a continuum of processed foods ranging from naturally preserved foods, like home-canned tomatoes or frozen berries, to completely denatured foods, such as high fructose corn syrup. Foods that undergo minimal processing can still be very nutritious, such as extra virgin olive oil, virgin coconut oil, and raw apple cider vinegar. Highly processed foods include man-made pseudo-foods such as artificial sweeteners and hydrogenated oils. Processed foods often have non-food constituents added to them like bleaching agents, solvents, and alkalizing agents and are often fortified with synthetic vitamins. For the purpose of this book, **processed foods** refer to those that are highly processed: those that are entirely man-made or have had parts removed from them or added to them, such as the refining of corn into high fructose corn syrup, or the bleaching and enriching of white flour.

What's in a Chicken Sandwich?
Take an unassuming grilled chicken sandwich with lettuce, tomato, and melted cheese. Let's throw in a side of fries and a diet soda as well. Seems pretty straightforward, right?

What you don't see are the large amounts of chemicals used on the genetically engineered grains or the arsenic added to the feed the chicken ate, whose meat now contains those chemicals, and the antibiotics that were added prophylactically to its feed. You don't see pesticide residues on the lettuce and tomato; chemicals never before tested for human safety. You don't see rBGH, a genetically engineered hormone that was injected into the cows to produce more milk and is now in your cheese.

What about the toxic combination of artificial sweeteners and caffeine in your soft drink? It has neuroexcitatory toxins that can kill brain cells, cause migraines and joint pain. How about a little sodium acid pyrophosphate, to maintain color, or dimethylpolysiloxane, to prevent foaming, in your fries? Unfortunately these chemicals are in most seemingly "natural" fries when you dine out.

Let's not forget about the bun; not only is it made from refined wheat—white flour—that can be highly inflammatory, but it most likely contains a list of ingredients you can't pronounce. If you wouldn't keep a jar of some of these unpronounceable ingredients in your kitchen cabinet, then they don't belong in your diet.

Loss of Nutrients
Not only are many processed foods full of genetically engineered ingredients and unnatural chemicals, but they are high in calories and low in nutrients. A diet of processed foods essentially starves your body while at the same time causing weight gain as the body, in its innate wisdom, keeps demanding more food in order to get the necessary vitamins, minerals, fats, and amino acids.

When a food is processed, such as in processing brown rice to make white rice, many essential nutrients and fibers are lost for properly digesting the grain. Blood sugar spikes more rapidly because the fibers that slow down the release of sugar into the blood stream have been removed and the majority of vitamins, minerals, and phytochemicals present in the outer portion of brown rice are lost. For example, thiamine and biotin help to utilize blood sugar by bringing glucose into the energy powerhouse of the cell—the mitochondria—to be burned for energy.

One of the first vitamins discovered was thiamine, or vitamin B1. In the late 1800's a Japanese medical doctor made the connection between the disease beri beri and a diet consisting mainly of polished rice. Thiamine is found in the outer portion of rice—the bran, which is removed when brown rice is polished into white rice. This is just one of a thousand examples where nutrients get depleted through processing.

Eating refined, processed foods overtime can deplete the body of essential nutrients needed for it to function properly. However, eating something refined on a very occasional basis shouldn't cause much harm if the body is well nourished from a whole foods diet.

Healthy Whole Foods

Whole foods are naturally more calming and nourishing. A whole food is something you can imagine growing or living in nature like kale, chicken, eggs, fish, almonds, carrots, millet, olives, apples, strawberries, brown rice, or avocados. These foods have not been processed, enriched, or denatured in any way. They contain a perfect balance of nutrients, just how nature intended.

Basing your diet around whole foods and using small amounts of minimally processed foods like olive and coconut oils, whole grain gluten-free flours, and natural sweeteners, you'll most likely see a dramatic improvement in you or your child's overall health.

Eat a Plant-Rich Diet

A plant-rich diet is one that focuses on foods such as vegetables, fruits, whole grains, legumes, nuts, and seeds; animal foods, while very nutrient-dense, make up a lesser proportion. Compared to all other foods, plants provide the body with the most gene-signaling molecules.

In nature, form equals function. Plants package themselves in their whole forms for brilliant reasons—the tougher outer portions are barriers against potential threats such as oxygen, temperature changes, bacterium, fungi, or insects and contain important chemicals that act as natural antioxidants, microbial deterrents, and insecticides. It so happens that these very same plant chemicals have numerous beneficial effects in the human body. Phenols, such as catechins, ellagic acid, and tannins, as well as pectin and other soluble fibers, are protective against cancer with some even binding readily to heavy metals and radioactive particles in the environment, allowing for proper excretion from the body. When the outsides of plants are broken or removed during processing, many of these protective compounds are lost. When you base your diet on whole plant foods, you get an abundance of phytochemicals, antioxidants, vitamins, and minerals that signal your genes to keep the immune system calm and the body healthy.

The Importance of Organics

A review published in 2010 found organic foods to contain higher levels of vitamin C, iron, and magnesium, as well as more of the important antioxidant phytochemicals like carotenoids, flavonoids, and anthocyanins. The higher mineral level is logical considering that organic farmers continuously add organic material to the soil, which nurtures the fruits, vegetables, grains, and animals that eat them. If you converse with an organic farmer for just a few minutes, you will quickly learn how important soil quality is to them for higher yields, better flavor, and keeping insects and disease away. They all know that well-fed plants are naturally more disease and insect resistant.

Chemical Use Changes How Plants Behave

Conventional farmers often use chemical fertilizers, pesticides, herbicides, and fungicides that may persist in the soil and environment for upwards of 50 years. Not only do these chemicals get into the food we eat, but they enter into the water, air, and soil harming the delicate balance of insects, aquatic life, soil microorganisms, and other living things that surround the farms. This can change the ability of the crops to interact with their environment, including the soil microorganisms, insects, competitive plants, and other natural stressors. It turns out these interactions are important in forcing the plants to produce protective chemical compounds. Anytime you stress a plant it forces the plant to defend itself and become "stronger." For example, when the sun strikes a plant with UV radiation, the plant will produce natural sunscreens like **carotenoids and flavonoids**. When plants are exposed to insects that nibble on the leaves, they can produce natural insecticides such as **sulfurophane** found in the cruciferous family of vegetables. If these same cruciferous vegetables are conventionally farmed and periodically sprayed with pesticides they are not likely to produce as much of these natural chemicals.

Impact of Chemical Farming

These same pesticides are likely to negatively impact all those whom consume them whether they are insects or humans. And why wouldn't they? That is exactly what they are engineered to do. Research gathered in California found that children of mothers living within 500 meters of field sites using the highest levels of organochlorine pesticides had a 6.1 times higher risk for having autism. Numerous studies examining pesticide exposure of neonates have determined there is a greater negative impact on brain function and intelligence measures as pesticide levels increase. One study showed a lowering of IQ by 7 points by the age of seven in those with the highest exposures.

Organic is the Most Nourishing Choice

Children who eat a conventional diet are continually exposed to pesticides. In one study, urinary levels of two commonly used pesticides—malathon and chlorphyrifos, which have been proven to lower IQ scores in children—were measured in children before, during, and after they ate a 5-day organic diet. Pesticide levels were elevated before the organic diet, and when the children returned to a conventional diet the level of pesticides jumped right back up. During the organic diet, however, the urinary levels of these two pesticides were almost non-detectible.

Clearly, buying and eating organic food is of utmost importance in order to decrease the amount of chemicals we are exposed to—not only for our children, but for everyone living around the farms. Ideally, this should begin before a child is conceived as the preconception time and the last two trimesters of pregnancy are the most vulnerable times for chemical exposure. Plants grown in nutrient-rich soil contain more vitamins, minerals, and phytochemicals than their conventional counterparts. These nutrients keep our bodies functioning properly, help grow resilient children, and protect us against disease.

Why Gluten-Free?

Food is made up of thousands of large molecules that need to be broken down into smaller molecules in order to be taken into the body and be used for fuel, as facilitators of many reactions, or incorporated into cell structures. This process of digestion and absorption can be altered by numerous factors, one of which may be the food itself—such as gluten. All people react differently to the ingestion of gluten. For some, the reaction may be an IgE mediated gluten allergy and for others it is the tearing down of the intestinal lining otherwise known as celiac disease. Others can have adverse symptoms without tearing down the gut lining known as a gluten sensitivity reaction. And yet far too many people have a gluten-initiated leaky gut.

Some people feel the effects of eating something containing gluten immediately with bloating and digestive upset, where others have "silent" symptoms ranging from infertility to osteoporosis. For example, it is actually possible to have celiac disease and have no symptoms other than anemia. There are just too many possible ways that gluten can cause harm so even if you do not have a gluten sensitivity or celiac disease, your digestion and overall health may benefit from a gluten-free diet.

Common Symptoms of Gluten Intolerance

Digestive
- Abdominal pain
- Bloating
- Diarrhea
- Constipation
- Fat malabsorption
- Multiple nutrient deficiencies
- Irritable bowl syndrome
- Crohn's disease
- Ulcerative colitis

Skin & Hair
- Acne
- Dermatitis herpetiformis
- Eczema
- Hair loss

Bone
- Osteoporosis
- Osteopenia
- Dental carries
- Dental enamel defects

Endocrine

- PCOS
- Thyroid disorders
- Addison's disease
- Diabetes (Type II)
- Weight loss
- Weight gain
- Infertility
- Recurrent miscarriages
- Stunted growth in children

Autoimmune

- Rheumatoid Arthritis
- Diabetes (Type I)
- Lupus
- Lou Gehrig's Disease

Neurologic & Behavioral

- Peripheral neuropathy
- Depression
- Dyslexia
- Autism
- ADHD
- Migraines
- Loss of memory

Blood

- Anemia
- Easy Bruising
- Bleeding Gums

General

- General weakness and fatigue
- Chronic fatigue syndrome
- Restless leg syndrome
- Inability to lose weight
- Muscle cramping
- Joint pain

What is Gluten?

Gluten is a composite of proteins joined with starch found in wheat, spelt, barley, and rye. It is what gives the chewy structure to bread, or what makes noodles hold together while cooking instead of turning to mush. The two main groups of proteins are gliadins and glutenins. Once broken down into smaller peptides—or chains of amino acids—these proteins, specifically the gliadins, can elicit multiple responses in the intestines. They can cause the release of antibodies and inflammatory chemicals that lead to the destruction of the intestinal lining leading to **Celiac Disease**. They can also increase the secretion of inflammatory chemicals that disrupt local and systemic inflammatory balance without tearing down the intestines leading to what is known as **Gluten Sensitivity**.

Interestingly, oats contain a protein called avenin, which when broken down through digestion, has a very similar peptide structure to the gliadin proteins. This means that it can have a similar effect on the body as gluten in some people, especially those with celiac disease.

Why is it so Damaging?

Gluten—particularly the gliadin peptides—differs from all other foods in that its consumption activates immune cells and the secretion of **leaky gut** proteins such as zonulin. This can lead to a permeable gut for a short time after eating in *all* humans and animals. In other words, you don't have to have celiac disease or a gluten sensitivity to have a reaction from consuming gluten! This could pose a problem for children who eat gluten for breakfast, lunch, dinner, and snacks.

Normally, intestinal cells are bound to one another by tight junctions, which control what is allowed into the intestinal cells and what is not. When the barrier is permeable that regulation is lost and the contents of the intestinal tract, including bacterium and undigested food proteins, are allowed to pass through the intestinal barrier unchecked. This leads to an alert and alarm—or inflammatory—response from the local immune cells and may also contribute to an increase in sensitivities to those food proteins.

Intestinal Degradation

In people with Celiac Disease—or a genetic alteration in immune cell function—this permeable gut will be sustained for an extended period of time after eating and contribute to the vicious cycle of gliadin exciting the secretion of inflammatory cytokines by immune cells. This cycle leads to atrophy of the villi (the small finger-like projections of the upper intestines), or the tearing down of the lining of the upper intestines. Unfortunately, this can drastically alter both the digestive and absorptive functions that are normally carried out in the upper intestines.

In addition to celiac disease, there are many other factors that can lead to this intestinal degradation. Parasitic infections like giardia, dairy and soy reactions, small intestinal bacterial overgrowth, and adverse medication reactions may lead to destruction of the villi as well.

Nutrient Deficiencies

Without sufficient villi in the small intestine, many nutrients are not absorbed properly. This can have devastating effects on a growing child or a pregnant woman because the body has such a high demand for nutrients during those times. Vitamins such as A, D, B12, and folates; minerals such as iron, iodine, and zinc; amino acids such as tryptophan; and other nutrients like essential fatty acids rely either directly or indirectly on the upper intestinal tract working properly for their utilization by the body.

Cross-Contamination

Becoming gluten-free means gaining a deeper understanding of our food supply. We need to learn where our food is grown, how it is processed, stored, transported, and sold. Are our grains being processed in the same facility as wheat is processed? When I am buying bulk sea salt at my local co-op, is there a bin of wheat flour above it that could be contaminating the salt?

Since gluten is everywhere in our food supply, getting it out of the diet 100 percent can be quite challenging. Certain foods such as millet and lentils are usually cross-rotated with wheat or barley in the field. Have you ever taken a look into your lentil jar? Look closely and you will usually find a few whole gluten grains in it. If you don't remove them and thoroughly rinse the lentils, you run the risk of consuming small doses of gluten and never feeling fully well. All foods that require processing, however minimal it might be, run the risk of contamination if the facility being used also processes wheat or another gluten-containing grain or flour. This includes coconut flour, coconut sugar, and gluten-free flours. It is best to contact the manufacturer to determine if their facility is gluten-free.

Other sources of cross-contamination include, restaurants, grills, salad bars, cutting boards, wooden rolling pins, toasters, pizza stones, countertops, and bulk bins.

Gluten Cross Contamination in Food:

No Risk	Low Risk	High Risk
Fresh Meats	Shelled Nuts and Seeds	Oats
Fresh Eggs	Nut and Seed Butters	Millet
Fresh Vegetables	Dry Beans	Buckwheat
Fresh Fruit	Brown Rice	Lentils
Most Cheeses	Quinoa	Processed Foods
Cow or Goat milk	Amaranth	
Coconut milk	Teff	
Almond Flour	Sorghum	
Honey	Corn	
Whole Nuts and Seeds (still in the shell)	Coconut Flour	
	Gluten-Free Flours	
	Cane Sugar	
	Coconut Sugar	
	Rice Noodles	
	Oils	
	Vinegar	
	Yogurt	
	Spices	

Why The Rise in Food Allergies and Sensitivities?

N o one can argue against the fact that children these days have more food-related problems than ever before. The factors indicated in this rise of food allergies and sensitivities are widespread, from our food and medical culture to our environmental health.

Wheat has been hybridized over the years for a high gluten content. Large scale conventional farming presides over organic farming. Genetically modified foods pervade our marketplace. Nutrient deficiencies are increasing. Antibiotics are overused. Fossil fuel use results in environmental toxicity. These practices reduce the nutrient content of food while invading the body with foreign substances resulting in an imbalanced gut and an over reactive immune system.

Common Symptoms of a Food Allergy or Sensitivity

Food Allergy
- Skin Issues (eczema, swelling, hives)
- Respiratory problems (wheezing, swelling of the throat, repetitive cough)
- Eyes (itching, watering, swelling)
- Gastrointestinal (nausea, vomiting, diarrhea, abdominal pain)
- Anaphylaxis

Food Sensitivity
- Skin Issues (acne, eczema, rashes, hives)
- Behavior Problems (hyperactivity, violence, moodiness)
- Sleep Disturbances (trouble falling asleep or staying asleep)
- Stomach Pains (gas, nausea, bloating, abdominal pain)
- Gastrointestinal (diarrhea, constipation)

Potential Causes of Food Allergies and Sensitivities

When the body launches an attack against a food or something found in the environment like pollen or pet dander, the immune system is reacting to a particular protein structure. The casein protein in cow's milk, some 15 different proteins in soy, albumen in eggs, and certain peptide chains in peanuts are at the root of the reaction. It is also theorized that it is not just these proteins that are causing the reaction, but rather certain starches that attach themselves to the protein and change the shape of the protein making them unrecognizable to the body. There are many things that can damage our ability to properly digest, absorb, and recognize foods as friends rather than foes, these are:

- Environmental toxins damaging the immune system
- Chronic Inflammation
- Overuse of antibiotics
- Overuse of non-steroidal anti-inflammatory drugs
- Leaky gut syndrome
- Low stomach acid
- Pancreatic enzyme insufficiency
- Not Breastfeeding
- Deficiency of key nutrients for normalizing immune response
- A diet high in processed, denatured foods, and refined sugars
- Increase in consumption of reactive foods like gluten, dairy, and soy
- Genetically modified foods
- Increase in stress

Environmental Toxicity

The primary job of the immune system is tolerance, or recognizing what is *not* foreign and leaving it alone. Our immune cells are constantly coming into contact with other molecules, cells, and organisms. It is their job to determine what is friend and what is foe. These days, our immune systems are constantly being bombarded with environmental toxins from those found in cleaning supplies and building materials to toxins found in foods consumed everyday.

Many children have what is described as a **toxicant-induced loss of tolerance** or TILT, meaning that their bodies are continually being exposed to certain chemicals from the home, environment, or food and they reach a point where they cannot tolerate them anymore. Their bodies begins to malfunction, and conditions of acquired allergy, food intolerance, and chemical hypersensitivity frequently result. This means that they can become sensitive to low levels of diverse and unrelated triggers in their environment such as commonly encountered chemicals, inhalants, or food antigens.

Toxins in Food
The highest amounts of chemicals in food are found in organ meats and the fats from animals. The pesticide DDT with a 50 year half life, PCBs from electrical transformers, PBDEs from flame retardants, and arsenic from animal feed and treated wood are just a few toxic chemicals that bioaccumulate in animal tissues, even organic pastured animals. These chemicals have been associated with asthma, cancer, and thyroid disorders. Arsenic in particular can cause immune system dysfunction, infertility, irritation of the stomach and intestines, and a decrease in white blood cells. This is one of the main reasons we advocate a diet revolving around organic whole plant foods.

Other food sources of chemicals include conventionally grown fruits and vegetables such as apples, grapes, celery, strawberries, bell peppers, peaches, spinach, potatoes, blueberries, raspberries, lettuce, and kale. The chemicals commonly sprayed on these foods include glyphosate (Roundup), chlorpyrifos, malathion, and endosulfan. These chemicals disrupt reproductive function, immune function, and mitochondrial function causing symptoms such as infertility, food allergies, learning disabilities, loss of coordination, neurologic problems, poor growth, and gastrointestinal disorders including low gastric acid secretion.

Chronic Inflammation

When you get injured or get an infection like the common cold, the immune system is triggered and a chain of events occurs, called the **inflammatory cascade**. The familiar signs of normal inflammation—heat, pain, redness, and swelling—are the first signals that your immune system is being called into action. These pro-inflammatory compounds signal white blood cells to do their job and clear out the infection or damaged tissue. Once the threat is neutralized, equally powerful anti-inflammatory compounds come in to begin the healing process. This ebb and flow between pro and anti-inflammatory compounds keeps the body healthy, but what happens when chronic inflammation occurs?

The Master Switch of Inflammation

The "master switch" that turns on the immune system's alert and alarm signals—or inflammation—is called **Nuclear Factor Kappa Beta** or NFkB. When levels of NFkB increase, hundreds of pro-inflammatory chemicals are turned on. When these pro-inflammatory chemicals don't turn off, the risk for every inflammatory disease increases, including heart disease, diabetes, arthritis, and irritable bowel disease. In one study, a fast food egg and sausage breakfast muffin with two hashbrowns was shown to cause a dramatic spike—a 500% increase—in the production of this master switch of inflammation shortly after eating this meal.

Which Foods Cause Inflammation?

Pro-inflammatory foods, or foods that contribute to inflammation, are polyunsaturated vegetable oils, meat from grain-fed animals, char-broiled meats, pasteurized cow's milk, sugar, and other highly refined starchy foods. Most vegetable oils like peanut, safflower, sunflower, corn, and soy, are high in linoleic acid, an omega-6 essential fatty acid that the body may convert into arachidonic acid, which has a predominantly pro-inflammatory effect. Grain-fed animals produce a high amount of arachidonic acid in their tissues. In contrast, grass-fed animals and wild cold-water fish contain a high level of omega-3 fatty acids—or anti-inflammatory compounds. It is hypothesized that our prehistoric ancestors ate a diet with an omega-6 to omega-3 ratio of 1:1. Our current ratio is anywhere between 10:1 and 25:1!

Refined sugar and other refined starchy foods with a high glycemic index raise insulin levels and put the immune system into an "alert and alarm" mode. This is because short-lived hormones inside our cells called eicosanoids act as either pro or anti-inflammatory compounds depending on their type. When insulin levels are high, eicosanoids become imbalanced, or skewed toward being pro-inflammatory. Additionally, excess sugar in the bloodstream can stick to proteins and change their shape. These misshaped proteins, or advanced glycated end products, trigger the immune system causing an increase in systemic inflammation.

Reducing Inflammation

You can reduce chronic inflammation by eliminating the pro-inflammatory foods previously mentioned, as well as limiting certain foods that may be causing inflammatory reactions in the gut—gluten and dairy being the most common. Be careful about switching to a diet of processed, packaged gluten-free and dairy-free foods as they are often high in sugar and refined starches, such as corn starch and potato starch, as well as canola oil—all of which contribute to inflammation. Consuming a diet high in anti-inflammatory foods such as raw organic berries and cherries, organic green vegetables like kale and broccoli, soaked raw nuts and seeds, slow-cooked whole grains, cold-water fish like wild salmon, and small amounts of sustainably-raised meats will reduce chronic inflammation by sending signals to the immune system to keep the body calm and balanced. A calm immune system is one that reacts to pathogenic bacteria and viruses and is less likely to react-to food and other things in the environment, like pet dander and pollen. The message? The food we eat either increases or decreases the alert and alarm signals of the body.

Leaky Gut Syndrome

In a healthy gut, intestinal cells are bound to one another by tight junctions that control what is allowed through to the bloodstream and what is not. When there is damage to the gut and that barrier becomes permeable—called a leaky gut—proteins can pass into the blood stream where the immune system recognizes them as foes and attacks. This can excite the immune system leading to an increase in food allergies, skin rashes and weight gain, as well as many chronic diseases. Remember from the chapter, "Why Gluten-Free?" that consuming gluten causes a leaky gut in all people, even if it just for a short time.

Normal Digestion

The two primary jobs of the intestinal tract are to recognize food particles and call for digestive hormones to be released; and to keep foreign molecules like bacterium, yeast, fungi, parasites and undigested food out of the blood stream. The intestinal cells do this by binding tightly to one another to form a barrier, and by secreting a protective layer of mucous and a compound called secretory immunoglobulin class A, or SIgA. When all is working well, food will enter into the stomach and be broken down into smaller parts by acid and churning. Stomach acid begins to destroy any harmful bacteria or fungi present in the food, as well as food lectins. After leaving the stomach, food moves into the upper intestine where cells recognize the food particles and call for secretions of bile and pancreatic enzymes to break down fats, proteins, and carbohydrates present in the food. When food particles are broken down enough they can then be properly absorbed and utilized by the body.

Compromised Digestion

When the body's digestive system is not functioning properly it means that the cells lining the stomach and intestines have lost their function. There are a number of things that can damage the entire digestive process such as environmental chemicals and certain foods. Damaging chemicals include heavy metals from amalgam fillings, fish consumption, or vaccines; cortisol from chronic stress; repeat antibiotic use; acid blockers; over-the-counter anti-inflammatory drugs; birth control pills; and chlorinated drinking water. Foods that can be quite damaging to the digestive system include gluten, dairy, and sometimes soy, as well as many processed foods—gluten-free or not—such as meat products, refined carbohydrates, simple sugars, juice, and alcohol. All of these factors contribute to the degradation of our digestive system and what is known as **leaky gut syndrome**.

Imbalanced Gut Microflora

Our bodies and our natural environment are made up of more bacteria that we could ever imagine! Our digestive tract is lined with a wide variety of **probiotics**—pro meaning *for*, biotic meaning *life*; or bacteria that support life. These beneficial bacteria are responsible for helping to digest your food by breaking down carbohydrates; degrading anti-nutrients; increasing mineral absorption; inhibiting viral, bacterial, or fungal issues; helping with immune system modulation; and degrading, metabolizing, and discarding toxins. In essence, a healthy number of beneficial bacteria signal the immune system to say: everything is okay, stay calm, don't overreact.

There are a few ways we can get a constant supply of beneficial bacteria, and there are a few ways we can deplete them. Eating fermented foods daily; taking a high-quality probiotic supplement; and letting our babies and children play with and eat dirt—yes, that's right, dirt—can all lead to the flourishing of healthy bacteria in our guts. Antibiotics, whether from eating animals that were fed antibiotics or from prescription medications; chlorine in the water; not breastfeeding; and stress can all lead to the depletion of beneficial bacteria in the gut.

Birthing

When women give birth they pass on strains of microflora in their guts to their babies. Cesarean section babies, who don't go through the birth canal, begin to get inoculated with the bacteria in the hospital and from the nurses who handle them instead of the beneficial bacteria from the birth canal. Since our twins were born via cesarean section, we brought in a bottle of a high-quality infant probiotic powder, which we let them suck off of our fingers within an hour after birth. Breastfeeding also provides a way for babies to become inoculated right after birth, as beneficial bacteria are present on the skin surrounding the nipple. If you have an older infant who was delivered by cesarean section you can still offer them probiotics, it's never too late. Look for a company who offers a high-quality probiotic supplement specifically designed for infants. Check our website, **www.WholeLifeNutrition.net**, for more information and links to companies we recommend.

Fermentation

Traditionally, all cultures fermented most of their grain flours into sourdough, whether it was injera from Africa, or sourdough rye bread from northern Europe. They cultivated the wild yeasts present on the grain and in the air. Lactobacilli bacteria also help in the sourdough process by creating an acidic environment in the starter, which keeps pathogenic bacteria out; helps to break down grain lectins; predigests the carbohydrates; and allows minerals to become more bioavailable by neutralizing phytic acid.

Fresh, *raw* milk obtained from cow's that ate grass—not grains—was fermented into clabber, kefir, and yogurt thereby breaking down lactose and rendering the proteins more digestible. A diet of grasses creates nutrient-dense milk, full of vitamins K and A.

Because refrigeration did not exist, vegetables were fermented to preserve the harvest. Cabbage was preserved into sauerkraut; cucumbers into pickles; soybeans into natto; and fruit into vinegar and wine. (See the Preserving the Harvest chapter, page 497, for fermented vegetable recipes).

People relied on these beneficial microbes present on vegetables, grains, and dairy to preserve their food, and in doing so they supported their own health and their ability to absorb nutrients. This synergistic interaction between humans, food, and the natural environment is missing in our modern civilization.

Let Them Eat Dirt!

This move to a modern lifestyle has also kept us indoors instead of continually interacting with our environment. Babies used to crawl and move in the natural environment instead of on carpeting or vinyl flooring that release chemicals such as flame-retardants and phthalates. Their toys were mud, rocks, sticks, and leaves—all things that are teaming with beneficial microorganisms. If you have been around a baby, you'll know that as soon as they can move, they begin to "sample" everything from their environment—or put everything in their mouths! This sampling is nature's way of assuring that their guts have a variety of bacteria to help them begin to digest solid foods. So go to the forest, the mountains, or the countryside and give your babies and young children the opportunity to crawl, play, and eat dirt!

Antibiotics in our Food

Antibiotics in meat and dairy products are a large contributor to the destruction of good bacteria. Most dairy products and beef you buy at the grocery store or eat at a restaurant came from animals raised in large factory farms. They were fed a diet of grains and soy, which they cannot properly digest because cows are ruminants, meaning they have multiple stomachs for digesting high-cellulose grasses, not grains. This creates a high need for antibiotics to be prophylactically administered in their feed. In fact, over 80% of the antibiotics used today are for animals! Chickens and eggs are also raised in large factory farms where they live so close together that they get sick easily. Antibiotics, as well as arsenic, are also prophylactically administered in their feed to keep profit margins high—they don't want too many of their chickens dying before slaughter. When you consume these animals or the eggs and milk that came from them, you are also consuming what they ate; you are continually ingesting small amounts of antibiotic residues that damage the beneficial flora in your gut.

Prescription Antibiotics

Prescription antibiotics, while life saving in some situations, are grossly overused by much of our population. Most children have had multiple rounds of antibiotics by the time they are five years old—mainly for ear infections, which are often times totally preventable with a proper diet. The word **antibiotic** means to go against life. Antibiotics kill both the harmful bacteria that are causing the infection and the good bacteria in the gut.

We have five children and have only used antibiotics once with one of them—our first daughter when she was seven years old. To keep her gut balanced, we gave her large amounts of probiotics the entire time she was taking the medication, and for weeks afterwards. Other than that one time, our children don't get infections that would necessitate the use of antibiotics. It *is* totally possible to raise healthy children!

Lack of Digestive Enzymes

After food has passed from our stomachs into the upper intestinal tract, cells located there will sample the digested food particles and signal the gallbladder and pancreas to secrete digestive aids, such as bile and pancreatic enzymes, that assist us in further digesting our food (breaking from large to small). Disorders of the upper intestinal tract such as celiac disease, dairy and soy enteropathies, and small intestinal bacterial imbalances have been shown to decrease the secretion of these digestive aids. Symptoms of pancreatic enzyme insufficiency include light-colored stools, chronic constipation, undigested food in the stool, and fat-soluble vitamin deficiencies such as A, D, E, K, and EFAs. The lack of proper digestion can lead to the incidence of food sensitivities because larger undigested food proteins are exposed to the immune system through a leaky gut. We already know that a leaky gut can be initiated through gluten ingestion, stress, antibiotic use, and many other factors.

Nutrient Deficiencies

Nutrient deficiencies during pregnancy are passed down to offspring and, if not rectified with proper diet and supplementation early in childhood, can lead to health issues, including allergies. Additionally, if one has a damaged upper intestine, then vitamins A, D, zinc, and essential fatty acids are not able to be properly absorbed. These nutrients are used by immune cells to determine how to react to insults and when to stop reacting. If there is a deficiency then immune cells can "misbehave" or recognize common food antigens as allergenic.

GMOs and Food Allergies

Research is clear that the use and consumption of GMOs is leading to more diseases in plants and animals, contributing to an increased use of potentially toxic herbicides and pesticides, is *not* increasing crop yields, and may be increasing the risk of food allergies.

The genetic engineering of food involves the insertion or deletion of genes in plants or animals. Rates of food allergies shot up after genetically engineered foods were introduced into the marketplace in 1996. Coincidence? For example, the incidence of peanut allergies doubled from 1997 to 2002! Also, there was a 50 percent increase in soy allergies just one year after the introduction of genetically engineered soy in 1996.

Genetically engineered foods, often called GM or GMO foods, are in everything these days, from shampoo to cooking oil and clothing. Over 90 percent of our major food and feed crops are now GMOs. They have infiltrated the market to a point now that they can be quite difficult to avoid unless you are cooking everything at home from 100 percent organic ingredients. Corn, soy, sugar beets, papaya, canola oil, zucchini, and milk (hormones injected into dairy cows) are the most common genetically engineered foods. This means that if you switch to a gluten-free diet and rely on many of the packed gluten-free products made from corn starch and canola oil, you might be increasing your intake of GMOs! For everyone's health, it is best to stick with naturally gluten-free whole foods that are organically grown.

GMO Pesticide found in Pregnant Women and Fetuses
Research carried out by a team at Sherbrooke University Hospital in Quebec found that

the toxic Bt insecticide protein Cry1Ab, engineered into GMO crops, was present in blood serum of 93% of pregnant women tested. The Bt toxin was also present in 80% of umbilical blood samples taken from fetuses, and in 67% of non-pregnant women. The researchers suggest that the most probable source of the toxin was the genetically engineered food consumed as part of a normal diet in Canada: "to our knowledge, this is the first study to highlight the presence of pesticides-associated genetically modified foods in maternal, fetal and non-pregnant women's blood. 3-MPPA and Cry1Ab toxin are clearly detectable and appear to cross the placenta to the fetus. Given the potential toxicity of these environmental pollutants and the fragility of the fetus, more studies are needed."

No Human Trials

The most frightening thing about genetically engineered foods is that there have been no human trials to test whether or not genetically engineered foods are safe for human consumption! In May 2009, the American Academy of Environmental Medicine called for a moratorium on genetically modified (GM) foods stating: "Avoid GM foods when possible.... Several animal studies indicate serious health risks associated with GM food....There is more than a casual association between GM foods and adverse health effects. There is causation....The strength of association and consistency between GM foods and disease is confirmed in several animal studies."

Organ Damage

European researchers at the University of Caen studied data on 90-day feeding trials with rats. They concluded that three varieties of GMO corn approved for consumption by safety authorities in the US, Europe, and other countries are linked to organ damage in mammals: "adverse impacts on kidneys and liver, dietary detoxifying organs, as well as different levels of damages to heart, adrenal glands, spleen and haematopoietic system."

Healing the Gut

To help heal the gut, reduce food sensitivities and allergies, as well as heal malabsorptive disorders such as osteoporosis and anemia, use the **4 R Program** as outlined by the Institute for Functional Medicine. You'll find the most benefit by following this program for at least 3 months, though most people usually see a dramatic shift in health within the first few weeks. For further assistance, consider talking with a functional medicine health care practitioner.

It is important to maintain the most nutrient-dense diet during this program. When the gut has been damaged for a long period of time the body is usually very deplete in certain nutrients. Be sure to soak or ferment your grains, beans, nuts, and seeds before consuming them (see the Getting Started chapter, page 51); consume nutrient-dense meats only from organic, pastured or grass-fed animals; eat a very high quantity of organic vegetables—both raw and cooked; and keep all processed foods and sugar out of the diet.

1. **Remove.** Removing offending foods is the first step in the healing process. If you never completely remove a food or food group from your diet—like dairy or gluten—you will never know how you feel without it. When testing to see if a food works for you, keep it out of the diet completely for at least 4 weeks, preferably 3 months. Then add it back in by eating it for 3 days straight, noting how you feel. This is the process of an Elimination Diet. For more information see our website,

www.WholeLifeNutrition.net. In addition to food, it is also important to consider removing exposure to environmental toxins such as those found in non-organic foods, chemicals at the work-place, cleaning supplies in the home, personal care products, and mercury in certain types of fish.

2. **Replace.** When the gut is not functioning properly, pancreatic enzymes, stomach acid, and bile are often not being produced in sufficient quantities. Taking high quality digestive supplements and adding in food sources of enzymes to your daily diet is essential to aid in the healing process. Food sources of enzymes include raw and sprouted foods, such as sprouted mung beans, broccoli sprouts, fresh pineapple, raw honey, and green leafy vegetables. Foods that stimulate bile and stomach acid production are artichokes and bitter foods including dandelion leaf, dandelion root tea, chamomile tea, gentian root, fresh ginger, and bitter salad greens.

3. **Reinocculate.** Start consuming foods rich in probiotics daily, such as raw sauerkraut, homemade coconut kefir, kombucha, cultured vegetables, and raw sour dill pickles (see the Preserving the Harvest chapter, page 497, for recipes). Taking a high-quality probiotic supplement may also be very beneficial to reinocculate the gut. Adding in prebiotics—foods that feed beneficial bacteria—is also very important. These foods include sunchokes, asparagus, dandelion greens, onions, garlic, leeks, buckwheat, quinoa, amaranth, millet, flaxseeds, and chia seeds.

4. **Repair.** Consider supplementation of key nutrients to help your body repair itself. Glutamine and glycine are amino acids that help to repair the gut lining. Homemade bone broths (see the Soups & Stews chapter, page 167) offer an easily assimilated source of glutamine and glycine, as well as gelatin in a flavorful form that work together to repair the gut. Raw sauerkraut is also an excellent source of glutamine and beneficial bacteria. Other nutrients that may be of benefit are zinc, vitamin D, and essential fatty acids. If you are still not feeling well, you may need to follow a strict diet for a period of time to further assist the gut in repairing, such as The Body Ecology Diet, GAPS diet, or SCD diet.

Raising Healthy Children

7 Ways to Help your Child THRIVE:

1. **Reduce your toxic load before conceiving**. If you have lived or worked near a chemically-laden environment; taken medications; consumed high amounts of alcohol; smoked; or eaten a diet of processed non-organic foods then you might consider a detoxification or cleansing program using herbs and raw foods six to twelve months before trying to get pregnant. Reducing toxic load may increase fertility as our ability to absorb key nutrients, such as zinc, is lessened from exposure to toxic chemicals.

2. **Decrease your family's chemical exposure**. Over 80,000 chemicals are registered for use in the U.S., and each year some 700 to 2,000 new ones are introduced for use in foods, drugs, household cleaners, lawn-care products, and personal-care items like shampoo and deodorants. Out of all of them, only 5 have been banned due to adverse effects! What can you do? Buy organic food! Use eco-friendly cleaning supplies and laundry detergents. Use natural personal care products. Avoid contact with toxic phthalates found in soft plastics, baby toys, vinyl flooring, and plug-in air fresheners. Replace plastic baby toys with uncoated natural wood toys, vinyl flooring with wood flooring, and air fresheners with 100 percent pure essential oils. Consider green building materials when remodeling or building a home. Question everything and ask, is this safe?

3. **Breastfeed your babies until at least 12 months of age**, preferably 24 months or longer. Breastmilk promotes the growth of friendly bacteria in your infant's gut, protects their immature immune system by building natural immunity, and promotes brain development through the types of fats found in human milk.

4. **Go 100% gluten-free**. Eliminating gluten from your diet decreases the chances of developing a leaky gut. When one has a leaky gut, even for short periods of time after the ingestion of gluten, large food molecules can enter the blood stream causing an adverse reaction to other foods. Gluten, in addition to casein and sometimes soy, can limit absorption of certain nutrients; increase inflammation in the body; and can send neuropeptides to the brain that can contribute to behavioral disorders in children.

5. **Eat a plant-rich, whole foods diet**. A diet high in fresh vegetables and fruits provides the most protection against all chronic diseases. Plants are naturally anti-inflammatory keeping the immune system calm and less likely to react to

things like food and pet dander. Consuming cruciferous vegetables everyday, like broccoli or raw sauerkraut, helps our bodies naturally get rid of toxins coming from our environment or food. Consuming sea vegetables once per week provides our bodies with sufficient iodine needed for proper thyroid function. Add in clean sources of animal foods as your body needs them—they provide important amino acids, minerals, and fats.

6. **Address nutrient deficiencies**. If a child has poor digestion, has not eaten a whole foods diet, is a picky eater, or is constantly getting sick, then he or she may have certain nutrient deficiencies. Children with ADD and autism usually have multiple nutrient deficiencies because they are either not consuming sufficient nutrients or not able to absorb or break them down in the gut. Talk with your health care practitioner about a "functional" lab analysis to get to the bottom of what might be going on.

7. **Rebalance the gut**. If the gut is out of balance—meaning there is an overgrowth of unfriendly bacteria and yeasts and not sufficient good bacteria—then inflammation increases, nutrient absorption decreases, lectins and phytates cannot properly be broken down, and brain function might be disturbed from bacterial metabolites and food neuropeptides. A diet high in raw plant foods naturally keeps the gut in good shape. Additionally, it is important to serve your child daily servings of fermented foods. These include kefir, homemade yogurt, kombucha, cultured coconut water, cultured vegetables, raw sauerkraut, and raw sour dill pickles. A high-quality probiotic supplement and specific diets for rebalancing the gut can also be very beneficial.

Nourishing your Growing Child

Feeding your children a whole foods diet rich in plant foods helps to nourish and protect them from diseases that can form later on in life. Plants—including whole grains, legumes, vegetables, seaweed, fruits, nuts, and seeds—contain an amazing array of protective compounds that keep their bodies functioning properly and assist in detoxifying environmental chemicals. Yet somewhere between 20 to 50 percent of children in the United States are described by their parents as picky eaters. Picky eating can lead to nutrient deficiencies, poor appetite, dental caries, lowered immunity, and obesity in children. Resolving picky eating issues while preparing daily nourishing meals allows children to get the nutrients they need so they have the best chance to grow into vibrant, healthy adults.

Given the opportunity and right environment, children are more likely to choose a diet that is best for them at any given moment. Have you ever noticed how one day your child may gag on a certain food and another day, beg for it? This is the innate self-regulation we all have with food. It is governed by our sense of taste and smell. Children who have undiagnosed sensitivities to gluten and casein, who have an imbalance in their gut microflora, who have a zinc deficiency, or who were overfed as infants may have temporarily lost this wisdom with food and crave only highly refined starchy and sugary foods. In addition, as parents, we all too easily focus on how to get our children to eat healthy instead of setting up an environment that supports their innate wisdom to choose foods that nourish. Raising children in such a supportive environment from pregnancy onward will result in a healthy diet as a normal and natural part of life.

If your children are picky eaters and suffering the consequences, it's not too late to bring them back to health. The human body is amazingly adaptable. Healing can happen quickly given the right ingredients and environment.

The First Three Years

The first three years of a child's life are critical as over 1,000 trillion neuronal connections form in the brain, setting up life-long behavioral patterns. By age two or three, most of a child's food preferences have formed as the brain and taste buds are the most malleable during these years. These food preferences are most influenced by the child's immediate surroundings: the family and home life. We've noticed that each of our children's eating habits differ slightly and can be linked to what foods we were consuming during each stage of their development. For example, we were not drinking green smoothies when our oldest daughter was in this critical first three-year period, it wasn't until she was about three and a half years old that we first began making them. She still isn't as fond of green smoothies like our younger children are. Not only are food preferences formed during the first three years but a child's ability to control food intake—when and how much to eat—develops during this time.

The first three years are also a time of imitation. What your children see you eat, even when they are infants, will set the stage for eating habits later on. Children see right though everything we do. We cannot expect a child to eat a healthy meal if a parent has just come back from a fast food restaurant. Children pick up on every nuance of our existence. It is a child's survival mechanism to first study what the adults around him or her are eating before choosing what and how to eat. If it is the norm in your house to make and drink a green smoothie every morning, your young child will naturally want to participate in this ritual. If they see you in the garden eating fresh carrots from the ground, they will do the same. Likewise, if they see you indulging in a bag of potato chips and drinking a soda, they will naturally want to do the same. Even before your child is born it is best to consider what foods your family eats and make changes accordingly; then you can bring your child into an already established environment of healthful food.

Pregnancy

Research shows that during pregnancy a mother's food preferences and eating patterns have a direct effect on her developing baby—children's food preferences and habits can actually be linked back to their time spent in the womb! Recent studies suggest that mothers who consume particular vegetables during pregnancy and breastfeeding have infants who display a quicker acceptance of those vegetables. For approximately 40 weeks a baby develops in the womb surrounded by amniotic fluid, which is comprised mainly of water with some carbohydrates, proteins, lipids, and electrolytes. Taste buds begin forming at around 5 weeks and by 12 weeks the baby begins to inhale and swallow this fluid. The flavors from the foods the mother consumes end up in the amniotic fluid and later on in the breastmilk as well. The amniotic fluid is the baby's first exposure to flavor.

By consuming a nutrient-dense diet full of healing whole foods a woman not only begins to set up her child's future food preferences, but also offers the developing fetus a wide variety of nutrients needed for proper growth. Additionally, when irritating foods like gluten are removed from the diet, a pregnant woman has a greater chance in absorbing sufficient key nutrients needed for the proper growth and development of her baby.

Clearly, the evidence proposes that eating habits begin prenatally, so this isn't the time to overindulge in unhealthy food. Pregnancy is the time to eat a diet that is as clean as possible, loaded with nutrient-dense foods.

> ### Ideal Foods for Pregnancy:
>
> Fresh organic fruits and vegetables; high-quality clean protein such as soaked and sprouted legumes, soaked nuts and seeds, grass-fed meats, pastured poultry and eggs, and wild fish; healthy fats such as avocados, fish oil, coconut oil, and olive oil; and slow-cooked gluten-free whole grains such as sweet brown rice, quinoa, amaranth, and teff.

Breastfeeding

Breastfeeding is one of the most important things you can do to nourish and protect your new baby against allergies and disease, for both short-term and long-term health. Breastmilk contains immune proteins to build up and protect your infant's developing immune system; oligosaccharides that feed beneficial bacteria in the colon; and beneficial fatty acids for proper neural and brain development. Interestingly, while the nutrient composition of breastmilk remains relatively constant among different diets, the types of fatty acids present change in response to the mother's diet. It has been found that DHA in human milk is significantly higher in women who eat a diet rich in seafood and lower in those who don't.

Formula doesn't contain these protective compounds and is often made from genetically engineered soy oil, corn syrup, and soy or whey protein, along with synthetic vitamins and minerals packed in BPA-lined containers. This can contribute to a pro-inflammatory state in the body. Formula feeding combined with a diet high in processed foods can lead to the development of food allergies and sensitivities in some children. **But what if you find you can't breastfeed or have an adopted child?** The best option would be to obtain pumped milk from several breastfeeding mothers for at least the first year. For babies 6 months and older a homemade formula made primarily from raw goat's milk is often used by parents. Lastly, you can try a pure amino acid formula prescribed by a doctor; these types of formulas don't have any antigens remaining that a baby could react to, but they also don't have the protective compounds found in breastmilk.

In addition to being health-protective, breastfeeding can also contribute to healthy eating habits. We are all born with an innate control system that alerts us to when we are hungry and to when we have had enough food. Babies who are breastfed on demand without much interference from the mother learn to control their own food intake—crucial for preventing overeating behaviors later on in life. When breastfeeding, you do not have a visual gauge of how much milk your baby is consuming which gives the baby full control. When bottle-feeding there is more external influence. When a mom encourages a baby to finish off a bottle, the baby goes beyond its internal satiety cues, which over time can disrupt this innate self-regulation of food intake, possibly leading to overeating later on in life.

A natural, drug-free childbirth will allow the hormones in the body to make breastfeeding initiation a pleasant experience for both mother and baby. When the mother is stressed or has had a medicated birth, hormones such as oxytocin are inhibited and the milk supply can take longer than normal to become established. Hiring a doula and having support during childbirth and during the post-partum period helps with both the initiation of breastfeeding and the continuance of exclusive breastfeeding during infancy. If you are having a difficult time breastfeeding your new baby, contact a trained lactation consultant, your local La Leche League support group, or talk with other breastfeeding mothers for support. Infant craniosacral therapy can be very beneficial for dealing with latch issues in the newborn. We had great success within in a few treatments right after birth with one of our babies.

If you are concerned about milk supply issues, please remember that your milk doesn't fully come in until about 3 days after birth. Your baby will be getting small amounts of immune-protective colostrum, often referred to as "liquid gold" during this time. There is no need to supplement with formula even if baby seems hungry. Babies build up fat stores during the last months of pregnancy to use for energy until the mother's milk supply is fully established. Once your milk is in you'll notice that your supply waxes and wanes throughout breastfeeding. Your baby may all of a sudden be constantly hungry and you might feel that your breasts are always empty. This is normal! I've doubted having enough milk with all of my babies when they were between 4 and 6 months old. Not by coincidence, formula manufacturers often send out free formula samples during this time! Babies naturally build your milk supply to the amount they need by nursing more often and more frequently. Trust in this natural rhythm and let the baby feed as long and as often as necessary to build up your supply to meet their needs. If formula or solid foods are introduced your milk supply will drop. Milk production is an "on demand" cycle: the more you nurse, the more milk is produced. Likewise, skipped feedings will lead to a decrease in milk supply.

Prolonged breastfeeding into the second and third year of life not only protects your child's gut and immune system, but also provides your child with ample nutrients for bone growth. Once your toddler is weaned there is no reason to introduce cow's milk or dairy-free milk substitutes. Feeding your toddler a plant-based whole foods diet provides ample nutrients for growth.

Foods to Increase Milk Supply:

Pastured chicken, wild salmon, yams, winter squash, carrots, beets, sweet brown rice, quinoa, lentils, leafy green salads, sea vegetables, nettles, fennel seed, coconut milk, coconut oil, pumpkin seeds, almonds, walnuts, and almond butter.

Introducing Solid Foods

If we follow the standard guidelines for introducing solid foods we find that by four to six months of age we should be introducing iron-fortified rice cereal. Humans have survived and thrived for hundreds of thousands of years without manufactured, highly processed baby cereals. Babies were breastfed until they were interested in food. They were then given mashed or pre-chewed bits of what the rest of the community or tribe were eating. It is best to avoid rice cereal as baby's first food for a few reasons. First, rice cereal is highly processed and causes a spike in blood sugar after consuming it. This could lead to cravings for processed grain products later on and may be a contributor to the obesity epidemic. Second, grains are difficult for babies to digest. Salivary and pancreatic amylase are enzymes needed to break the polysaccharide bonds found in grains and form simple sugars for absorption and utilization in the body. Newborn babies don't produce any salivary amylase as salivary amylase only begins to be produced in small amounts after about three months of age. Pancreatic amylase doesn't begin production in large amounts until after two years of age—about the time when the molar teeth fully emerge for chewing—though research does show that pancreatic amylase production can vary among 6 to 24 month old babies; some babies at 6 months may be able to properly digest very small amounts of complex starches from cereal grains, while others may not. When you are ready to introduce grains, soak them for 12 to 24 hours, and then slow cook them (see our Whole Grains chapter, page 253, for instructions). You can also serve your older baby or toddler a pancake—also called Injera—made out of gluten-free Sourdough Starter, page

122. Simply heat a cast iron skillet over medium heat, add a few teaspoons of coconut oil and pour in ¼ to ½ cup of starter; cook for 1 to 2 minutes on each side. Fermented flours are highly digestible and a good way to introduce grains into your child's diet, plus their taste buds will develop early to favor soured foods.

Don't babies require supplemental iron from rice cereal so they don't become anemic? It is true that we do have a worldwide iron deficiency epidemic among infants and toddlers. Upon closer examination of the diets among deficient infants and toddlers, it appears that these children are not exclusively breastfed. Exclusive breastfeeding—no supplemental feedings of formula or solid foods—allows the iron in breast milk to be properly absorbed. It is important to also note that fetuses store iron during the last month of a full-term gestation. Exclusively breastfed pre-term babies can become iron deficient during the first six months since they do not have the same amount of stored iron as full-term babies, therefore introducing some heme iron sources at six months might be beneficial. It is also theorized that since iron competes with zinc, breast milk is naturally lower in iron to allow for zinc to be properly absorbed. Zinc is a mineral needed for optimal development of an infant's nervous and immune systems. Breastmilk has adequate zinc as long as the mother is consuming and absorbing enough zinc-rich foods.

The introduction of solid foods can begin around six months of age, but certainly should not be done before as an infant's digestive system is still developing. For exclusively breastfed babies that were born full-term, solid foods can even wait until nine or twelve months or until the child is interested in eating. Offer your baby a wide variety of flavors and nutrients with easily digestible fresh, in season raw or lightly cooked fruit and steamed vegetables. Steer away from jarred, processed baby foods to allow your child's taste buds to develop a preference for fresh foods, instead of something that comes in a package or a can. I wouldn't feed anything to my baby that I wouldn't eat myself. Have you tried jarred, strained spinach? Yuck! These first few months of eating solids are not so much about getting a lot of nutrients in—as milk is still a the primary nutrient source—but rather an exploratory phase of flavor, textures, and learning to swallow. Start slowly with just a few flavors and textures and gradually offer a wider variety during the first three years. This will set the stage for a life-long love of nutritious food. On average, it can take up to ten introductions of a food before a child will accept it into their diet.

Remember that each child will develop differently. I remember our second daughter at seven months refused to eat even a mashed banana, but by eight months she was very ready to eat. Our twin boys were very interested in food early on so we started them on solids around six months. Since it was summertime, their first food was pureed raw cantaloupe melon. They were so interested in food that by the time they were nine months old they were eating more than their toddler sister! Our youngest daughter started eating solids at about seven and a half months; first with nori seaweed and then a little wild salmon and roasted organic chicken, as these were the foods she was most interested in eating. By the time she was eight months old she was feeding herself a whole meal of baked wild salmon, steamed broccoli, and frozen blueberries! When our twin boys were a year old we were offering mixed green salads with a little homemade dressing on top. Since they didn't chew it thoroughly I am sure they didn't get much nutrition out of it, but now they beg for salads and will eat a whole plate of greens with just about any type of homemade dressing drizzled on top.

When introducing solids, be sure to keep potentially allergenic or hard to digest foods out of baby's diet until at least 12 months of age, preferably 24 months. These foods are egg whites, cow's milk, tree nuts, peanuts, gluten grains, corn, and soy. When and if you introduce them, make sure that they are offered in their most digestible forms. For example, use yogurt made from raw milk sweetened only with a little maple syrup; tree nuts soaked overnight in water and then blended into a smoothie; gluten grains sprouted or fermented into a sourdough starter and made into bread; masa harina for the introduction of corn; and soy that has been fermented into miso, tamari, or tempeh.

> ### Great First Foods for Baby:
> Steamed carrots and winter squash, blueberries, cherries, applesauce, sea vegetables, ripe bananas, avocado, mango, sautéed zucchini, roasted turnips, watermelon, and pears. For an older baby try slow-cooked organic chicken, wild salmon, finely chopped kale cooked in homemade chicken stock, Injera, cultured vegetables, small amounts of brine from raw sauerkraut, and celery sticks to teeth on.

Key Nutrients for Proper Development

In order to grow into healthy, resilient adults, children need to consume a wide variety of nourishing foods. Highlighted below are some of the nutrients that are key for proper growth and development in utero and in childhood. Of course all vitamins and minerals are necessary for good health, but the nutrients discussed here are typically deficient or difficult to absorb in a large portion of our population. If you are consuming a plant-rich whole foods diet, you'll most likely be getting plenty of vitamin C, B vitamins, potassium, beta-carotene, vitamin E, and trace minerals. By combining a high intake of plant foods along with small amounts of sustainably-raised, organic animal foods your child will have the best chance to thrive.

Omega-3 Fatty Acids

Omega-3 fatty acids lower chronic inflammation; in fact, they are a prime modulator of inflammatory hormones in the body, key to preventing and healing food allergies. Omega-3 fatty acids are also critical in modulating fetal and infant growth and development of the central nervous system. In fact, over 18% of an infant's brain is DHA!

Omega-3 fatty acids come from plants as ALA, and from animals as DHA and EPA. ALA can be converted into DHA and EPA in the body, but the process is not very efficient as it requires numerous cofactors such as zinc, magnesium, and B6. When we consume a lot of omega-6 vegetable oils in our diet the body will prioritize enzymes to convert those oils into arachidonic acid instead of using them to convert EPA to DHA. The take home message: greatly reduce the consumption of vegetable oils and increase the consumption of DHA and EPA.

To optimize pregnancy outcomes and fetal health, consensus guidelines have recommended that pregnant women consume at least 200 mg of DHA per day. In 2004, the FDA advised all pregnant women to limit seafood consumption to two 6-ounce servings per week in order to decrease fetal exposure to trace amounts of neurotoxins. This amount of consumption would provide the necessary 200mg DHA per day if consuming fish rich in EPA and DHA. Alternatives to fish include DHA-enriched eggs, which contain about 150 mg DHA per serving, or fish oil supplements. A new method of fish oil purification called "Super Critical CO2 Extraction" has demonstrated some of the cleanest oil products to date, so consider spending the extra money on these if you are concerned about environmental exposures. DHA does not pass easily through the placenta without EPA so it is of utmost importance to consume fish oil supplements that combine EPA and DHA while pregnant.

> **Signs of Deficiency:** Lower growth rate in infants and children, dry skin and dry scaly rashes, decreased wound healing, and an increase in infections.

> **Contributors of Deficiency:** Low intake, high stress levels, high circulating insulin, fat malabsorption from celiac disease, and degradation of the small intestine from various factors including candida overgrowth, antibiotic use, and gluten.

> **Food Sources:** Salmon, halibut, sardines, pastured eggs, grass-fed beef, leafy greens, walnuts, chia seeds, and flax seeds.

> **Recipes:** Orange Pepper Salmon, page 315. Thai Coconut Fish Sticks, page 320. Kale and Egg Scramble, page 98. Green Chia Smoothie, page 75. Creamy Herb Salad Dressing, page 346.

Vitamin D

Vitamin D is an essential nutrient for bone formation and proper immune system functioning. When you have adequate vitamin D you can bind and absorb 30-80% of intestinal calcium, whereas a person with a low vitamin D status is lucky to get between 10-15% absorption of intestinal calcium. So which is more practical: taking large amounts of calcium for bone development, or efficiently absorbing the calcium that is in your intestines by having adequate vitamin D? Beyond the effects on bone, vitamin D levels have been associated with reducing autoimmune diseases and infections in growing children. Unfortunately many pregnant women are deficient in vitamin D, and thus their offspring are most likely deficient in utero and at birth. Breastmilk is often a poor source for vitamin D so building up stores prior to and during pregnancy may be of utmost importance.

Research has found that women who supplement with 4,000 IU of vitamin D during pregnancy significantly decreased the risk of pregnancy complications, such as small-for-gestations age babies, high-blood pressure or preeclampsia, and gestational diabetes. A minimum of 4,000 IU a day is required during pregnancy, however, taking 6,000 IU a day was found to get circulation levels of vitamin D (25-OHD) to levels beneficial for a healthy pregnancy.

Year round, in areas of the US below the 35th parallel, vitamin D naturally forms in the skin upon exposure to UVB radiation from midday sun. In the winter months, native peoples in northern latitudes typically consumed animal organ meats and fat—rich sources of vitamin D. Now these foods are too contaminated with environmental toxins to be considered safe. If supplementation is needed to maintain adequate levels in you or your child, be sure to choose a supplement that is free of artificial preservatives such as sodium benzoate, BHT, or BHA, and GMO carrier oils such as soy oil. Nutrition experts have agreed that 1000 IU per 25 pounds of body weight appears to be a valid equation for meeting the needs of young children. For an infant, use 200 IU per 5 pounds of body weight.

Signs of Deficiency: Rickets, osteoporosis, osteopenia, osteomalacia, elevated parathyroid hormone, bone pain, inflammation, weakness, and fatigue.

Contributors of Deficiency: Lack of sun exposure, use of sunscreen, having dark skin, fat malabsorptive disorders including celiac disease and cystic fibrosis. In infants, low maternal vitamin D status during pregnancy.

Food Sources: Lard, organ meats, fatty fish, mushrooms, eggs.

Recipes: Garlic Ginger Salmon, page 314. Cream of Mushroom Soup, page 178. Basil Zucchini Frittata, page 99.

Vitamin K

There are two types of vitamin K used by the body. Vitamin K1 (phylloquinone) and vitamin K2 (menaquionone). K1 is primarily used in clotting functions of the blood. K2 is used for putting calcium into the bones, which is essential for growing bones and healthy teeth in young children. Vitamin K1 is primarily found in plants and can be converted into K2 two different ways. Certain tissues in the body, including the pancreas, testes, and blood vessels can directly convert K1 into K2 (MK4). The other method is in the intestines where non-pathogenic e-coli bacteria convert K1 into K2 (MK7).

Signs of K1 deficiency: Easy and pronounced bruising, bleeding gums, nosebleeds, heavy menstrual bleeding, and bleeding in the gastrointestinal tract.

Signs of K2 deficiency: Osteoporosis, osteopenia, increased fracturing, and dental carries.

Contributors of Deficiency: Malabsorptive disorders including celiac disease and cystic fibrosis, bacteria imbalances in the colon, pancreatic enzyme insufficiency, low dietary intake.

Food Sources for K1: Kale, collards, spinach, brussels sprouts, romaine lettuce, and broccoli.

Food Sources for K2: Natto, meat, eggs, pastured butter and raw cheese.

Recipes: Pan-Fried Steak Salad, page 223. Spring Green Smoothie, page 77. Mini Quiches with a Sweet Potato Crust, page 101. Sautéed Winter Greens with Caramelized Onions, page 240.

Calcium

Calcium is needed to mineralize teeth and bones in growing children, for muscle contractions, and to signal damaged cells to destroy themselves (apoptosis). For young girls, the most important time to have adequate calcium intake is during the pre-teen and teenage years, from about 9 to 19 years of age, as this is the peak of bone mass formation. The emphasis has always been on consuming a lot of calcium in order to have strong bones, however, this is only a small part of a larger picture. It may be that vitamin D and K deficiencies as well as chronic inflammation play a larger roll in bone health than calcium intake.

Signs of Deficiency: Rickets, dental carries, muscle spasms, tingling and numbness, and bone fractures.

Contributors of Deficiency: An inability to process oxalates, caffeine consumption, excessive animal protein intake, diet high in phytic acid, and high intake of sodium.

Food Sources: Sea vegetables, agar flakes, collard greens, kale, broccoli, sesame tahini, raw almonds, hazelnuts, black-eyed peas, canned salmon or sardines, and raw goat or cow's milk or fermented dairy like yogurt and kefir.

Recipes: Spicy Black-Eyed Pea Soup, page 194. Raw Breakfast Tacos, page 92. Strawberry Almond Smoothie, page 71. Raw Blueberry Cheesecake, page 435. Raw Kale Salad with Lemon Tahini Dressing, page 229. Overnight Quinoa Hot Cakes, page 107. Raspberry Almond Pudding, page 424. Baby Green Smoothie, page 73.

Magnesium

Magnesium is one of the most important minerals in the human body. It is a cofactor for over 300 different enzymes needed for proper function in the heart, skeletal muscle, bone, cardiovascular system, nervous system, and digestive system. Magnesium helps to regulate blood sugar, maintain normal blood pressure, and keep the bones strong—in fact over 50 percent of the body's magnesium is found in the bone! One of the reasons that magnesium is so essential for human health is that it allows ATP, the primary energy currency of cells, to be moved around in the body. Magnesium also acts to block the stimulation of an excitatory receptor in the brain (NMDA receptor) that can lead to increased cases of ADD/ADHD and anxiety. Magnesium is one of the most common nutrient deficiencies in our society.

Signs of Deficiency: Anxiety, insomnia, high blood pressure, muscle cramping, weakness, tremors, headaches, restless leg syndrome, and irregular heartbeat.

Contributors of Deficiency: Stress, kidney disease, malabsorptive disorders, chronic diarrhea, and alcoholism.

Food sources: Nuts, seeds (pumpkin seeds are highest), legumes, leafy greens, chocolate, and whole grains—particularly oats.

Recipes: Oatmeal Cinnamon Muffins, page 156. Chocolate Brownie Cupcakes, page 461. Sweet and Spicy Kale Chips, page 400. Cashew Orange Date Balls, page 407. Herb and Olive Oil Hummus, page 375. Raw Kale Salad with Lemon Tahini Dressing, page 229.

Zinc

Unfortunately, mild to severe zinc deficiencies exist in most of our global population. Women in third world countries are at the highest risk because overall caloric intake is low and because cereal grains make up most of the diet. Zinc is needed as a cofactor in over 200 reactions in the human body. Zinc keeps the immune system functioning properly, aids in wound healing, helps to make the active form of thyroid hormone, and is involved in DNA synthesis and cell division. Zinc is needed to properly be able to taste and smell things; in fact, one of the most common symptoms of zinc deficiency in children is picky eating and a loss of appetite. Since the body has no way of storing zinc, a daily supply is needed to maintain optimal health. A recent article found an association between low maternal and infant zinc with the incidence of autism. When you are zinc deficient you up-regulate the formation of receptors in the small intestine for absorbing zinc; those zinc receptors are not selective for only zinc and will also absorb heavy metals from the diet such as cadmium and arsenic from rice, potatoes, and root crops grown with chemical pesticides and fertilizers. Therefore, consider purchasing only organic food and make sure to consume a zinc-rich diet.

Signs of Deficiency: Picky eating, growth retardation, mood and behavioral issues, hair loss, poor wound healing, diarrhea, and even Down's syndrome. Skin rashes, learning disabilities, lowered immunity, and infertility are also strongly associated with a zinc deficiency. A zinc deficiency during pregnancy can lead to structural abnormalities and low birth weight in offspring; intrauterine growth retardation; prolonged labor; and learning disabilities in offspring, such as dyslexia.

Contributors of Deficiency: Low intake; food grown in poor soil conditions; undiagnosed celiac disease and gluten enteropathies; damage to the small intestine from candida; high consumption of phytic acid from unfermented or unsoaked cereal grains, and unfermented soy (soy milk, fake meats, soy protein isolate, soy flour). See the Whole Grains chapter, page 253, for more details on phytic acid.

Food Sources: Animal sources include venison, beef, lamb, chicken, and turkey. Oysters also have a high amount of zinc, but because of the high chance of mercury contamination it is not a good idea to eat them. Plant sources include pumpkin seeds and whole grains, but these need to be soaked or fermented for the best availability.

Recipes: Turkey Quinoa Meatballs, page 335. Nori Rolls with Pumpkin Seed Pate, page 390. Grain-Free Chicken Nuggets, page 331. Cream of Mushroom Soup, page 178. Overnight Quinoa Hot Cakes, page 107. Slow Cooked Beef Stew, page 337.

Iron

Iron deficiency anemia is one of the most common nutritional concerns for most of the globe, affecting 20 to 50 percent of the global population. Iron is an essential component of hemoglobin—a protein in red blood cells used for oxygen transport. In fact, over two-thirds of iron in the body is found in hemoglobin! Iron is also used for cell growth and differentiation—critical during pregnancy and growth in childhood. The requirements for iron nearly double during pregnancy as it is needed for the development of the placenta, for the fetus' iron needs, for the increase in maternal red blood cells, and to cope with blood loss at delivery. Iron deficiency anemia during pregnancy increases the risk of low birth weight in neonates. It has also been associated with preterm labor and premature rupture of the membranes, although some studies give conflicting results. Babies store iron during the last month of pregnancy, which is why preterm infants are at a much higher risk for becoming anemic. Research demonstrates that when the mother is deficient in iron during pregnancy the fetus cannot store as much, and therefore could become anemic in infancy. Infants born from mothers who are not anemic during pregnancy usually have enough stored iron to last 6 to 8 months.

It is important to note that iron is classified as heme (from animals), or non-heme (from plants). While heme iron is generally better absorbed by most people, it can also be quite toxic in large amounts. This is yet another reason to consume a diet high in plants with a smaller proportion of animal foods.

Signs of Deficiency: Eating less, gaining weight poorly, paleness, weakness, and tiring easily. Symptoms of iron deficiency in children are not apparent until they are very deficient. They may have frequent respiratory and intestinal infections, and may develop pica. It also can lead to impaired development in behavior, cognition, and psychomotor skills.

Contributors of Deficiency: Low intake of vitamin C (needed to absorb iron); undiagnosed celiac disease and gluten enteropathies; damage to the small intestine from candida; high consumption of phytic acid from unfermented or unsoaked cereal grains, and unfermented soy (soy milk, fake meats, soy protein isolate, soy flour). See the Whole Grains chapter, page 253, for more details on phytic acid.

Food Sources: Iron is found in high concentrations in all animal tissues, otherwise known as heme iron. Plant sources of iron—or non-heme iron—include nettles, dandelion leaf, broccoli, bok choy, teff flour, quinoa, sprouted lentils, and tempeh.

Recipes: Slow Cooker Chicken Stew, page 197. Grass-Fed Beef Chili, page 199. Smoked Salmon Salad with Honey Mustard Vinaigrette, page 231. Lentil Minestrone (preferably made with sprouted lentils), page 188. Sautéed Tempeh and Spinach, page 305. Spring Green Smoothie, page 77. Sourdough Teff Bread, page 124. Quinoa and Lentil Salad with Caramelized Onions, page 276.

Iodine

Iodine is primarily used in the human body to make the thyroid hormones T3 and T4. These hormones are three and four iodine molecules, respectively, attached to one tyrosine (an amino acid). Zinc and selenium are needed to convert the inactive form of thyroid hormone, T4, into the active form, T3. Did you know that every cell in the human body has receptors for thyroid hormones? Without sufficient thyroid hormones, you cannot properly convert beta-carotene from plants into the active form of vitamin A—something to consider if you are raising a vegan child.

Iodine deficiency is the most frequent cause of mental retardation as it is needed for brain development during the first trimester in the developing fetus. An iodine deficiency and low thyroid hormones have been linked to infertility in women and sperm abnormalities in men. They can negatively effect cognitive development in children and even cause a severe stunting in physical and mental growth called cretinism. One study found that 63.6% of children born to women with hypothyroxinemia developed ADHD. The opposite is also true in that iodine supplementation during pregnancy can increase head circumference and cognitive functioning in offspring. The World Health Organization has recently raised recommended levels during pregnancy from 200 to 250 mcg/d.

Signs of Deficiency: Cretinism, cognitive impairment, goiter, multiple miscarriages, hypothyroidism, weakness and fatigue, weight loss resistance, and weight gain.

Contributors of Deficiency: Low dietary intake and consumption of arsenic from non-organic chicken may interfere with the uptake of iodine by the thyroid gland. Cruciferous vegetables and soy are often avoided by people with thyroid issues out of fear that their consumption might lead to goiter. After close examination of the literature, it appears that this only occurs in populations that have iodine and selenium deficiencies.

Food Sources: The best sources of iodine are sea vegetables such as kombu, arame, hijiki, dulse, and nori. Fish appears to vary wildly in iodine content. Yogurt, milk, eggs, and strawberries also contain smaller amounts of iodine.

Recipes: Quinoa Salad with Arame and Daikon, page 273. Nori Rolls with Salmon and Mustard Greens, page 391. Homemade Chicken Stock, page 170. Cucumber Arame Salad, page 214.

Folate

Folate, or vitamin B9, is needed in the body to help convert the food you eat into energy. It also helps to make RNA, DNA, and red blood cells. The developing fetus needs a continual supply of folate to assist in these processes, especially early on in the first trimester. Additionally, elevated blood homocysteine levels, considered an indicator of folate deficiency, have been associated with increased incidence of miscarriage as well as pregnancy complications like preeclampsia and placental abruption. Folate is also used for methylation or "remodeling" reactions in the human body. For example, methylation of DNA can turn on and off the reading of certain genes, called epigenetics, depending on where the methyl group is placed. This is important for preventing childhood cancers and cardiovascular disease.

A lot of foods are now fortified with folic acid (the synthetic form of folate), like orange juice and all-purpose flour. But, did you know that the form of folic acid used in fortification and in most supplements is not absorbable in a certain percentage of our population? Further more, studies show that this synthetic form of folic acid can actually be quite toxic to the human body. This is not a metabolically active form of vitamin B9 and has to be metabolized to different folate forms—folinic acid and 5-methyltetrahydrofolate (5MTHF)—before it can be used by the body. If a person has a challenged ability to transform the synthetic folic acid to a biologically active form, the synthetic folic acids can build up in the body and may be associated with an increase risk of cancer. Therefore, when supplementation is necessary, it would make logical sense to use folinic acid and 5MTHF exclusively and avoid folic acid all together.

Signs of Deficiency: Anxiety, depression, memory issues, headaches, loss of appetite, bleeding gums, elevated homocysteine levels, macrocytic anemia, low birth weight in babies, and colon cancer.

Contributors of Deficiency: Low amounts of gastric acid, acid-blocking medications, celiac disease or other causes of irritation of the upper intestinal tract (bacterial overgrowth, parasitic infections, non-celiac food reactions, Crohn's disease), weight loss surgeries, and alcoholism.

Food Sources: Dark leafy greens, salad greens, legumes.

Recipes: Apple Cider Baked Beans, page 290. Arugula Salad with Shaved Fennel, page 207. Greek Salad with Chickpeas, page 217. Pear Pomegranate Salad with Orange Vinaigrette, page 224. Winter Green Smoothie, page 79.

Vitamin B12

Like folate, vitamin B12 is used by the body for methylation reactions. It also builds new blood cells in the bone marrow and helps to orchestrate all functions of metabolism. B12 is involved with balancing hormones, digesting food, eliminating waste, and utilizing oxygen.

B12 and folate act synergistically to prevent miscarriage. You cannot properly develop a fetus without sufficient B12 and folate. The metabolically active forms of vitamin B12 for supplementation are adenosylcobalamin and methylcobalamin.

> **Signs of deficiency**: Anemia, neurological symptoms such as depression, poor memory, numbness and tingling of the hands and feet, and loss of balance.

> **Contributors of Deficiency:** Low amounts of gastric acid, acid-blocking medications, celiac disease or other causes of irritation of the upper intestinal tract (bacterial overgrowth, parasitic infections, non-celiac food reactions, Crohn's disease), weight loss surgeries, and alcoholism.

> **Food Sources:** Sardines, salmon, lamb, and beef.

> **Recipes:** Sloppy Joes, page 336. Slow Cooked Beef Stew, page 337. Tandoori Salmon, page 317. Quinoa Salmon Burgers, page 313.

Moving from Processed Foods to Whole Foods

Why cook from scratch? Isn't it just easier to just go out to eat or pick up a frozen meal from the grocery store? It may be easier, but by preparing your own food you have control over the quality and freshness of ingredients—no hidden MSG, flavor enhancers, GMOs, or gluten. Moving away from convenience may take more effort at first, but in the long run you and your family will be healthier because of it.

Changing the Diet

When we look at diet as a continually evolving process rather than an end goal, making changes becomes easier. It's okay if you didn't start your child out with a lot of fresh fruits and vegetables, or a green smoothie every day—what's important is that you are making the changes now. If you are feeling overwhelmed, then add one new change a week or a month until you adjust. Let's say you start by going gluten-free, then a few months later you remove all highly processed foods from your house, and six months later you add in a green smoothie twice a week. Maybe a year or two down the line you begin to soak your grains, soak and dehydrate raw nuts and seeds, and make sourdough bread. During each step of the way, know that you are improving your health and the health of your family.

Often the younger the child is, the easier it is to make changes. Some parents find that making small changes over time is easier while others find that a complete kitchen overhaul is needed. Whichever method you choose, stick with it even when it looks like nothing is working and you feel your child may starve. Don't worry, your children's survival instincts will kick in and they will begin to eat what you offer. If your children are older, involving them in the process can be rather exciting. Together you can look for new recipes to try, create a menu plan, and have them help you grocery shop. Keeping the process positive and upbeat will go a long way.

My Child Has a Very Limited Diet and Won't Change

Healthy children have healthy appetites and want to expand their diets. A child who is a picky eater or who doesn't have an appetite often has a compromised digestive system, is addicted to certain foods, or has nutrient deficiencies—notably zinc—that affect the sense of taste. Sometimes a child gets comfortable eating only five different foods because they have constant bellyaches and have a difficult time digesting their food. Often parents don't even realize their child has an issue because he or she has always had a compromised digestive tract and doesn't know what it is like to be well. Food sensitivities are often at the root of stomach pain and disinterest in all but a limited variety of food.

A large percentage of the population lacks a particular enzyme called dipeptyl peptidase, or DPP4, that breaks down gluten and casein. DPP4 can be damaged by mercury; whether from amalgam fillings, vaccines, or environmental toxicity such as coal-burning power plants. If gluten and casein are only partially broken down they create partial proteins, or peptides, that are similar to **opiates**. These opiates act like morphine once in the bloodstream creating a high and then a low, leading to cravings for more gluten and casein-containing foods, thus perpetuating the cycle. Additionally, incomplete digestion of these proteins damages the villi of the small intestine potentially causing inflammation, digestive discomfort, malabsorption, and nutrient deficiencies. Remember, a damaged gut lining or "leaky gut" often results in a number of other food allergies and intolerances.

When food is not properly broken down and absorbed, unfriendly gut bacterium and yeasts feed off of the undigested food and grow out of balance. These organisms can cause mood changes, and increased cravings for sweet and refined foods. When this occurs the child's digestive tract becomes so irritated and inflamed that he or she simply does not want to eat. In this case, you might consider a diet for rebalancing the gut such as the Body Ecology Diet, GAPS diet, or Specific Carbohydrate Diet. Supporting the digestive system with enzymes, high-quality probiotics, and amino acid supplements is also very beneficial. A great way to offer all of these digestive-supporting nutrients is by offering raw kombucha, a pleasing fizzy, fermented beverage. Our children consider this "soda" and love to drink it! Homemade bone broths and raw sauerkraut also offer many gut-healing nutrients and should be consumed daily for best results.

A **zinc deficiency** can also be at the root of extreme picky eating behaviors. Zinc is needed to properly taste and smell things. If a child has an altered sense of taste and smell, he or she may develop picky eating habits. Pregnancy is also a time when the body's demand for zinc increases. Interestingly, zinc deficiencies can be passed down from mother to child. Second, third, and subsequent children are at most risk if the mother was not consuming or absorbing enough zinc from her diet. You may want to consider talking to your health care practitioner about zinc supplementation until the child's diet contains enough zinc-rich foods.

Once digestion is supported and nutrient deficiencies are addressed, it is best to do a complete kitchen overhaul: eliminate all gluten and casein from your house and any unhealthy foods in the pantry, refrigerator, and freezer. Start by offering healthier gluten-free casein-free versions of what they know and then move on to unfamiliar foods. They may protest, scream, cry, and not eat much for a week or more. This is especially true for a child who is addicted to gluten and casein foods because of the opiate-like reaction described above.

Since bacteria in the gut respond to the types of food we eat, there may be a die-off of unfriendly bacteria and yeasts when the diet is drastically changed. This is a good thing. Eventually the child will eat, even if just part of the whole meal. It is easy to give the child whatever he or she will eat because of the false notion that something is better than nothing. This just encourages the child to continue eating a limited number of foods, many of which lack essential nutrients or are high in sugar. Long-term health and well-being are the goals, not temporary satiation. Children are naturally very adaptable and quick to heal, so once the process has begun you'll begin to see results almost immediately.

Education is Key

Invariably children will be exposed to the billion-dollar snack food industry, whether though TV, school, or friends. Forbidding these foods can backfire and cause binging later on, but if instead children are educated about what those foods really are, where they come from, and how they react in our bodies, they can make empowered choices about their food.

So what can we do as parents? If we keep junk food out of our children's diet for as long as possible, their taste buds will be set to prefer healthy foods over junk food later on. We can educate our older children on the importance of eating organic food, non-GMO food, and a healthy diet—giving them the tools to make healthy choices when away from home. It is important to make the lesson positive and inspirational to keep their interest and energy focused on the benefits of eating nourishing meals.

The time to begin educating your children depends upon their development. A child's nature is to see the good in the world and we want to help them develop in that bubble for as long as possible. Once they are ready to explore global situations and how other people live they will be ready for detailed information on food and nutrition. For our family this has seemed to be between eight and nine years of age. At this time we discuss the details of organic versus non-organic food and how our planet is affected by these different growing methods. We discuss what genetically modified foods are and what we can do to not support that industry. We explain about the factory farming of animals, which is something that can create a lot of fear in young child, so make sure your child is ready for this before delving into it. Other points of discussion can be how eating a diet rich in fruits and vegetables prevents disease—particularly cancer—and how our food choices affect our planet and the people living on it. Education early on will empower our children to say no to food choices that don't support their individual health and the health and well-being of our entire planet.

A Home Environment for Health

We are often asked how we get our children to eat a healthy, nourishing diet. We have found that by only having foods available in our home that we are comfortable with our children eating at any point in the day, our children will naturally consume a diet that is good for them. This is the key factor in eliminating food battles. **No food to battle over, no battle**.

Snacking

If our children are hungry for a snack, they reach into the freezer and serve themselves a bowl full of frozen organic berries and cherries; they cut up apples and carrots; or eat whatever fruit we have ripe in our fruit basket. I also keep a few jars of soaked and dehydrated nuts on the counter for them to grab at any time. Occasionally, I have other homemade snacks on hand for them (see the Snacks and Treats Chapter, page 397).

If your children are hungry before dinner and the meal is not quite ready yet, consider offering raw vegetables such as carrot and celery sticks or raw cauliflower and broccoli.

A small bowl of raw sauerkraut is also a great food to keep them busy. These foods will fill them up slightly for a short time and then actually increase their appetite and digestion for the meal ahead of them.

Snacking before bedtime can be a tricky thing. If your children don't eat a meal, and then ask for a bedtime snack, the message they are receiving is that it is okay not to eat dinner. This can set up a cycle where the parent works hard to create healthy meals; the children don't eat them, and then get hungry before bed. Breaking the cycle may be hard at first, but your children will learn to eat dinner as long as they know there won't be any more bedtime snacks.

Family Mealtimes

Food is the source of many family traditions. Family mealtimes nurture connectivity and security between family members. Research shows that children who participate in family meals are more likely to eat a balanced diet full of fresh fruits and vegetables, are generally happier with higher self-esteem, and have lower obesity rates.

It is important to begin the family mealtimes during your child's infancy. All of our babies snuggled in our arms at the dinner table from the time they were newborns. When they were able to sit up we put them in a chair that hooked onto the dinner table. Babies that don't yet have teeth and are not eating can be given a raw carrot or celery stick to teethe on.

Once our first daughter was eating solid foods, we would feed her a part of our meal. So if I was making a soup with carrots she had, mashed, steamed carrots.

Children learn to love food by eating with us and watching what and how we eat. In fact, parents are the best role models for healthy eating behaviors. Humans are social creatures and want to feel included. If parents prepare and enjoy eating nourishing foods at every meal, children will eventually want to try those same foods—they don't want to feel excluded! Just make sure never force your children into eating anything, that just sets up a separation between parent and child. A child who is a picky eater can eventually enjoy a diverse array of healthy foods; it may just take some time and patience.

Kids in the Kitchen

Involving your child in the kitchen is key to developing a love of food. This is a wonderful time to have them participate in the process of family meals. Young children, even toddlers, can help set the table and bring dishes of food to the table. They can even participate in the planning of the meal. As they grocery shop or garden with you they begin to know ingredients and where food comes from. Having them help prepare a meal creates a lot of excitement and an eagerness to eat the finished product. It may seem to take more energy at first, but it pays off in the long run for everyone to be working as a team.

Children as young as two years old can help with a variety of tasks—I remember giving our oldest daughter, when she was about two and a half years old, a small paring knife and a pile of green beans to trim. I set the pot right next to her for her to fill as she had them cut. She was thrilled with this task. By the time she was nine years old she was cooking an entire meal, even creating her own recipes (that actually tasted good).

A three year old can keep busy peeling carrots or potatoes, while an older child chops the vegetables. We have let all of our children cook at the stove from an early age. They have all burned themselves once and only once. One time is enough to learn how to safely navigate around a hot stove. A three year old will love to participate in sautéing vegetables. Older children can help measure ingredients for baking and whisk things together. A child who is reading can read a recipe to you as you cook. If you want to double a recipe, this is the perfect time for a math lesson in fractions! Involving your children in the menu planning, grocery shopping, and meal preparation sets up an environment for healthy eating and a strong sense of belonging.

What's Served is Served
We don't make special meals for our children if they don't like what we make. We don't even ask them want they want for breakfast, lunch, or dinner. We just make a meal and serve it; if they don't want to, or are not hungry enough, they don't have to eat. We live in a time with a fairly constant food supply. Your child won't go hungry if she or he doesn't eat much one night or occasionally skips a meal. Usually, if one of our children doesn't like what we make there is still something at the table they will eat like steamed broccoli or cooked quinoa. Just make sure that everything you are serving is nutrient-dense, this way your children will get the most out of what they do eat.

Sometimes mealtime battles come into play when we are overly concerned with what our children are or are not eating. Instead of focusing on the food and who is eating what at mealtimes, try to focus on something completely different such as what each family member did that day. There are so many things to discuss other than the food. This is a time to slow down and connect with those around you, to simply relax and know that they are getting enough food. Most of the time, if children don't eat much for dinner one evening they will eat a large breakfast the next morning.

By letting your children set the pace of their eating you empower them; allowing them learn how to control their intrinsic metabolism and eating patterns. If we constantly cater to our children's food preferences, we rob them of the opportunity to expand their horizons of likes and dislikes. Some evenings a child might not be hungry enough to try a new food whereas other times your child may be so hungry that they will eat anything.

Make it a Lifestyle!

We are all doing the best we can to raise our children given the information we have and our available resources. The more information we can gather about food and nutrition, the more educated we are to make changes and stick with them. Searching out local health food stores, food co-ops, organic farmers, and online sources of ingredients will make eating nourishing food a lifestyle. By consuming a nutrient-dense whole foods diet, as well as reducing chemical exposure and rebalancing the gut, the body will have the best chance to not only survive, but to thrive! Our children learn so much from us. Not only do our children learn to eat by watching us, but they also learn the process of positive change and growth as we journey though life.

Packing a Healthy Lunchbox

A healthy school lunch is essential to building health and resilience in a growing child. Most hot school lunches don't provide the necessary vitamins, minerals, and phytochemicals in an easily digestible and absorbable form. Plus, they are usually full of chemical pesticide and herbicide residues, made from GMO ingredients, and may contain too much sodium and refined oils. Luckily though, the school lunch scene is beginning to change as more and more parents and health care practitioners demand something different for our children.

There are so many ways to quickly pack a school lunch, even without bread! In fact, bread is NOT at all a necessary component of a healthy lunch. It has become so ingrained that we need to have bread for sandwiches that it can be difficult to think of other options. Although a few slices of homemade gluten-free bread can sure come in handy once in a while, our goal here is to emphasize other lunchbox ideas that are healthy and naturally gluten-free. Please visit our blog, **www.NourishingMeals.com** to print off our full color "Packing a Healthy School Lunch" chart. Post it on the refrigerator and let your children learn how to pack their own balanced lunches. They will be more likely to eat what they pack themselves.

Growing Foods

The following ideas are nutrient-dense "growing" foods our children frequently pack in their lunch. We always have four child-sized thermoses clean and ready to be used for school lunches. Leftover soups and stews, or cooked beans and a whole grain can form the foundation of a healthy school lunch.

- Lentil and vegetable soup
- Chicken vegetable soup
- Reheated frittata
- Black beans and brown rice
- Curried vegetables over quinoa
- Organic turkey slices and raw cheese wrapped in a lettuce leaf
- Quinoa and bean salad
- Smoked salmon
- Hardboiled pastured eggs
- Chicken salad wrapped in a lettuce leaf, page 395

- Container of homemade Hummus, page 375
- Nutty Granola, page 89
- Nori Rolls with sticky brown rice, tempeh, and carrots

Fresh Fruits and Vegetables

We have a kitchen drawer full of different sized stainless steel and glass containers for our children to pack fresh fruits and vegetables in. We only use organic produce in our house. We encourage you, for the long-term health of your children, to only use organic produce or produce from farms that use organic farming practices though they may not be certified organic.

- Sliced cucumbers
- Carrot sticks
- Celery sticks
- Lettuce leaves
- Napa cabbage leaves
- Apple slices

- Orange slices
- Banana
- Fresh berries
- Grapes
- Raw Sauerkraut, page 504
- Raw Sour Dill Pickles, page 508

High Quality Fats

We have a few very small containers for our children to pack dips for apples, carrots, and celery sticks. High quality fat is needed for proper brain function both in and out of school. We also give each of them a krill oil supplement every morning before school for their daily dose of DHA.

- Mashed avocado with lime and sea salt
- Raw walnuts
- Raw macadamia nuts
- Coconut oil truffle
- Chicken stock heated with cooked beans, fish, rice, or vegetables
- Chia seed coconut fruit smoothie
- Soaked almond smoothie

Snacks and Treats

Sugar is a stimulant that can lead to hyperactivity and learning impairment in children. Choose a treat made from whole foods that is naturally sweetened. The dessert recipes in this book use small amounts of natural sweeteners such as coconut sugar, maple syrup, or honey along with other whole food ingredients to create nutrient-packed sweet treats.

- Raisins
- Dried mango
- Homemade naturally sweetened cookie
- Pudding, such as the Raspberry Almond Pudding, page 424
- Homemade yogurt
- Candied nuts
- Homemade popcorn cooked in coconut oil
- Nut and date energy ball

The Recipes

Getting Started

What does a nourishing meals kitchen look like? Imagine opening your pantry to find jars of whole grains, dry beans, dried fruit, homemade canned jam, applesauce, canned organic coconut milk, coconut flour and whole grain gluten-free flours lining your shelves. A box of potatoes and yams sits on your pantry floor. Imagine opening your refrigerator to find drawers stocked full of leafy greens; organic pastured butter and eggs on the door shelf; pure maple syrup, nut butters, and homemade cultured vegetables on the top shelf; organic apples in the bottom drawer; and a leftover pot of soup on the main shelf. In the freezer you find containers of organic berries and fruit, organic raw nuts, almond flour, grass-fed meats, and pastured poultry. On your kitchen counter you see a small bowl of raw almonds soaking, a jar of bubbling gluten-free sourdough starter, a large bowl of beans soaking, a jar of lentils sprouting, a small basket of onions and garlic, and a large basket of fresh organic fruit. Next to the stove you find a small container of unrefined sea salt, a black pepper grinder, a big jar of organic virgin coconut oil, and a bottle of extra virgin olive oil. Your cabinets are full of fresh organic spices, dried herbs, organic vinegars, and a jar of local raw honey. This is what our kitchen looks like; it's what works for us. Maybe some of these things might work for you too? Choose one thing that excites you most and work on changing that first. Remember to set a pace of dietary change that feels right to you.

Caloric Information?

You'll notice that we don't provide caloric information with each recipe. Calories are only a small fraction of the overall picture of health. What's most important is the quality of your food, not the quantity. Your body functions properly when you have all of the necessary vitamins, minerals, and phytochemicals in your daily diet. Managing weight can be effortless when you combine regular exercise with a plant-rich whole foods diet.

But how do we know if we are getting the recommended daily amount of nutrients? Here's the thing, we all have this intrinsic, intuitive process with food—when given the opportunity, we will choose the exact foods that we need on a daily basis. One day you may crave raw cauliflower, and the next day it may cause you to gag. We've witnessed our children do this too. Some weeks all they want to eat is seaweed, and at other times they want nothing to do with it. Listen to these cues for certain foods—they are telling you what your body really needs. This is far more important than regulating caloric intake.

Guide to Ingredients

This section includes commonly used ingredients found in this book. Most can be found at your local health food store or ordered in bulk online. In fact, to save money we order many of these products either in bulk though our local food co-op or through online food buying companies such as Azure Standard. Larger quantities of dry foods often come in paper bags, which easily biodegrade, reducing packaging and cutting down on waste.

Fresh Organic Produce

Organic produce usually takes up most of the space in our shopping carts and in our refrigerator. We like to purchase perishable vegetables more frequently like lettuce, parsley, and cilantro. Root vegetables and tubers such as yams, carrots, potatoes, rutabagas, and beets can be purchased less frequently because they store for long periods of time. For optimal levels of nutrients, it is best to consume produce in season. This way you are consuming the majority of your food from local sources—meaning it didn't have to travel very far from farm to plate and will be fresher. In the spring, look for baby salad greens, kale, collards, asparagus, radishes, strawberries, garlic greens, and peas. In the summer look for all types of stone fruits, melons, berries, cucumbers, carrots, string beans, corn, bell peppers, fresh onions, zucchini, tomatoes, and carrots. In the fall look for beets, carrots, onions, garlic, broccoli, cauliflower, kale, collards, mustard greens, lettuces apples, and pears. In the winter use root crops stored from the fall such as rutabagas, turnips, potatoes, carrots, celery root, and sweet potatoes, as well as cabbages, onions, and winter squash.

Grass-Fed Meat and Organic Poultry

Most meat you buy at the grocery store or eat from a restaurant contains varying amounts of antibiotic and hormone residues; dyes and other additives; and is often irradiated. With the rise in consciousness of the way most meat and poultry is mass-produced, people are searching for sustainably raised animals instead. With this rise in demand, new farms are popping up all over the country. Invariably, you have a number of very small farms near you where you can directly buy whole chickens, cuts of beef, pork, or lamb. Ask around for contact information or search websites like **www.EatWild.com** or **www.LocalHarvest. org**. Animals raised on organic pasture land have meat that is more nutritious; contains a more even balance of omega 3 and omega 6 fats; the animals are usually healthier requiring little or no antibiotics; and their waste is naturally composted into the earth instead of polluting the water supply and nearby farms. Since their meat is more nutrient-dense, you'll find that you don't need to eat as much, thereby supporting the environment and everyone's health. Having an extra freezer is ideal for storing meat you buy in large quantities directly from a farm. It is best to use frozen meat within a year of purchasing it.

Eggs

Allergies and sensitivities to eggs are certainly on the rise, but for many eggs still offer an excellent source of nutrition. Large-scale egg production creates eggs that are far less nutritious than their pastured counterparts. Chickens are often fed genetically engineered grains that have arsenic and antibiotics added to them to keep parasites and disease at bay. Raising backyard egg-laying chickens is becoming quite popular for a healthy source of eggs. You can also check your local food co-op, Farmer's Market, or small family farms for pastured eggs—or eggs from chickens that are raised outside on grass and fed vegetable scraps and minimal organic grains. Pastured eggs have dark orange yolks and are far richer in nutrients such as vitamins E, D, and A, as wells as omega-3 fatty acids. They may cost more than "free range" or organic eggs, but you'll end up saving money in the long run because you won't need to spend as much on expensive vitamin supplements!

Dairy

While some adults and children—especially of Northern European decent—can digest dairy products, the vast majority cannot, especially those with damaged upper intestines. It is actually quite common for the body to recognize dairy proteins as foreign and launch an immune attack against them. Dairy products are not a necessary component of a healthy diet, but if you do choose to eat them or feed them to your child it is important to purchase the healthiest forms. Dairy products that undergo a lot of processing, such as through the pasteurization and homogenization process, are far less digestible and less nutritious than raw or fermented dairy products.

In fact, research shows that pasteurizing milk causes the loss of key nutrients either through the destruction of carrier proteins or the nutrient itself. Vitamin C, iron, calcium, vitamin A, folate, B6, and B12 are all affected. The process of homogenization breaks apart larger fat molecules into smaller ones. These smaller fat particles present a dramatically increased surface area onto which allergenic milk proteins can adhere to. In raw milk, many of the antigenic proteins are located inside casein micelles. In homogenized milk, the amount of exposed antigenic proteins is reported to increase. These small fat particles with attached casein proteins might be a large contributor to the increase in inflammatory diseases, food allergies, and heart disease we see today.

Find a local source of raw milk produced from cows or goats raised on grasses. If you can't find raw milk, the next best thing is to buy fermented organic dairy products from milk that was not homogenized—like "cream at the top" yogurt. It is important to note that many people feel better when removing dairy from the diet, even raw and cultured dairy products. If you are looking for an alternative to cow's milk, check out our Beverage chapter, page 477, for homemade dairy-free milk and kefir recipes.

Gluten-Free Whole Grains

You can find a variety of gluten-free whole grains in the bulk section of your local food co-op or health foods store, but you need to be very careful about cross-contamination. Some stores are very knowledgeable and place wheat berries and wheat flours away from everything else, but most do not. Flour dust can linger in the air and contaminate surrounding bins. We prefer to order organic quinoa and brown rice in 25-pound bags from Azure Standard. Millet, raw buckwheat groats, and rolled oats need to be purchased from a place that offers certified gluten-free versions, such as Bob's Red Mill. Place your grains in large glass jars and store them in a cool dark pantry where they will keep for up to 9 months.

The optimal way to prepare grains is to soak them for 12 to 24 hours in warm water with the addition of something acidic, such as lemon juice or apple cider vinegar. Doing this will help to neutralize phytic acid and allow for better absorption of minerals such as iron, zinc, calcium, and magnesium. See the Whole Grains Chapter, page 253, for details on how to soak and cook whole grains.

Legumes

We buy dry beans in bulk from our local food co-op or in 25-pound bags from Azure Standard. For optimal nutrient availability it is best to soak beans in warm water for 8 to 48 hours. Beans, just like whole grains contain phytic acid, which can block mineral absorption in some people. Soaking them helps to neutralize phytic acid as well as eliminate most of the lectins—a family of proteins abundant in uncooked beans and grains that are believed to be natural insecticides. Lectins can be hard on the digestive tract if not broken down before consuming. Soaking and cooking, as well as having adequate stomach acid and a healthy population of friendly bacteria in the gut, all help to break down lectins found in beans and whole grains.

To cook beans, drain off soaking water, place beans into a large pot, and cover with fresh water; add one strip of kombu seaweed. Bring beans to a boil, then reduce heat to low and simmer until soft. Most beans take 45 minutes to 2 hours of cooking time. You'll know when they are done if they mash easily in your mouth. Don't add salt or acids, such as vinegar or tomatoes, to them during cooking as this can inhibit the beans from cooking properly. We always add salt and acids to beans after they are cooked and then simmer them for an extra 20 to 30 minutes to allow the flavors to meld.

For a higher protein content and even better nutrient profile you can sprout your beans after soaking and then slow cook them. This changes the ratio of starches and protein. If you or your child has weak digestion and multiple nutrient deficiency symptoms, then sprouting is the best route to go when preparing dry beans. If you are new to soaking and sprouting beans then start with lentils—they are one of the fastest legumes to sprout! For more details on cooking legumes, please refer to our first book, *The Whole Life Nutrition Cookbook*.

Nuts and Seeds

Raw, organic nuts and seeds are best purchased in bulk from your local food co-op or health food store. Make sure the store you are buying from has a high turnover rate if not, they could be rancid. We prefer to buy 30-pound boxes of raw organic, unpasteurized almonds directly from farms in California. We order 10 pounds of chia seeds at a time and pour some into a quart jar for our refrigerator and store the remaining seeds in our freezer until ready to use. Other nuts and seeds we buy in bulk though our local food co-op and store them in our freezer until ready to use.

For optimal nutrient availability and digestibility, soak your nuts and seeds in warm filtered water for 8 to 24 hours (less time for seeds, more for nuts), then rinse and drain, and dehydrate at 110 to 115 degrees F until crispy, usually about 24 to 48 hours. Check them for doneness by eating a few, if they don't feel crispy let them dehydrate an hour or two longer.

Like grains and beans, nuts and seeds contain phytic acid as well as enzyme inhibitors, which lock down enzymes and nutrients until the seed is ready to germinate. By soaking your nuts and seeds in warm water you are essentially mimicking the process of nature. Dehydrating them makes them "shelf stable" and usable for all recipes where raw nuts and seeds are called for. This process creates a highly digestible nut or seed that is rich in live enzymes! We store jars of soaked and dehydrated nuts on our kitchen counter so our children can have access to a quick, nutritious snack and so we can use them in recipes. Roasting nuts and seeds is another way to reduce phytic acid and enzyme inhibitors, though soaking seems to work more efficiently. The remainder of our nuts and seeds are stored in the refrigerator or freezer until we have time to soak and dehydrate, or roast them. Please note that chia and flax seeds should not be soaked and dehydrated before using as they create a thick gel when exposed to liquid.

Gluten-Free Flours

Most gluten-free flours can be found at your local health food store or food co-op. They come in small packages in the baking section. To reduce wasteful packaging, consider ordering flours directly from the mill in 25-pound paper bags. We order flour and grains directly from Bob's Red Mill, except for teff flour—we save the most money by buying a 25-pound bag of teff flour from Azure Standard. You can use a kitchen scale and divvy up the flour among friends.

If you want to take your health one step further, consider using *sprouted* gluten-free flours in cookies, bars, and breads, which offer even more nutrients than regular whole grain flours. Sprouting wakes up the grain for germination, which increases nutrients, reduces phytic acid, and changes starches into a more digestible form. If you are making sourdough breads, rolls, pancakes, etc., there is no need to buy sprouted flours—the process of making a sourdough starter renders the grain flours very digestible with a high nutrient availability. Additionally, when using blanched nut flours or coconut flour there is no need for soaking or sprouting.

Fats & Oils

For most of our recipes we use either organic virgin coconut oil or organic extra virgin olive oil. Coconut oil is rich in medium-chain triglycerides, such as caprylic, capric and lauric acids, which help to boost your metabolism and strengthen your immune system. Medium chain triglycerides (MCTs) are absorbed differently than long-chain fatty acids. In fact, in weight loss trials, there is evidence that diets higher in medium chain triglycerides can contribute to greater fat loss. Coconut oil is more stable at higher temperatures than olive oil, but we still use olive oil on occasion for roasting veggies.

When purchasing olive oil, it is important to look for one that is labeled "extra virgin" and preferably is organic. A 2004 article in the *Journal of Nutrition* noted that potent plant chemicals in the olive oil, specifically protocatechuic acid and oleuropein, protected vessels and cholesterol from oxidative damage by signaling genes to express more powerful antioxidant enzymes like glutathione reductase and glutathione peroxidase. When comparing types and qualities of olive oils, researchers found that extra virgin high-quality oils with higher phenolic compounds have a much more profound beneficial effect than the lower quality, more refined oils.

Some members of our family also use organic, pastured butter on occasion. Pastured means that the cows were grazing on grasses instead of eating grains, which is what their bodies are designed to be doing. This makes their milk and butterfat a good source of nutrients such as vitamins A and K2, which allows for proper utilization of both calcium and phosphorous leading to strong bones and teeth. Though given the levels of environmental toxicity in the world, it is best to limit the consumption of butter—even organic pastured butter—because toxins are found in highest amounts in the fats of animals. To replace butter in recipes such as biscuits and pie crusts, we suggest using organic palm shortening. High quality organic extra virgin olive oil, organic virgin coconut oil, and organic palm shortening can all be found at your local food co-op or health food store.

Vinegars

Raw apple cider vinegar and raw coconut vinegar are some of the healthiest vinegars. Taking a spoonful before a meal can improve digestion. They are living foods, rich in live enzymes that can help digest parts of your meal. We use vinegar weekly for homemade salad dressings and also medicinally to steep herbs in.

Wine vinegars can also make a nice addition to your pantry. Adding a tablespoon or two to a finished bean soup can boost flavors without the need for more salt. Be sure to purchase organic wine and apple cider vinegars as grapes and apples are routinely sprayed with a variety of toxic chemicals.

Natural Sweeteners

Most natural sweeteners can be found at your local health food store or food co-op. If you live in an area where maple syrup is produced then search out a small local farm and purchase directly from them. Every town has a few beekeepers to buy directly from. Look for a place that sells raw honey, as the glycemic index is generally lower and it contains more nutrients. We buy medjool dates in large boxes from Azure Standard—they keep for many months in our garage refrigerator. For an alternative to granulated white sugar we use coconut sugar, another low-glycemic sweetener. For a more detailed look into natural sweeteners, see our Desserts chapter, page 413.

Tomato Products

Canned tomato products often contain BPA, a hormone-disrupting chemical, in the lining of the can. To avoid this, we use freshly diced tomatoes in most recipes. We like to freeze whole roma tomatoes in the summertime to use during the winter months. Simply let a few thaw on your counter for 10 minutes then dice them up to add to your soup. Also, look for organic tomato sauce and tomato paste in glass jars at your local food co-op or health food store—Bionaturae is a brand we like to use.

Coconut Milk

Coconut milk is rich and thick, perfect for baking grain-free cakes with or making puddings and curries. We prefer to use coconut milk from the can as it is less processed and contains only coconut milk (and usually a small amount of guar gum). To avoid BPA in cans, we use the brand, Native Forest.

Chocolate

I usually have a few different forms of chocolate around for baking and raw desserts. Dagoba's bittersweet chocolate is perfect for baking, I store it in my freezer. I also prefer to use raw cacao powder instead of roasted, as it is higher in antioxidants and lower in caffeine. Make sure the company you purchase it from is gluten-free! We also use dark chocolate chips and cacao nibs for baking and special snacks. Again, make sure the company you are purchasing from is gluten-free. Additionally, if you want to avoid soy, then look for a company that doesn't use soy lecithin in their products.

Extracts and Flavorings

You'll notice that some of our recipes call for almond flavoring or vanilla extract. We use organic almond flavoring, which can be found in the baking section of your local health food store or food co-op. A small amount goes a long way! Placing a few organic vanilla beans in a jar of organic vodka and letting it sit for a few months is a way to make homemade vanilla extract. Non-alcoholic vanilla is made using a glycerin extract and is ideal for raw desserts where the alcohol won't get cooked off.

Unrefined Sea Salt

Be sure to purchase sea salt that is unrefined. This means that all of the minerals and trace minerals still exist in the salt. Celtic sea salt or Real Salt are good choices. For baking, be sure to use a fine-grained sea salt. Using coarse sea salt will alter how much sodium is in the recipe. I like to use coarse sea salt for sprinkling into a pot of cooking soup or on top of meats before roasting. We also like to use a natural salt seasoning called Herbamare. Organic herbs and vegetables are steeped in unrefined sea salt to create a flavorful seasoning that can be used in soups, meat dishes, beans, or whole grain salads.

Baking Powder

Baking powder is often made with cornstarch and sometimes can contain gluten and aluminum. Rumford brand is gluten-free and the cornstarch they use is GMO-free. However, you can easily make your own corn-free baking powder very easily. Simply mix together 2 parts arrowroot powder, 2 parts cream of tarter, and 1 part baking soda. Place baking powder mixture into a glass jar and label it!

Essential Kitchen Equipment

Creating great recipes requires a few specific tools. These are all items that I use daily in my kitchen and tools I find essential in any working kitchen.

High-Powered Blender

All of the recipes created in this book that require a blender were created using a high-powered blender, such as a Vita-Mix or Blendtec. These types of blenders have powerful motors that can blend very thick sauces or fillings into a smooth creamy consistency. They also work very well at breaking down tough greens into a pleasant, fine-textured green smoothie. Some of the recipes have notes in the directions for using a regular blender and some recipes simply cannot be made without a high-powered blender, such as our Raw Blueberry Cheesecake.

Immersion Blender

This is a relatively inexpensive hand-held blender that works great for quickly pureeing cream soups or blending small amount of ingredients, such as a salad dressing. I recommend buying a stainless steel immersion blender if you plan to use it for hot soups. Otherwise the plastic will leach chemicals into the hot soup.

Food Processor

For making nut-based truffles or raw nut crusts, a food processor is essential. I also use it to make fish or bean burgers, meatballs, and to mince vegetables. A food processor can also be used with the slicing or grating disc in place to thinly slice or grate a variety of vegetables in very little time. I use a 14-cup Cuisinart Food Processor, though the 11-cup size will work for all of my recipes as well.

Food Dehydrator

A food dehydrator is essential if you are preparing nuts and seeds for optimal digestibility, meaning that they are being soaked and then dehydrated before being used in recipes or eaten as a snack. You can also soak, sprout, and dehydrate whole grains and then grind them into flour. We get the most use out of our dehydrator in late summer and early autumn when the fresh produce is at its peak. Kale chips, dried tomatoes and homemade fruit leathers are always being made! An Excalibur dehydrator is one of the best on the market, but an American Harvest works just as well with a cheaper price tag. If you are looking to avoid plastic, then the Excalibur is your best bet.

Pots and Pans
I use both stainless steel and cast iron pots and pans. Many of my recipes suggest using a deep 11-inch skillet—I find this pan to be one of the most convenient and useful pans for a variety of recipes. I also recommend purchasing a good quality stockpot, 8-quart or larger. We usually cook our grains in 2 or 3-quart pots. Small skillets are also very useful. When purchasing stainless steel, make sure that the bottom has a thick aluminum core. This prevents food, such as whole grains and pancakes, from sticking and burning. We never recommend using non-stick pots and pans. When heated, these pans release toxic gases, some of which have been found to be carcinogenic.

Stone Baking Pans
I bake all of my muffins and most of my quick breads using stoneware. This type of cookware never sticks, heats evenly, and cleans up quickly. I have a stone muffin pan, mini-loaf pan (contains 4 mini loaves), bundt pan, cookie sheet, and pizza stone. I use the Pampered Chef brand, which is relatively inexpensive. I also feel that this type of cookware is earth-friendly, meaning when the time comes for it to break, it will actually biodegrade in the earth since it is made only of uncoated clay.

Glass Baking Pans
For all other baking and roasting, I prefer to use glass Pyrex pans. I have a few 9 x 13-inch pans as well as one 10 x 14-inch pan. 8 x 8-inch pans work well for baking small cakes and bars. All of the pie plates I use are glass as well. I have a few deep dish and a few regular pie plates in a variety of sizes; they are great for roasting small batches of nuts too.

Stainless Steel Baking Pans
I have a large stainless steel jelly roll pan that I use for everything from roasting homemade oven fries to baking cookies and flatbread. The size I use is 11 x 17 inches. I also have a few stainless steel 9-inch round cake pans for baking layered cakes.

Oven Thermometer
Since baking temperature is crucial to the end product, a simple oven thermometer is essential. They cost around $5. Many ovens, even newer ones, can be off sometimes by as much as 25 degrees. Use the oven thermometer to adjust the temperature as needed.

High Quality Knives
Heavy-duty, sharp knives are indispensable for anyone who cooks regularly. I recommend going to your local kitchen store and checking out a few different brands. They should be comfortable for the size of your hand. I like the brand, Wusthof. Since good quality knives can be a bit pricy, try adding just one at a time.

Liquid Glass Measures

I use everything from a 1-cup to an 8-cup liquid glass measure. It is important to always measure your liquid ingredients in a liquid measure and your dry ingredients in dry measuring cups. I use Pyrex brand and always stick with glass. When measuring hot liquids it is really important to be using glass and not plastic as plastic can leach toxic chemicals into your food.

Garlic Press

I use a heavy-duty stainless steel garlic press. The cheaper ones tend to break easily creating unnecessary waste. I use crushed garlic in most of my recipes calling for garlic. The brand I use and highly recommend is Rosle. This garlic press is so sturdy that you don't need to peel the garlic before putting into the press, saving a lot of time.

Microplane

This is an indispensable type of grating tool for cooks. I use mine to grate lemon or orange zest, fresh ginger, and nutmeg.

Fine Mesh Strainer

Along with a few colanders for draining noodles or chicken stock, I use a fine mesh strainer for rinsing small grains such as quinoa and amaranth. A fine mesh strainer also works well for straining the pulp out of homemade raw almond milk.

Food Storage

We store all of our leftover food in a variety of glass storage containers. I also have a number of small stainless steel containers for packing lunches as well as a few larger ones for food storage. Each child also has their own small stainless steel Thermos for packing hot soup or warm grains and beans in their school lunches.

Smoothies

Green smoothies are a fantastic way to consume large amounts of raw, green leafy vegetables. In fact, it is difficult to eat enough green vegetables without having a green smoothie each day. We use a Vita-Mix for all of our smoothie recipes. This type of high-powered blender has a 2-plus horsepower motor, which effectively breaks down whole foods—including the leaves, peels, and stems—allowing the valuable phytonutrients stuck inside the plant fibers to become fully bioavailable. High-powered blenders can make smooth and creamy homemade "ice cream," frozen fruit smoothies, and green smoothies. We highly recommend a high-powered blender as an investment in your health.

Introducing Smoothies to Children

Smoothies are one of the best ways to get concentrated nutrients and fiber into anyone, but especially young children. We have found that the earlier you introduce green smoothies to your children, the more likely they will enjoy them and have an eagerness to drink them throughout their childhood and beyond. Begin to serve citrus-free green smoothies between 8 ½ and 10 months of age. We have seen some children react to citrus with rashes if introduced earlier than twelve months. Start with a small amount of greens and then gradually add more when first introducing green smoothies to your child's diet.

Sometime between twelve and twenty-four months is a good time to introduce nuts to your child's diet. When first introducing nuts we like to soak them overnight to aid in digestibility and nutrient availability. Soaked nuts form the basis of many of the smoothies in this chapter. If desired, you can replace some of the nuts called for in these recipes with other nuts or seeds. For example, try replacing almonds with raw cashews, sunflower seeds, or macadamia nuts.

Hiding Supplements in Smoothies
Smoothies are also a great way to "hide" supplements. When we were working on healing our daughter's gut we made special smoothies with powdered glutamine, probiotics, liquid vitamin D & K, and fish oil. She loved them and couldn't taste the supplements.

10 Tips for Making Smoothies:

1. **A high-powered blender will easily blend up whole chia seeds into a smoothie**. If you don't own one, first grind the chia seeds in a coffee grinder or small electric grinder before adding them to the smoothie.

2. **We try to freeze as much fruit as possible in the summer and fall so we have local fruit to use throughout the seasons before the new crops arrive**.

3. **When making green smoothies**, adding fresh lemon juice will preserve the smoothie and keep it bright green for days in the refrigerator.

4. **If you are allergic to citrus**, then use a tart granny smith apple and fresh or frozen cranberries in your green smoothies to add the tart flavor normally provided by the lemon.

5. **If your green smoothie tastes too bitter add one to three pitted medjool dates**, 10 to 20 drops of liquid stevia, or an extra pear to add sweetness.

6. **Add additional water or organic apple juice for a thinner smoothie**.

7. **Add a few tablespoons of fat**, whether in the form of flax seeds, chia seeds, avocado, or virgin coconut oil, to help you to absorb the carotenoids in the greens.

8. **Use frozen organic fruit and coconut water to create a simple**, refreshing smoothie in the summertime.

9. **Use uncommon fruits for making smoothies**. Honeydew melon, fresh mint, and ice cubes create a frosty fresh smoothie for a hot day.

10. **Leftover smoothies can be either stored in glass jars in the refrigerator or poured into popsicle molds and frozen for a fun treat later on**.

Berry Orange Smoothie

During our Pacific Northwest summers, our kitchen is usually filled with a variety of freshly picked berries. For this smoothie try using blueberries, strawberries, blackberries, marionberries, or raspberries for a refreshing afternoon antioxidant snack. Pour any leftover smoothie into popsicle molds for a fun treat later on for your children.

3 cups fresh organic berries
2 cups freshly squeezed orange juice
2 cups ice cubes

Place all ingredients into a blender and blend until smooth. Serve immediately.

Yield: About 6 cups

Ingredient Tip:

If your berries are tart, you can add a few drops of liquid stevia to this smoothie to sweeten it if needed.

Blueberry Cucumber Smoothie

Serve this ice cold, refreshing smoothie for a late afternoon summer snack. It is thirst-quenching and full of powerful antioxidants. It can also be frozen into popsicle molds for a nutritious, kid-friendly snack.

1 large cucumber, peeled and sliced
2 cups fresh blueberries
1 cup apple juice or water
2 cups ice cubes

Place all ingredients into a blender and blend on high for about 60 to 90 seconds. Serve immediately.

Yield: About 5 cups

Ingredient Tip:

Cucumber peels are packed with nutrients, particularly minerals such as silica, potassium, and magnesium, but sometimes they can be quite bitter and blending the cucumbers with the peels intact will only increase the bitterness. Younger, fresher cucumbers often have peels that aren't bitter. I suggest peeling a little off and tasting it before deciding whether or not to use the peel.

Blueberry Cherry Smoothie

This simple smoothie is packed with cell-protective antioxidants. It is naturally sweetened using fruit and provides easily assimilated protein from the raw almond milk and chia seeds.

2 cups frozen blueberries
2 cups frozen cherries
1 small banana
2 to 4 tablespoons chia seeds
2 cups Raw Almond Milk (page 481)

Place all ingredients into your blender and blend on high until very smooth. If you do not own a high-powered blender then you will want to grind your chia seeds in a small electric grinder or coffee grinder prior to adding them to the smoothie. Drink immediately or pour into popsicle molds to freeze any leftovers.

Yield: About 6 cups

Nutrition Tip:

Studies show that consuming blueberries helps to balance the gut. Blueberries—specifically the lowbush or wild variety—can decrease the risk of a negative reaction to foodborne pathogens while preserving the function of beneficial bacterium in the intestines. These blueberries appear to have a potent antimicrobial effect on foodborne pathogenic bacterium including E. coli, Salmonella Typhimurium, and Listeria, yet the beneficial Lactobacillus rhamnosus is spared. Additionally, research has demonstrated that blueberry consumption can lead to an increase in bifidobacterium counts, further balancing the intestines with beneficial bacterium.

Blueberry Kefir Smoothie

This smoothie idea came from our good friend Phyllis, a vibrantly healthy woman in her mid-sixties. She makes her own kefir from organic raw goat's milk and tells me that this smoothie keeps her energized and full until well after lunchtime. If you don't have any blueberries then try cherries or Italian plums instead.

1 cup kefir (cow, goat, or coconut)
1 cup fresh or frozen blueberries
½ avocado
1 tablespoon chia seeds
5 to 7 drops liquid stevia (optional)

Place all ingredients into a blender and blend until smooth. For a thinner smoothie, add water, a few tablespoons at a time, until desired consistency is reached.

Yield: About 2 ½ cups

Variation:

Replace the blueberries with frozen cherries for a slightly sweeter smoothie.

Creamy Cashew Peach Smoothie

This semi-sweet smoothie feels more like a treat than anything, but it packs in the protein and magnesium, making it a perfect "treat" to give to your children. Any leftovers can be poured into popsicle molds and frozen for another time.

1 ½ cups raw cashews
2 cups water
2 large peaches, pitted and frozen
2 to 4 medjool dates, pitted
2 tablespoons chia seeds
1 tablespoon non-alcoholic vanilla or 1 whole vanilla bean

Place the cashews and water into a high-powered blender and blend until smooth and creamy. Then add the peaches, dates, chia seeds, and vanilla; blend again, pulsing as needed, until the peaches break down and the smoothie is blended and creamy.

Yield: 5 cups

Kitchen Tip:

If you don't own a high-powered blender then first soak the cashews in water for 3 hours then drain. Also, make sure your frozen peaches are chopped up, and use ground chia seeds.

Mango Banana Almond Smoothie

This smoothie is helpful in repairing the gut. We often recommend this recipe for children as part of a gut-healing plan after being diagnosed with Celiac disease. I prefer to use frozen mango as it creates a thick, cold, creaminess that you can't achieve by using all fresh fruit. I also use homemade raw almond milk, but you could use coconut milk, hemp milk, or cashew milk if desired.

2 cups chopped fresh or frozen mango
2 ripe bananas
2 cups Raw Almond Milk (page 481)

Place all ingredients into a blender and blend for about 60 seconds or until all of the mango pieces are broken down and pureed.

Yield: About 4 to 5 cups

Variation:

Homemade Cashew Milk, page 483, can be used in place of the raw almond milk.

Nutrition Tip:

Both mangos and bananas are beneficial for the gut. Mangos are a good source of glutamine, the amino acid which helps repair a damaged gut—especially one healing from celiac disease, and bananas are high in pectin, a substance that helps to normalize movements of the large intestines. Mangos are also an excellent source of cancer-protective pectins, phenols, and enzymes.

Orange Creamsicle Smoothie

This smoothie was inspired by a drink served at Thrive, one of our favorite restaurants in Seattle, and is more like a frosty beverage than a thick smoothie. It is quite refreshing on a very hot day. If you don't want to use raw almond milk or have a nut allergy then use hemp milk or any milk of your choice. I prefer freshly squeezed orange juice over store-bought because all of the enzymes needed to help digest the sugars remain intact. This is another recipe that can be frozen in popsicle molds for a frosty treat later on.

4 cups Raw Almond Milk (page 481)
2 cups freshly squeezed orange juice
2 medium frozen bananas
1 to 2 handfuls ice cubes

Place the almond milk, orange juice, and bananas into a high-powered blender and blend for about 60 seconds or until smooth. Add ice cubes and blend again.

Yield: About 8 cups

Ingredient Tip:

I like to use Valencia oranges for their high juice content.

Pecan Berry Blast

This antioxidant and protein-packed smoothie makes an excellent snack or quick breakfast on the run.

1 cup raw pecans, soaked for 3 to 6 hours
2 to 3 pitted medjool dates, soaked for 3 to 6 hours
2 tablespoons chia seeds
2 cups water
1 cup frozen blackberries
1 cup frozen blueberries
1 cup frozen pitted plums or raspberries

Place the pecans into a small bowl and cover with water. Place dates into a separate small bowl and cover with water. Once they are done soaking, drain them and place into a blender along with the chia seeds and water. Blend until very smooth and creamy. Add the frozen fruit and blend again until completely smooth. Add more water for a thinner smoothie. Serve immediately.

Yield: About 5 cups

Variation:

If you do not have any dates on hand then substitute 2 tablespoons honey or coconut nectar.

Nutrition Tip:

Choosing organic or wild blueberries over conventionally grown makes a difference! One study revealed that organic blueberries had 33% more antioxidant activity, over 35% more anthocyanins, and 40% total phenolic content than their conventionally grown counterparts.

Strawberry Almond Smoothie

It is important to plan ahead when you want to make this smoothie or a variation of it. Before I go to bed, I briefly plan out the next day and consider if I need to soak any nuts or beans. It only takes a few minutes to get the nuts out and pour water over them. You'll want to give them about 8 to 10 hours of soaking time. In the morning be sure to drain off the soaking water and rinse well in a colander. Use any frozen or fresh fruits you have on hand in place of the strawberries if desired.

1 cup raw almonds, soaked overnight
1 ½ to 2 cups water
2 to 3 cups fresh or frozen strawberries
1 whole vanilla bean or 1 tablespoon non-alcoholic vanilla
1 tablespoon raw honey (optional)

Rinse and drain the soaked almonds. Place the almonds and water into a high-powered blender or a blender fitted with a sharp blade and blend until very smooth, about 30 to 60 seconds. Then add the berries, vanilla bean, and honey; blend again until smooth adding more water if necessary. Serve immediately.

Yield: About 6 cups

Variation:

Replace the strawberries with fresh or frozen Italian plums.

Raw Cacao Hemp Seed Smoothie

This smoothie makes a great nutritious dessert or a sweet afternoon energizing drink. It is nut-free and high in plant-based protein. Additionally, hemp and chia seeds are excellent sources of omega-3 fatty acids. Raw cacao is very high in antioxidants, even more than regular cocoa powder. The pear can be replaced with one frozen banana if desired, just make sure to add extra water to compensate for the water lost in the pear.

½ cup hemp seeds
1 cup water
1 tablespoon chia seeds
1 ripe pear, cored and chopped
3 to 4 tablespoons raw cacao powder
2 to 3 tablespoons coconut nectar or honey
1 whole vanilla bean (optional)

Place the hemp seeds and water into a blender. Blend until ultra smooth and creamy, about 60 seconds, then add the remaining ingredients. Blend again until smooth. Taste and add more coconut nectar and raw cacao if needed. Blend again. Serve immediately or chill for 2 hours before serving.

Yield: About 2 ½ cups

Nutrition Tip:

Pears are an excellent source of soluble fibers. These fibers act as a sponge to mop up toxins that are released from the liver via the bile and excreted into the intestinal tract.

Baby Green Smoothie

This recipe is designed for older babies who are just getting introduced to green smoothies. Most babies will be ready for their first cup between 8 ½ and 10 months. Children's taste buds develop during the first three years of life so beginning healthy eating habits right from the start—in infancy—is very important. The flavor of this smoothie is very mild and slightly sweet.

1 medium apple, cored
1 small cucumber, peeled
2 large collard greens
1 cup water

Place all ingredients into a blender and blend on high until smooth.

Serve immediately or pour smoothie into a glass jar and store in your refrigerator for up to 2 days.

Yield: About 3 cups

Variation:

You can replace the apple with a ripe pear, peach, or a couple of plums if desired.

Cherry Beet Detox Smoothie

This beautiful, ruby-colored smoothie is just as delicious as it is detoxifying. Beets have unique detoxification support chemicals, called betalains, which help the liver process toxins while keeping antioxidants levels high. If the beet flavor is too strong for you, add more cherries or an extra pear.

1 small raw beet, peeled
1 medium ripe pear, cored
1 cup frozen pitted cherries
1 cup chopped cabbage
1 cup water

Place all ingredients into a high-powered blender and blend until smooth. Add more water if desired.

Yield: 3 ½ cups

Nutrition Tip:

Cabbage is beneficial for both the healing of the intestinal tract and for reducing cancer risk. The fibers in cabbage and the high content of the amino acid glutamine, which is used by intestinal cells for repair, contribute to the healing of the intestinal tract. Cabbage also contains cancer-fighting compounds called glucosinolates. Glucosinolates are sulfur-containing molecules that have glucose attached to them. When cabbage is blended up the enzyme myrosinase is released, which removes the glucose from the sulfur compounds. One such sulfur compound called sulforaphane has an amazing ability to turn on a part of our genes called the Antioxidant Response Element. When it does this, we start producing more antioxidant and detoxification enzymes that provide 72 hours of protection from environmentally and internally produced toxins. Doctors from John's Hopkins say that sulforphane may be one of the best-known cancer protective substances on the planet.

Green Chia Smoothie

Adding chia seeds to our morning smoothies boosts the protein and fat content, which helps to stabilize blood sugar and make them feel more like a meal with actual staying power. The coconut water in this smoothie helps to make it a great pre or post workout drink. Coconut water is very high in potassium, but if you need to replace electrolytes post-workout, be sure to add a pinch of sea salt to each serving to replace sodium.

1 tart apple, cored
1 large mango, peeled and pitted
3 to 4 large kale leaves
3 handfuls baby spinach
½ medium cucumber
2 to 3 tablespoons whole chia seeds
2 to 3 cups water or coconut water

Place all ingredients into a high-powered blender and blend until smooth and creamy. Serve immediately.

Yield: 2 servings

Variation:

Freeze part of the coconut water into ice cube trays and add the coconut ice cubes after you have blended the other ingredients and blend again. This makes a refreshing, cool drink in the summertime.

Low Fructose Green Smoothie

Some people have a difficult time digesting fructose. Apple and pears, which we use in many of our smoothie recipes, are very high in fructose. Mandarins, blueberries, and strawberries are lower in fructose and therefore good to use in green smoothies in place of apples and pears. Adding the avocado boosts absorption of beneficial carotenoids in the greens. It also slows the digestion of the smoothie, which helps to maintain blood sugar and keep you satisfied longer.

3 cups water
2 tablespoons whole chia seeds
½ cup freshly squeezed lemon juice
2-inch piece fresh ginger
2 cups frozen strawberries
1 cup frozen blueberries
1 peeled mandarin orange
1 avocado
½ bunch collard greens
½ bunch kale

Add the water, chia seeds, lemon juice, and ginger to a high-powered blender. Blend on high until the chia seeds are pureed. Then add the cherries, blueberries, and peeled orange. Blend again until smooth and creamy. Then add the greens and blend until combined.

Yield: About 8 cups

Variation:

If you do not have a fructose sensitivity, consider replacing some of the frozen berries with frozen cherries.

Spring Green Smoothie

The first vegetables of spring happen to be bitter greens, making this time of year a season of cleansing. Many of these early spring greens can be harvested around your neighborhood, such as dandelion greens, nettles, bittercress, and lamb's quarters. Bitter greens stimulate the liver to wake up and get rid of any stored toxins from the winter. We let our kale, collard, and sorrel plants die back in the winter, then when the weather is warm enough—usually in late winter here—the greens begin to grow again.

2 apples, cored
2 pears, cored
1 lemon, juiced (optional)
2 to 3 cups water
1 cup sorrel leaves
2 cups chopped kale or collard greens
½ cup fresh nettles
½ cup dandelion leaves

Place the fruit, lemon juice, and water into a high-powered blender and blend until smooth. Add in the greens and blend again until very smooth. Add more water if necessary.

Yield: About 6 cups

Kitchen Tip:

Don't forget to use gardening gloves when handling fresh nettles!

Super Antioxidant Smoothie

This smoothie is a great way to introduce greens into your child's diet without overwhelming them with the color "green." Start with a little spinach and then add more as their taste buds adjust. You can even add a few drops of liquid stevia to sweeten if you would like a sweeter flavor. I think the consistency is best if some of the fruit is frozen. I use frozen plums, blackberries, and blueberries.

1 peach, pitted and cut into chunks
1 apple, cored and cut into chunks
3 Italian plums or 1 large plum, pitted
1 cup blueberries
1 cup blackberries
4 cups packed spinach leaves
2 cups water

Place all ingredients into a blender and blend on high until smooth. Store any unused portions in a glass jar and place in the refrigerator for up to 2 days.

Yield: About 5 to 6 cups

Nutrition Tip:

Does it make a difference if blueberries are organic, raw, cooked, juiced, dried, or frozen? Yes! The antioxidant effect of blueberries is similar in fresh, frozen, and dried blueberries, yet cooking or pasteurizing the juice does decrease some important components. For example, one study found 64% higher levels of antioxidant anthocyanidin levels in fresh blueberries compared to blueberry juice.

Winter Green Smoothie

Remember that a smoothie made without lemon will need to be consumed the day it is made; otherwise the fruit will begin to oxidize. This smoothie has Granny Smith apples and cranberries, which add tartness. You can also vary the recipe by adding in frozen blueberries, cherries, or peaches, though your smoothie won't be green anymore (and may not look very appetizing).

2 Granny Smith apples, cored and cut into chunks
2 pears, cored and cut into chunks
handful of fresh or frozen cranberries
1 to 2-inch piece of fresh ginger
2 cups of water
6 to 7 large kale leaves
4 to 5 large collard greens
large chunk of green cabbage (about 1 to 2 cups chopped)
handful of fresh parsley

Place apples, pears, cranberries, ginger, and water into a high-powered blender and blend until smooth. Stuff the greens into the blender and blend again until smooth. Add more water for a thinner smoothie.

Store in a glass jar in the fridge for up to a day.

Yield: About 6 to 7 cups

Nutrition Tip:

Kale is an outstanding source of vitamin K1 with one cup having over 1000% of the recommended daily value. Recent research has pointed to the importance of vitamin K2 in maintaining optimum calcium balance in the body. Vitamin K2 is formed from dietary K1 in reactions with beneficial bacterium in the intestines. When vitamin K2 is sufficient, it works to allow the protein osteocalcin to put calcium into bone (osseus tissue), and allows for another protein, Matrix-GLA, to clean up calcium from soft tissue areas. In essence, when vitamin K is low the body is less likely to put calcium where it's needed and will leave it where it's not.

Breakfast

For most of us, breakfast while growing up included some form of refined wheat, dairy, eggs, and sugar. Starting the day out with these foods—whether in the form of cereal with milk, pancakes from a mix made with milk and eggs, or some sort of fast food breakfast item—causes the day to begin not only with a sharp rise in blood sugar, but an increase in inflammation in the body. Research shows that children who eat a healthy breakfast concentrate, behave, and learn better in school. This cookbook includes a variety of healthy breakfast options that allow the body to wake up and begin the day with energy such as scrambled eggs and kale, raw breakfast tacos, overnight quinoa hot cakes, green smoothies, and teff breakfast bars.

Starting the Day with a Healthy Breakfast

Research shows that only about 40 percent of Americans actually eat breakfast—cold cereal with milk being one of the most popular choices. Starting the day with something high in refined carbohydrates and sugar, like cold cereal, causes a dramatic spike in blood sugar. When there is a high amount of circulating blood sugar in the body, inflammatory chemicals are released. This can cause our immune system to become confused and attack things entering the system that wouldn't otherwise cause a problem—like certain foods, pollen, and pet dander—creating allergies or sensitivities to compounds in food and the environment.

Let's Rethink Breakfast

If your child has mood swings, learning disabilities, is hyperactive, or is ravenously hungry within an hour or two after eating, it might be time to rethink breakfast. Serving complex carbohydrates with protein and fat is essential first thing in the morning. Scrambled eggs with sourdough bread and raw sauerkraut, or warm beans and sticky brown rice in broth are good choices. A whole grain pancake made with coconut oil topped with almond butter and fresh berries is another great choice. A small piece of pan-fried grass-fed beef with salad greens can also be a nutrient-dense breakfast providing essential protein, minerals, vitamins, and fats for proper growth and brain function. Fruit, nut, and green smoothies can be a good option for people with strong digestion as cold foods can be hard on a weak digestive system. I'm always amazed how long our children can go on a green smoothie made from blueberries, avocado, apple, chia seeds, lemon juice, and kale! Starting the day with nutrient-dense foods that won't cause a blood sugar roller coaster will help keep inflammation in check, thereby reducing the chances of your children developing a food allergy or sensitivity. Prioritizing a healthy breakfast also helps to strengthen their immune systems, protect their digestive health, and increase cognitive functioning.

What about skipping breakfast?

It is commonly known that starvation is a major stressor of the body—it increases the secretion of the stress hormone **cortisol**. In other words, skipping breakfast stresses you out. Stress has been associated with numerous health disorders that may, in certain individuals, cause an increase in weight as well. Many people believe that skipping meals is a good idea because of the misconception that weight is all about a simple equation of "calories in and calories out." Unfortunately, this is not how the body works.

If we do not regularly receive signals from food then our cells have to adapt and alter their function. When there is a drop in fuel intake, lean muscles cells are forced to turn off and another type of cell takes over with calorie management: **the fat cell**. Prolonged fasting that occurs from sleeping and then skipping breakfast increases the body's insulin response, which in turn, leads to fat storage. People who skip breakfast are often overweight, stressed out, have low energy, and do not sleep well.

Research shows that eating meals frequently throughout the day keeps your cells constantly burning energy. Lean muscle cells need fuel to stay active. If you supply fuel evenly throughout the day, muscles can remain healthy and productive. Eating a balanced breakfast first thing in the morning usually decreases the total amount of food eaten in a day, significantly decreases late afternoon and evening snacking, and boosts overall metabolism.

10 Quick and Healthy Breakfast Ideas:

1. **Two poached or fried eggs served with a leftover cooked grain**, such as quinoa, and a fermented vegetable, such as raw sauerkraut.

2. **Steamed yams**, scrambled eggs, and fresh greens.

3. **A quick salad of lettuce**, sprouts, and hardboiled eggs. Drizzle it with a mixture of lemon juice and olive oil and season with salt and pepper.

4. **A nutritious nut and fruit smoothie**. Soak nuts overnight then blend with your favorite fruits.

5. **Green smoothie along with a slice of toasted gluten-free bread spread with sunflower seed butter**.

6. **Leftover cooked quinoa topped with fresh blueberries**, raspberries, chopped walnuts and a dollop of dairy or non-dairy yogurt.

7. **A bowl of fresh cut fruit**, berries, avocados, and soaked nuts drizzled with a little fresh lime or lemon juice.

8. **Quesadilla made with refried beans and two gluten-free tortillas**. To cook, add a little coconut or olive oil to a heated 11-inch skillet on the stove; cook each side for about 90 seconds, then cut into wedges using a pizza cutter.

9. **A bowl of cooked beans**, cooked brown rice, and avocado topped with lime juice and salt.

10. **Last night's leftover dinner**!

Cream of Rice Cereal

We like to make this simple breakfast for busy weekday mornings. The rice grinds up in seconds and can then cook unattended on the stove for 5 to 10 minutes while we prepare a green smoothie and make sure the kids have packed themselves a good lunch. If you have a small family you may want to cut this recipe in half. We like to top this cereal with ground raw almonds, frozen blueberries, and a sprinkling of coconut sugar for a simple, nutritious breakfast.

2 cups long grain brown rice
6 to 8 cups water
¼ teaspoon sea salt

Optional Toppings:
ground raw almonds
coconut sugar or maple syrup
cinnamon
frozen blueberries
raisins

Place the rice into a coffee grinder or high-powered blender and grind into a very fine meal, not as fine as flour, but not as coarse as cornmeal either. We use the dry container of our Vita-Mix to grind the rice and then the almonds for the topping.

Place the water into a 3-quart saucepan and heat over medium heat until warm. Pour in the ground rice, whisk immediately otherwise it will begin to clump up. Turn heat up and bring cereal to a boil, stirring constantly.

Once boiling, reduce heat to medium or medium-low. Cover and simmer for about 10 minutes. Remove lid and whisk cereal occasionally, adding more water if necessary depending on desired thickness. Cook for a few more minutes then remove from heat. Cereal will thicken as it cools.

Scoop into serving bowls and serve with your favorite toppings.

Yield: 4 to 6 servings

Ingredient Tip:

We like to use Lundberg brand brown jasmine rice or brown basmati rice, both of which work well in this recipe. Lundberg Farms from California supplies high-quality organic rice that does not carry with it the concerns of high levels of arsenic and cadmium like some of the Asian and Midwestern US grown rice.

Rice and Nut Milk Hot Cereal

We often have one or two different types of whole grain cooked and ready to be used for any meal. On really busy mornings, I like to reheat leftover cooked short grain brown rice with a high-protein nut milk. I will use either freshly made Cashew Milk, page 483 or Creamy Macadamia Nut Milk, page 484. We like to top the cereal with ground raw almonds, a little coconut sugar, and frozen blueberries.

3 cups cooked short grain brown rice
2 cups nut milk or your favorite unsweetened milk
pinch sea salt
few dashes maple syrup (optional)

Optional Toppings:
ground raw walnuts or almonds
hemp seeds
coconut sugar or maple syrup
frozen blueberries or blackberries
cinnamon

Place all ingredients into a small pot and heat over medium heat, stirring occasionally for 5 to 7 minutes or until thickened and warm.

Scoop into serving bowls and sprinkle with your favorite toppings.

Yield: 2 to 3 servings

Nutrition Tip:

Whole grains, such as brown rice, quinoa, and millet, are considered complex carbohydrates. This means they provide a steady, slow release of sugar into your bloodstream keeping you energized for hours!

Quinoa Currant Porridge

The cinnamon in this recipe creates a slightly sweet porridge without having to add any sweeteners. I like to use homemade almond milk though any unsweetened non-dairy milk will do. If you use a thicker milk, such as coconut milk or whole raw cow's milk, you may need to add a little extra water.

1 cup uncooked quinoa, rinsed
4 cups milk
¼ cup currants
1 teaspoon cinnamon
pinch sea salt

Garnish:
chopped nuts
hemp seeds

Rinse the quinoa well and drain though a fine mesh strainer. Place the quinoa, milk, currants, cinnamon, and salt into a 2-quart pot. Bring to a boil, reduce heat to medium-low, cover, and simmer for 20 to 25 minutes.

Serve warm. Sprinkle each bowl with chopped nuts or raw hemp seeds.

Yield: 4 servings

Cinnamon Raisin Teff Breakfast Bars

My mother-in-law inspired this recipe; she pours leftover teff porridge into a pan and then cuts it into bars the next day. These bars make a great snack packed in your child's lunchbox! Serve with a green smoothie for a nourishing breakfast.

2 cups water
1 to 1¼ cups milk
1 cup teff grain
½ cup raisins or currants
2 to 3 tablespoons maple syrup
1 tablespoon cinnamon
½ teaspoon sea salt

Optional Additions:
chopped pecans
sunflower seeds
chopped dried apple
hemp seeds

Oil an 8 x 8-inch glass baking pan with coconut oil; set aside.

Place the water and milk into a 3-quart pot, cover, and bring to a boil. Add the teff grain, raisins, and maple syrup. Whisk together then cover, reduce heat to a simmer, and cook for about 15 minutes. Stir the teff a few times while cooking. If the teff seems a little thick, add up to ¼ cup more milk. Add the cinnamon and salt; stir again. Stir in any optional additions at this time. Cover and simmer for another 5 minutes.

Immediately pour the cooked teff into the prepared pan. Spread out with the back of a wet spoon. Chill in the refrigerator for about 3 hours, then slice and serve.

Teff bars will keep for up to a week in the refrigerator.

Yield: 9 bars

Pumpkin Pie Granola

Homemade granola is one of the easiest things to make. Your children can help measure and stir the ingredients together and then patiently wait for the pan to come out of the oven. Serve this granola over your favorite dairy or non-dairy yogurt. It can also be added as a special treat to your child's lunchbox.

Dry Ingredients:
3 cups gluten-free rolled oats
2 cups raw pumpkin seeds
1 tablespoon pumpkin pie spice
½ teaspoon sea salt

Wet Ingredients:
½ cup melted coconut oil
½ cup maple syrup
½ cup pumpkin puree
1 teaspoon vanilla

Optional Additions:
½ to 1 cup currants
½ to 1 cup chopped dried apple

Preheat oven to 300 degrees F. In a large bowl, mix together the dry ingredients. In another smaller bowl, whisk together the wet ingredients. Pour the wet into the dry and mix together well.

Pour mixture onto a large rimmed cookie sheet or into two 9 x 13-inch pans. Spread evenly into a single layer. Bake for 45 to 60 minutes, stirring 2 to 3 times during baking. Once the granola is done and out of the oven, stir in the currants and chopped dried apples, if using. Let the pan sit on the counter until the granola is completely cooled. The granola will crisp up as it cools. Store in a large glass jar for up to two weeks in your pantry.

Yield: 5 to 6 cups

Kitchen Tip:

I often have freshly baked winter squash stored in my refrigerator during the fall and winter months. To use baked squash or pumpkin that is not pureed, measure ½ cup of the cooked flesh and add it to a blender with the other wet ingredients. Blend until combined and smooth and pour over your dry ingredients. Continue as the recipe directs. .

Nutty Granola

This grain-free granola is packed with protein and healthy fats. With just a smidgen of sweetener to help hold it together and boost flavors you can enjoy this treat for breakfast sprinkled over your favorite dairy or dairy-free yogurt. Top it off with fresh berries or diced bananas for a balanced breakfast or snack.

1 cup raw almonds
1 cup raw pecans
1 cup raw walnuts
½ cup raw sunflower seeds
½ cup raw pumpkin seeds
2 to 3 tablespoons whole chia seeds
2 teaspoons cinnamon
¼ teaspoon nutmeg
¼ teaspoon sea salt
¼ cup maple syrup
¼ cup melted coconut oil
½ to 1 cup dried cranberries or raisins

Preheat oven to 300 degrees F. Line a large baking dish, rimmed cookie sheet, or jelly roll pan with parchment paper.

Place the almonds, pecans, and walnuts into a food processor fitted with the "s" blade. Process until you have a chunky, coarse meal. Pour into a medium-sized mixing bowl. Add the sunflower seeds, pumpkin seeds, chia seeds, cinnamon, nutmeg, and sea salt. Stir together to evenly distribute the spices and salt. Add the syrup and mix together using a large spoon.

Spread onto the parchment-lined cookie sheet and bake for about 35 to 40 minutes. Remove from oven and stir in the dried cranberries or raisins.

Let cool completely on the cookie sheet then transfer to a glass jar for storage.

Yield: 4 to 5 cups

Kitchen Tip:

Lining your metal cookie sheet with parchment paper keeps the granola from burning.

Nutrition Tip:

Soaking your nuts and seeds overnight and then dehydrating them until crisp not only makes them more digestible, but also allows their nutrients to become more bioavailable. You can do this before using them in a granola recipe like this. See the Getting Started chapter, page 51, for details.

Fruit and Avocado Bowls with Hemp Seeds

On days when we want a lighter breakfast we make fruit and nut bowls along with a green smoothie. Any fruit combination works, but the avocado-mango duo is quite luscious! You'll want to eat this right after it is made, as it will spoil quickly.

1 ripe pear, cored and chopped
1 large ripe mango, peeled, and cubed
1 large avocado, peeled and cubed
½ lemon or lime, juiced
¼ cup hemp seeds
2 tablespoons whole chia seeds
handful of raw macadamia nuts or raw sunflower seeds

Place the fruit and avocado into a small serving bowl and toss together. Add the lemon or lime juice and toss again. Sprinkle hemp and chia seeds over the top of fruit and add macadamia nuts or raw sunflower seeds if desired. Serve and enjoy right away!

Yield: 2 servings

Almond-Chia Breakfast Parfaits

This recipe is perfect to make in the summertime when fresh, organic fruit is abundant! It is light, refreshing, and nourishing—just the thing to wake you up and give you energy before your morning jog or yoga routine. My favorite types of fruit to use in this recipe are fresh strawberries, blueberries, peaches, nectarines, cherries, and apricots.

2 cups Raw Almond Milk (page 481)
6 tablespoons whole chia seeds
1 to 2 tablespoons maple syrup
4 cups fresh fruit
hemp seeds

Place the almond milk, chia seeds, and maple syrup into a glass jar, cover, and shake. Place in your refrigerator overnight, or for about 8 hours.

In the morning, it should be pudding-like and thick. Place four parfait cups on the counter and fill each with one cup of fruit. Top with equal amounts of the chia-almond pudding. Serve immediately or chill and serve within a few hours. Top each parfait with a sprinkling of hemp seeds if desired.

Yield: 4 servings

Nutrition Tip:

Chia seeds have been used since pre-Columbian times as a dietary staple in both the Aztec and Mayan cultures. It is said that Aztec warriors, and runners of Mexico and Guatemala, considered it a prize food for performance. A single one-ounce serving of dry chia seeds contains almost 10% of your daily value of protein, over 40% of your daily fiber, and more omega-3 fatty acids than flax seeds.

Raw Breakfast Tacos

This is my go-to recipe when we have a busy morning. If I make the filling the night before, all I need to do in the morning is slice an avocado and mango and put everything into a lettuce leaf. I like to use romaine lettuce or napa cabbage for the "taco shell" but any variety of lettuce will work. I like to add the whole chili pepper, seeds and all, because I like things really hot. However, if you don't want the filling too spicy, or are serving this to young children, remove the seeds before adding it to the food processor.

Filling:
1 cup raw almonds, soaked for 8 to 10 hours
3 to 4 brazil nuts, soaked for 8 to 10 hours
3 green onions, ends trimmed
handful fresh cilantro
1 hot pepper, such as Serrano or jalapeno, seeded
1 small lime, juiced
½ teaspoon sea salt or Herbamare

Other Ingredients:
lettuce leaves
sliced avocado
sliced mango
lime wedges

To soak the nuts, place them into a bowl and cover with at least an inch of filtered water. Leave them on your counter to soak overnight or for the day, about 8 to 10 hours. When they are done, drain and rinse them.

Place the soaked nuts into a food processor fitted with the "s" blade and add the remaining filling ingredients. Pulse/process until the nuts and vegetables are ground to the desired consistency. Taste and add more salt if necessary.

To assemble the tacos, place a few dollops of the filling into a lettuce leaf and top with avocado and mango slices. Serve with lime wedges.

Yield: 4 to 6 servings

Adzuki Bean and Yam Hash

As long as you have cooked adzuki beans on hand, this recipe can be prepared in short order. The key is to dice the yams very small so they cook quickly without burning. Serve over cooked quinoa for a hearty breakfast.

2 tablespoons extra virgin olive oil
1 small onion, diced
2 small yams, peeled and diced small
½ to 1 teaspoon ground cumin
few pinches crushed red chili flakes
2 cups cooked adzuki beans
4 collard greens, finely chopped
Herbamare and black pepper to taste
½ cup chopped cilantro

Heat an 11 or 12-inch skillet over medium heat. Add olive oil, onions and a few dashes of salt. Sauté for a few minutes or until softened.

Then add yams, cumin, and chili flakes; sauté for a few minutes uncovered, then cover your pan and cook for about 15 to 20 minutes, stirring occasionally, until yams are tender. Watch carefully so they don't burn.

Add adzuki beans and collard greens. Sauté a few minutes more, or until collards are tender. Add Herbamare and pepper to taste. Sprinkle with chopped cilantro and serve.

Yield: 4 to 6 servings

Kitchen Tip:

To finely chop collard greens, first stack the leaves on top of each other. Then tightly roll. Use a sharp knife to thinly slice the collards, and then cut those slices crosswise into small pieces.

Bean and Rice Breakfast Bowls

This is another favorite recipe of ours to make for just about any meal, but it does make a very nutritious, energizing breakfast. It can be made very quickly if you don't have much time in the morning as long as you have cooked rice and beans on hand. Cooked quinoa also works great. The sauerkraut adds a nice salty-sour flavor and some crunch. It is also full of beneficial microorganisms that balance the gut flora and aid in healing a damaged gut lining.

2 cups cooked short grain brown rice
1 cup cooked black beans
1 large avocado, diced
½ cup raw sauerkraut
Herbamare, to taste

Optional Additions:
chopped mustard greens
baby arugula
thinly sliced green onions

Divide the rice, beans, diced avocado, and raw sauerkraut equally between two bowls. Sprinkle each with a little Herbamare. Add any optional additions you desire. Serve immediately.

Yield: 2 servings

Black Bean and Potato Breakfast Burritos

The first time I made this recipe, my children all sat down for breakfast and at first bite said, "Mom these are so good, you just have to put this in your new cookbook!" They happily devour these every time I make them. To make breakfast time go a little quicker, I suggest making up a big batch of the filling the night before and then reheating what you need in the morning. It will last for up to 5 days stored in the refrigerator.

Filling:
2 to 3 tablespoons extra virgin olive oil
1 small onion, diced small
1 teaspoon dried marjoram or oregano
¼ teaspoon chipotle chili powder
1 teaspoon sea salt or Herbamare
2 ½ cups diced potatoes, cut into ¼-inch cubes
2 cups cooked and drained black beans
½ cup chopped cilantro

Other Ingredients:
gluten-free tortillas or blanched collard greens
baby arugula or mixed greens
guacamole
salsa
sour cream

Heat an 11 o 12-inch over medium heat. Add the oil and then the onion; sauté for about 5 minutes or until softened. Then add the herbs, chili powder, and salt; sauté for 30 seconds more. Add diced potatoes and sauté for about 10 minutes. Add cooked black beans, cover, and cook until black beans are heated through and potatoes are cooked, a few more minutes. Turn off heat and add chopped cilantro.

Place about ½ cup of filling in the center of each heated tortilla or blanched collard green. Add any additional ingredients such as mixed greens and salsa. Fold in the top and bottom edges then roll.

Yield: About 4 to 6 burritos

Variation:

For a nightshade-free recipe, replace the potatoes with yams, sweet potatoes, winter squash, or rutabagas.

Kitchen Tip:

To heat gluten-free tortillas so they will roll without falling apart, you will need to steam them. I steam one at a time over the cooking filling or I place a pot of water on the stove to boil, set a wire rack over the pot, and steam one tortilla at a time for about 60 seconds each.

Breakfast Potatoes

Our family loves these breakfast potatoes though we only make them on the weekends because they are a little more time consuming to prepare. Serve them with poached eggs or cooked black beans and sautéed greens for a balanced meal.

2 to 4 tablespoons extra virgin olive oil or coconut oil
1 medium red onion, diced
3 pounds red or yellow potatoes, scrubbed and cut into ¼ -inch cubes
1 red bell pepper, seeded and diced
Herbamare and freshly ground black pepper

Garnish:
snipped fresh chives

Heat an 11 or 12-inch skillet over medium heat. Add about 1 tablespoon of the oil then the onion; sauté for 5 minutes. Add potatoes and sauté for 10 more minutes, keep them moving in the pan and add more oil if necessary so they don't stick.

Add pepper and sauté a few minutes more. Cover pan with a lid and cook for 5 to 10 more minutes or until potatoes are tender. Remove lid, let extra liquid cook off. Season with Herbamare and black pepper to taste.

Yield: 4 to 6 servings

Kitchen Tip:

Using a well-seasoned cast iron skillet to cook potatoes will keep them from sticking and will cook them properly. Cast iron skillets are inexpensive and a great addition to your kitchen!

Variation:

For a nightshade-free version, replace the potatoes with diced rutabagas, celery root, or sweet potatoes and omit red bell peppers.

Winter Vegetable Hash

Before refrigeration, people used to harvest and place foods into their root cellars to store for the winter; foods like root vegetables and tubers—such as carrots, parsnips, celery root, turnips, beets, rutabaga, sunchokes, and potatoes—as well as winter squash, cabbages, and onions. Along with any homemade vegetable ferments, these were the only vegetables available during the colder months in northern climates. Use any combination of the above winter vegetables for this hash recipe. I like to use part yellow potato, part carrot, and part winter squash for a simple, flavorful combination. Serve with poached eggs or cooked beans for a hearty breakfast.

¼ cup extra virgin olive oil, organic butter, or coconut oil
1 small onion, minced
8 cups grated winter vegetables
1 teaspoon Herbamare or to taste
freshly ground black pepper

If you are using potatoes you will need to first grate them and then place them into a large bowl filled with cold water. Stir them around a bit to loosen the starches. Then strain through a clean towel, squeezing out all of the moisture. Place into a large bowl, then add any other grated winter vegetables. If you are using winter squash be sure to peel it first.

Heat a large skillet over medium heat. The best type of skillet to use for this recipe is an 11 or 12-inch seasoned cast iron skillet. The hash won't stick to the bottom of the pan in one of these. Add part of the oil and the onion; sauté for a minute. Add the grated vegetables and sauté for a few minutes adding the remaining oil as needed. Cover the skillet and cook for 10 minutes, uncovering to stir once after 5 minutes, then uncover and sauté until cooked through—usually, it takes about 15 minutes total. Add Herbamare and black pepper and sauté a minute more. Serve hot.

Store leftovers in your fridge for up to 5 days and reheat as needed.

Yield: 4 to 6 servings

Kale and Egg Scramble

This tasty and nourishing recipe has been a staple breakfast food during many of my pregnancies. It is quick to prepare and can easily be made on a busy weekday morning. I like to serve it with the Breakfast Potatoes, page 96, and a spoonful of raw cultured vegetables to maximize digestion.

2 teaspoons organic butter or coconut oil
2 cups finely chopped kale
4 large organic eggs
sea salt and black pepper to taste

Heat a 10-inch skillet over medium heat. I like to heat the skillet for a few minutes before I add anything to the pan. This helps keep the food from sticking to the pan. Add the butter or coconut oil, then the chopped kale; sauté for about 5 minutes adding a tablespoon or two of water if needed to help the kale soften.

While the kale is cooking, crack the eggs into a bowl and whisk. Before adding the eggs, push the kale to the side of the pan and add a few more teaspoons of butter or coconut oil. This will prevent the eggs from sticking to the bottom of the pan while cooking. Then add the eggs and scramble into the kale. Cook for about 2 minutes turning constantly.

Remove from heat, season with sea salt and black pepper to taste. I usually drizzle my portion with hot sauce.

Yield: 2 to 4 servings

Nutrition Tip:

Eggs are a great source of choline and phosphatidylcholine, which are beneficial for proper nerve and brain function. It is estimated that 90% of the US population may be choline deficient with the elderly and pregnant women being the most susceptible to deficiencies.

Basil Zucchini Frittata

Frittatas are basically oven omelets. They are usually made by first lightly sautéing the vegetables in an ovenproof skillet. The beaten eggs are added and the whole thing is finished off in the oven. I don't like over-cooked zucchini so I simply add the raw slices to a pie plate along with the basil and then add the eggs and bake it in the oven. You can do it either way. I also like to make this recipe for a quick, nutritious lunch in the summertime. I usually serve it with a bowl of cooked quinoa and a green salad.

1 medium zucchini, thinly sliced
½ cup thinly sliced fresh basil
6 large organic eggs, beaten
sea salt and freshly ground black pepper
¼ cup grated Parmesan cheese (optional)

Preheat oven to 375 degrees F. Lightly butter or oil a 9-inch pie plate.

Place the zucchini slices on the bottom of the pie plate, sprinkle with the basil. Then add the beaten eggs. Sprinkle with salt and pepper. Add the grated Parmesan cheese if using.

Bake for about 25 minutes. Slice and serve.

Yield: 4 to 6 servings

Roasted Squash and Corn Frittata

This recipe is perfect for lazy weekend breakfasts or large family brunches in early autumn when the fresh corn and squash are in abundance. If fresh corn is out of season, use about 1½ cups of frozen organic corn instead. Serve with the Baby Arugula Salad, page 209, and Buckwheat Cinnamon Rolls, page 141, for a hearty weekend brunch.

1 ½ cups peeled and cubed butternut squash
1 tablespoon extra virgin olive oil
pinch sea salt
3 to 4 green onions, cut into rounds
1 to 2 small jalapeno peppers, seeded and diced
2 ears fresh corn, cut off the cob
½ teaspoon Herbamare
6 large organic eggs
¼ to ½ cup crumbled cotija cheese or feta (optional)

Preheat the oven to 350 degrees F.

Toss the cubed squash in the olive oil and salt and place into an 8 x 8-inch baking dish. Roast for about 35 minutes or until tender. Let cool slightly before adding to the egg mixture.

Lightly grease a 9-inch deep-dish pie plate with butter or olive oil. Place the green onions, jalapeno peppers, and corn into the pie plate. Sprinkle with the Herbamare. Add the roasted squash and gently toss together.

In a separate bowl, whisk the eggs together. Pour the eggs over the vegetables in the pie plate. Sprinkle with cotija cheese if using.

Bake for about 25 to 30 minutes or until frittata is cooked through. Slice and serve.

Yield: 4 to 6 servings

Kitchen Tip:

Use leftover roasted squash from a previous meal to cut prep time in half.

Mini Quiches with a Sweet Potato Crust

This recipe makes a large enough batch that you can reheat them as needed for breakfasts throughout the week. I reheat mine in a small, covered skillet with a few tablespoons of water. Use any combination of vegetables, herbs, and cheese. Some of my favorite combinations are chive, asparagus, and feta; broccoli, jalapeno, onion, and cilantro; and cauliflower, mushroom, and spinach. You can add crumbled, cooked bacon or sausages too if desired. The "crust" is made from grated sweet potato but other starchy vegetables work as well, such as red potatoes, parsnips, or rutabaga.

1 medium sweet potato or yam, peeled and grated
1 tablespoon olive oil
2 cups diced vegetables
10 large organic eggs
¼ cup water or milk
½ teaspoon Herbamre or sea salt
freshly ground black pepper

Optional Additions:
thinly sliced fresh basil
chopped cilantro
grated raw organic cheddar cheese

Preheat oven to 325 degrees F. Grease a 12-cup muffin pan with butter or coconut oil.

Divide the grated sweet potato among the 12 muffin cups and evenly press into the bottoms of each.

Heat a 10-inch skillet over medium heat. Add about a tablespoon of olive oil, then add the diced vegetables; sauté for about 5 minutes to soften. Divide the vegetables evenly among the 12 muffin cups.

Crack the eggs into a medium-sized mixing bowl and add the water or milk; whisk together. Pour beaten eggs over the vegetables. Sprinkle on cheese if using.

Bake for about 35 minutes. Use a knife to gently nudge them out of the muffin cups. Serve hot or store in a covered glass container for up to 5 days.

Yield: 12 mini quiches

Coconut Banana Breakfast Cake

Our children think that having cake for breakfast is quite a treat, although this is not your typical cake; it is high in protein and low in sugar. In fact, it is completely free of any sweetener other than mashed ripe bananas! Since this cake is made with coconut flour, you will not be able to replace the eggs with an egg-substitute in this recipe. Serve with sliced fresh bananas and a dollop of sunflower butter or peanut butter.

Dry Ingredients:
½ cup coconut flour
¾ teaspoon baking soda
½ teaspoon sea salt

Wet Ingredients:
1 heaping cup mashed ripe banana
⅓ cup coconut oil
6 large organic eggs

Preheat oven to 350 degrees F. Oil a 9-inch round cake pan with coconut oil.

In a medium-sized mixing bowl, whisk together the dry ingredients.

Place the wet ingredients into a blender and blend until smooth and creamy. Pour the wet ingredients into the dry and whisk together.

Pour batter into cake pan and bake for approximately 40 minutes. Let pan cool for about 10 minutes before turning pan over and releasing cake onto a large plate. Serve warm or at room temperature.

Yield: one 9-inch round cake or 8 slices

Zucchini Almond Pancakes

I like to make these savory grain-free, protein-packed pancakes on a summer morning before we head out for the day. Combined with a green smoothie they create an energizing breakfast! These store well in the refrigerator, but if you prefer to make a smaller batch halve the recipe. Top each pancake with a dollop of sour cream or Cashew Sour Cream, page 369, and chopped parsley if desired.

4 large organic eggs
3 cups grated zucchini
¾ to 1 cup almond flour
½ cup minced onion
½ to 1 teaspoon Herbamare or sea salt
freshly ground black pepper
olive oil or butter for cooking

Mix all ingredients except the oil together in a medium-sized bowl. Batter will thin a little as it sits.

Heat a 10-inch stainless steel skillet or cast iron skillet over medium-low heat. Be sure to heat your pan long enough before adding the oil and batter, otherwise the pancakes will stick. Add about 1 tablespoon olive oil. Drop batter by the ¼ cup into the hot skillet. Cook for a few minutes on each side. Repeat with remaining batter, adding a little oil or butter to the skillet before cooking each pancake.

Yield: 10 to 12 pancakes

Kitchen Tip:

A well-seasoned cast iron skillet keeps pancakes from sticking to the bottom of the pan and is especially useful in this recipe.

Grain-Free Pancakes

These high-protein pancakes can be made in a snap by blending all of the ingredients together in a blender. I've tried whisking them together, but the flours tend to clump up. A food processor works as well. They key to cooking these all the way through without burning is to make sure the pan is well heated, but not too hot, before adding the batter. I cook mine on low heat but let the pan heat up for about 5 minutes before I begin cooking. Serve pancakes topped with fresh berries and Whipped Coconut Cream, page 476, for a decadent yet healthful breakfast.

6 large organic eggs
1 large, ripe banana
2 tablespoons melted coconut oil or organic butter
1 tablespoon maple syrup or honey
2 cups almond flour
2 tablespoons coconut flour
½ teaspoon baking soda
½ teaspoon sea salt
coconut oil or butter for cooking

Heat a 10 or 11-inch heavy bottomed skillet over low to medium-low heat.

Place all ingredients into a blender or food processor and blend until smooth. Add a teaspoon or two of coconut oil or butter to the pan and pour batter by the ¼ to 1/3 cup-full at a time onto the hot skillet. Cook for about 90 seconds on each side. Repeat with remaining batter, adding a little coconut oil or butter before cooking each pancake.

Yield: 8 to 10 pancakes

Sourdough Buckwheat Crepes

We love the flavor of soured buckwheat flour and so do our children. We like to make these and set out different fillings for everyone to make their own crepe. Our favorite fillings are sautéed apples with cinnamon; Vanilla Plum Butter, page 513; homemade blueberry-honey jam; sautéed spinach and caramelized onions; and fresh peach slices with almond butter.

1 cup freshly ground buckwheat flour
1 cup water
2 teaspoons cultured coconut water or kefir
3 large organic eggs
2 tablespoons melted organic butter or coconut oil
1 to 2 tablespoons coconut sugar or maple syrup
¼ teaspoon sea salt

Place the flour and water into a quart jar and add the cultured coconut water or kefir; whisk together. Place a towel over the top of the jar and set in an undisturbed part of your kitchen for 48 hours. When the mixture is ready it should be bubbly and smell slightly sour.

Pour soured buckwheat-water mixture into a medium-sized mixing bowl and whisk in the remaining ingredients.

Heat a 10-inch skillet over medium to medium-low heat. Add a little butter or coconut oil then add about ⅓ cup batter and spread it out by moving the pan in a swirling motion. Cook for about one minute then carefully flip using a very thin, wide spatula. Cook for about 20 seconds on the other side. Repeat with remaining batter, adding a little butter or coconut oil before cooking each crepe. Serve warm.

Yield: 6 to 8 crepes

Quinoa and Mung Bean Dosas

Dosas are traditional Indian pancakes or crepes made from soaked and fermented whole grains and beans. Making dosas is a two-part process—first you soak the grains and beans overnight, then you blend them into a batter and let it ferment. This is one of the most digestible ways to prepare grains and beans. I am using quinoa and mung beans in this recipe but you can use brown basmati rice, millet, lentils, or chickpeas. Serve one for breakfast along with sautéed greens and a dollop of yogurt or Spicy Peach Chutney, page 3800. They also pair well with curried vegetables or a lentil dal for dinner.

Day 1:
1 cup dry quinoa
½ cup dry mung beans
1 tablespoon apple cider vinegar
warm water to cover

Day 2:
1 ½ cups water
1 teaspoon whole cumin seeds
1 teaspoon sea salt

Rinse the quinoa through a fine mesh strainer. Place it into a small mixing bowl along with the mung beans, apple cider vinegar, and water. Make sure there is at least an inch of water covering the quinoa and mung beans as they will expand quite a bit during soaking. Let them soak for 6 to 12 hours or up to 24 hours. Then drain and rinse.

Add the soaked quinoa and mung beans to a blender along with the water; blend on high until smooth and creamy. Add the cumin seeds and salt; blend on a very low speed to incorporate. Pour mixture into a mason jar or bowl, cover with a kitchen towel, and let the mixture ferment for 24 to 48 hours. It will turn slightly sour and a little bubbly.

When ready to cook, heat a cast iron skillet over medium heat. Once it is hot, add a few teaspoons of coconut oil. Pour ⅓ to ½ cup batter into the hot skillet; spread into a thin pancake in a circular motion using the back of a spoon. Cook for about 2 minutes. Dosa will pull easily from bottom of pan when cooked, if it sticks leave it on there for another 30 seconds or so. Then flip and cook for about 1 minute on the other side. Place dosa onto a plate. Continue with remaining batter, adding coconut oil each time. Serve warm.

Yield: About 8 dosas

Overnight Quinoa Hot Cakes

Griddle cakes, hot cakes, pancakes—they are all the same thing—a whole grain flour mixture usually made into a thin batter with milk and eggs. Back in the day when raw milk soured naturally due to lack of refrigeration and farm fresh eggs were outside your back door, pancakes were made because those ingredients needed to be used up. Soaking your grains overnight in some sort of acidic liquid begins to break down phytic acid and release some of the grain's minerals. Feel free to substitute other whole grains for the ones used in this recipe.

Day 1:
½ cup uncooked quinoa
½ cup uncooked buckwheat groats
½ cup gluten-free rolled oats
1 cup plain kefir or yogurt (cow, goat, or coconut)
½ cup water

Day 2:
2 large organic eggs
1 tablespoon maple syrup or honey
¾ teaspoon baking soda
¼ teaspoon sea salt
butter or coconut oil for cooking

Optional Additions:
cinnamon
chopped banana
chopped nuts
fresh or frozen berries

Before you go to bed at night, place the grains into a bowl and pour the kefir or yogurt and water over them; stir to combine. Set a plate over the bowl and leave it on the counter overnight or for about 8 to 10 hours.

In the morning, pour the grains and kefir into a blender. Add the eggs, maple syrup or honey, baking soda, and salt. Blend until smooth. Stir in any of the optional additions.

Heat a cast iron or stainless steel skillet over medium-low heat. Add a little butter or coconut oil to the pan and drop batter by the ¼ cup. Cook for 60 to 90 seconds on each side. Repeat with remaining batter.

Yield: 10 to 12 pancakes

Nutrition Tip:

Buckwheat groats are high in phytase, the enzyme that breaks down phytates in the grain. Rolled oats contain very little phytase. By combining the two grains in kefir overnight, the phytase from the buckwheat helps to break down the phytates in the oats, allowing for better mineral absorption.

Teff Banana Pancakes

Teff, a very small Ethiopian grain, is now cultivated in Idaho. It is low in phytic acid and rich in minerals—particularly iron—and when ground into flour, these minerals become more accessible. These pancakes will give you staying power until lunchtime, especially if combined with a green smoothie. For more banana flavor, chop up a small banana and fold it into the batter. We usually make a double batch of this recipe to feed our family.

Dry Ingredients:
1 cup teff flour
¼ cup tapioca flour
1 teaspoon baking powder
½ teaspoon baking soda
¼ teaspoon sea salt

Wet Ingredients:
1 cup water or milk, warmed
2 tablespoons ground flax seeds
¼ cup mashed ripe banana (about 1 small banana)
2 tablespoons melted virgin coconut oil
1 tablespoon maple syrup

In a small bowl mix together the dry ingredients. In a separate bowl or liquid measuring cup, whisk together the warm milk or water and ground flax; let rest for a minute to thicken. Add the remaining wet ingredients and whisk together. Add the wet ingredients to the dry and whisk together until combined.

Heat a cast iron or stainless steel skillet over medium-low heat until hot. Add a little coconut oil. Drop batter by the ½-cupful onto the hot skillet. Flip pancake after tiny bubbles form. Cook for another minute then transfer to a plate. Repeat with the remaining batter, adding about ½ teaspoon coconut oil before cooking each pancake.

Yield: About 5 pancakes

Variation:

For those of you who cannot tolerate bananas, you may replace the mashed banana with unsweetened applesauce.

Apple Cinnamon Teff Pancakes

As summer begins to fade into autumn my children begin to ask for these pancakes in the morning. I like to make a simple apple-cinnamon topping for these by simmering one sliced apple in a little water with a few dashes of maple syrup and ground cinnamon for about 10 minutes. Put a spoonful of this topping on top of each pancake with a few tablespoons of chopped walnuts.

Dry Ingredients:
2 cups dark brown teff flour
½ cup tapioca flour
1 tablespoon cinnamon
2 teaspoons baking powder
¾ teaspoon baking soda
½ teaspoon sea salt

Wet Ingredients:
2 cups milk or water
½ cup unsweetened applesauce
2 large organic eggs
3 tablespoons melted virgin coconut oil or butter
3 tablespoons pure maple syrup

Whisk the dry ingredients together in a medium-sized mixing bowl. Add the wet ingredients. Whisk together.

Heat a 10-inch skillet over medium heat. Add a few teaspoons of coconut oil. Once the pan is hot, use a ½-cup measure to pour the batter into the pan. Cook for 60 to 90 seconds on one side, then flip and cook for 30 to 60 seconds on the second side. Add about ½ teaspoon of oil before cooking each pancake. Adjust the cooking temperature as needed. On my stove, I cook pancakes just under medium heat. Serve with pure maple syrup or a warm apple topping.

Yield: About 10 pancakes

Buckwheat Hazelnut Pancakes

I like to serve these healthy pancakes with warm Blueberry Syrup, page 115. I use Bob's Red Mill Hazelnut Meal but you could try grinding your own raw hazelnuts to a very fine meal if desired. Use any milk you prefer in the batter, I usually use homemade hemp milk or almond milk. Serve pancakes with a green smoothie for a balanced breakfast.

Dry Ingredients:
1 ¾ cups freshly ground buckwheat flour
1 ½ cups hazelnut meal
1 ½ teaspoons baking powder
¾ teaspoon baking soda
½ teaspoon sea salt

Wet Ingredients:
2 cups milk
2 large organic eggs
2 to 3 tablespoons maple syrup
2 to 3 tablespoons melted butter or coconut oil

Begin by heating a heavy-bottomed 10-inch stainless steel skillet over medium heat. For cooking pancakes it is really important to let the pan heat on the stove for a few minutes before using it so your pancakes don't stick. Melt the coconut oil or butter in the heating pan at this point.

Whisk together the dry ingredients in a medium-sized mixing bowl. Add the wet ingredients and whisk together again.

Use a ½-cup measure to pour batter into pan. Cook for 30 to 60 seconds on each side. Adjust temperature if needed. I usually cook mine just under medium heat. Add a little coconut oil or butter before adding more batter and continue to cook until batter is gone.

Yield: About 10 pancakes

Kitchen Tip:

I usually grind at least 3 cups of raw buckwheat groats at a time and then store the extra flour in a glass jar in my pantry.

Buckwheat Banana Waffles

These healthy, vegan waffles can also be made into pancakes. This recipe is one of our family's favorite and most requested breakfast recipes! I use homemade Hemp Milk, page 482, for the milk in this recipe but any dairy-free milk will work. Serve with pure maple syrup, chopped walnuts, and sliced fresh banana.

Dry Ingredients:
1 ½ cups freshly ground buckwheat flour
1 ½ teaspoons baking powder
½ teaspoon baking soda
½ teaspoon sea salt

Wet Ingredients:
2 tablespoons ground chia seeds
¼ cup hot water
¾ cup mashed banana
1 cup milk
2 tablespoons melted coconut oil
1 tablespoon maple syrup

Heat a waffle iron. Coat it lightly with coconut oil.

Whisk together all of the dry ingredients in a medium-sized mixing bowl. In a smaller bowl, add the ground chia and hot water; whisk together immediately. Add the dry ingredients to the chia water and whisk together well. Then add the wet ingredients into dry and mix together.

Add the batter to your hot, oiled waffle maker and gently spread with the back of a spoon (egg-free batter is a tad thicker than batter made with eggs). Cook according to your waffle iron's instructions.

Yield: About 4 Belgian waffles

Variation:

Use applesauce or pureed peaches in place of the mashed banana.

Nutrition Tip:

Compounds, such as rutin, in buckwheat are helpful in maintaining a steady blood glucose level after eating.

Whole Grain Waffles

This gluten-free waffle is crispy on the outside and soft on the inside, just like a waffle should be. These waffles can be frozen and then reheated in a toaster, or toaster oven, for convenience. To make breakfasts even easier, plan a day to mix up a few batches of the dry ingredients and store them in separate sealed containers, then place the directions and list of wet ingredients on each container.

Dry Ingredients:
1 cup teff flour
¾ cup tapioca flour
½ cup brown rice flour
½ cup sorghum flour
½ cup millet flour
½ cup quinoa flour
1 tablespoon baking powder
2 to 4 teaspoons cinnamon
1 teaspoon baking soda
½ teaspoon sea salt

Wet Ingredients:
3 large organic eggs
6 tablespoons melted coconut oil or melted butter
4 tablespoons maple syrup
2 ½ to 3 cups milk

Heat your waffle iron. Coat it lightly with coconut oil or butter.

In a large bowl whisk together the dry ingredients. In a separate bowl, whisk together the wet ingredients. Add the wet ingredients, start with 2 ½ cups of milk, to the dry and whisk well.

Make one waffle and if it seems too dry, add more milk. It will depend on how you measure, some of us over-measure slightly and some of us under-measure.

Cook waffles according to your waffle iron's instructions.

Yield: About 8 waffles

Whole Grain Pancake and Waffle Mix

It is very helpful to have a pancake mix ready in the pantry when I need to make a quick breakfast for my children. This easy mix combines some of the most nutritious gluten-free flours—the teff and quinoa flours make it higher protein. If quinoa flour is too strong for you or your child then replace it with buckwheat, teff, or millet flour. Follow the directions on the next page to make basic egg-free pancakes or waffles.

1 ½ cups brown rice flour
1 cup teff flour
1 cup millet flour
1 cup tapioca flour
½ cup quinoa flour
4 teaspoons baking powder
2 teaspoons baking soda
1 teaspoon sea salt

Place all ingredients into a large bowl. Using a wire whisk, mix well. Place mix into an airtight container.

This mix can be stored in your pantry for up to 4 months, for longer storage place container in the freezer.

Yield: 5 cups or 5 batches of pancakes

Basic Egg-Free Whole Grain Pancakes or Waffles

These pancakes are light and fluffy like when made with eggs. I've tried this recipe with eggs in place of the ground flax, hot water, and applesauce but the pancakes didn't turn out as well. This egg-free version has better taste and texture. Serve with the Blueberry Syrup, page 115, or the Nut Butter Syrup, page 116.

1 heaping tablespoon ground flax seeds (use 2 tablespoons for waffles)
2 tablespoons very hot water
2 tablespoons unsweetened applesauce
2 tablespoons melted virgin coconut oil
1 tablespoon maple syrup
¾ cup milk (use 1 cup for waffles)
1 cup Whole Grain Pancake and Waffle Mix, page 113

Heat a 10-inch skillet over medium-low heat.

Place the ground flax seeds and hot water into a medium-sized mixing bowl; quickly whisk together until the flax forms a thick gel. Sometimes this doesn't happen right away so keep whisking until the gel forms. Add the applesauce, oil, syrup, and milk and whisk together well. Then add the cup of pancake mix. Whisk together until the batter is smooth.

For making pancakes, add a teaspoon or two of coconut oil to the hot skillet. Wait until it has melted, then add the batter by the ½ cup-full. Cook until bubbles form on the top, about 60 seconds, then flip and cook for another minute or so. Add a little coconut oil in between cooking each pancake.

For making waffles, cook according to your waffle iron's directions.

Yield: About 5 Pancakes or 4 Waffles

Blueberry Syrup

Either fresh or frozen blueberries work in this recipe. To vary this recipe, use blackberries, raspberries, or strawberries or a mix of all of them. Serve this syrup with freshly made pancakes or drizzled over a slice of cake as an alternative to frosting.

1 cup fresh or frozen blueberries
¾ cup water
2 to 3 tablespoons honey or maple syrup
1 tablespoon arrowroot powder

Place all ingredients into a blender and blend on high until smooth. Pour liquid into a small saucepan and heat over medium heat until little bubbles form, reduce heat just slightly and continue to cook while whisking until thickened and clear. It only takes about 5 minutes total cooking time. Just remember to keep whisking.

Serve hot syrup over pancakes or waffles. Store the remaining syrup in a glass jar in the refrigerator. The syrup will solidify a little in the fridge and needs to be reheated before using.

Yield: About 1 ½ cups

Variation:

In place of the arrowroot I sometimes use kudzu starch, which is very healing to the intestines. Use $\frac{1}{2}$ tablespoon kudzu in place of 1 tablespoon arrowroot.

Nut Butter Syrup

I like to mix maple syrup or honey with a creamy nut butter to sneak in a little extra protein and fat into our children's breakfasts. Use organic sunflower butter, almond butter, or cashew butter. Don't heat the syrup or it will thicken considerably.

¼ cup creamy nut butter
4 to 6 tablespoons maple syrup or honey

In a small bowl, whisk together the nut butter and syrup or honey. Use a spoon to scoop it out and drizzle over hot pancakes or waffles.

Yield: About ½ cup

Nutrition Tip:

Pure maple syrup is more than just glucose and sucrose, it is full of antioxidant phenolic compounds that are beneficial for health and longevity. In fact, over 26 phytochemicals have been found! Maple syrup is made by boiling down the sap of the sugar maple tree, thereby concentrating beneficial nutrients contained in the sap.

Breads, Muffins, and Crackers

When you are just transitioning to a gluten-free diet having bread and muffin recipes that mimic the flavor and texture of wheat-based products can be so helpful. Therefore, I have worked over the years to create healthy and simple gluten-free baking recipes that are nourishing, and best of all, taste great. They aren't meant to be consumed everyday—no mater how nutritious the ingredients are, eating a diet based off of baked goods won't benefit your health. We prefer to revolve our diet around vegetables, whole grains, beans, nuts, fruits, and meats. With the exception of sourdough bread, baked gluten-free treats are prepared only a few times a month in our home.

Gluten-Free Baking Basics

If you are new to gluten-free baking you might find the amount of different flours and different baking methods a bit overwhelming. Once you have a little practice, you'll get the hang of it, and baking gluten-free will become second nature. Keep in mind that your gluten-free baking won't be completely gluten-free if you are also using wheat flour in your kitchen. Flour dust can linger in the air for a day or more and land on countertops, dishes, and cooking utensils. It only takes a minute amount of gluten to cause a reaction in a gluten-sensitive person. It is best to keep the kitchen gluten-free for sensitive family members.

Whole Grain Flours

Many gluten-free products and recipes rely on the typical white rice flour, potato starch, and tapioca flour combinations. These refined flours and starches are devoid of many natural fibers, vitamins, minerals, and phytochemicals and can create a sharp rise in blood sugar. For people with functioning blood sugar regulation this can cause a large spike in insulin, with a subsequent quick drop in circulating sugar (hypoglycemia), which may lead to fatigue, foggy thinking, anxiety, and cravings for sweets. For others with dysfunctional blood sugar regulation, this may lead to extended elevated levels of blood sugar and insulin leaving them susceptible to increased inflammation, and at increased risk for numerous chronic diseases.

In my recipes, I rely on either whole grain gluten-free flours or grain-free flours and use as little starch as possible, or none at all. My favorite flours are teff and buckwheat, but I also use coconut, almond, sorghum, millet, and brown rice flours and I like to add in ground nuts whenever possible to add flavor and protein.

It saves quite a bit of money and packaging if you buy your flours in bulk (see resources). If you don't use your gluten-free flours frequently, it is best to store them in glass jars in your refrigerator. Otherwise store them in your pantry. If you buy twenty-five pounds of flour at a time, freeze three quarters of it and store the rest in your pantry or refrigerator.

Milk
The protein content of milk provides structure and flavor in baked goods. You'll notice that my recipes simply call for milk. We don't drink cow's milk, so for us this means homemade hemp milk, almond milk, cashew milk, or coconut milk. If you'd prefer, any type of animal milk can be used with good results, such as fresh cow or goat milk. I also use "banana milk" on occasion, which is made by blending up a ripe banana with a few tablespoons of water until thin and milky. See the Beverage chapter, page 477, for homemade dairy-free milk recipes.

Natural Sweeteners
The only refined cane sugar I have in the house is for making cultured drinks like kombucha. I prefer to use sweeteners that still contain the beneficial phytochemicals, vitamins, and minerals to help metabolize the sugar—coconut sugar is one we commonly use. It is a granulated sweetener that has a glycemic index of about 35 and comes from the dehydrated sap of the coconut palm. If you do not have coconut sugar you can replace it with another granulated sweetener, such as Sucanat (whole cane sugar). Raw local honey, pure grade B maple syrup, and coconut nectar are my choice in liquid sweeteners. Other natural sweeteners that can be used are mashed bananas, applesauce, pureed ripe peaches, yacon syrup, and stevia. For a more detailed look into natural sweeteners, see our Dessert chapter, page 413.

Healthy Fats
Adding fat into baked goods provides tenderness, moisture, and flavor. I use coconut oil, organic palm shortening, organic pastured butter, and olive oil, but mostly prefer to use virgin coconut oil for the majority of my baking recipes.

Occasionally I will use melted butter in a recipe instead of coconut oil, mainly for cornbread. When purchasing butter, look for one labeled "pastured." This means that the animals grazed on grasses instead of being fed corn and soy (which are commonly genetically engineered).

Olive oil can also be used on occasion for quick breads and muffins if you would prefer everything didn't taste like coconut, though it isn't as stable with heat like coconut oil is. Organic palm shortening is best used where you need a saturated fat, such as in biscuits, scones, and pie crusts. I never use butter substitutes or refined oils such as canola or safflower in my cooking or baking. These fats are highly refined, most often genetically engineered, and can transform into trans fats during high heat cooking.

Natural Binders
You'll notice that the majority of my recipes don't contain any xanthan gum. This is because xanthan gum isn't a real food. Xanthan gum is an ingredient that is commonly used in gluten-free baking to help bind ingredients together, provide elasticity, and hold moisture. It is a hydrocolloid, meaning it forms a gel in the presence of water. Xanthan gum is most

often produced using corn though it can also come from wheat, dairy, or soy. Labeling laws don't require manufacturers to list where it comes from. Xanthan gum is created from the excrement of the bacteria, *Xanthomonas campestris*, which normally grows on rotting vegetables, such as broccoli, and creates a sticky substance. Food manufacturers use corn syrup to feed this bacteria, then they dry the excrement and sell it as powder.

Instead of xanthan gum, I use—alone or in combination—ingredients such as chia seeds, flax seeds, and psyllium husks. Chia and flax help to bind ingredients together while psyllium holds moisture. Together these ingredients work in a similar fashion to xanthan gum. Using eggs also helps bind gluten-free flours together.

There isn't an exact science or perfect ratio to replacing xanthan gum. I have found that experimentation is your best bet. Often times it is simply easier and more effective to create a new recipe using ground seeds and psyllium rather than try to replace the xanthan gum in an old recipe.

10 Tips for Successful Gluten-Free Baking:

1. **High Altitude**. When baking my recipes at a high altitude you might find slightly different results. We live at sea level in a moist climate so my gluten-free flours retain a little more moisture compared to ingredients stored in very dry climate. Recipes baked at a high altitude often rise much faster when using baking powder or baking soda, and can turn out denser, drier, and a tad more crumbly than recipes baked at sea level. You may need to decrease baking powder and soda by $1/8$ to $1/4$ teaspoon per teaspoon called for, while increasing liquids by 2 to 4 tablespoons per cup of liquid called for.

2. **Measuring**. When measuring, be sure not to pack down your flours. I usually just scoop my flours out of the jar and then gently level them off. Always use dry measuring cups for the dry ingredients and liquid measures for the liquid ingredients.

3. **Varying Oven Temperatures**. Oven temperatures can vary widely so be sure to buy a little oven thermometer and stick it in the oven to get a correct reading. Ovens can sometimes be off by as much as fifty degrees!

4. **Stoneware for baking**. I suggest investing in stone baking pans for many of my baking recipes. I use stoneware from Pampered Chef. It works beautifully for gluten-free baked goods. I use a stone muffin pan, mini-loaf pan, bundt pan, and pizza stone.

5. **Glass loaf pans**. I like to bake my yeast breads in glass Pyrex bread pans. All of the bread recipes in this chapter were tested using this type of pan.

6. **Grind your own flour or purchase from a grain mill**? Gluten-free grain flours, other than oats and buckwheat, are best bought from a company that specializes in grinding flour. Even a Vita-Mix has a difficult time getting a fine enough flour with hard grains such as brown rice or teff. I prefer to use Bob's Red Mill gluten-free flours in my baking recipes. Teff flour I purchase through The Teff Company. Superfine flours are wonderful to have on hand for making pie crusts and biscuits. I purchase these through Authentic Foods.

7. **Making your own buckwheat flour**. You'll notice that many of my recipes call for freshly ground buckwheat flour. This type of flour is made by grinding raw buckwheat groats in a coffee grinder, grain grinder, or Vita-Mix for a minute or so until a fine powdery flour forms. It is a soft grain and grinds up quite easily. This flour is very different than the strong-flavored roasted buckwheat flour found in grocery store isles. The mild taste of raw buckwheat flour is quite pleasing. You won't have the same results in my recipes if you use store-bought, roasted buckwheat flour. I like to grind a large amount of raw buckwheat groats at once and then store the flour in a glass jar in my pantry. Be sure to use certified gluten-free buckwheat as most

buckwheat you find in the bulk bins from your local health food store is cross-contaminated with gluten grains!

8. **Making fresh oat flour**. Oat flour is best ground fresh just before using. Oat flour purchased from a grocery store is most often rancid by the time you buy it. The rancid flavor will completely throw off the recipe. Use gluten-free rolled oats and grind them as you do buckwheat in a coffee grinder, grain grinder, or Vita-Mix.

9. **Using chia and flax seeds**. Chia seeds and flax seeds are high in omega-3 fatty acids that can spoil quickly if not stored in the refrigerator. Use your coffee grinder, small electric grinder, or Vita-Mix to grind chia and flax seeds into a fine meal. Store them separately in glass jars in your refrigerator for up to a week. Since they tend to clump up once ground, I use a small sifter to sift the measured amount needed into the recipe. Chia seeds and flax seeds are not interchangeable in equal amounts. Chia seeds have about twice the binding power of flax so you would need to use about twice as much ground flax in a recipe calling for ground chia seeds.

10. **Using psyllium**. Whole psyllium husks and psyllium husk powder are two different things. Be sure to read the recipe carefully and use the correct one. You cannot interchange the two. Once you whisk warm water in with the psyllium husk it will begin to absorb water immediately. You need to be ready with your dry ingredients otherwise the mixture will become too thick to work with.

Gluten-Free Sourdough Starter

This starter recipe can be used to make the recipes on the following pages or used to create your own variations of breads, rolls, muffins, or pancakes.

About the Sourdough Process

Wild yeasts are abundant on whole grain flours. Traditionally, bread was made by cultivating the wild yeasts present on the grain—you couldn't just go to a store and buy baker's yeast back then. Wild yeasts will become active when the environment is right—they prefer an acidic environment. I have found that adding a little apple juice on the first day of making the starter helps to get the fermentation process going, though it is not always necessary. After about 48 hours you should see a bit of bubbling. Often times the first microbes to grow are the ones that prefer a more neutral pH. They eat up some of the starches in the flour and produce acids as a by-product. As the environment becomes more acidic, the wild yeasts wake up, usually when the pH drops below 4. It usually takes at least 7 days to create a viable starter. If your house is cooler, it may take 10 days. Generally, starters should not be used until they are at least a week old for bread baking, this way the wild yeasts have proliferated enough to be able to rise the bread. You'll find that after about a month or two your starter will create a better textured and flavored bread than it did at a week old.

Types of Flours Needed

You can use any gluten-free flour for your starter. I prefer to start with teff flour and then add in any combination of millet, brown rice, sorghum, quinoa, amaranth, and buckwheat flours. Using buckwheat in your starter will cause it to become considerably thicker so you will need less flour when making the actual loaf of bread. If I add too much buckwheat flour and the starter becomes too thick I usually just thin it out with extra water.

Filtered Water

Remember to always use filtered water for making sourdough starters. Chlorine in city water can inhibit microbial activity and we certainly don't want that when making a sourdough starter!

Making the Starter

Day 1: Place 1 cup whole grain gluten-free flour, 1 cup water, and 2 tablespoons apple juice into a large wide-mouthed half-gallon or gallon-sized glass jar; whisk together. Place a thin dishtowel or cloth napkin over it and place it into an undisturbed warm spot in your kitchen.

Day 2: After 24 hours, add ½ cup flour and ½ cup filtered water; whisk together.

Day 3: After 24 hours, add another ½ cup flour and ½ cup water; whisk together. By now you should be seeing a lot of bubbling and a distinct sour smell.

Day 4 and Beyond: Feed your starter every 12 to 24 hours; 12 if your kitchen is very warm, 24 if your kitchen is cooler. After every feeding you should see the starter become very active, and then rise and fall within a twelve-hour period. Make sure to feed your starter when you see very few bubbles and a layer of dark liquid on top. This liquid is called *hooch* and is an alcohol by-product of fermentation—it means your starter is starving and needs to be fed! Some people like to pour it off, while others stir it back in before feeding it. I've done it both ways with good results. Making a starter is not an exact science. It is about tuning into those lovely little microbes in your jars. Once you do it a few times, you'll gain a better understanding of the cues that determine when to feed it and when to wait.

Keep feeding your starter every 12 to 24 hours, and by day 7 you should have a viable starter to bake bread with.

Using Your Starter

When your starter is ready to use, measure out the amount needed for your bread recipe and then add 1 cup gluten-free flour and 1 cup filtered water. You can keep your starter going by feeding it every 12 hours a mixture of ½ cup gluten-free flour plus ½ cup filtered water. This way you can use it every few days to make breads or rolls. If you see a lot of crusting on the jar then pour it into a clean jar every week.

Taking a Break

If you go on vacation or don't plan on using your starter for a while just stick it in the refrigerator with a lid on and feed it equal amounts of flour and water every 2 to 3 weeks. When ready to use again, place the jar on your counter and begin to feed it every 12 hours.

Sourdough Teff Bread

The art of sourdough bread baking is an art, not an exact science. Each loaf I make yields slightly different complex and unique flavors. The best time to use your starter for bread baking is a few hours after you feed it—when it is in its "active and bubbly" stage. Use this beautiful, nutritious loaf for sandwiches or as a compliment to your main meal.

4 cups sourdough starter, active and bubbly
½ cup warm water
2 teaspoons sea salt
2 tablespoons extra virgin olive oil
2 tablespoons maple syrup
4 tablespoons ground chia seeds
4 tablespoons whole psyllium husks
1 to 1 ¾ cups teff flour
¼ cup tapioca flour or arrowroot powder

Place the sourdough starter into a medium-sized mixing bowl. Whisk in the warm water, salt, olive oil, and maple syrup. Then whisk in the ground chia and psyllium husks. Let the mixture rest for no more than 2 minutes; then add the flours. Use a fork to mix them together. The dough should feel slightly wet and sticky, but stiff enough to hold shape. If the dough is too dry it won't rise properly. Add a little water if it feels dense and dry. If it is too wet, add a little extra flour. It should feel wetter than my yeast-risen recipes.

Place dough into an oiled 9 x 5-inch bread pan and smooth the top with your fingers. Place a plastic produce bag or piece of parchment paper over it and set it in a warm spot to rise for 3 to 6 hours. I usually set it on top of my refrigerator where my sourdough starters sit. To help the dough rise a bit faster I sometimes set the rising loaf in a pan of warm water. You can also set the pan in a warm, sunny spot. Warm rising should only take about 3 hours. If your kitchen is very cool rising time may take up to 8 hours. You should see the dough almost double in size during rising time.

Preheat oven to 375 degrees F. Bake bread for 60 to 75 minutes. Let cool for about 10 minutes and then remove from pan and continue to cool on a wire rack.

Yield: 1 loaf

Kitchen Tip:

I reuse biodegradable produce bags for covering my rising bread. We don't buy plastic wrap and find we never need to use it.

Variation:

Replace the teff flour with any combination of whole grain gluten-free flours.

Sourdough Buckwheat Burger Buns

These sourdough buns are soft and spongy. Use them for sandwiches, burgers, or as an accompaniment to a meal. We like to serve them with the Sloppy Joe's, page 336, and some sort of lacto-fermented vegetable. It makes a nice, cozy wintertime meal.

3 cups sourdough starter, active and bubbly
½ cup warm water
1 ½ teaspoons sea salt
2 tablespoons extra virgin olive oil
1 tablespoon maple syrup
2 tablespoons ground chia seeds
2 tablespoons whole psyllium husks
1 cup freshly ground buckwheat flour
¼ cup tapioca flour or arrowroot powder

Place the sourdough starter into a medium-sized mixing bowl. Whisk in the water, salt, olive oil and maple syrup. Then whisk in the ground chia and psyllium husks. Let the mixture rest for about 2 minutes. Slowly add the flours until the dough thickens. Use a fork to mix together. The dough should feel slightly wet and sticky, like thick cake batter. If it feels dense and dry then add water, a little at a time, until it lightens up. If the dough is too dry it won't rise properly and you will have hockey pucks instead of burger buns!

Place a piece of parchment paper onto a cookie sheet. Place 8 oiled English muffin rings onto the cookie sheet. Scoop out dough with a spoon and evenly distribute it among the rings. Drizzle a little olive oil, melted butter, or milk over the top of each bun (this will keep the tops of the buns from drying out during rising and baking). Place a plastic produce bag or piece of parchment paper over them and set the cookie sheet in a warm sunny spot to rise for about 3 to 6 hours or until doubled in size.

Preheat oven to 350 degrees F. Bake buns for about 35 minutes. Wait about 10 minutes and then pop the buns out of the metal rings. Cool on a wire rack before slicing in half.

Yield: 8 buns

Burger Buns

Use these buns to create a nutritious hamburger using grass-fed beef, salmon patties, or vegan veggie burgers. Our children like to make hummus, cucumber, and sprout sandwiches with these buns and pack them in their school lunch. You will need English muffin rings to create the bun shape. These can be ordered online for a minimal cost. You have the option to make them larger or smaller by the number of English muffin rings you use. After the buns have cooled, cut them in half and freeze some for later use.

Wet Ingredients:
1 ½ cups warm water (105 to 110 degrees F)
1 tablespoon active dry yeast
1 teaspoon maple syrup
½ cup ground golden flax seeds
¼ cup whole psyllium husks
2 tablespoons extra virgin olive oil
2 tablespoons coconut sugar

Dry Ingredients:
1 cup freshly ground buckwheat flour
1 cup teff flour
¾ cup tapioca flour
1 ½ teaspoons sea salt

Topping:
sesame seeds

Place water into a small bowl. Add yeast and syrup to water; whisk then let rest until foamy and bubbly. Add ground flax seeds and psyllium husks; quickly whisk together. Add oil and sugar; whisk together.

In a mixing bowl whisk together the dry ingredients. Add the wet to the dry and mix together using a wooden spoon until thickened. Dough will feel thick and sticky.

Lightly oil a large pan with olive oil. Oil the insides of 6 to 8 English muffin rings and place them onto the pan. Scoop dough evenly into the muffin rings. Smooth out using lightly oiled hands. Sprinkle each with sesame seeds. Let rise in a warm place for 45 to 60 minutes. If your spot is very warm, they may only need about 30 minutes of rising time.

Preheat oven to 350 degrees F. Bake for about 30 to 35 minutes. Use a spatula to take them off of the baking pan. Place onto a wire rack to cool. Once cooled, pop off the muffin rings. Cut each bun in half using a serrated knife.

Yield: 6 to 8 buns

Everyday Sandwich Bread

This is the bread recipe our children like best. I've substituted nearly all of the flours with good results. The bread will remain moist and ready to eat without needing to toast it. It is great for sandwiches or hot out of the oven!

Wet Ingredients:
2 ½ cups warm water (105 to 110 degrees F)
1 tablespoon active dry yeast
1 teaspoon maple syrup or organic cane sugar
2 tablespoons extra virgin olive oil
2 tablespoons maple syrup
⅓ cup ground chia seeds
⅓ cup whole psyllium husks

Dry Ingredients:
1 to 1 ½ cups sorghum flour
1 cup brown rice flour
1 cup tapioca flour
¾ cup almond flour
½ cup millet flour
1 ½ teaspoons sea salt

Place the warm water in a bowl or 4-cup liquid glass measure. Add the yeast and teaspoon of maple syrup, whisk together. Let rest for 5 to 10 minutes to activate the yeast. The mixture should get foamy or bubbly. If not, dump it out and start over.

While the yeast is activating, mix 1 cup of the sorghum flour with the remaining dry ingredients together in a large bowl.

After the yeast is activated whisk in the olive oil, additional maple syrup, ground chia seeds, and psyllium husks into the water-yeast mixture. Let stand for no more than 2 minutes to let the chia and psyllium release their gelatinous substances. Whisk again.

Pour the wet ingredients into the dry and mix together with a large wooden spoon until thick. Turn dough out onto a floured wooden board. Add more sorghum flour (¼ to ½ cup), a little at a time, until the dough holds together and isn't too sticky.

Form dough into an oblong ball, and place it into an oiled 9 x 5-inch bread pan. Cover with a damp towel or piece of waxed paper and place into a warm spot to rise. I like to place the bread pan in another larger pan of warm water. Let dough rise for an hour or until nearly doubled in size. Rising time will depend on the temperature of the environment around the dough.

Preheat the oven to 375 degrees F. Bake bread for about 55 to 60 minutes or until top is lightly golden and a nice crust has formed. Let pan cool for about 10 to 20 minutes before removing the bread. Then release it with a knife and turn it over. Cool on a wire rack.

Yield: 1 loaf

Dark Teff Sandwich Bread

Most people think this tastes a lot like whole wheat bread. We love it for making sandwiches or for toast in the morning.

Wet Ingredients:
2 ½ cups warm water (105 to 110 degrees F)
1 tablespoon active dry yeast
1 teaspoon maple syrup or organic cane sugar
2 tablespoons extra virgin olive oil
2 tablespoons maple syrup
⅓ cup ground chia seeds
⅓ cup whole psyllium husks

Dry Ingredients:
3 to 3 ½ cups teff flour
½ cup tapioca flour or arrowroot powder
1 ½ teaspoons sea salt

Place the warm water in a bowl or 4-cup liquid glass measure. Add the yeast and teaspoon of maple syrup; whisk together. Let rest for 5 to 10 minutes to activate the yeast. The mixture should get foamy or bubbly. If not, dump it out and start over.

While the yeast is activating, mix 3 cups teff flour and the rest of the dry ingredients together in a large bowl.

After the yeast is activated whisk in the olive oil, additional maple syrup, ground chia seeds, and psyllium husks into the water-yeast mixture. Let stand for no more than 2 minutes to let the chia and psyllium release their gelatinous substances. Whisk again.

Pour the wet ingredients into the dry and mix together with a large wooden spoon until thick. Turn dough out onto a floured wooden board. Add more teff flour, a little at a time, until the dough holds together and isn't too sticky.

Form dough into an oblong ball, and place it into an oiled 9 x 5-inch bread pan. Cover with a damp towel or piece of waxed paper and place into a warm spot to rise. I like to place the bread pan in another larger pan of warm water. Let dough rise for an hour or until nearly doubled in size. Rising time will depend on the temperature in your kitchen.

Preheat the oven to 375 degrees F. Bake bread for about 55 to 60 minutes or until top is lightly golden and a nice crust has formed. Let pan cool for about 10 to 20 minutes before removing the bread. Then release it with a knife and turn it over. Cool on a wire rack.

Yield: 1 loaf

Variation:

If I reduce the teff flour and replace it with sorghum flour our children refer to it as "gluten-free wheat bread." Use 2 cups sorghum flour, 1 ½ cups teff flour, and ½ cup tapioca flour. I knead in extra teff or sorghum flour until the dough isn't sticky.

Breads

Buckwheat Cinnamon Raisin Bread

Our family enjoys this bread so much that I need to make a two loaves at a time. For best storage, once the bread has cooled slice it, wrap in paper and a plastic bag, and then freeze. This way you can take a slice or two out of the freezer for toast when needed. I usually keep one loaf on the counter and freeze the other. This bread makes great almond butter and jam sandwiches for school lunches!

Wet Ingredients:
2 ½ cups warm water (105 to 110 degrees F)
1 tablespoon active dry yeast
1 teaspoon maple syrup or organic cane sugar
2 tablespoons extra virgin olive oil
4 tablespoons maple syrup
⅓ cup ground chia seeds
⅓ cup whole psyllium husks

Dry Ingredients:
3 ½ to 4 cups freshly ground buckwheat flour
½ cup arrowroot powder
2 tablespoons cinnamon
1 ½ teaspoons sea salt
½ to 1 cup raisins

Place the warm water in a bowl or 4-cup liquid glass measure. Add the yeast and teaspoon of maple syrup, whisk together. Let rest for 5 to 10 minutes to activate the yeast. The mixture should get foamy or bubbly. If not, dump it out and start over.

While the yeast is activating, mix 3 ½ cups of buckwheat flour with the remaining dry ingredients together in a large bowl.

After the yeast is activated whisk in the olive oil, additional maple syrup, ground chia seeds, and psyllium husks into the water-yeast mixture. Let stand for about 2 minutes to let the chia and psyllium release their gelatinous substances. Whisk again.

Pour the wet ingredients into the dry and mix together with a large wooden spoon until thick. Turn dough out onto a floured wooden board. Add more buckwheat flour, a little at a time, until the dough holds together and isn't too sticky. Don't add too much flour, otherwise the dough will become very dense; it should still be slightly sticky.

Form dough into an oblong ball, and place it into an oiled 9 x 5-inch bread pan. Cover with a damp towel and place into a warm spot to rise. I like to place the bread pan in another larger pan of warm water. Let dough rise for an hour or until nearly doubled in size. Rising time will depend on the temperature of the environment around the dough.

Preheat the oven to 375 degrees F. Bake bread for about 60 minutes or until top is lightly golden and a nice crust has formed. Let pan cool for about 10 to 20 minutes before removing the bread. Then release it with a knife and turn it over. Cool on a wire rack.

Yield: 1 loaf

Farmhouse Seed Bread

This artisan bread reminds me of a hearty seeded whole wheat bread. If you have a corn allergy, try replacing the cornmeal with almond meal. I have made this bread with many different flour combinations so feel free to experiment, but this one is my favorite for flavor and texture. The bread gets its crusty crust from being baked on a stone pan with a pan of water on the lower oven rack. The steam from the water helps to form the crust. The bread will be a little gummy hot out of the oven so be sure to let it cool a bit before cutting into it. Slice and serve with a good quality olive oil for dipping. It is also delicious spread with either almond butter or hummus!

Wet Ingredients:
2 ½ cups warm water (105 to 110 degrees F)
1 tablespoon active dry yeast
1 teaspoon maple syrup or organic cane sugar
2 tablespoons extra virgin olive oil
2 tablespoons maple syrup
⅓ cup ground chia seeds
⅓ cup whole psyllium husks

Dry Ingredients:
1 cup teff flour
1 cup sorghum flour
½ cup sweet rice flour
½ cup cornmeal
¼ cup raw sunflower seeds
¼ cup uncooked millet
2 tablespoons poppy seeds
2 tablespoons flax seeds
1 ½ teaspoons sea salt

Place the warm water in a bowl or 4-cup liquid glass measure. Add the yeast and teaspoon of maple syrup, whisk together. Let rest for 5 to 10 minutes to activate the yeast. The mixture should get foamy or bubbly. If not, dump it out and start over.

While the yeast is activating, mix together the dry ingredients in a large bowl.

After the yeast is activated whisk in the olive oil, maple syrup, ground chia seeds, and psyllium husks into the water-yeast mixture. Let stand for about 2 minutes to let the chia and psyllium release their gelatinous substances. Whisk again.

Pour the wet ingredients into the dry and mix together with a large wooden spoon until thick. Then knead the dough in the bowl to incorporate the flour. Add more teff and sorghum flours, a little at a time, until the dough holds together and isn't too sticky. Form dough into a ball, place onto a cookie sheet lined with parchment paper. Place in a warm spot to rise. I like to place the cookie sheet over a pot of warm water. Let dough rise for an hour or until doubled in size. Rising time will depend on the temperature of the environment around the dough. Drizzle the top of the risen bread with olive oil.

Preheat the oven to 375 degrees F.

Place a stone cookie sheet or pizza stone on the middle rack to heat up. Place a pan of water on the bottom rack of the oven. I usually use a 9 x 13-inch glass pan filled ¾ of the way full.

Lift the bread and parchment paper onto the stone pan in the oven. Bake for about 55 to 60 minutes. Remove from oven and let cool 30 to 60 minutes before cutting into it. The texture of bread will be very gummy hot out of the oven, but perfect once cooled.

Yield: 1 loaf

Ingredient Tip:

I use Arrowhead Mills cornmeal because it is the only brand I have found to be both organic and certified gluten-free.

Variation:

For an olive-rosemary bread omit seeds and add 1 cup sliced, pitted kalamata olives and 2 to 4 tablespoons chopped fresh rosemary.

Yeast-Free Seed Bread

This hearty, high protein sandwich bread doesn't use any yeast to make it rise. The simple combination of baking soda and vinegar does the trick. This also means no waiting for the bread to rise, just mix the ingredients together and pop it in the oven! This bread can spoil quickly so it is best to slice and freeze it or store it in the refrigerator.

Dry Ingredients:
1 cup teff flour
1 cup freshly ground buckwheat flour
½ cup arrowroot powder
1 cup raw pumpkin seeds, finely ground
1 cup raw sunflower seeds, finely ground
1 ½ teaspoons baking soda
1 teaspoon sea salt

Wet Ingredients:
2 cups water
¼ cup ground chia seeds
¼ cup whole psyllium husks
2 tablespoons extra virgin olive oil
2 tablespoons maple syrup
2 tablespoons apple cider vinegar

Preheat oven to 375 degrees F. Oil an 8.5 x 4.5 glass bread pan with olive oil.

In a large bowl, whisk together the dry ingredients. I grind my seeds in the dry container of my Vita-Mix. You can also use a food processor. Use your hands to break up any clumps of ground seeds in the dry ingredients.

In a medium-sized mixing bowl, whisk together the water, ground chia seeds, and whole psyllium husks. Let stand for 2 minutes. Then whisk in the oil, syrup, and vinegar.

Pour the wet ingredients into the dry and mix together with a large wooden spoon. Add more flour if the dough seems very sticky. It should be a little sticky but not too much. You might end up adding an extra ½ cup or more of either buckwheat or teff flour.

Place dough into oiled bread pan and use slightly oiled hands to smooth the top into a loaf shape. Sprinkle with pumpkin and sunflower seeds if desired. Bake for 60 to 70 minutes. Remove from oven and let bread cool in pan for about 10 minutes, then remove and place onto a wire rack to cool.

Yield: 1 loaf

Rosemary Sea Salt Breadsticks

I like to make up a batch of this dough and give it to my children to knead and make shapes out of. It is a relaxing afterschool activity for them and they help contribute to the evening meal! Use this recipe for breadsticks or omit the dried rosemary and form dough into balls to bake into dinner rolls. You can sprinkle the tops with sesame seeds or add seeds—such as sunflower, pumpkin, flax, and poppy—to the dough. This recipe is very versatile. Have fun with it!

Wet Ingredients:
2 cups warm water (105 to 110 degrees F)
1 tablespoon active dry yeast
1 teaspoon maple syrup or organic cane sugar
2 tablespoons extra virgin olive oil
1 tablespoon maple syrup or honey
½ cup ground golden flax seeds
¼ cup whole psyllium husks

Dry Ingredients:
1 ¼ cups brown rice flour
1 cup teff flour
¾ cup tapioca flour or arrowroot powder
1 to 2 tablespoons dried rosemary
1 ½ teaspoons sea salt

Place the warm water in a bowl or 4-cup liquid glass measure. Add the yeast and teaspoon of maple syrup, whisk together. Let rest for 5 to 10 minutes to activate the yeast. The mixture should get foamy or bubbly. If not, dump it out and start over. While the yeast is activating, mix together the dry ingredients in a large bowl.

After the yeast is activated whisk in the olive oil, additional maple syrup, ground flax seeds, and psyllium husks into the water-yeast mixture. Let stand for 2 to 3 minutes to let the flax and psyllium release their gelatinous substances. Whisk again.

Pour the wet ingredients into the dry and mix together with a large wooden spoon until thick. Turn dough out onto a floured wooden board. Add more flour (rice, teff, or tapioca) a little at a time, until the dough holds together and isn't too sticky.

Divide dough into eight equal-sized balls. On the floured board, roll each ball into a long log. Place each breadstick onto a well-oiled cookie sheet. Place cookie sheet in a warm place to rise. I like to place it on top of a large pan filled partially with water that is set on the stove on low heat. Let rise for 45 to 60 minutes.

Preheat oven to 375 degrees F. Bake breadsticks for 30 to 35 minutes or until done. Cool for about 10 minutes before serving. Serve with a homemade marinara sauce or a good olive oil for dipping.

Yield: About 10 breadsticks

Chia Dinner Rolls

Serve these hearty rolls with a baked chicken dinner or a vegetable bean soup. Because of the amount of chia seeds, the dough will feel a little different than my other bread recipes. The tendency will be to add more flour, but try not to. The dough should remain slightly sticky.

Wet Ingredients:
2 cups warm water (105 to 110 degrees F)
1 tablespoon active dry yeast
1 teaspoon maple syrup
3 tablespoons olive oil or melted butter
2 tablespoons maple syrup
2 tablespoons coconut sugar

Dry Ingredients:
3 cups sorghum flour
1 cup ground chia seeds
1 ½ teaspoons sea salt

Place water into a small bowl. Add yeast and teaspoon of syrup to water; whisk then let rest until foamy and bubbly. Add oil or butter and additional syrup and sugar; whisk together.

In a mixing bowl whisk together the dry ingredients. Add the wet to the dry and whisk together until thickened. Whisk quickly so it doesn't form lumps. Then turn out onto a well-floured wooden board. Knead for a few minutes incorporating more flour until dough isn't too sticky, but be careful not to add too much flour. I usually add ½ to 1 cup more flour.

Divide dough into 6 to 8 equal balls and place into an oiled 9 x 13-inch pan. Cover with a cloth or parchment paper. Let rise in a warm place for 1 hour.

Preheat oven to 350 degrees F. Brush the tops with milk if desired. Then bake for about 30 to 40 minutes, depending on the size of the rolls.

Yield: 6 to 8 rolls

Kitchen Tip:

To help the rolls rise, I like to place the pan of rising rolls into another larger pan filled partially with very hot water. You can also set the pan atop a pot of heated water.

Nutrition Tip:

Baking with chia seeds not only improves the texture of the final product, but also slows the release of carbohydrates into the bloodstream.

Almond Herb Pizza Crust

Use the Homemade Pizza Sauce, page 360, and your favorite toppings to make healthy gluten-free pizza! I've used a number of different gluten-free flours in place of the brown rice flour and they all work well lending different flavors—try amaranth, quinoa, or sorghum flour. I've also used sprouted brown rice flour with great results. Any type of almond flour will work here, such as Bob's Red Mill almond meal or the finely ground blanched almond flour listed in the Resources section at the back of this book.

Wet Ingredients:
¾ cup warm water (105 to 110 degrees F)
1 package active dry yeast (2 ¼ teaspoons)
1 teaspoon maple syrup
2 tablespoons extra virgin olive oil

Dry Ingredients:
1 ½ cups almond flour
1 cup brown rice flour
¾ cup arrowroot powder or tapioca flour
2 to 3 teaspoons dried Italian herbs
2 teaspoons psyllium husk powder
1 teaspoon sea salt

Place the warm water into a small bowl or 1-cup liquid glass measuring cup. Add the yeast and maple syrup. Whisk together then let stand until the mixture gets foamy and/or bubbly.

In a medium-sized mixing bowl whisk together the dry ingredients. Pour the wet mixture into the dry and stir together using a wooden spoon. Form dough into a ball, cover bowl, and let rise in a warm spot for about an hour.

Preheat oven to 375 degrees F. Oil your pizza stone or baking sheet with a little olive oil. Punch down dough and place it in the center of the pan. Drizzle a little olive oil over the top of the dough so the rolling pin doesn't stick to it. Roll out into a thin crust, about ¼-inch thick. You can also press the dough into a flat circle using your hands.

Prebake for about 15 to 20 minutes. Then remove from oven and top with your favorite toppings and bake again for another 10 to 15 minutes or until toppings are cooked to your liking. If you want to use your crust as flatbread or spread raw toppings onto it and not bake it a second time, bake for approximately 25 minutes total.

Yield: one 12 to 14-inch pizza crust

Variation:

If you would like to lessen the amount of starch in this recipe you can replace half of it with another whole grain flour, though we found that the consistency is best using ¾ cup.

Buckwheat Pizza Crust

Use this yeast-free recipe to make your favorite pizza. Since the crust needs to be completely cooked before adding the toppings you'll need to make sure veggies, such as mushrooms, are cooked prior to adding them as a topping. I like to roast my veggies in the oven (tossed in olive oil and sea salt) to top the pizza.

Dry Ingredients:
2 ¼ cups freshly ground buckwheat flour
½ cup tapioca flour
½ teaspoon sea salt
½ teaspoon baking soda
¼ teaspoon garlic powder

Wet Ingredients:
1 cup warm water
¼ cup extra virgin olive oil
1 tablespoon honey or maple syrup
1 tablespoon apple cider vinegar

Preheat oven to 375 degrees F.

In a medium-sized mixing bowl, combine the dry ingredients. Whisk together well.

In a separate bowl combine the wet ingredients. Pour the wet into the dry and whisk together well, until you see long dough strings formed. The dough will be thinner, more like cake batter. If it is too thick to whisk, add a tad more water.

Oil a pizza stone generously with olive oil. Scoop out the dough (it will begin to thicken as it sits) and with oiled hands work the dough into a thin sheet covering the pan. I use a 12 x 15-inch stone baking sheet, though I think a larger pan would produce a thinner, crispier crust. You may need to add extra olive oil to the top of the dough or your hands to prevent sticking. Once it is shaped, bake the crust for about 15 to 20 minutes. The timing can be very different depending on the oven and altitude. The crust is cooked when it is just slightly golden on top. You can pull some off the side to check for doneness, you'll know when it is cooked. If you like it crispier leave it in the oven a little longer.

Top with pizza sauce and your favorite toppings. Return to the oven until desired doneness. I usually put it back in for another 10 minutes or so.

Yield: one 12 to 14-inch pizza crust

Whole Grain Pizza Crust

Pizza is so versatile. You can make a simple vegetable pizza and serve small slices as a party appetizer or load on the toppings for a full meal. This is a thin crust with a crispy bottom and a slightly chewy center. I bake it on my 15-inch round pizza stone. Sometimes we fully bake the crust and then add a layer of pesto, fresh baby spinach, sliced cherry tomatoes, a few dollops of Cashew Sour Cream, page 369, and serve it fresh.

Wet Ingredients:
1 cup warm water (105 to 110 degrees F)
1 package active dry yeast (2 ¼ teaspoons)
2 teaspoons maple syrup
2 tablespoons ground chia seeds
¼ cup extra virgin olive oil

Dry Ingredients:
1 cup teff flour
1 cup brown rice flour
½ cup tapioca flour
1 teaspoon sea salt

Place the water in a small bowl or a 2-cup liquid glass measure. Add the yeast and maple syrup. Whisk together then let stand until the mixture gets foamy and/or bubbly. Whisk in the ground chia seeds and olive oil until the mixture thickens and a thin gel forms.

In a medium-sized mixing bowl whisk together the dry ingredients. Pour the wet mixture into the dry and stir together using a wooden spoon. Knead the dough a few times while it is still in the bowl. Add more flour if the dough seems sticky. Form dough into a ball, cover bowl, and let rise in a warm spot for about an hour.

Preheat oven to 400 degrees F.

Oil your pizza stone or baking sheet with about a tablespoon of olive oil. Punch down dough and place it in the center of the pan. Drizzle a little olive oil over the top of the dough so the rolling pin doesn't stick to it. Roll out into a thin crust, about ¼-inch thick.

Prebake for about 15 minutes. Then remove from oven and top with your favorite toppings and bake again for another 10 minutes or until toppings are cooked to your liking. If you want to use your crust as flatbread or spread raw toppings onto it and not bake it a second time, bake for approximately 20 minutes total.

Yield: one 12 to 14-inch pizza crust

Coconut Flour Flatbreads

This simple bread recipe is niceb to make once in a while if you are following a grain-free or low-carb diet. It is quite filling and the texture is very bread-like. Serve it with your main meal or use two of them to make a sandwich. They are also delicious slathered with homemade jam and sunflower seed butter!

½ cup ground golden flax seeds
½ cup hot water
2 tablespoons melted coconut oil or olive oil
1 tablespoon apple cider vinegar
6 tablespoons coconut flour
¼ teaspoon sea salt
¼ teaspoon baking soda

Optional Additions:
sliced kalamata olives
chopped fresh rosemary
snipped fresh chives
sesame seeds

Preheat oven to 350 degrees F. Line a cookie sheet with parchment paper.

In a food processor fitted with the "s" blade add the ground flax and hot water; pulse a few times. Let rest for about 3 minutes to thicken. Then add the oil and vinegar and process again to combine. Add the coconut flour, salt, and baking soda and process until the dough has formed a ball. Add in any optional additions at this time and pulse to combine.

Use wet hands to form four balls. Flatten the balls into individual flatbreads. Place onto the cookie sheet. Brush with oil and sprinkle with sesame seeds if desired.

Bake for about 30 to 35 minutes, flipping each flatbread half way though baking. Cool completely then serve.

Yield: 4 small flatbreads

Pita Bread

These simple, yeast-free pita breads can be made in just minutes. Use them to make pita sandwiches or use as flatbreads to serve with soup, curried stews, or as a crust for individual pizzas. I like to fill them with Chicken Salad, page 395, or Sweet Potato Falafels, page 310, and cultured vegetables and lettuce. My daughters like to stuff them with turkey, lettuce, and sliced Raw Sour Dill Pickles, page 508, for their school lunches.

Wet ingredients:
1 ¼ cups warm water
6 tablespoons ground golden flax seeds
2 tablespoons extra virgin olive oil
1 tablespoon apple cider vinegar

Dry Ingredients:
1 ½ cups sorghum flour
½ cup sweet rice flour
½ teaspoon sea salt
½ teaspoon baking soda

Preheat the oven to broil (550 degrees F). Line one or two cookie sheets with parchment paper. Position your oven rack so it is in the center of the oven, not directly underneath the broiler.

In a medium-sized mixing bowl, whisk together the warm water and ground flax seeds. Let rest for about five minutes to thicken. Then whisk in the olive oil and cider vinegar.

Add the dry ingredients to the wet and use a fork to mix together. You should be able to form a ball of dough that is neither too sticky nor too dry. If the dough seems sticky, add a little more sweet rice flour; I sometimes add up to ¼ cup more flour. If the dough seems too dry add a dash of water.

Divide the dough into five equal pieces. Using wet hands, roll each piece of dough in the palms of your hands. If your cookie sheet is large enough you should be able to fit all of them onto it, otherwise use two cookie sheets. Flatten each with your hands until they are about 5 to 6 inches in diameter and place onto the parchment-lined cookie sheets.

Bake for 10 to 12 minutes, flipping each flatbread after about 6 or 7 minutes. They should bubble slightly and be golden around the edges when done. After they have cooled, slice them in half and if need be, cut into the bread to form a pocket. Some of them bubble enough that this isn't necessary.

If you are not serving them right away, then layer them in between waxed paper and store in a sealed container. They may also be frozen.

Yield: five 6-inch pita breads

Buckwheat Cinnamon Rolls

Cinnamon rolls have always been a favorite of mine. I have fond childhood memories of making homemade cinnamon rolls with my mother. I like to makes this special treat around Christmas time and then again on Easter. Try some of the variations below for the filling. Children love to help sprinkle cinnamon and sugar into the filling and then spread frosting onto the cooked rolls. We like to use the Dairy-Free Cream Cheese Frosting, page 474.

Dry Ingredients:
3 to 4 cups freshly ground buckwheat flour
1 cup tapioca flour
1 tablespoon baking powder
1 teaspoon sea salt
½ teaspoon baking soda

Wet Ingredients:
1 cup cooked, mashed sweet potato
1 cup unsweetened applesauce
⅓ cup maple syrup
⅓ cup melted virgin coconut oil
1 tablespoon vanilla

Filling:
¼ to ½ cup softened coconut oil (or butter)
¼ to ½ cup coconut sugar or another granulated sugar
2 to 4 tablespoons cinnamon

Preheat oven to 350 degrees. Oil two 8 or 9-inch cake pans.

In a large mixing bowl, add 3 cups of the buckwheat flour and the remaining dry ingredients; whisk together.

Place all of the wet ingredients into a blender or vita-mix and blend until very smooth and creamy. Pour the wet into the dry ingredients and whisk together. Once it becomes too thick to whisk, use a wooden spoon. Add more buckwheat flour until the dough forms a ball but is still a little sticky.

Generously flour a work surface using buckwheat flour or tapioca flour. Turn the dough out onto the floured surface. Sprinkle the top of the dough with flour if it is too sticky. The trick here is to add just enough flour to be able to roll out the dough but not too much otherwise the cinnamon rolls become too dense.

Roll out dough into a large rectangle using a floured rolling pin. Spread with softened coconut oil. Don't use melted coconut oil or another oil, as it will leak out of the dough from all sides and make it impossible to roll and hold shape. Sprinkle with sugar and cinnamon, or your filling of choice.

Begin to roll from the long end down towards you. If your dough is sticking to the work surface then try coaxing it with a large, thin spatula coated with flour. Once the dough has been rolled up, slice it with a serrated knife, and place the rolls into your oiled pans. Bake for about 30 to 35 minutes.

Yield: About 10 rolls

Nutrition Tip:

Buckwheat has many nutritional benefits. It helps to maintain blood glucose levels and has been shown to be beneficial for diabetics. Buckwheat is high in the flavonoid, rutin, which helps to prevent disease through its antioxidant effects. It is also a rich source of magnesium. Magnesium acts as a cofactor for over 300 enzymes in the human body! All reactions that involve ATP, the energy currency of our cells, depend on magnesium.

Variation:

Process some dates and walnuts in a food processor and spread over the dough. Another favorite is a fig puree made from dried mission figs, boiling water, and orange zest. I would still add a little cinnamon and coconut sugar to these variations.

Baking Powder Biscuits

This biscuit recipe is a great transition recipe if you are just beginning a gluten-free diet and are accustomed to flakey biscuits made from wheat flour. The sweet rice flour creates a soft texture and a structure that will remind you of traditional biscuits. Do not replace the superfine brown rice flour with regular brown rice flour or you will end up with very dense biscuits. The millet flour adds a luscious nutty flavor to the otherwise bland rice flours. The xanthan gum helps to add structure but isn't necessary, in fact, I don't use it but if you are accustomed to traditional biscuits then its use might help with the transition into the gluten-free world.

1 cup superfine brown rice flour
1 cup superfine sweet rice flour
½ cup millet flour
½ cup tapioca flour
1 tablespoon baking powder
½ teaspoon xanthan gum (optional)
1 teaspoon sea salt
8 to 10 tablespoons cold unsalted butter or organic palm shortening
1 ¼ to 1 ½ cups cold milk

Preheat oven to 425 degrees.

Place the flours, baking powder, xanthan gum if using, and salt into a medium mixing bowl and whisk together well. Add the butter or shortening. Cut in with your fingers or a pastry cutter. I use my fingers until flat, coarse crumbs are formed. Then add the milk and quickly mix it in with a fork or spoon until combined.

Turn dough out onto a lightly floured cutting board, lightly knead to incorporate the flour and liquid, and then gently pat into about a 1 ½ to 2-inch thick round. Do not overwork the dough. Cut into biscuit shapes with a cup or biscuit cutter. I take a large, sharp knife and slice them into squares, which is much quicker than using a biscuit cutter. Place onto ungreased cookie sheet and bake for about 15 minutes, depending on the size of your biscuits.

Biscuits are best consumed the day they are made, but can be stored for up to 2 days.

Yield: About 1 dozen

Ingredient Tip:

I usually use Hemp Milk, page 482, or Cashew Milk, page 483 in this recipe. Using richer milk such as these will produce a tender and better flavored biscuit. You can also use cow or goat milk if you prefer.

Coconut Flour Biscuits

This low-glycemic, grain-free biscuit recipe is very simple and quick to prepare! Serve them with organic bacon and sautéed kale for breakfast, or with a bean and vegetable stew for dinner. You can also cut this recipe in half and use it to top the Chicken Pot Pie, page 328.

Dry Ingredients:
1 cup coconut flour
1 teaspoon baking soda
¼ teaspoon sea salt

Wet Ingredients:
8 tablespoons butter or organic palm shortening
6 large organic eggs
1 cup milk

Preheat oven to 375 degrees F. Lightly grease a large cookie sheet with coconut oil.

Place the dry ingredients into a food processor and pulse a few times to incorporate. Add the butter or shortening and process until fine crumbs form. Then add the eggs and milk; process until smooth. The dough will look watery and thin at first. Just turn off the food processor and let the dough rest for a few minutes to thicken up.

Drop about 10 to 12 equal-sized biscuits onto the cookie sheet. Lightly reshape with your hands if desired. Bake for 20 to 25 minutes.

Yield: 10 to 12 biscuits

Ingredient Tip:

For the milk, I prefer to use homemade cashew cream but any type of thick, rich milk will work.

Oat Currant Scones

Serve these high-fiber, protein-rich scones with a glass of herbal tea as an afternoon treat. I always grind my own oat flour from gluten-free rolled oats for all baking recipes requiring oat flour. Oat flour that is sold in the stores is often quite rancid and tastes bitter. Use a coffee grinder or blender to grind the oats. It only takes a minute.

1 ¼ cups gluten-free oat flour
1 cup hazelnut flour
½ cup sweet rice flour
1 tablespoon baking powder
½ teaspoon sea salt
4 tablespoons coconut sugar
½ cup cold unsalted butter or organic palm shortening
½ cup rolled gluten-free oats
½ cup currants
1 teaspoon orange zest
¾ cup milk

Preheat oven to 425 degrees F.

In a large mixing bowl whisk together the flours, baking powder, salt, and sugar. Cut in the butter or coconut oil with a pastry cutter or your fingers until small pea-sized crumbs form. Work quickly so the fat doesn't begin to melt. Stir in the rolled oats, currants, and orange zest. Then add the milk and stir it in with a fork. If the dough seems too wet, add more oat flour, a tablespoon or two at a time, until you can form a ball.

Place dough ball onto a lightly floured board. Pat into a flat circle, about 1½ inches high. Cut the dough, using a large sharp knife, into quarters and then eighths so you have 8 triangles.

Place the scones onto an ungreased cookie sheet. Bake for 15 to 20 minutes. Cool on a wire rack. These scones are best served warm.

Yield: 8 scones

Pumpkin Scones

There is nothing more scrumptious than spiced pumpkin scones and hot tea on a chilly autumn morning. If you can tolerate dairy then replace the shortening with cold, organic unsalted butter and use either cow or goat's milk. I usually make my own cashew milk for these or use unsweetened Hemp Milk, page 482.

1 cup sorghum flour
½ cup sweet rice flour
4 tablespoons maple sugar or coconut sugar
2 teaspoons baking powder
½ teaspoon sea salt
1 teaspoon cinnamon
½ teaspoon ground ginger
¼ teaspoon ground nutmeg
6 tablespoons organic palm shortening
2 tablespoons ground chia seeds
2 tablespoons hot water
6 tablespoons cold pumpkin puree
½ cup cold milk

Optional Toppings:
milk
maple sugar

Preheat oven to 425 degrees.

Place the flours, sugar, baking powder, salt, and spices into a medium mixing bowl and whisk together. Add the shortening. Cut in with your fingers or a pastry cutter. I use my fingers until coarse crumbs are formed.

Place the ground chia seeds and hot water into a small bowl and immediately whisk together with a fork. Add the pumpkin and milk; whisk again. Sometimes I add the ground chia, water, pumpkin, and milk to my blender and blend on high to incorporate them.

Combine the pumpkin mixture to the flour and quickly mix in with a fork or spoon until just combined. Only mix the dough until it comes together otherwise you will end up with a doughier scone rather than a flakey one. Dough should be slightly sticky.

Turn dough out onto a lightly floured cutting board and pat into a circle of about 1-inch of thickness. Do not overwork the dough. With a large, sharp knife cut the dough into quarter and then eighths so you have 8 triangles. Brush tops with milk, sprinkle with maple sugar if desired.

Yield: 8 Scones

Apple Almond Muffins

This recipe is very versatile. You can replace the apple with diced peaches or pears, add different spices such as cardamom and nutmeg, and replace some of the brown rice flour with another flour such as millet or sorghum flour. These muffins are perfect hot out of the oven with a cup of hot apple cider. They will also stay moist for days. My children beg me to make these muffins any time of year!

Dry Ingredients:
1 ½ cups brown rice flour
1 ½ cups almond flour
1 tablespoon psyllium husk powder
1 tablespoon baking powder
1 to 2 teaspoons cinnamon
½ teaspoon baking soda
½ teaspoon sea salt

Wet Ingredients:
1 cup milk
½ cup unsweetened applesauce
½ cup coconut sugar
¼ cup melted coconut oil or olive oil

Other Ingredients:
1 apple, diced small

Preheat oven to 350 degrees F. Grease a 12-cup muffin pan or line with paper liners.

Whisk the dry ingredients together in a large bowl. In another smaller bowl, whisk together the wet ingredients. Pour the wet ingredients into the dry and whisk together well. Since this batter is egg-free it will be slightly thicker than muffin batter made with eggs. Fold in the diced apple.

Fill each muffin cup to the top. You may want to smooth the tops with wet fingers before baking if desired. Bake for approximately 30 minutes. Cool muffins on a wire rack.

Yield: 1 dozen muffins

Apricot Almond Quinoa Muffins

I wanted to create a muffin recipe that was high in protein but didn't rely entirely on nut flours. This recipe is what evolved from that thought. I make these muffins often at night after the children are in bed. I love having breakfast ready on the counter when we wake up. Serve these with a green smoothie for a quick, nutritious breakfast or bedtime snack.

Dry Ingredients:
1 cup teff flour
1 cup quinoa flakes
½ cup almond meal
½ cup tapioca flour
2 tablespoons ground chia seeds
2 tablespoons ground flax seeds
2 teaspoons baking powder
½ teaspoon baking soda
½ teaspoon sea salt

Wet Ingredients:
1 cup unsweetened applesauce
½ cup milk
⅓ cup extra virgin olive oil
⅓ cup maple syrup
2 large organic eggs
¼ cup almond butter
2 teaspoons vanilla

Other Ingredients:
1 cup chopped dried apricots

Preheat oven to 350 degrees. Oil a 12-cup muffin pan or line with paper liners.

Whisk together the dry ingredients in a large mixing bowl. In a separate mixing bowl, whisk together the wet ingredients.

Pour the wet into the dry and whisk together until the batter thickens. Fold in the dried apricots. Spoon batter into prepared muffin pan. Fill each muffin cup to the top.

Bake for 30 to 35 minutes. Cool on a wire rack.

Yield: 1 dozen muffins

Variation:

You can also make these into banana-walnut muffins using 3 mashed, ripe bananas in place of the 1 cup of applesauce and replacing the dried apricots with chopped walnuts.

Banana Buckwheat Muffins

This egg-free muffin recipe is light and airy and perfectly sweet with ripe bananas in every bite. By using freshly ground buckwheat flour from raw groats, you create a muffin that is light and flavorful without a strong buckwheat flavor. People who don't like buckwheat will most likely have no idea that the main flour is buckwheat. Add one of these muffins to your child's lunchbox for a healthy treat!

Dry Ingredients:
2 ¼ cups freshly ground buckwheat flour
¼ cup tapioca flour or arrowroot powder
2 teaspoons baking powder
½ teaspoon baking soda
½ teaspoon sea salt

Wet Ingredients:
2 cups mashed ripe bananas
½ cup coconut sugar
⅓ cup melted coconut oil
2 teaspoons vanilla extract
1 cup milk

Preheat oven to 350 degrees F. Grease a 12-cup muffin pan or line with paper liners.

In a large bowl, whisk together the dry ingredients.

In another medium-sized mixing bowl combine the wet ingredients, starting with ¾ cup of milk. Whisk together well. If the batter seems too thick (it will thicken as it rests for a few minutes) then add more liquid so the batter will easily fall off of a spoon but not too much that the batter is runny and thin. How you measure your dry ingredients will affect how much liquid you need.

Pour the wet ingredients into the dry and whisk together. Fill each cup up all the way for 12 muffins or fill each about ¾ of the way full for 18 muffins.

Bake for 20 to 25 minutes. Cool on a wire rack. Store in an airtight container for up to 3 days or freeze for longer storage.

Yield: 12 to 18 muffins

Kitchen Tip:

It can take quite a few bananas to equal 2 cups mashed. Count on at least 4 to 5 large ones—more if your bananas are smaller.

Blueberry Teff Muffins

This super nutritious, dark, whole grain muffin is an absolute favorite at our house. My children devour them as they come out of the oven and then ask to take one in their lunchbox the next day. If you don't have blueberries on hand try using diced apples and a few teaspoons of cinnamon. Raspberries or blackberries also work well.

Dry Ingredients:
2 cups teff flour
½ cup tapioca flour
2 teaspoons baking powder
½ teaspoon baking soda
½ teaspoon sea salt

Wet ingredients:
2 tablespoons ground chia seeds
¼ cup hot water
2 large eggs
½ cup coconut sugar
½ cup unsweetened applesauce
⅓ cup melted coconut oil or olive oil
1 cup milk
1 to 2 teaspoons orange zest

Other Ingredients:
1 cup fresh or frozen blueberries

Preheat oven to 350 degrees F. Grease a 12-cup muffin pan or line with paper liners.

In a large bowl whisk together the dry ingredients.

In another medium-sized mixing bowl add the ground chia seeds. Pour the hot water over them and quickly whisk together until a thick slurry forms. Add the eggs, coconut sugar, applesauce, oil, milk, and orange zest. Whisk together well.

Pour the wet ingredients into the dry and whisk together. Fold in the blueberries. Scoop batter into prepared muffin pan. Fill each cup up all the way.

Bake for 30 minutes. Cool on a wire rack. Freeze muffins once cooled or store in an airtight container for up to 3 days.

Yield: 1 dozen muffins

Carrot Almond Muffins

These muffins are grain-free and more of a savory muffin than a sweet one. They are high protein and low-glycemic, perfect for a quick breakfast on the go or and afternoon snack. If you would like to omit the sweetener altogether then replace it with more applesauce. You can also add a ¼ teaspoon of liquid stevia if you prefer to add in more sweetness without the sugar.

Dry Ingredients:
2 cups raw almonds, finely ground (2 ½ cups ground)
¼ cup ground golden flax seeds
1 teaspoon baking soda
½ teaspoon sea salt
½ teaspoon cinnamon

Wet Ingredients:
2 cups grated carrots
¼ cup olive oil or melted coconut oil
¼ cup honey or maple syrup
¼ cup unsweetened applesauce
4 large organic eggs

Preheat oven to 350 degrees F. Line a 12-cup muffin pan with paper liners.

Use a food processor fitted with the "s" blade to finely grind the almonds. Most of them should be very fine and powdery with some small chunks that don't grind up completely. The total amount of ground almonds should equal about 2 ½ cups.

Mix the ground almonds with the other dry ingredients in a large mixing bowl. Add in the wet ingredients and whisk everything together. Spoon batter into muffin pan. Fill each cup to the top.

Bake for about 30 minutes. Cool on a wire rack.

Yield: 1 dozen muffins

Coconut Raspberry Muffins

Pairing fresh raspberries, coconut flour, and eggs creates a flavorful, light grain-free muffin. Plus, with so few ingredients, this recipe can be whipped up in very little time. You can replace the raspberries with huckleberries, blackberries, blueberries, or finely diced fresh peaches if desired. I have found that whisking the coconut flour with the wet ingredients creates a lumpy batter so it is best to use a food processor to mix the wet and the dry ingredients together.

Wet Ingredients:
6 large organic eggs
¼ cup unsweetened applesauce
¼ cup honey or maple syrup
¼ cup melted coconut oil or organic butter
1 teaspoon vanilla extract
½ teaspoon almond flavoring

Dry ingredients:
½ cup coconut flour
1 teaspoon baking soda
½ teaspoon sea salt

Other Ingredients:
1 cup fresh or frozen raspberries

Preheat oven to 350 degrees F. Line a 12-cup muffin pan with paper liners.

Add all of the wet ingredients to a food processor fitted with the "s" blade and process until pureed. Add dry ingredients and process again until combined. Scoop the batter evenly into each muffin cup. The batter should fill each muffin cup about half full. Drop the raspberries on top of the batter of each muffin cup. Gently press them into the batter.

Bake for 25 to 30 minutes. Remove muffins and let cool on a wire rack or enjoy warm, spread with butter and honey.

Yield: 1 dozen muffins

Nutrition Tip:

To make coconut flour, coconut meat is dried, defatted, and then finely ground into a powder. Coconut flour is very high in fiber; in fact, about 58% of its carbohydrates are fiber! Because of this, coconut flour absorbs a lot of liquid. If you are not accustomed to consuming coconut flour, you may want to drink an extra glass or two of water before or after a meal containing coconut flour.

Cranberry Orange Muffins

This healthy vegan muffin recipe most often makes its appearance around the holidays but can be varied to create many different flavors. Try omitting the cranberries and orange zest and replacing them with grated zucchini or carrots, blueberries, blackberries, or raspberries. Apple juice or milk can replace the orange juice.

Dry Ingredients:
2 cups freshly ground buckwheat flour
2 teaspoons baking powder
½ teaspoon baking soda
¼ teaspoon sea salt
1 to 2 teaspoons orange zest
1 teaspoon cinnamon
½ teaspoon nutmeg

Wet Ingredients:
2 tablespoons ground chia seeds
½ cup hot water
½ cup freshly squeezed orange juice
⅓ cup coconut sugar
¼ cup unsweetened applesauce
¼ cup melted coconut oil or olive oil

Other Ingredients:
½ to ¾ cup fresh or frozen cranberries

Preheat oven to 350 degrees F. Line a 12-cup muffin pan with paper liners.

In a medium-sized mixing bowl, whisk together the dry ingredients.

Place the ground chia seeds and hot water into a blender. Blend for a few seconds to combine; let rest for about 2 minutes to form a gel. Add the remaining wet ingredients to the blender and blend until combined.

Pour wet mixture into dry and whisk together. It should be sticky and stringy. Fold in the cranberries. Spoon batter into muffin cups. You will fill each one half full.

Bake for approximately 25 minutes. Cool on a wire rack.

Yield: 1 dozen muffins

Date Walnut Cinnamon Swirl Muffins

These cozy little muffins are perfect paired with a hot cup of spice tea on a chilly winter day. Serve them as a healthy treat on Christmas morning or as part of a spring brunch. I like them best topped with the Dairy-Free Cream Cheese Frosting recipe, page 474.

Cinnamon Swirl:
½ cup raw walnuts
½ cup medjool dates, pitted
1 tablespoon coconut oil or organic butter
2 to 3 teaspoons cinnamon
¼ cup coconut sugar (optional)

Wet Ingredients:
6 large organic eggs
¼ cup unsweetened applesauce
¼ cup honey or maple syrup
¼ cup melted coconut oil or organic butter

Dry ingredients:
½ cup coconut flour
1 teaspoon baking soda
½ teaspoon sea salt

Preheat oven to 350 degrees F. Line a 12-cup muffin pan with paper liners.

Place the walnuts into a food processor fitted with the "s" blade and process until very finely ground and pasty. Add the dates, oil, and cinnamon; process again until you have a smooth, thick paste. Add the coconut sugar and pulse until combined. Remove the cinnamon swirl mixture from the food processor and set aside.

Rinse out the food processor, add all of the wet ingredients, and puree until smooth. Then add the dry ingredients and process again until combined.

Scoop the batter evenly into each muffin cup and drop a heaping spoonful of the cinnamon swirl mixture on top of each muffin; use a knife or spoon to fold it in.

Bake for about 30 minutes. Remove muffins and let cool on a wire rack. Cool completely if you plan on frosting.

Yield: 1 dozen muffins

Hazelnut Banana Muffins

A luscious smell fills the kitchen when these muffins are baking. They are high in protein and low in sugar. Eat one for breakfast with a green smoothie for a protein-packed breakfast or share them with your children for a healthy after-school snack.

Dry Ingredients:
3 cups hazelnut flour
2 tablespoons ground chia seeds
¾ teaspoons baking soda
½ teaspoon sea salt

Wet Ingredients:
4 large organic eggs
1 cup mashed banana
¼ cup honey
¼ cup melted coconut oil or butter
2 teaspoons vanilla extract

Preheat oven to 325 degrees. Grease a 12-cup muffin pan or line with paper liners.

In a large bowl, whisk together the dry ingredients.

In a smaller bowl, crack the eggs and whisk them together. Then add the remaining wet ingredients and whisk them together.

Pour the wet into the dry and whisk together. Scoop batter into prepared muffin cups.

Bake for about 30 minutes. Let cool in the pan for about 5 to 10 minutes before removing and placing on a wire rack to cool completely. They will hold together once cooled.

Yield: 1 dozen muffins

Ingredient Tip:

To make your own hazelnut flour, first soak 4 cups of raw hazelnuts overnight in warm water. Then drain, rinse, and place into your food dehydrator. Set the temperature to 110 degrees F. Dehydrate for 24 to 48 hours or until dry and crispy. Then place the nuts into your food processor and grind into a fine meal.

Kitchen Tip:

Make sure all ingredients are at room temperature before starting. Otherwise the melted coconut oil or butter can clump up once added to cold whisked eggs.

Lemon Blueberry Muffins

Beautiful and light, these egg-free muffins are bursting with lemon and juicy, sweet berries. You can use either fresh or frozen blueberries in this recipe, making it a perfect treat anytime of the year.

Dry Ingredients:
2 ¼ cups brown rice flour
¼ cup tapioca flour or arrowroot powder
1 tablespoon baking powder
½ teaspoon baking soda
½ teaspoon sea salt

Wet Ingredients:
¼ cup ground golden flax seed
2 tablespoons whole psyllium husks
1 ¼ cups milk
2 tablespoons freshly squeezed lemon juice
⅓ cup maple syrup
⅓ cup melted coconut oil or olive oil
½ cup unsweetened applesauce
2 teaspoons vanilla extract
1 to 2 teaspoons lemon zest

Other Ingredients:
1 to 1 ½ cups fresh or frozen blueberries

Preheat oven to 350 degrees F. Grease a 12-cup muffin pan or line with paper liners.

In a medium-sized mixing bowl whisk together the dry ingredients and set aside.

In a separate bowl combine the ground flax and psyllium husks. Use your fingers to break apart any clumps in the ground flax. Whisk in the milk and lemon juice. Let the mixture rest for about 2 minutes to thicken. Then whisk in the remaining wet ingredients.

Pour the wet mixture into the dry and combine using a large spoon. Since this batter is egg-free it will be thicker than muffin batter made with eggs. Fold in blueberries. Fill each muffin cup to the top. You may want to smooth the tops with wet fingers before baking.

Bake for 30 minutes. Cool muffins on a wire rack.

Yield: 1 dozen muffins

Variation:

Replace the blueberries with raspberries, blackberries, or diced peaches.

Oatmeal Cinnamon Muffins

This recipe uses whole grains instead of flours. By soaking the whole grains overnight in an acidic medium, stored minerals become more available and starches become more digestible. Making muffins this way is actually much easier and faster than using a flour-based recipe.

1 cup gluten-free rolled oats
1 cup raw buckwheat groats
2 cups kefir (cow, goat, or coconut)
1 large organic egg
⅓ cup honey
2 tablespoons ground chia seeds
1 tablespoon cinnamon
¾ teaspoon baking soda
½ teaspoon sea salt
2 teaspoons vanilla

Place the oats and buckwheat groats into a medium-sized bowl. Pour the kefir over them and stir together. Cover the bowl with a plate and leave it on your kitchen counter for 12 to 24 hours.

Preheat oven to 350 degrees F. Line a 12-cup muffin pan with paper liners. Pour the kefir-grain mixture into a high-powered blender. Add the egg and honey; blend on high until pureed. Then add the chia seeds, cinnamon, baking soda, sea salt, and vanilla; blend again until combined.

Pour batter into muffin cups. Bake for 25 to 30 minutes. Cool on a wire rack.

Yield: 1 dozen muffins

Ingredient Tip:

Be sure to use certified gluten-free buckwheat groats as most buckwheat in the United States is cross-contaminated with gluten grains. Bob's Red Mill offers certified gluten-free buckwheat groats that are also organic.

Breads

Vegan Corn Muffins

Serve these perfectly tender and mildly sweet corn muffins with your favorite chili recipe, such as the Three Bean Vegetable Chili, page 195.

Dry Ingredients:
1 ½ cups yellow cornmeal
1 cup sorghum flour
¼ cup tapioca flour
1 tablespoon baking powder
1 teaspoon sea salt

Wet Ingredients:
¼ cup ground golden flax seeds
½ cup hot water
⅓ cup coconut sugar
⅓ cup melted coconut oil, butter, or olive oil
⅓ cup unsweetened applesauce
1 ½ cups milk

Preheat oven to 350 degrees F. Oil a 12-cup muffin pan or line with paper liners.

Place the dry ingredients into a large mixing bowl and whisk together.

In a medium-sized mixing bowl, whisk together the ground flax seeds and hot water. Let them rest for about 4 to 5 minutes or until thickened. Then add the coconut sugar, oil, and applesauce; whisk until incorporated. Add the milk and whisk again.

Pour the wet ingredients into the dry and whisk batter together for a minute or two. The batter should be a little stringy and on the thicker side. Spoon batter into prepared muffin pan. You will fill each muffin cup to the top.

Bake for 25 to 30 minutes. Run a knife around each muffin to gently release. Cool on a wire rack.

Yield: 1 dozen muffins

Ingredient Tip:

I like to use Arrowhead Mills brand of cornmeal in this recipe because it is both gluten-free and organic.

Coconut Almond Bread

Serve a slice of this high-protein, grain-free bread with a fried egg for a quick, nutritious breakfast. I also like to spread it with homemade honey-sweetened jam or my Vanilla Plum Butter, page 513, for a real treat! I have made this bread several different ways. It can work without adding the arrowroot powder if you don't want any starches, but I prefer the texture with the arrowroot in it. I have also made it without any sweetener and it still tastes great.

Wet Ingredients:
5 large organic eggs
½ cup creamy roasted almond butter
¼ cup unsweetened applesauce
¼ cup melted coconut oil or butter
1 tablespoon honey or maple syrup

Dry Ingredients:
½ cup coconut flour
¼ cup ground golden flax seeds
2 tablespoons arrowroot powder
1 teaspoon baking soda
½ teaspoon sea salt

Preheat oven to 350 degrees. Grease an 8.5 x 4.5 loaf pan.

Add all of the wet ingredients to a food processor or high-powered blender and blend on a medium speed until pureed. Add dry ingredients and blend again until combined.

Scoop batter into loaf pan. Bake for about 45 minutes. Cool on a wire rack for about 10 minutes and then remove bread from pan and continue to cool on a wire rack.

Yield: 1 loaf

Nutrition Tip:

If you need to lower your carbohydrate intake then this bread is ideal. It is very low in carbs and high in protein, perfect for someone with blood sugar regulation issues.

Chocolate Banana Bread

Chocolate lovers don't have to wait for dessert to enjoy chocolate! This bread is light, yet rich with chocolate flavor with chunks of sweet banana melting in your mouth with every bite. Have a slice with your breakfast smoothie or as a mid-afternoon snack. Our favorite is always fresh out of the oven!

Dry Ingredients:
1 ¾ cup teff flour
¼ cup tapioca flour or arrowroot powder
6 tablespoons cocoa powder
2 teaspoons baking powder
1 teaspoon baking soda
½ teaspoon sea salt

Wet Ingredients:
2 tablespoons ground chia seeds
¼ cup warm water
1 ½ cups mashed banana
¾ cup coconut sugar
½ cup melted coconut oil
2 large eggs
2 teaspoons vanilla

Optional Additions:
chopped dark chocolate bar
chopped walnuts

Preheat oven to 350 degrees F. Grease two 4.5 x 8.5-inch bread pans with coconut oil.

In a large bowl whisk together the dry ingredients.

In a separate mixing bowl add the ground chia and warm water; whisk together immediately so the chia doesn't clump up. Then add the remaining wet ingredients and whisk together.

Pour the wet ingredients into the dry and mix together using a large wooden spoon. Fold in any optional additions. Pour batter into the two bread pans. Bake for about 35 to 40 minutes. Cool for about 20 minutes and then remove bread from pans and continue to cool on a wire rack.

Yield: 2 small loaves

Pumpkin Cornbread

Both gluten-eating and gluten-free folks will enjoy this cornbread recipe. It is moist, slightly sweet, and full of that traditional cornbread flavor we have all come to know and love. If you don't have any sugar pie pumpkins on hand to make your own puree, you can use canned pumpkin or any type of winter squash puree, such as butternut, kabocha, or acorn. Sprouted brown rice flour works well here in place of regular stone-ground flour.

Dry Ingredients:
1 ½ cups cornmeal
1 cup brown rice flour
1 tablespoon baking powder
¾ teaspoon sea salt

Wet Ingredients:
1 cup pumpkin puree
1 cup milk
⅓ cup melted coconut oil or butter
⅓ cup honey
2 large organic eggs

Preheat oven to 350 degrees F. Oil a 7 x 11-inch glass baking dish.

In a medium-sized bowl, whisk together the dry ingredients. In a separate large bowl, whisk together the wet ingredients. Pour the dry into the wet and whisk together well. Scoop batter into oiled baking dish and spread it out evenly with the back of a spoon.

Bake for about 35 minutes. Let cool slightly before serving.

Yield: 8 to 10 servings

Ingredient Tip:

I use Arrowhead Mills corn meal because it is both organic and gluten-free.

Spiced Butternut Squash Bread

This bread makes an excellent after-school snack for children. Serve it with sliced fresh apples and almond butter. It is also excellent served as a quick breakfast spread with almond or sunflower butter and served with a green smoothie.

Dry Ingredients:
2 ½ cups freshly ground buckwheat flour
¾ cup tapioca flour
2 teaspoons baking powder
1 teaspoon baking soda
½ teaspoon sea salt
1 tablespoon pumpkin pie spice

Wet Ingredients:
2 cups cooked butternut squash
¾ cup coconut sugar
½ cup melted coconut oil
¾ cup apple cider or apple juice
¼ cup ground chia seeds
2 teaspoons vanilla extract

Preheat oven to 350 degrees F. Grease 4 mini loaf pans. The mini-loaf pans I use are about 6 x 3.5 x 2.5 inches each.

In a large bowl, whisk all of the dry ingredients together.

Place all wet ingredients into a blender and puree until smooth, start with the lesser amount of apple cider and then and more if necessary once you have mixed the wet and dry ingredients together.

Pour the wet into the dry and whisk together well. Pour batter into prepared loaf pans.

Bake for approximately 35 to 40 minutes or until toothpick inserted in the center comes clean. Let it cool completely before slicing. When this bread is hot out of the oven it can be a little gummy. Once cooled, the texture changes completely.

Yield: 4 mini loaves

Zucchini Almond Bread

This moist and delicious bread is a great way to use up the massive amounts of garden zucchini available during the summer months. Use the grating disc on your food processor to quickly grate the zucchini or offer the task to your child to be done with a hand grater. To bake this bread, I use stone mini loaf pans that evenly distribute the heat and don't cause any sticking. They are available through Pampered Chef.

Dry Ingredients:
1 ½ cups sorghum flour
1 cup almond flour
½ cup sweet rice flour
2 tablespoons ground chia seeds
1 tablespoon baking powder
1 teaspoon cinnamon
½ teaspoon baking soda
½ teaspoon sea salt

Wet Ingredients:
½ cup olive oil or melted coconut oil
¾ cup coconut sugar
2 large organic eggs
2 cups grated zucchini, packed
½ cup almond milk

Optional Additions:
½ cup mini chocolate chips

Preheat oven to 350 degrees. Oil four mini-loaf pans. The mini-loaf pans I use are about 6 x 3.5 x 2.5 inches each.

In a large bowl, whisk all of the dry ingredients together well.

In a separate bowl, whisk together the oil, sugar, and eggs. Add the zucchini and milk and stir together.

Pour the wet ingredients into the dry and mix together using a whisk or wooden spoon until the batter thickens. Immediately fold in the chocolate chips, if using.

Evenly distribute batter amongst the four loaf pans. Smooth the tops with your finger if desired (I always do this). Bake for about 35 minutes. Remove loaves from pans after about 5 to 10 minutes and place onto a wire rack to cool.

Yield: 4 mini loaves

Amaranth and Sun-Dried Tomato Crackers

These crackers are beautiful, speckled with black chia seeds and little chunks of red tomato. Serve them with pesto for dipping or a good quality raw organic cheese. When I make this recipe I double, or triple it so I can have a jar of crackers on the counter ready for school lunches or an on-the-go snack. In this recipe, I use my own homemade Sun-Dried Tomatoes, page 514, but you can also use organic dehydrated tomatoes found at your local health food store.

¼ cup sun-dried tomatoes, cut into small pieces
2 tablespoons whole chia seeds
½ cup hot water
3 tablespoons extra virgin olive oil
½ teaspoon Herbamare or sea salt
1 cup amaranth flour

Preheat oven to 350 degrees. Set out a large cookie sheet.

Use scissors to cut the dried tomatoes into tiny pieces. Place them into a medium-sized bowl along with the whole chia seeds, then add the hot water. Whisk together with a fork and let soak for 5 to 7 minutes, then add the olive oil and salt, whisk again. Add the flour and stir it in using a fork until the dough forms a ball.

Place the ball in between two pieces of parchment paper and roll using a rolling pin until you have a very thin sheet of dough. Place the rolled dough and parchment onto the cookie sheet. Remove the top layer of parchment. Then take a pizza cutter and cut into cracker sized squares.

Bake for 20 minutes, then remove from oven and take out the ones that are crisp. If there are some that still feel soft put them back into the oven for a few more minutes, or until crisp.

Yield: varies depending on the size of your crackers

Herbed Sunflower Seed Crackers

For the fresh herbs use any combination of chives, rosemary, marjoram, thyme, and oregano. The trick to making crispy crackers is to roll them as thin as possible! Serve these crackers with a good quality cheese, hummus, or roasted red pepper dip.

½ cup raw sunflower seeds
3 to 4 tablespoons fresh herbs
1 cup cooked quinoa (warm or at room temp)
1 cup amaranth flour
½ to ¾ teaspoon Herbamare
6 tablespoons extra virgin olive oil
2 tablespoons water

Preheat oven to 325 degrees F.

Place the seeds and herbs into a food processor fitted with the "s" blade. Process the seeds and herbs until they are resemble a finely ground meal. Add the quinoa, flour, and salt. Process again until combined and finely ground. With the processor running, add the oil and water until the dough forms a ball.

Place a large piece of parchment paper over a large cookie sheet. Place the ball of cracker dough in the center of it then cover with another sheet of parchment. Roll out as thin as possible covering the entire cookie sheet. Remove the top piece of parchment paper and use a pizza cuter to cut into cracker-sized squares.

Bake for about 35 minutes or until lightly browned around the edges. Cool completely before serving. Crackers will become crispier as they cool. Store in tightly sealed quart jars in a cool dark place for up to two weeks.

Yield: varies depending on the size of your crackers.

Variation:

For a milder flavor, replace the quinoa with cooked millet, and the amaranth flour with superfine sorghum or brown rice flour.

Breads

Sesame Thins

I think we all like something crunchy and slightly salty to munch on every now and then. These crackers are crispy and thin, perfect for dipping into your favorite dip or eating with a slice of an artisan cheese. I like to serve them with the Roasted Red Pepper Cashew Dip, page 370.

1 cup cooked millet (warm or at room temp)
1 cup sorghum flour
½ to ¾ teaspoon sea salt or Herbamare
½ cup sesame seeds
6 tablespoons extra virgin olive oil
2 tablespoons water

Preheat oven to 325 degrees F.

Place the millet, flour, and salt into a food processor fitted with the "s" blade. Process until combined and finely ground. Add the sesame seeds and process again until just combined. With the processor running, add the oil and water until the dough forms a ball.

Place a large piece of parchment paper over a large cookie sheet. Place the ball of cracker dough in the center of it then cover with another sheet of parchment. Roll out as thinly as possible covering the entire cookie sheet. Remove the top piece of parchment paper and use a pizza cuter to cut into cracker-sized squares.

Bake for about 35 minutes or until lightly browned around the edges. Cool completely before serving. Crackers will become crispier as they cool. Store in tightly sealed quart jars in a cool dark place for up to two weeks.

Yield: varies depending on the size of your crackers.

Ingredient Tip:

Using Authentic Foods superfine sorghum flour in this recipe produces the best results, though regular stone-ground flour works as well. I've also used sprouted quinoa and brown rice flours in this recipe with good results.

Soups and Stews

The art of soup making is one of the oldest forms of cooking. Vegetables, meats, and beans simmered for hours in stock made from animal bones has been an easily digestible source of nourishment for humans throughout the ages; a traditional remedy to treat the weak and sick.

Soups and stews are often a main dish in our house during the winter months. I find it very easy to make a large pot of soup for dinner and serve it with a cooked whole grain or homemade bread. Just before serving, I like to add finely chopped kale, spinach, collard greens, or parsley. The bright green color adds a lovely contrast as well as additional flavors and nutrients.

Adding beans or meat to a soup boosts protein content, which helps to quickly satisfy hunger. Since all of the vegetables, herbs, and meat are cooked directly in the liquid, their nutrients are released into the broth. This nutrient-rich broth helps to signal the brain that you are full—meaning that by consuming such nutrient-dense foods you end up eating less. Using homemade bone broths in your soups helps to boost nutrient and mineral content even more.

Homemade Bone Broths

Historically, stock has been used to treat disorders of the gastrointestinal tract, joints, lungs, blood, and skin. With our fast-paced lifestyles many people no longer routinely make homemade stocks, yet, homemade stock is far more nutritious than store-bought, even the organic brands. Homemade stocks add depth and richness to soups, vegetable purees, and cooked whole grain dishes that couldn't be achieved with just water.

Downfall of Commercial Stock

Commercial stocks—whether chicken, beef, or vegetable—use many different "natural" flavorings. These flavorings can be made of anything, but most often it is a man-made chemical often containing MSG (free glutamic acid).The FDA classifies MSG as "natural" and by using other terms such as "natural flavoring" or "yeast extract," manufacturers can deceive label-reading consumers into buying their products.

The flavoring industry is an incredibly lucrative business; most of us won't buy a product that doesn't taste good. Humans have receptors on their tongues for glutamate, the amino acid we recognize as the common "meat" flavor in foods. Using MSG in foods such as chicken stock is a way to cut corners and create a cheap food for a profit. Unfortunately, MSG is a neurotoxic substance that causes headaches and, in large amounts, can lead to brain damage (in B6 and magnesium deficient people). Preparing stocks with high-quality ingredients infuses so much flavor that nothing else needs to be added.

Benefits of Homemade Stock

Homemade stock made from animal bones contains nutrients that strengthen digestion, heal the intestinal tract, and sooth joints—specifically gelatin and the amino acids proline, glycine, and glutamine. Homemade stock also contains many minerals in an easily absorbable form, including calcium, magnesium, and fluoride. Once you begin making your own stock and noting the benefits in your health and the flavors in your meals, it will be easier to add it to your weekly or monthly cooking routine.

I know we are all very busy and for some of us, just the thought of making our own stock seems overwhelming, but it doesn't need to be. Stocks can be simmered slowly for hours on the stove or in a crockpot with very little supervision. When you roast a whole chicken and have pulled all the meat from the bones, simply toss it in an eight quart stockpot, add some vegetables, water, vinegar, and salt and then cover and simmer for 6 hours or more. If you don't have time to make stock within a few days of roasting the chicken then put the chicken carcass in the freezer and take it out when you are ready.

10 Tips for Making Stocks and Soups:

1. **When making homemade stock,** add very little salt to it. This way, when you go to use it in a soup, you can salt the soup to your liking.

2. **Add a tablespoon or two of vinegar to your simmering stock to help release minerals from the bones**. I always use apple cider vinegar.

3. **For large batches of soup,** a high quality stainless steel 8-quart stockpot is essential. Most of the recipes in this chapter use this size of pot.

4. **Be sure to heat the soup pot first before adding the oil,** then add oil and let it heat for about 20 to 30 seconds before adding the onions or other ingredients called for.

5. **Start soup by sautéing an onion to create a flavor base from which to work from**. If you are not using a homemade stock in your soup, I suggest sautéing the onion for at least 10 minutes to create a rich depth of flavor.

6. **When using lentils for soup,** be sure to sort though them and pick out any gluten grains. Lentils are often cross-contaminated with gluten grains during growing, harvesting, and processing. Be sure to rinse and drain the lentils well before using them.

7. **When a recipe calls for diced tomatoes,** use fresh or frozen, not canned. Canned tomatoes often contain high levels of BPA, see page 56 for more details.

8. **To make a pureed soup**, use a high quality stainless steel immersion blender, or pour the soup into a blender and puree in batches.

9. **Add chopped fresh herbs to the soup after you turn off the heat.**

10. **Most soups freeze very well**. The exceptions are soups made with potatoes or noodles as these absorb water in the freezer and can create a very mushy soup when reheated.

Soups

Homemade Chicken Stock

Every time we roast a chicken I make stock. I pour it into glass mason jars and freeze the majority of it right away. This way my freezer is continually stocked with homemade organic stock. Use stock to make soups and stews, or to replace the water used for cooking whole grains. You can add it to mashed potatoes, sauces, or basically anywhere a liquid is needed for a savory dish. If I am making soup and need stock—and have not thought about thawing it out—I will take a jar out of the freezer and put it into a pot of hot water. By the time my vegetables are chopped and I am ready to add some liquid, enough of it will be thawed out to use in the soup. For this reason I always use wide-mouthed glass pint or quart jars.

1 chicken carcass (from a 3 to 4 pound organic chicken)
4 chicken wings (optional)
1 large onion, chopped
1 head garlic, cut in half cross-wise
1 to 2 leeks, rinsed well and chopped
4 stalks celery, chopped
2 carrots, chopped
½ bunch parsley
few sprigs fresh rosemary and thyme
1 strip kombu or wakame
1 teaspoon whole black peppercorns
2 to 3 teaspoons Herbamare or sea salt (optional)
1 to 2 tablespoons apple cider vinegar
12 to 14 cups water

Add all ingredients to an 8-quart stockpot. Gently bring to a simmer. Make sure that it is a gentle simmer, on low or medium-low heat. Cook, covered, for 3 to 6 hours. The longer cooking times will extract more nutrients and produce a richer flavored stock.

Place a large colander over another large pot or bowl. I use a colander over an 8-cup Pyrex liquid glass measure because it is easy to pour from. I only pour half of the stock through at once to make pouring into the jars easier. If using a bowl or another pot, use a ladle to put the stock into jars. Discard the solids.

Once all of the jars are filled, let them cool for about 30 minutes, then freeze them uncovered. Once frozen you can screw the lid on. Doing it this way prevents the jars from cracking. If you plan on using your stock within a few days then refrigerate until ready to use.

Yield: About 3 quarts

Nutrition Tip:

The vinegar in the stock is needed to help extract the minerals from the chicken bones. The stock won't have a vinegary taste as long as you don't add too much.

Variation:

In springtime we harvest fresh nettles and then add about 2 cups of the leaves and stems to the pot. This is a great way to add even more minerals to the stock.

Vegetable Mushroom Stock

This nutrient-dense vegan stock obtains much of its flavor from slowly sautéing onions and mushrooms before adding water. Any type of mushroom, or a combination of a few, can be used to make this stock. Try white button, cremini, portabella, shiitake, or oyster mushrooms. The addition of the seaweed adds trace minerals, antioxidants, and algin, which is an important nutrient for gut health. If you want to add more nutrients to this stock, consider adding some organic beef bones and a few tablespoons of raw apple cider vinegar.

1 tablespoon extra virgin olive oil
1 large onion, chopped
1 leek, chopped
1 pound mushrooms, chopped
1 head garlic, cut in half cross-wise
1 large carrot, chopped
2 to 3 stalks celery, chopped
2 large strips kombu
1 bay leaf
1 teaspoon whole black peppercorns
3 sprigs fresh thyme
handful fresh parsley
2 to 3 teaspoons sea salt
12 to 14 cups water

Heat an 8-quart stockpot over medium heat. Add the oil, then add the onions; sauté for 10 to 15 minutes, lowering the heat if needed so the onions don't brown too much. Then add the leeks and mushrooms; sauté about 10 minutes more.

Add the remaining ingredients, cover the pot, and simmer for approximately 3 to 4 hours. Place a large colander over another pot or large bowl and pour your stock through it discarding the solids. Pour your stock into quart jars, cover, and refrigerate. If you plan on freezing it be sure to let the jars cool down first and freeze them uncovered.

Yield: 3 quarts

Hot and Sour Soup

The key to this soup is a good stock—using a store-bought stock doesn't even compare in flavor and nutrition to a homemade stock. I prefer to use homemade chicken stock but a homemade Vegetable Mushroom Stock, page 171, works well too. Serve with Thai rice noodles, zucchini noodles, or a scoop of cooked spaghetti squash for a light meal.

10 cups chicken or vegetable stock
8 ounces white button mushrooms, thinly sliced
3 carrots, cut into matchsticks
3 cloves garlic, crushed
4 tablespoons brown rice vinegar or coconut vinegar
4 tablespoons wheat-free tamari or coconut aminos
1 to 3 tablespoons hot pepper sesame oil
3 cups thinly sliced napa cabbage
1 bunch green onions, sliced into rounds
1 cup chopped cilantro
Herbamare or sea salt

Pour the stock into a 4-quart pot. Add the mushrooms, carrots, and garlic. Cover pot, bring to a boil, then reduce heat and simmer for about 20 minutes or until carrots and mushrooms are tender.

Then add the vinegar, tamari or coconut aminos, hot pepper sesame oil, cabbage, green onions, and cilantro. Simmer another 2 to 3 minutes. Taste and add a little Herbamare or sea salt if necessary.

Yield: 6 to 8 servings

Glorious Greens Soup

This soup tastes best fresh. It is great to make on days when you might be feeling a little under the weather. I always use homemade chicken stock for its healing properties. See page 170 for instructions on making your own stock. If I have fresh tomatoes in the house I might add one chopped to this soup, but it is delicious just the way it is.

2 tablespoons extra virgin olive oil
1 medium onion, cut into crescent moons
6 to 7 cloves garlic, crushed
1 to 2 teaspoons dried thyme
10 cups chicken stock
8 cups chopped dark leafy greens (kale, chard, collard, spinach)
2 to 4 cups cooked cannellini beans
1 lemon, juiced
Herbamare or sea salt and freshly ground black pepper to taste

Heat a 6-quart pot over medium heat. Add the oil, then add the onions; sauté until soft, about 5 to 10 minutes. Add the garlic, sauté a minute more. Then add stock and simmer for about 5 minutes so the onions soften a little more.

Add the greens and beans. Cover and simmer 10 to 20 minutes or until greens are tender. Timing will depend on how large your greens are. Young, fresh greens will only take a few minutes, while large greens may need about 20 minutes. Add lemon juice and season with salt and pepper to taste.

Yield: 6 to 8 servings

Healing Ginger Miso Soup

We like to serve miso soup as a nourishing breakfast with leftover fish and cooked brown rice. This recipe also makes a light dinner when feeling under the weather. We use gluten-free miso from The South River Miso Company. In addition to making gluten-free miso, they also make soy-free miso made out of adzuki beans or chickpeas. Our favorite variety is their Garlic-Red Pepper Miso. Serve with a scoop of brown rice in each bowl. Top with leftover halibut or salmon if desired.

6 cups water
3 tablespoons chopped fresh ginger
3 to 6 cloves garlic, chopped
1 strip wakame seaweed, broken into pieces
3 carrots, peeled and sliced
½ teaspoon red chili flakes (optional)
1 to 2 cups thinly sliced savoy cabbage
4 green onions, sliced into thin rounds
handful fresh cilantro, chopped
2 tablespoons tamari or coconut aminos
4 to 5 tablespoons miso
2 to 3 teaspoons coconut vinegar or brown rice vinegar

Place the water, chopped ginger, garlic, seaweed, carrots, and chili flakes into a 3-quart pot. Cover and simmer until carrots are tender, about 10 to 12 minutes. Add the cabbage, green onions, and cilantro; simmer about 2 minutes more.

Turn off heat and add tamari or coconut aminos, miso, and vinegar. Make sure to get the miso completely stirred into the soup. Taste and adjust seasonings if necessary.

Yield: 6 servings

Healing Quinoa Cabbage Soup

The large sweet onion in this recipe is sautéed for a long time and then garlic, ginger, and carrots are added. Once the water is added a beautiful, flavorful clear broth forms. Then with the addition of Herbamare, the flavors deepen. Complexity is formed when the quinoa and cabbage are dropped in. With the final touch of cilantro, you have a bright, colorful, and flavorful soup just waiting to help your cells and liver detoxify!

2 to 3 tablespoons extra virgin olive oil
1 very large sweet onion, cut into crescent moons
2 to 3 cloves garlic, crushed
1 to 2 teaspoons grated fresh ginger
4 large carrots, cut into matchsticks
6 cups water
2 to 3 teaspoon Herbamare
2 cups cooked quinoa
2 to 3 cups sliced Savoy cabbage
½ cup chopped cilantro
freshly ground black pepper to taste

Heat a 6-quart pot over medium heat. Add the olive oil, then add the onions; sauté for 10 to 15 minutes. Make sure your heat isn't too high or your onions will brown too much and cause the broth to be off in flavor. Lower the temperature if necessary.

Add garlic, ginger and carrots; sauté 5 minutes more. Add water, Herbamare, and cooked quinoa and simmer for about 10 to 15 minutes or until carrots reach desired tenderness. Add in cabbage and cook a few more minutes.

Turn off heat; add cilantro and freshly ground black pepper. Taste and adjust salt and seasonings if necessary. Stir together and serve.

Yield: 6 servings

Kitchen Tip:

To create carrot matchsticks, first cut the carrots into ¼-inch thick diagonal rounds and then cut them lengthwise into thin strips.

African Peanut and Red Quinoa Soup

This is a favorite spicy, but not too spicy, soup of ours. It's full of vegetables with the addition of red quinoa for extra protein and energy. Red quinoa holds its shape better than regular quinoa and has a lovely nutty flavor. If you can't find red quinoa simply use the regular cream-colored variety that is widely available. This soup makes a great light lunch!

Soups

1 to 2 tablespoons extra virgin olive oil or coconut oil
1 medium onion, cut into crescent moons
4 to 5 cloves garlic, crushed
2 to 3 tablespoons grated fresh ginger
4 carrots, peeled and cut into 4-inch strips
2 small red bell peppers, chopped
8 cups water, vegetable stock, or chicken stock
6 to 7 tablespoons creamy peanut butter
½ teaspoon crushed red chili flakes
2 cups thinly sliced savoy cabbage
large handful fresh cilantro, chopped
3 to 4 cups cooked red quinoa
1 to 3 teaspoon Herbamare or sea salt

Heat an 8-quart stockpot over medium heat. Add the oil, then add onions; sauté for 5 to 10 minutes or until softened. Add garlic and ginger; sauté a minute more. Then add carrots and red bell pepper; sauté for another 3 to 5 minutes.

Add water or stock, peanut butter, and red chili flakes. Cover and simmer for 15 to 20 minutes or until vegetables are tender. Stir in savoy cabbage, cilantro, and cooked quinoa. Add salt to taste. If you are using a salted stock you may not need much salt at all.

Simmer for a few more minutes, or until cabbage is tender. Serve each bowl with an extra sprinkling of crushed red chili flakes if desired.

Yield: 8 servings

Cream of Broccoli Soup

This dairy-free soup gets its creaminess from a small amount of Yukon Gold potatoes and cashew butter. My children love this soup and will take it packed in a small Thermos for their school lunches. I always use homemade chicken stock, which adds extra nutrients and a depth of flavor you can't get with just water. If you use water then you will need to add extra Herbamare, garlic, and herbs to bring up the flavor.

2 to 3 tablespoons extra virgin olive oil
1 large onion, chopped
3 cloves garlic, chopped
2 to 3 small Yukon gold potatoes, peeled and chopped
2 pounds broccoli, chopped
6 to 7 cups chicken stock or water
1 to 2 teaspoons dried tarragon
½ cup cashew butter
sea salt and black pepper to taste

Garnish:
chopped fresh parsley

Heat an 8-quart stockpot over medium heat. Add the oil, then add onions; sauté for 5 to 10 minutes or until softened. Then add chopped garlic, potatoes, and broccoli; sauté for about a minute then add chicken stock or water and dried tarragon. Cover and simmer for 20 to 30 minutes or until broccoli is tender but still bright green.

Add the cashew butter and simmer for about 5 minutes more. Use an immersion blender to puree the soup in the pot, or blend in batches in your blender.

Pour the soup back into the pot and add salt and pepper to taste. Heat on low until ready to serve. Serve each bowl garnished with chopped fresh parsley if desired.

Yield: 6 to 8 servings

Ingredient Tip:

If you don't have any dried tarragon on hand substitute it with about ¼ cup fresh basil or a few teaspoons of dried thyme or oregano.

Cream of Mushroom Soup

I considered adding coconut milk to this soup for the "cream" but I thought the deep earthy flavor of the mushrooms wouldn't mingle well with the tropical coconut flavors. Instead I chose to use cashews. If you are avoiding grains you can omit the sweet rice flour—it helps to thicken the soup and provide a creamy feel, but it isn't totally necessary. Serve soup with a vegetable salad for a light, nutritious lunch or dinner.

¼ cup extra virgin olive oil, butter, or ghee
1 medium onion, chopped
4 cloves garlic, chopped
3 large carrots, chopped
1 pound cremini mushrooms, chopped
5 cups water, vegetable stock, or chicken stock
few sprigs fresh thyme (pull the leaves from the stems)
few sprigs fresh rosemary
1 teaspoon freshly ground black pepper
2 to 3 teaspoons Herbamare, or to taste
½ cup raw cashews
2 tablespoons sweet rice flour (optional)

Heat a 6-quart pot over medium heat. Add the oil, then add onions; sauté for 5 to 10 minutes or until soft. Add garlic, carrots, and mushrooms; sauté for a few minutes more. Add water, herbs, pepper, and salt; cover and simmer for about 25 to 30 minutes.

Remove from heat and ladle some of the soup into a blender. Add cashews and sweet rice flour. Blend on high until smooth and creamy; transfer to a clean pot. Puree the remaining soup in batches (you can blend it for just a short time for more texture or longer for a smoother consistency).

Stir the soup together to mix cashew cream in with the rest of the blended batches. Taste and adjust salt and seasonings if necessary. Add more water for a thinner consistency. Simmer over low heat for a few minutes to meld the flavors. Garnish each bowl with sliced and sautéed mushrooms, chopped fresh parsley, and edible flowers.

Yield: 6 servings

Nutrition Tip:

Antibodies are secreted in the gastrointestinal tract to combat harmful bacterium and viruses. The most common antibody is called Sectratory IgA. Research has shown that higher levels of this important antibody have reduced incidences of colds and flus. One great way to increase Secratory IgA (SIgA) is to eat cremini mushrooms. A recent study found that eating 100 grams a day of blanched cremini mushrooms raised SIgA levels by 53%. Interestingly, those levels stayed elevated by 56% for an additional week after ceasing of the mushroom consumption. The take home message: eating approximately three ounces of cremini mushrooms a day for a week may boost your immunity for two weeks.

Creamy Potato Leek Soup

I like to use Yukon gold potatoes in this recipe though any variety will do. If you use Russets you may want to peel them. For all other varieties it is fine to leave the peel on. Serve this delicious dairy-free soup with the Chia Dinner Rolls, page 134, and a fresh garden salad with Ranch Dressing, page 355.

3 to 4 tablespoons extra virgin olive oil
2 large leeks, sliced into rounds
4 stalks celery, chopped
4 carrots, peeled and chopped
2 to 3 teaspoons Herbamare or sea salt
1 teaspoon freshly ground black pepper
1 to 2 teaspoons dried dill
1 teaspoon dried thyme
2 pounds potatoes, chopped (about 4 medium)
6 cups water

Garnish:
cooked or smoked salmon
chopped fresh parsley

Heat a 6 to 8-quart pot over medium heat. Add the oil, then add leeks; sauté for about 4 to 5 minutes to soften, being careful not to brown. Add celery, carrots, salt, pepper, and herbs; sauté 5 to 10 minutes more to soften the vegetables and deepen the flavors. Add potatoes and water, cover pot, and simmer for about 45 minutes.

Use an immersion blender to puree part of the soup in the pot or remove half of the soup at a time and puree in a blender. Return pureed soup to pot and stir together. Taste and add more salt and pepper if necessary.

Garnish each bowl with cooked salmon and chopped parsley.

Yield: 6 to 8 servings

Creamy Summer Zucchini Soup

This soup is a great way to make use of extra zucchini growing in your vegetable garden! You can use green zucchini, yellow zucchini, or patty pan squash in this recipe. For the liquid, I like to use Homemade Chicken Stock, page 170, which adds a nice depth of flavor and many important gut-healing nutrients. It is very rare that we consume white rice, however, it works quite nicely in this soup to provide creaminess without the use of nuts or dairy. If you would like to replace it with something else, use either uncooked quinoa or one cup of cooked brown rice. Uncooked brown rice will not work, as it will not cook fully in the 15 to 20 minutes needed to simmer the soup.

2 to 3 tablespoons extra virgin olive oil
1 large onion, chopped
2 to 4 cloves garlic, chopped
1 teaspoon ground cumin
8 to 10 cups chopped zucchini (about 5 to 6 medium zucchini)
½ cup uncooked white rice
8 cups chicken stock or vegetable stock
1 small bunch cilantro, coarsely chopped
2 tablespoons freshly squeezed lemon juice
sea salt or Herbamare to taste

Heat a 6 to 8-quart pot over medium heat. Add the oil, then add onion; sauté for 8 to 10 minutes or until onion softens and is beginning to change color. Add garlic and cumin; sauté a minute more. Add chopped zucchini, white rice, and stock; cover and simmer for 15 to 20 minutes or until zucchini is tender and rice is cooked. Then add cilantro and lemon juice to the pot.

Remove from heat and puree in batches. I puree just enough so it is creamy but still has some texture. Pour soup into another clean pot or bowl, stir batches together, and taste. If it needs a flavor boost, add Herbamare or sea salt to taste.

Soup will last in the fridge for up to 5 days or can be frozen for up to a year.

Yield: 8 servings

Creamy Tomato Asparagus Soup

This fantastic recipe was inspired by a soup I tasted while traveling in Kauai. The original version used all local produce grown on Kauai including mushrooms, sweet potatoes, summer squash, leeks, tomatoes, fennel, basil, carrots, celery, and asparagus. You can add different vegetables to this soup. I have made it several ways and it is always delicious! My children love it too.

2 to 3 tablespoons extra virgin olive oil
I heaping cup diced shallots
1 leek, ends trimmed and chopped
4 to 5 cloves garlic, chopped
1 teaspoon dried thyme
¼ teaspoon crushed red chili flakes (optional)
2 to 3 teaspoons Herbamare
1 teaspoon ground black pepper
1 large yam (about 1 pound), peeled and diced
1 pound asparagus, ends trimmed and chopped
4 cups diced tomatoes
2 cups cooked garbanzo or cannellini beans
6 cups water, vegetable stock, or chicken stock
1 large handful fresh basil leaves

Heat an 8-quart stockpot over medium heat. Add the oil, then add shallots and leeks; sauté for about 5 to 10 minutes. Add garlic, thyme, chili flakes, salt, and pepper; sauté a minute more. Add yams, asparagus, tomatoes, beans, water, and basil; cover and simmer for about 25 minutes.

Puree in batches, taste, and adjust salt and seasonings if necessary. Leftovers can be frozen in jars for future use.

Yield: 8 to 10 servings

Spiced Pumpkin Soup

A soup my sister-in-law made while we were visiting for Christmas one year inspired this recipe. I didn't have her original recipe so improvised based on memory. Serve soup with cooked quinoa and a cabbage slaw for a balanced meal.

2 to 3 tablespoons extra virgin olive oil
1 large onion, chopped
1 to 2 tablespoons finely chopped ginger
4 to 5 large carrots, peeled and chopped
4 to 5 celery stalks, chopped
2 Granny Smith apples, cored and chopped
10 cups water, vegetable stock, or chicken stock
8 cups sugar pie pumpkin puree
2 to 3 cups cooked white beans
2 to 3 teaspoons pumpkin pie spice
3 to 4 teaspoons Herbamare or sea salt
½ to 1 teaspoon ground black pepper

Garnish:
coconut milk
chopped cilantro

Heat an 8-quart stockpot over medium heat. Add the oil, then add onion; sauté for about 5 minutes. Then add ginger, carrots, celery, and apples; sauté 5 to 10 minutes more. Add the water, cooked pumpkin, pumpkin pie spice, salt, and pepper. Bring to a boil, then reduce heat to a simmer and cook for about 20 minutes, covered.

Puree soup in batches. Taste and adjust salt and seasonings if necessary. Garnish each bowl with a swirl of coconut milk and chopped cilantro.

Yield: 8 to 10 servings

Kitchen Tip:

If you don't have any previously made pumpkin puree on hand you can bake two sugar pie pumpkins as directed in the recipe for Homemade Pumpkin Puree, page 511, and skip the pureeing part. No need to do that step since your soup will be pureed.

Carrot Lentil Ginger Soup

Serve this warming, nourishing soup with a swirl of coconut milk in each bowl. Use South River Miso Company's Adzuki Bean miso, which is gluten-free and soy-free. Remember to sort through your lentils and pick out any gluten grains, then rinse very well.

2 tablespoons extra virgin olive oil or coconut oil
1 medium onion, chopped
3 cloves garlic, crushed
2 tablespoons chopped fresh ginger
8 large carrots, peeled and chopped
1 cup red lentils, rinsed
8 cups water
2 teaspoons Herbamare, or to taste
¼ cup gluten-free miso
handful fresh cilantro, chopped

Heat a 6-quart pot over medium heat. Add the oil, then add onions; sauté for 5 minutes or until softened. Add garlic and ginger; sauté a minute more. Then add chopped carrots, lentils, water, and Herbamare. Cover and bring to a boil, then reduce heat and simmer for about 40 minutes or until lentils are cooked and carrots are soft.

Add the miso. Use an immersion blender to puree or blend in batches using your blender. Return soup to pot, stir in cilantro. Taste and add more miso or Herbamare if desired.

Yield: 6 to 8 servings

Red Lentil Dal

This dal is quite easy to prepare and comes together rather quickly. Serve over red quinoa or brown jasmine rice along with the Raw Mango Chutney, page 379, and Chili-Garlic Fermented Green Beans, page 505.

2 cups red lentils, rinsed
6 cups water
1 teaspoon turmeric
1 teaspoon ground cumin
¼ teaspoon cayenne pepper
4 tablespoons coconut oil
1 tablespoon finely chopped fresh ginger
1 tablespoon cumin seeds
1 tablespoon brown mustard seeds
1 large onion, cut into crescent moons
2 teaspoons sea salt
2 cups diced tomatoes

Add lentils to a 6-quart pot along with the water, turmeric, cumin, and cayenne. Cover and simmer over medium heat for about 30 minutes.

While the lentils are cooking, heat a large skillet over medium-high heat. Add the oil, then add ginger, cumin seeds, and mustard seeds; sauté for 20 to 30 seconds. Add the onions and salt; sauté for 10 to 12 minutes or until the onions are very soft and beginning to change color. Add tomatoes and sauté 2 minutes more.

Add onion-tomato mixture, scraping the bottom of the pan to get all of the spices out, into the pot of cooked lentils; simmer for 10 to 15 minutes more.

Yield: 6 to 8 servings

Soothing Red Lentil Soup

Serve this nourishing tomato-free soup with a scoop of cooked quinoa or brown basmati rice. You can freeze portions of it before adding the greens. When you are ready to use it, heat it up in a small pot and add a handful of greens. This will keep the soup tasting fresh and the colors bright.

2 tablespoons extra virgin olive oil
1 tablespoon whole cumin seeds
1 large onion, chopped
2 to 3 cloves garlic, crushed
1 to 2 teaspoons grated fresh ginger
1 tablespoon mild curry powder
1 ½ teaspoons ground black pepper
2 ½ cups red lentils, rinsed and drained
10 cups water, vegetable stock, or chicken stock
4 cups thinly sliced greens (kale, spinach, collards)
2 to 3 tablespoons freshly squeezed lemon juice
2 teaspoons Herbamare or sea salt

Heat a 6 to 8-quart pot over medium heat. Add the oil, then add the cumin seeds; sauté for about 30 seconds. Then add the onions and sauté for about 5 minutes. Add the garlic, ginger, curry powder, and black pepper; sauté a minute or so more. Add the red lentils and water or stock, cover, and simmer for about 30 minutes.

Then add the greens, lemon, and salt. Stir it all together and simmer, uncovered, for about 5 to 10 more minutes. Taste and adjust salt and seasonings if necessary.

Yield: 8 servings

Variation:

Add in diced carrots, fresh or frozen peas, or diced zucchini for more flavor and nutrition.

Curried Lentil and Yam Soup

This is one of our favorite quick and easy evening meals. Serve it with a scoop of cooked quinoa and a dollop of Raw Cilantro Lime Chutney, page 378, for a balanced family meal.

2 to 3 tablespoons extra virgin olive oil or coconut oil
1 medium onion, chopped
1 to 2 teaspoons grated fresh ginger
1 tablespoon ground cumin
2 teaspoons curry powder
1 teaspoon ground coriander
½ teaspoon turmeric
2 yams, peeled and diced (about 4 to 5 cups)
2 cups French lentils, rinsed
8 cups water
2 to 3 teaspoons Herbamare

Heat an 8-quart stockpot over medium heat. Add the oil, then add onions; sauté for 5 to 10 minutes or until onions are soft and beginning to change color. Add ginger, cumin, curry powder, coriander, turmeric, and yams; sauté for another few minutes.

Stir in the lentils and water, cover, and bring to a boil. Reduce heat to a simmer and cook for 35 to 40 minutes or until lentils are cooked. Add salt and simmer a minute more. Taste and adjust salt and seasonings if necessary. Leftover soup can be frozen.

Yield: 8 servings

Moroccan Lentil and Cabbage Soup

Our children love anything with curry, but are especially fond of the flavors of Morocco. I always ate a lot of curried dishes while pregnant and breastfeeding and then offered them curried dishes by twelve months of age. From these experiences, their taste buds adapted to accept and enjoy these flavors. We like to make this recipe on a busy weeknight and serve it over cooked quinoa for a simple, balanced meal.

2 to 3 tablespoons extra virgin olive oil
1 medium onion, diced
4 carrots, peeled and diced
2 teaspoons curry powder
1 teaspoon ground cardamom
½ teaspoon garam masala
pinch cayenne pepper (optional)
2 cups French lentils, rinsed
10 cups water or chicken stock
6 tablespoons tomato paste
4 cups sliced Savoy cabbage
2 teaspoons Herbamare or to taste

Heat an 8-quart stockpot over medium heat. Add the oil, then add onions; sauté for 5 to 10 minutes until softened and beginning to change color. Add carrots and spices and sauté a minute more.

Add lentils, water, and tomato paste. Cover and simmer for about 35 to 40 minutes or until the lentils are cooked. Turn off heat, stir in cabbage and salt. Taste and adjust salt and seasonings if necessary.

Yield: 8 servings

Lentil Minestrone

Serve this soup as a main dish with a loaf of crusty gluten-free bread. This soup freezes well as long as you don't add the noodles to the portion that will be frozen.

3 to 4 tablespoons extra virgin olive oil
1 large onion, chopped
1 tablespoon Italian seasoning
2 teaspoons smoked paprika
2 cups sliced carrots
2 cups chopped celery
4 to 5 cloves garlic, crushed
2 cups French lentils, rinsed
10 to 12 cups water, chicken stock, or vegetable stock
2 cups chopped tomatoes
1 cup chopped Italian parsley
2 to 3 teaspoons Herbamare or to taste
freshly ground black pepper
½ package brown rice elbow noodles

Heat an 8-quart stockpot over medium heat. Add the oil, then add onions; sauté for 5 to 10 minutes or until softened and beginning to change color. Add Italian seasoning, paprika, carrots, celery, and garlic; sauté a minute more. Add lentils, water, and tomatoes. Cover and simmer for about 45 minutes.

While soup is cooking, cook the pasta al dente according to the directions on the package.

Once lentils are cooked, turn off heat and add parsley, Herbamare and black pepper. Gently stir in cooked rice noodles. Serve.

Yield: 8 to 10 servings

Kitchen Tip:

Remember to sort through your lentils before you use them and pick any gluten grains. Lentils are often cross-contaminated during growing and harvesting.

Gingered Yellow Split Pea Dal

This dal is a bit thicker than most other dals we make. We like to serve a scoop of it along side other Indian flavored recipes, such as the Fresh Vegetable Curry, page 299, or the Red Quinoa Masala, page 279.

2 tablespoons extra virgin olive oil or coconut oil
2 teaspoons whole cumin seeds
1 teaspoon brown or black mustard seeds
1 medium onion, finely diced
3 tablespoons grated fresh ginger
2 cloves garlic, crushed
2 teaspoons ground coriander
1 teaspoon turmeric
2 cups yellow split peas, rinsed and drained
6 cups water
1 lemon, juiced
2 teaspoons Herbamare or sea salt

Heat a 3-quart pot over medium heat. Add the oil, then add the cumin and mustard seeds; sauté for about 30 to 60 seconds or until the seeds begin to pop and you smell a fragrant aroma. Immediately add onions to the seeds don't burn; sauté for 5 to 7 minutes. Add ginger, garlic, coriander, and turmeric; sauté a minute more.

Add split peas and water; cover and bring to a boil. Then reduce heat to a simmer and cook for about 40 to 60 minutes, stirring occasionally, until the split peas have turned into a creamy, thick stew. Add more water if you prefer a thinner stew. Stir in lemon juice and salt. Taste and adjust salt and seasonings if necessary.

Yield: 6 servings

Chipotle Black Bean and Yam Stew

Serve this spicy tomato-free stew with a large scoop of Cilantro Cabbage Slaw, page 213. Sometimes we also add a scoop of cooked brown rice. If using canned black beans it will take about four cans. Be sure to save the bean cooking liquid from the cans. I prefer to use bean cooking liquid rather than water in this recipe to create a thicker stew. You can also replace the yams in this recipe with a small butternut squash that has been peeled and diced.

2 tablespoons extra virgin olive oil
1 medium yellow onion, chopped
2 teaspoons ground cumin
½ teaspoon dried oregano
½ to 1 teaspoon chipotle chili powder
2 to 3 teaspoons Herbamare or sea salt
2 medium yams, peeled and diced (about 4 cups)
4 cloves garlic, crushed
6 cups cooked black beans
4 cups bean cooking liquid or water
1 medium red bell pepper, diced
1 lime, juiced (about 2 to 3 tablespoons)

Heat a 6 or 8-quart pot over medium heat. Add the oil, then add onions; sauté for 5 to 7 minutes. Then add the spices, Herbamare, yams, and garlic and sauté a minute or two more.

Add the black beans and bean cooking liquid; simmer uncovered for 10 to 15 minutes or until yams are barely tender but not yet cooked. Timing will depend on what size you dice your yams.

Then add diced peppers and simmer for 10 minutes more. Taste and adjust salt and spices if necessary. Remove from heat and stir in lime juice.

Yield: 6 to 8 servings

Nutrition Tip:

More and more research is pointing to the importance of consuming foods that make your intestinal bacterium happy. Researchers in Mexico have found that black beans do a great job at that. Black beans contain higher quantities of fibers that are not digestible (indigestible fractions) by our enzymes, but are digested by organisms in our intestines. These undigested black bean portions feed certain beneficial bacteria and allow them to produce a substance called butyric acid. It just happens that butyric acid is one of the preferred sources of energy for the cells lining the colon allowing them to function properly and remain healthy.

Curried Lima Bean Soup

Lima beans are often called butter beans because of their soft buttery texture. They can be found in bulk at your local food co-op or health food store. Be sure to soak them in warm water for at least 12 hours, preferably 24 hours, to aid in digestibility. Feel free to add any vegetables to the soup in place of the yams and peas such as carrots, potatoes, kale, or zucchini.

3 cups dry lima beans, soaked for 12 to 24 hours
2 tablespoons coconut oil
1 large onion, chopped
1 tablespoon curry powder
1 teaspoon ground cumin
1 teaspoon ground coriander
12 to 14 cups water
2 medium yams, peeled and cut into cubes
2 to 3 cups fresh or frozen peas
2 to 3 teaspoons Herbamare or sea salt
freshly ground black pepper, to taste

Garnish:
chopped cilantro

Sort through the beans and remove any discolored, shriveled, or moldy ones. Rinse them and add them to a large bowl; cover with a few inches of warm water. Leave the bowl on your counter and let the beans soak for 12 to 24 hours. Then drain and rinse using a large colander. Set aside.

Heat an 8-quart stockpot over medium heat. Add the oil, then add onions; sauté for 5 to 10 minutes or until softened and beginning to change color. Add the spices; sauté a minute more.

Add the soaked beans and water, cover, bring to a boil then reduce heat to low and simmer for 45 to 60 minutes or until the beans are tender and cooked through. Then add yams, peas, salt, and black pepper; simmer uncovered for about another 20 minutes or until vegetables are tender. Taste and adjust salt and seasonings if necessary.

Garnish each bowl with chopped cilantro. Leftovers can be frozen.

Yield: 10 servings

Ginger Coconut Mung Bean Soup

We often serve this for a main meal with a scoop of brown basmati rice in each bowl. Since mung beans are one of the easiest legumes to digest, people with compromised digestive systems often tolerate it very well. The fresh ginger and spices further help with digestion.

1 to 2 tablespoons coconut oil
1 medium onion, diced
2 tablespoons grated fresh ginger
3 to 4 cloves garlic, crushed
2 teaspoons garam masala
1 to 2 teaspoons crushed red chili flakes
½ teaspoon ground coriander
½ teaspoon turmeric
1 ¾ cups dry mung beans
8 cups chicken stock or water
2 large carrots, peeled and diced
1 medium yam, peeled and cut into cubes
1 can coconut milk
3 to 4 cups thinly sliced greens (kale, collards, or chard)
1 to 2 teaspoons sea salt, or to taste

Heat an 8-quart stockpot over medium heat. Add the oil, then add onions; sauté for 5 to 10 minutes or until softened and beginning to change color. Add ginger, garlic, and peppers; sauté a minute more. Then add garam masala, coriander, and turmeric.

Rinse the mung beans in a fine mesh strainer and add them to the pot. Add the chicken stock or water, cover, and cook for about 25 minutes. Add carrots, yams, and coconut milk; cover and simmer for another 25 to 30 minutes or until vegetables are tender.

Turn off heat and add the sliced greens and salt. Taste and adjust salt and seasonings if necessary.

Yield: 6 to 8 servings

Italian White Bean Soup

Our children beg me to make this soup. They love to heat it up in the morning and pack it in their school lunchbox. We like to serve it with a scoop of sticky brown rice. Of course a good crusty loaf of bread pairs well with this soup too. In the wintertime I use whole frozen tomatoes that I thaw in a bowl of warm water while I am chopping the other vegetables. Within ten minutes their skins easily peel off and they become soft enough to chop. This soup can be frozen in jars and reheated when needed.

2 to 3 tablespoons extra virgin olive oil
1 large onion, chopped
3 to 4 cloves garlic, crushed
1 teaspoon paprika
1 teaspoon ground black pepper
2 tablespoons Italian seasoning
4 to 5 carrots, diced
3 to 4 stalks celery, chopped
½ pound green beans, cut into 2-inch pieces
12 cups chicken stock
4 cups diced tomatoes
3 to 4 tablespoons tomato paste
6 cups cooked navy beans
2 to 3 cups thinly sliced kale
½ to 1 cup chopped parsley
3 teaspoons Herbamare or sea salt

Heat an 8-quart pot over medium heat. Add olive oil, then add onion; sauté for 8 to 10 minutes or until very soft and beginning to change color. Add garlic, spices, and herbs; sauté a minute more. Then add the carrots, celery, green beans; sauté abut 2 minutes. Then add stock, tomatoes, and tomato paste. Cover and simmer for about 20 to 25 minutes or until vegetables are tender.

Stir in cooked beans, kale, and parsley; simmer 5 minutes more. Add salt; taste and adjust salt and seasonings if necessary. Store leftovers in the refrigerator for up to a week.

Yield: About 12 servings

Spicy Black-Eyed Pea Soup

We like to serve this soup with sautéed collard greens and Chipotle Yam Fries, page 246. It is also delicious served with a scoop of polenta. Sprinkle extra chili flakes on top of individual servings for an added kick.

page 246

2 to 3 tablespoons extra virgin olive oil
1 large onion, chopped
4 to 5 cloves garlic, crushed
2 tablespoons ground cumin
½ to 1 teaspoon crushed red chili flakes
½ teaspoon freshly ground black pepper
2 cups dry black-eyed peas
8 to 10 cup water
3 to 4 carrots, peeled and sliced
1 large red bell pepper, seeded and diced
3 cups broccoli florets
3 teaspoons sea salt or Herbamare

Heat an 8-quart pot over medium heat. Add olive oil, then add onion; sauté for 6 to 7 minutes or until soft. Add garlic and spices; sauté a minute more. Add beans and water, cover and bring to a boil, then reduce heat to a simmer and cook for 25 minutes.

Add carrots and cook for about 10 to 15 more minutes. Add red pepper and broccoli and simmer until vegetables are tender and beans are cooked, about 45 minutes total cooking time. Stir in sea salt; taste and adjust salt and seasonings if necessary.

Yield: 8 to 10 servings

Three Bean Vegetable Chili

Serve this colorful chili recipe when the weather begins to get chilly. It is great served with the Pumpkin Cornbread, page 160, or over cooked short grain brown rice with sliced avocado on top.

2 tablespoons extra virgin olive oil
1 onion, chopped
4 cloves garlic, crushed
4 teaspoons chili powder
2 teaspoons ground cumin
2 to 3 teaspoons Herbamare or sea salt
3 to 4 carrots, diced small
4 cups diced tomatoes
2 cups cooked black beans
2 cups cooked kidney beans
2 cups cooked pinto beans
2 to 4 cups water
½ pound fresh or frozen corn
½ bunch curly green kale, chopped finely
1 cup cilantro, chopped

Heat an 8-quart stockpot over medium heat. Heat the oil, then add onions; sauté for about 10 minutes. Add garlic, spices, and salt; sauté a minute more.

Add carrots, tomatoes, beans, water, and corn. Cover and simmer for about 60 minutes. Add chopped kale and cilantro. Simmer another 5 minutes. Serve hot!

Yield: 8 to 10 servings

Nutrition Tip:

Use diced fresh or frozen tomatoes to avoid canned tomatoes. Most canned tomatoes contain BPA in the lining of the can, which easily migrates into the tomatoes because of their acidity. BPA is a hormone-disrupting chemical, its effects ranging from birth defects, reproductive dysfunction, and increased incidence of miscarriages to cancer. Testing has found that pregnant women and infants who eat even a single serving of some canned foods are exposed to unsafe doses of BPA.

Chicken and Chard Chili

We like to make this recipe on a very busy weeknight. I can toss all of the ingredients into the pot in ten minutes and then let the chili simmer on the stove while I work with my children on practicing their music, reading, or writing. You can accompany this stew with a batch of Vegan Corn Muffins, page 157, or a simple pot of short grain brown rice.

2 to 3 tablespoons extra virgin olive oil
1 medium onion, chopped
3 cloves garlic, crushed
1 to 2 jalapeno peppers, seeded, and finely diced
2 organic chicken breasts, chopped into small pieces
1 tablespoon ground cumin
1 tablespoon mild chili powder
1 teaspoon smoked paprika (optional)
2 cups tomato sauce
3 cups water
5 to 6 cups cooked pinto or red beans
2 teaspoons Herbamare, or to taste
2 cups chopped chard

Heat a 6-quart pot over medium heat. Add the olive oil, then add onions; sauté for 5 to 10 minutes or until onions are soft and beginning to change color. Add crushed garlic, jalapeno peppers, and chicken; sauté for 2 to 3 minutes more. Add cumin, chili powder, and smoked paprika; sauté a minute more.

Add tomato sauce, water, beans, and Herbamare. Stir, cover, and simmer on medium-low heat for 45 to 60 minutes. Once the chicken is very tender and the flavors have melded, add chard and simmer for 5 minutes more. Turn off heat, taste, and adjust salt and seasonings if necessary.

Yield: 6 to 8 servings

Ingredient Tip:

I use Bionaturae Strained Tomatoes in place of the tomato sauce. I like that this product comes in glass jars and not in a can. I use it everywhere you would normally use canned tomato sauce.

Slow Cooker Chicken Stew

I don't have many crock-pot recipes because I usually get inspired to cook when I'm hungry, close to dinnertime, but this recipe came to me early one day and I knew I just had to pull out my old slow cooker. The flavors come together beautifully and the chicken is so tender you'll hardly need to chew! Serve this stew over basmati rice alongside a salad of crispy romaine lettuce. It is also pairs well with the Farmhouse Seed Bread, page 130.

1 cup diced shallots
3 stalks celery, diced
4 carrots, peeled and diced
1 ½ pounds boneless chicken breasts, cut into chunks
2 cups diced tomatoes
1 cup water
¼ to ½ cup dry white wine
¼ cup extra virgin olive oil
1 tablespoon Italian seasoning
1 to 2 teaspoons Herbamare or sea salt
freshly ground black pepper

Add all ingredients to your slow cooker and cook on high for 4 to 5 hours or on low for 6 to 8 hours.

If you do not have a slow cooker, place all ingredients into a covered casserole dish and bake in the oven for about 2 ½ hours at 300 degrees F.

Yield: 4 to 6 servings

Chicken, Ginger, and Cabbage Soup

This recipe is a two-part process. First you make a flavorful broth by slow cooking chicken and vegetables together. Then you strain it, pull the meat from the bone, add fresh vegetables to the strained broth, and then add back in the cut-up chicken. You can add the veggies from making the broth into pureed soups, serve them to your toddler as a soft finger food, or just compost them as most of the nutrients are now in the broth. If you don't like spicy food then omit the Thai chilies when making the soup part of this recipe. You can add noodles to the finished soup if desired—try rice noodles, kelp noodles, or homemade raw zucchini noodles.

For the Broth:
3 to 4 bone-in organic chicken breasts
10 cups water
1 large onion, chopped
3 stalks celery, chopped
1 large carrot, chopped
1 whole head garlic, cut in half cross-wise
¼ to ½ cup finely chopped fresh ginger (or more)
2 to 3 Thai chilies, chopped or 1 teaspoon crushed red chili flakes
2 cups finely chopped shiitake mushrooms
1 stalk fresh lemongrass, chopped
cilantro stems
1 teaspoon whole black peppercorns
3 teaspoons Herbamare or sea salt

For the Soup:
1 medium onion, cut into crescent moons
3 to 4 stalks celery, sliced into diagonals
3 carrots, cut into matchsticks
2 to 3 cups sliced shiitake mushrooms
4 cups chopped fresh napa cabbage
1 cup chopped fresh cilantro
2 fresh Thai green chilies, chopped (optional)
sea salt and freshly ground black pepper to taste

To make the broth, place all ingredients for broth into a 6-quart pot. Cover and bring to a boil, reduce heat to medium-low and simmer for 1 ½ to 2 hours. Strain broth into a large bowl or another pot using a colander. Place chicken breasts onto a plate to cool. Pour the broth back into the pot. Once chicken has cooled enough to handle it, remove the skin, pull the meat from the bone, and chop the chicken into bite-sized pieces.

To make the soup, place the onion, carrot, celery, and shiitake mushrooms into the pot with the broth. Cover and simmer for about 15 to 20 minutes. Add the chopped cabbage, cilantro, chilies, and chicken. Season with salt and pepper to taste. Simmer a minute or two more or until vegetables are cooked to your liking. Ladle soup into bowls and serve.

Yield: 8 servings

Grass-Fed Beef Chili

When purchasing red meat, be sure to always purchase grass-fed, organic beef. This is the most sustainable and nutritious form of red meat. Serve this chili with the Pumpkin Cornbread, page 160, and a spoonful of raw cultured vegetables to maximize digestion.

1 tablespoon extra virgin olive oil or coconut oil
1 large onion, finely chopped
6 cloves garlic, crushed
1 tablespoon ground cumin
1 tablespoon chili powder
1 red bell pepper, diced
1 jalapeno pepper, finely diced (optional)
1 pound ground beef
4 cups cooked red beans
2 cups tomato sauce
2 cups water
2 teaspoons Herbamare or sea salt
½ cup chopped cilantro

Heat a 6-quart pot over medium heat. Add the oil, then add the onions; sauté for about 10 minutes or until very soft and beginning to change color. Add the garlic, cumin, chili powder, red bell pepper, jalapeno pepper, and ground beef; sauté for a few minutes.

Add the cooked red beans, tomato sauce, water, and salt; cover and simmer for about 35 minutes, stirring occasionally. Stir in chopped cilantro. Taste and adjust salt and seasonings if necessary.

Yield: 6 servings

Halibut and Potato Chowder

A bowl of hot chowder is welcoming to come home to after a long afternoon of skiing, sledding, or just playing in the snow. This chowder is wonderful served with a slice of freshly baked Sourdough Bread, page 124, and a large serving of sautéed dark leafy greens.

2 tablespoons extra virgin olive oil
1 large onion, diced
2 slices organic bacon (optional)
4 cloves garlic, crushed
1 to 2 teaspoons dried thyme
1 to 2 teaspoons dried dill
2 to 3 large carrots, peeled and diced
3 stalks celery, diced
6 large red or yellow potatoes, peeled and diced
5 to 6 cups chicken or vegetable stock
1 to 2 pounds fresh halibut, skin removed and cut into 1-inch chunks
large handful of fresh parsley, chopped
Herbamare and freshly ground black pepper, to taste

Heat a 6-quart pot over medium heat. Add the oil, then add onions; sauté for 5 to 7 minutes, or until soft and starting to turn a little golden. Add bacon slices, garlic, and herbs; sauté a minute or so more.

Add diced carrots, celery, and potatoes; sauté a few minutes more. Then add stock and simmer, covered, for about 30 minutes or until vegetables are very soft. Take a large spoon and mash some of the potatoes up against the side of the pot to make the chowder creamy.

Add halibut and simmer for about 5 minutes more. Remove bacon slices and discard. Add chopped parsley and stir. Add salt and pepper to taste.

Yield: 6 servings

Salads and Vegetables

Making vegetables the centerpiece of your meals is one of the healthiest choices you can make for your family. Vegetables are vital to all aspects of human health and contain literally thousands of phytochemicals offering innumerable health benefits. Vegetables have been touted as the go-to foods for decreasing the risk for a multitude of diseases including cancer, hypertension, type II diabetes, age-related macular degeneration, obesity, and early stage cognitive decline.

Vital Phytochemicals

Plant phytochemicals signal our cells to produce antioxidant and detoxification proteins after eating. Why would this be important? We hear from the media on a daily basis about all of the harmful chemicals we are exposed to in the environment—BPA in plastics and the lining of cans, pesticides on our produce, and heavy metals like arsenic in our water or mercury in the air from coal plants. Every one of these substances needs to be filtered from our body by the liver, and we need extra antioxidants to protect our cells from the damaging effects of these chemicals.

Sulforaphane from broccoli, cauliflower, brussels sprouts, collards, cabbage, kale, and kohlrabi initiates the reading of an incredible portion of our genes called the Antioxidant Response Element, which leads to the production of antioxidant and detoxification proteins for more than 72 hours! As a result, our body's overall ability to survive in an increasingly toxic world gets a boost.

How much should I eat?

Incorporating vegetables into breakfast, lunch, and dinner is necessary if you want to continuously bath your cells with disease-fighting nutrients. A step further would be to use green smoothies and chopped raw vegetables as snacks.

The daily minimum: consume 2 to 3 cups each of the following daily:

- Leafy greens such as lettuce, arugula, and spinach.
- Cruciferous vegetables such as broccoli, kale, and cabbage.
- Brightly colored vegetables such as carrots, beets, and peas.
- Fresh or frozen fruit.

It is best to start a meal with a salad or plate of vegetables, before the starchy or meat-based parts of the meal are served. Our taste buds are hard-wired to seek out salt, starch, and fat, for survival. Oftentimes we need to retrain the taste buds to accept new and interesting flavors. Starting out the meal with raw vegetables can help in both the training of the taste buds and the stimulation of digestion.

Getting Kids to Eat More Veggies

Fresh fruits and vegetables are some of the easiest foods to snack on, but if your home is stocked with other snack foods filled with empty calories your children will most likely seek those first. We have found that our children will reach into the refrigerator and snack on carrots, radishes, celery, cucumbers, and snap peas or into the freezer for frozen blueberries, cherries, and peaches when there is nothing else available in the house to eat that doesn't require some sort of preparation. If I have made cookies, muffins, or bread they usually go for those first. I make it a habit to bake treats only on occasion so fresh fruits and vegetables can easily make up the bulk of the diet.

Gardening with Children
Gardening with children also provides a way for them to connect with how food grows and have easy access to fresh vegetables. I once lived next door to two young boys that loved eating sweets and junk food. Their mom often asked me how to get the boys to eat vegetables. I promptly went into my garden with the boys and marked off rectangular areas for them to plant their own mini-vegetable patch. I then handed them a box of vegetable seeds and had them dig the soil and plant the vegetables that they wanted. Over the next few months, they came by often to check on their vegetable plants and admire how quickly they grew. When they were ready to harvest, we found both boys eating raw kale, collards, broccoli, and peas! From then on, their attitude changed, and they had a completely different relationship with vegetables.

Cooking with Children
Cooking with your children also provides a non-threatening way to be introduced to vegetables. Imagine sitting at a table and being told you can't leave the table until you have finished eating your cauliflower and peas. But what if your children helped in the chopping and prepping of dinner? They might be more inclined to taste one of those brightly colored, fresh, raw vegetables on their own. I remember our first daughter cutting cauliflower with us when she was a toddler. She would sample the raw cauliflower we were chopping and ended up eating about a cup or more during the meal preparation!

10 Tips for Adding More Vegetables to your Child's Diet:

1. **Make sure your children are hungry and have not been snacking all afternoon or evening**. Hungry children are more likely to try and eat new foods, including vegetables.

2. **Serve the new vegetable or salad first**. This is especially true for young children between 2 and 4 years of age.

3. **Sit down as a family and talk about everything but the meal**. Focusing on the food can lead to food battles.

4. **Suggest a "try-it-bite" for a child who seems really uncomfortable about trying something new**. They may spit it out and that is okay. Sometimes it can take 10 "try-it-bites" over a series of weeks for a child to accept a new food.

5. **Start early**! As soon as a child is old enough to chew he or she begin munching on raw or cooked greens. A one year old won't digest much of it but will gain so much in the way of programming the taste buds to accept these types of foods.

6. **Model eating vegetables**. Young children learn how to eat and what to eat by watching the adults and caregivers around them. This starts from infancy on.

7. **Cook and garden with your children**. When given the opportunity, young children are naturally curious to try new things, including vegetables like brussels sprouts! Cooking with your children and planting a small backyard vegetable patch provide non-threatening ways to be introduced to new foods.

8. **When grocery shopping with your children**, have them pick out one vegetable that they get to try and possibly help incorporate into a meal. This can't be the usual carrots or celery. This "vegetable treat" can be exciting to have as part of your grocery shopping routine.

9. **Only have snacks and foods around your house that you are comfortable with your child eating at any time**. When they are hungry they will learn to reach for what is easily available. Fresh vegetables and fruits are the easiest and most nutritious snacks!

10. **Give your children green smoothies**! We can't think of a better way to pack a lot of vegetables into one snack. Adding carrots, beets, cucumbers, leafy greens and fruit to a blender along with a little water creates a delicious, refreshing drink! See our Smoothie chapter, page 61, for recipes.

10 Tips for Storing Fresh Vegetables and Fruits

1. **Store potatoes and sweet potatoes in a dark**, cool place such as a pantry or root cellar. Light causes them to turn green and begin to sprout. When potatoes turn green, it is an indicator that solanine—a toxic compound—has increased. If this happens it is best to not eat them.

2. **Cut the leafy green part off of root vegetables before storage**. If trimmed off, the nutrients and water will continue to flow into the leafy parts causing limp root vegetables. This includes carrots, beets, radishes, parsnips, celery root, and turnips. For best storage, wrap the root vegetables in damp kitchen towels and place them into your refrigerator's crisper drawer.

3. **Onions and garlic do best stored away from other vegetables and fruits**. I store mine in a large open box in my pantry and keep a few out on my counter in a separate basket.

4. **Place bunched fresh herbs in small glasses of water and cover loosely with a produce bag**. This includes parsley, cilantro, mint, dill, thyme, and oregano.

5. **Store apples in the refrigerator to keep them fresh and crispy**. Some varieties of apples can be stored like this for three months or more. We dedicate one whole drawer in our refrigerator just for apples!

6. **Citrus fruits and tomatoes need to be stored in a place with airflow**, such as an open basket on your counter.

7. **Berries like to be kept dry and cool**. Never wash your berries before placing them into your refrigerator. A paper bag can be used for strawberries. Other berries can be stored in shallow layers in open rectangular glass containers.

8. **Kale, collards, napa cabbage, and lettuce** liked to be wrapped in a damp kitchen towel and stored in a plastic bag or loosely covered glass container in the refrigerator.

9. **Freshly picked zucchini can be left on the counter for a few days**. For longer storage place them into your refrigerator's crisper drawer. We do the same with cucumbers, peppers, and eggplant.

10. **Winter squash like to be stored in a cool**, dark well-ventilated area. After harvesting squash from our garden we set them inside our house at room temperature to cure for about 2 weeks. Then we put them in shallow cardboard boxes in our garage. Winter squash store best at 50 to 55 degrees F where they should keep until March.

Apple Walnut Salad with Fig-Balsamic Vinaigrette

Heirloom apples are available in early autumn at your local Farmer's Market or health food store. Each variety has its own unique set of flavors. The dressing recipe was inspired by something I tasted at the lovely Café Gratitude in California. The blended figs work as a natural emulsifier in the dressing—meaning that the oil and vinegar won't separate. The figs also add a seedy texture and a touch of sweetness. Any variety of fresh figs work in this recipe.

Salad:
8 to 10 cups mixed organic baby greens
1 cup Candied Walnuts (page 404)
2 organic heirloom apples, cored and sliced thin
5 to 6 fresh figs, quartered

Dressing:
5 fresh figs, stems removed
6 tablespoons balsamic vinegar
1 to 2 tablespoons maple syrup
½ teaspoon sea salt or Herbamare
½ cup extra virgin olive oil
freshly ground black pepper, to taste

Optional Addition:
crumbled feta cheese

Place all ingredients for the salad into a large bowl. Add feta cheese if desired.

To make the dressing, place the figs, balsamic vinegar, maple syrup, and salt in a blender and blend on medium until combined and the figs are lightly pureed. With the motor running on a low speed, slowly pour in the olive oil. Add black pepper if desired and blend on low speed, slightly, to incorporate.

Pour desired amount of dressing over salad. Transfer remaining dressing to a glass jar. It will last in the refrigerator for 7 to 10 days.

Yield: 6 servings

Asian Chicken Salad

This high-protein, low carbohydrate salad is the perfect thing to serve for lunch—it will keep you energized for hours! You could use sliced almonds in place of the slivered. Try adding daikon radish, chopped cilantro, and sliced green onions to this salad as well.

Salad:
6 to 8 cups thinly sliced greens (kale, collards, savoy cabbage, bok choy)
2 to 3 cups shredded cooked chicken
2 large carrots, julienned
1 cup slivered almonds, lightly toasted
sesame seeds for garnish

Dressing:
4 tablespoons extra virgin olive oil
1 tablespoon sesame oil
3 tablespoons coconut vinegar or brown rice vinegar
3 tablespoons coconut aminos or wheat-free tamari
2 to 3 teaspoons honey
1 clove garlic
1-inch piece of fresh ginger, peeled

Toss all of the ingredients for the salad into a large bowl if serving immediately. If you want to stretch the salad over a few days place all ingredients into separate containers and store in the fridge. Use what you would like for each serving.

To make the dressing, place all ingredients into a blender and blend on high until combined.

Pour dressing over salad, toss and serve. Garnish with sesame seeds if desired. Leftover dressing will keep in the fridge for up to a week.

Yield: 4 servings

Kitchen Tip:

To thinly slice the greens, stack them on top of each other then roll them. Take a sharp knife and cut into thin slices. This cutting method is called chiffonade.

Arugula Salad with Shaved Fennel

This simple salad is perfect to serve as part of a Sunday brunch or a weeknight dinner. Serve it with poached eggs and roasted vegetables for brunch or for dinner try pairing it with the Mushroom Millet Risotto, page 271, and the Poached Salmon with Spring Onions, page 316. I like to add Roasted Golden Beets, page 245 to this salad for more color, flavor, and nutrients.

Salad:
2 bunches arugula, rinsed and spun dry
1 large fennel bulb, ends trimmed
¼ cup snipped fresh chives

Dressing
3 tablespoons extra virgin olive oil
3 tablespoons champagne vinegar
1 teaspoon Dijon mustard
sea salt and freshly ground black pepper to taste

Tear the arugula into pieces and place it into a large salad bowl. To shave the fennel, take a sharp knife and thinly slice the entire bulb. Place the shaved fennel into the bowl with the arugula. Add the chives and toss together.

In a small bowl, whisk together the ingredients for the dressing. Just before serving, pour the dressing over the salad and toss together. Serve immediately.

Yield: 6 to 8 servings

Nutrition Tip:

Besides being an excellent source of vitamin C, fennel has an important compound called *anethole* that can block the response of a potent inflammatory chemical called *tumor necrosis factor*. Researchers are examining the role that anethole may play in reducing cancer incidence.

Avocado and Yam Salad with Lime

This simple salad can dress up a plate of plain brown rice and black beans for a tasty, nutritious meal. It is also great served at potlucks or as part of a large family taco dinner!

2 medium yams, peeled and cut into ½-inch cubes
3 small ripe avocados, peeled and cubed
¼ cup finely chopped cilantro
2 small limes, juiced
2 to 3 tablespoons extra virgin olive oil
1 clove garlic, crushed
¼ teaspoon sea salt or Herbamare
pinch red chili flakes

Place cubed yams into a steamer basket fitted over about an inch of water. Cover and steam until fork tender, about 10 minutes. Be careful not to overcook otherwise the yams will become too mushy in the salad. Remove steamer basket from pot and let cool completely in the basket.

Place the yams to a medium-sized bowl; then add the avocado, cilantro, lime juice, olive oil, garlic, salt, and chili flakes. Gently toss together. Taste and add more salt and chili flakes if desired. Serve immediately.

Yield: 4 to 6 servings

Nutrition Tip:

The area closest to the skin of the avocado has concentrated amounts of the carotenoids zeaxanthin, beta-carotene, lutein, and beta-cryptoxanthin. Use the nick-and-peel method to keep this part in your salad instead of your compost.

Vegetables

Baby Arugula Salad with Zucchini Lime Dressing

Baby arugula is slightly spicy and pungent, but milder and sweeter than fully mature arugula. The zucchini adds a luscious creaminess to this dressing. Serve this salad to go along with the Roasted Squash and Corn Frittata, page 100, for a festive Sunday brunch. It is also delicious served with cooked black beans and quinoa for an easy, nutritious weekday meal.

Salad:
8 cups baby arugula
½ small onion, sliced into very thin rounds
1 ear corn, cut from the cob
1 small red bell pepper, diced
1 small avocado, diced
½ cup pumpkin seeds, toasted

Dressing:
⅓ cup finely diced zucchini
⅓ cup freshly squeezed lime juice
⅓ cup extra virgin olive oil
⅛ to ¼ teaspoon ground cumin
¼ teaspoon Herbamare

Place the arugula, sliced onion, corn kernels, red bell pepper, and avocado into a large salad bowl and toss together. Set aside.

To toast the pumpkin seeds, heat a 10-inch skillet over medium heat. Add the seeds and keep them moving in the pan until they begin to pop and turn slightly golden, about 5 minutes. Set aside on a plate to cool.

To make the dressing, add all ingredients to a blender and blend until smooth. Taste and adjust salt and seasonings if necessary.

Sprinkle cooled pumpkin seeds atop of salad, pour desired amount of dressing over salad, and serve. If you have leftover dressing, store it in a small glass jar in the fridge for up to a week.

Yield: 6 servings

Blanched Kale Salad with Green Apple Dressing

Blanching kale begins to break down its tough fibers while still keeping nutrient levels intact. Also, blanching for a minute or less turns the kale a beautiful bright green color that is very attractive in a salad. Use extra kale for other salads or to toss into an egg scramble, burritos, or soup. I usually use any type of cold leftover cooked salmon I may have in the fridge. If you don't have any simply omit it. This salad pairs well with a side of baked winter squash.

Salad:
2 bunches curly kale, chopped
1 cup cooked salmon
1 pomegranate, arils removed
½ cup sunflower seeds, toasted

Dressing:
1 medium Granny Smith apple
½ cup water
⅓ cup extra virgin olive oil
1 to 2 cloves garlic
1-inch piece of fresh ginger, peeled
Herbamare or sea salt to taste

Fill an 8-quart stockpot with filtered water about ¾-full and bring to a rapid boil. Quickly add all of the kale, pushing it down with a large spoon. Blanch for about 60 seconds, or until bright green and tender. Pour kale and boiling water through a colander set in your sink and immediately run icy cold water over the kale to stop it from cooking any longer. Gently squeeze the water out of the kale.

Place desired amount of kale onto each plate, top with cooked salmon, pomegranate arils, and toasted sunflower seeds.

To make the dressing, place all ingredients for dressing into a blender and blend about 60 seconds until smooth and creamy. Taste, add a little more salt if needed, and blend again.

Drizzle dressing over each salad. Store leftover dressing in a sealed glass jar in the fridge for up to a week. Store remaining kale in the fridge in a sealed glass container.

Yield: 4 servings

Cabbage Salad with Mandarins and Mung Bean Sprouts

This easy and nutritious salad is best paired with the Garlic Ginger Salmon, page 314, along with a side of mashed sweet potatoes or cooked quinoa. If you don't have slivered almonds or have a nut allergy, use sunflower seeds instead.

Salad:
5 cups thinly sliced napa cabbage
1 cup thinly sliced red cabbage
2 mandarin oranges, peeled and sectioned
3 to 4 green onions, sliced into thin rounds
1 cup mung bean sprouts
½ cup slivered almonds, toasted

Dressing:
¼ cup extra virgin olive oil
2 tablespoons toasted sesame oil
¼ cup coconut vinegar or brown rice vinegar
1 tablespoon creamy peanut butter or cashew butter
2 to 3 teaspoons honey
½ teaspoon Herbamare

Place the cabbage, mandarin sections, green onions, and mung bean sprouts into a large bowl and set aside.

To toast the almonds, heat a large skillet over medium heat. Add the slivered almonds and keep them moving in the pan. Once they are lightly golden in color, and are very fragrant, remove them from the pan and place onto a plate to cool. It should only take a few minutes to do this.

Whisk together the dressing ingredients in a separate bowl. Pour dressing over salad and sprinkle with the toasted slivered almonds. Serve immediately.

Yield: 4 to 6 servings

Cherry Pecan Salad with Cherry Balsamic Vinaigrette

We like to make this salad a few times a week when the sweet cherries are in season. To keep the dressing an appealing darker color, use a dark red cherry variety such as lapin or bing. We like to serve this salad with the dressing on the side, that way each person can add as much as they want. I usually pour the dressing into a tall jam jar to serve it and then store leftovers in the fridge.

Salad:
1 head red leaf lettuce, rinsed and spun dry
1 cup pecans, roasted
1 cup fresh cherries, pitted and cut in half

Dressing:
½ cup fresh or frozen pitted cherries
½ cup extra virgin olive oil
5 to 6 tablespoons balsamic vinegar
1 tablespoon maple syrup
¼ teaspoon sea salt

Tear the lettuce into bite sized pieces and place into a salad bowl. Chop the pecans and sprinkle them on top of the lettuce. Add the cherries.

Place all ingredients for the dressing into a blender and blend until smooth and creamy. Pour into a glass jar for serving. Pour dressing over salad or serve along side the salad. Serve immediately.

Yield: Serves 6

Ingredient Tip:

To roast the pecans, place them into a small glass baking dish or pie plate. Roast in a preheated 350 degree oven for 10 to 15 minutes. Cool on a plate before chopping.

Cilantro Cabbage Slaw

One of our children's favorite vegetables is napa cabbage, therefore this recipe makes a frequent appearance on our dinner table. Serve this fresh-tasting slaw atop the Chipotle Black Bean and Yam Stew, page 190 or with a piece of grilled chicken.

5 cups thinly sliced napa cabbage
2 cups chopped cilantro
2 to 3 green onions, sliced into thin rounds
the juice of one lime
1 to 2 tablespoons extra virgin olive oil
½ teaspoon Herbamare

Place all ingredients into a medium-sized mixing bowl and toss together. Be sure to dress only what you will eat with your meal. Otherwise it will become soggy and unappealing on the next day.

Yield: 4 to 6 servings

Nutrition Tip:

Cilantro can assist with heavy metal detoxification in the body. Heavy metals enter the body through amalgam fillings, vaccines, pesticides and herbicides in conventional food; paint from old buildings, the water supply, and through flame retardants found in children's pajamas, crib mattresses, and furniture. Most people have varying levels of heavy metals in their systems that can be chelated with regular consumption of cilantro.

Cucumber Arame Salad

Incorporating sea vegetables into your weekly diet is one of the healthiest things you can do. Seaweed is a rich source of iodine—a mineral needed to make thyroid hormones. Serve this refreshing salad with adzuki beans and rice, or grilled fish.

¼ cup arame
water for cooking
2 medium cucumbers
3 green onions, sliced into thin rounds
½ chopped cilantro
3 tablespoons brown rice vinegar or coconut vinegar
2 tablespoons extra virgin olive oil
1 to 2 teaspoons grated fresh ginger
¾ teaspoon sea salt

Place the arame into a small pot and cover with about 2 cups of water. Bring to a boil, then reduce heat to low and simmer for 5 to 7 minutes. Remove from heat and pour through a fine mesh strainer to drain off the water. Set the strainer over the pot to finish draining and cool while you prepare the other ingredients.

Cut the cucumbers in half lengthwise, then slice into thin half moons; place them into a medium-sized bowl. Add the cooked arame and remaining ingredients; toss together. Taste and adjust salt and vinegar if necessary. Serve.

Store in a covered glass container in your refrigerator for up to 3 days.

Yield: 6 servings

Nutrition Tip:

The thyroid hormones triiodothyronine (T3) and thyroxine (T4) are primarily composed of iodine. T3 literally stands for one tyrosine amino acid attached to three iodine molecules, and T4 has four iodine molecules attached to tyrosine. Out of all the foods found in nature, sea vegetables are the best source of iodine. Arame is also a particularly rich source of a carotenoid called fucoxanthin. This powerful antioxidant compound has been researched for its effects on increasing the burning of body fat leading to weight loss. Fucoxanthin appears to have anti-cancer and anti-diabetic effects as well.

Fresh Cauliflower Salad

The displays of fresh, organic cauliflower at the Farmer's Market or at the grocery store always inspire me to create new recipes using this beautiful vegetable. Of course, often times we cut it into florets and use it to dip into a bean or nut spread. Serve this refreshing salad with grilled fish or cooked quinoa and beans for a simple, nutritious meal.

1 medium head cauliflower, stemmed and chopped
3 to 4 green onions, sliced into thin rounds
large handful fresh parsley, finely chopped
3 to 4 tablespoons extra virgin olive oil
3 to 4 tablespoons freshly squeezed lemon juice
Herbamare or sea salt to taste

Optional Additions:
sliced kalamata olives
halved cherry tomatoes
grated carrots
thinly sliced fresh basil

Remove the stem from the cauliflower and chop the head into bite-sized pieces. Add it to a large bowl along with the green onions, parsley, olive oil, and lemon juive. Toss together. Add salt to taste and any optional additions. Toss again.

Serve immediately or store in the refrigerator for a few hours. Bring to room temperature before serving.

Yield: 4 to 6 servings

Grapefruit, Radish, and Cabbage Salad

This salad is very quick to prepare. It has a light dressing that doesn't overpower the flavors of the grapefruit or vegetables. Serve with grilled chicken breasts or baked salmon and cooked quinoa.

Salad:
6 cups thinly sliced napa cabbage
2 pink grapefruit, peeled
5 to 6 small radishes, sliced thin

Dressing:
2 tablespoons extra virgin olive oil
2 tablespoons champagne vinegar
freshly ground pepper
few pinches sea salt

Garnish:
1 to 2 tablespoons snipped chives

Place the napa cabbage into a medium-sized salad bowl, set aside.

To cut the grapefruit, first trim the top and bottom off. Then place the grapefruit on one of the cut ends and begin taking the peel and pith off with a sharp paring knife. Slice the peeled grapefruit into rounds and cut each round into quarters. Add the grapefruit to the salad along with the radishes.

Whisk together the ingredients for the dressing. Pour over salad and toss together. Sprinkle the chives over the salad. Serve immediately.

Yield: 4 to 6 servings

Greek Salad with Chickpeas

This salad is a complete meal. Serve it in the summertime when your garden is overflowing with fresh tomatoes, cucumbers, and lettuce. This salad pairs well with the Rosemary Sea Salt Breadsticks, page 133.

Salad:
1 head romaine lettuce, rinsed and spun dry
2 cups cherry tomatoes, cut into halves
2 cups cooked chickpeas, rinsed and drained
1 cup pitted kalamata olives, sliced
½ small red onion, diced
1 large cucumber, sliced

Greek Dressing:
½ cup extra virgin olive oil
6 tablespoons freshly squeezed lemon juice
1 to 2 cloves garlic
2 tablespoons fresh oregano leaves
½ teaspoon sea salt
½ teaspoon freshly ground black pepper

Optional Additions:
fresh mint leaves
crumbled feta cheese

Chop the romaine lettuce and place it into a large salad bowl and top with the remaining salad ingredients. Add fresh mint leaves and feta cheese if desired.

Place all ingredients for the dressing into a blender and blend until smooth. Pour dressing over salad and toss together or pour dressing into a small glass jar and let each person dress his or her own salad.

Store extra salad in the refrigerator for up to 2 days. Dressing will last about 10 days in the fridge.

Yield: 6 servings

Variation:

To make this dressing citrus-free, replace the lemon juice with organic red or white wine vinegar.

Jalapeño-Lime Kale Slaw

Eating raw food, especially raw vegetables and greens, as part of your meal can help digest other parts of your meal. Serve this salad with cooked black beans and quinoa for a simple, nutritious meal.

Salad:
5 to 6 cups thinly sliced lacinato kale
½ to 1 cup diced red bell pepper

Dressing:
¼ cup packed cilantro
1 jalapeño pepper, seeded
1 clove garlic
4 tablespoons extra virgin olive oil
3 tablespoons fresh squeezed lime juice
¼ teaspoon sea salt or Herbamare

Place kale and diced red pepper in a large bowl, set aside.

Place all ingredients for the dressing into a blender and blend on medium until combined. I like to place the ingredients into a wide mouth jar and use my immersion blender. This way I don't dirty the whole blender!

Pour dressing over salad and toss together. Taste and add more salt if needed. Let dressing mingle with the kale for 2 to 24 hours. The kale will tenderize and become softer the longer it sits.

Yield: 4 to 6 servings

Nutrition Tip:

Kale is high in lutein, a carotenoid that helps to prevent age-related macular degeneration. It has been shown that an increased consumption of green leafy vegetables can lead to a 35% reduction in overall neurologic decline. Kale is also high in fiber, which helps to keep cholesterol levels in check.

Kale Apple Walnut Salad

Serve this crispy salad in autumn when kale and green apples are at their peak. I use one medium Granny Smith apple when making this recipe. Half goes into the salad and the other half into the dressing. Use the candied walnut recipe or simply roast a cup of walnuts in the oven for about 10 minutes; either way works well. This salad pairs well with a bean soup and a whole grain salad or served with the Roasted Chicken with Root Vegetables, page 325.

Salad:
1 bunch kale, rinsed
½ green apple, diced
1 cup Candied Walnuts (page 404)

Dressing:
½ green apple
6 tablespoons extra virgin olive oil
4 tablespoons apple cider vinegar
1 clove garlic
½ teaspoon sea salt

Remove the thick stem from the middle of each kale leaf. If your kale is young and tender you don't need to do this step. Then chop or tear into bite-sized pieces.

Toss kale in a medium-sized bowl with the diced apple. If you are serving this salad immediately after preparing it then toss in the candied walnuts now. If not, wait until ready to serve to add the walnuts.

Place all ingredients for the dressing into a blender and blend until smooth. Pour dressing over kale and apples. Toss together. Serve.

Yield: 4 to 6 servings

Kohlrabi Apple Slaw

I was first introduced to kohlrabi when I worked at a local state park the summer after my first year in college. A fellow co-worker, 65-year old Ben, grew much of his own produce and used to bring me sliced kohlrabi packed in cold water. It was so refreshing and crispy! Ever since then I have been enjoying it and finding new ways to prepare it. If you don't have any dairy-free yogurt on hand you can substitute Almond Mayonnaise, page 367, but thin it out with water. Homemade Coconut Kefir, page 479, works well here too.

Slaw:
3 kohlrabi, peeled, sliced, and cut into matchsticks
3 carrots, grated
2 small apples, cut into matchsticks
3 to 4 green onions, thinly sliced

Dressing:
¾ cup plain yogurt or kefir (cow, goat, nut, or coconut)
1 tablespoon honey
1 tablespoon apple cider vinegar
½ teaspoon Herbamare

Place the kohlrabi matchsticks, grated carrots, apple matchsticks, and sliced green onions into a bowl.

In a small bowl, whisk together the ingredients for the dressing. Pour over the slaw. Toss together. Let it sit for about 20 minutes, then toss again, and serve.

Yield: 6 servings

Nutrition Tip:

Being part of the brassica family, kohlrabi is high in isothiocyanates. These amazing phytochemicals help protect against cancer by not allowing carcinogens that have entered your body to activate and also by counteracting carcinogens that have already been activated. Isothiocyanates also help with the speedy removal of carcinogens from your body, making kohlrabi an awesome cancer fighting food!

Lemon Walnut Green Bean Salad

This salad is very quick to prepare and quite addicting to eat. Blanching green beans for a few minutes cooks them perfectly so they still have a bit of crispness to them. I always drain them in a colander, then run them under icy cold water to stop the cooking process. This salad can be made ahead of time though I would suggest leaving the walnuts out until you are ready to serve, otherwise they will get quite soggy within a few hours.

1 ½ pounds fresh green beans, ends trimmed
1 cup walnuts
2 to 4 tablespoons snipped fresh chives
2 tablespoons extra virgin olive oil
2 tablespoons freshly squeezed lemon juice
½ teaspoon lemon zest
½ teaspoon Herbamare
freshly ground black pepper

Preheat oven to 400 degrees F.

Bring a medium sized pot of water to a boil. Add the green beans and blanch for about 4 to 5 minutes or until desired doneness. Drain using a colander and run under icy cold water to stop the cooking process. Place into a large bowl.

Place the walnuts into an 8 x 8-inch baking dish and roast for about 10 minutes in the preheated oven. Place on a plate to cool, then chop. Add to the green beans.

Add the remaining ingredients to the bowl and toss together well. Serve and enjoy!

Yield: 4 to 6 servings

Orange Wasabi Cabbage Salad

This festive winter salad is a nice addition to a holiday celebration meal. And since it comes together quickly, it can also be made as part of a weeknight dinner. You can add the dressing up to 30 to 60 minutes before serving to improve the flavors.

Salad:
3 to 4 cups thinly sliced green cabbage
3 to 4 cups thinly sliced red cabbage
4 to 5 large carrots, peeled or shredded
3 to 4 green onions, sliced into thin rounds

Dressing:
½ cup freshly squeezed orange juice
¼ cup extra virgin olive oil
2 tablespoons apple cider vinegar or coconut vinegar
1 to 2 tablespoons wasabi powder
½ teaspoon Herbamare

Use either your food processor fitted with the slicing disc to cut the cabbage or slice it thinly with a sharp knife. For the carrots you can use a vegetable peeler to make wide, thin strips or shred them. Place all salad ingredients into a large bowl and toss together.

To make the dressing, add all ingredients to a blender, or use an immersion blender in a glass jar, and blend on high for 30 seconds or so. I find that the wasabi powder doesn't mix in very well unless blended. Pour dressing over salad, toss, and serve.

Yield: 6 servings

Pan-Fried Steak Salad with Sesame Ginger Dressing

Remember to always purchase organic grass-fed beef for the best health benefits. Use either fillet mignon or sirloin steak. Fillet mignon is more tender but also more expensive. Plan for about 3 to 4 ounces per person. Serve this delicious, nourishing salad as a main dish with a side of Coconut-Lime Cauliflower Rice, page 236, or baked yams.

Steak:
1 pound fillet mignon or sirloin steak
toasted sesame oil
wheat-free tamari or coconut aminos
white pepper

Salad:
1 head romaine lettuce, rinsed and thinly sliced
3 to 4 green onions, sliced into thin rounds
2 to 3 carrots, shredded
½ cup slivered almonds
handful fresh cilantro, chopped

Dressing:
¼ cup sesame seeds, lightly toasted
¼ cup extra virgin olive oil
3 tablespoons brown rice vinegar or coconut vinegar
1 tablespoon toasted sesame oil
1 to 2 tablespoons wheat-free tamari or coconut aminos
2 tablespoons chopped celery
1-inch piece of fresh ginger, peeled
1 to 2 cloves garlic

Heat a skillet over medium-high heat for a few minutes until very hot. While it is heating, rub the steak with a little sesame oil and tamari on both sides then sprinkle with a small amount of white pepper.

Add a few teaspoons of sesame oil to the pan. Add the steak and cook on each side for 3 to 5 minutes or until desired doneness. Three minutes for a rare steak and 5 minutes for medium to medium-well. It depends on the thickness of the steak. Use tongs to pick up steak to cook the sides. Cook each side for about one minute. Remove steak from pan and place onto a plate. Let the steak rest for 5 minutes to keep the juices in. It will continue to cook a little. Then slice into thin strips with a sharp knife.

Toss the salad ingredients together in a large bowl, set aside.

To make the dressing, place all ingredients into a blender and blend on high until smooth and creamy. Just before serving, placed the sliced steak on top of the salad and pour the dressing over it. Serve immediately.

Yield: 4 servings

Pear Pomegranate Salad with Orange Vinaigrette

This salad makes a beautiful addition to your holiday table. To prep this salad ahead of time, first make the dressing and store it in a tightly sealed glass jar in the fridge. Prep the pomegranate by removing the arils (beautiful juicy red seeds) and storing them in a covered container in the fridge. Toast the pecans, cool them, and store in a sealed container on the counter. Then just before serving the salad, slice the pear and toss all ingredients together in a large salad bowl.

Salad:
8 to 10 cups mixed organic greens
1 pomegranate
1 ripe, firm pear, cored and sliced thin
1 cup pecans, roasted

Dressing:
¼ cup extra virgin olive oil
2 tablespoons freshly squeezed orange juice
2 tablespoons apple cider vinegar
½ teaspoon Herbamare or sea salt
¼ teaspoon freshly grated orange peel
pinch cinnamon

Add the greens to a large bowl. Cut the pomegranate in half and gently remove the arils; add them to the greens. Add the sliced pear and roasted pecans set aside.

To make the dressing, place all ingredients into a glass jar and shake well. Pour dressing over salad and toss again. Serve immediately.

Yield: 6 servings

Ingredient Tip:

To roast the pecans, place them into a small glass baking dish or pie plate. Roast in a preheated 350 degree oven for 10 to 15 minutes. Cool on a plate before chopping.

Kitchen Tip:

When you take a salad dressing made with olive oil out of the refrigerator it will need to warm up before using it. Some of the fats in olive oil naturally harden at refrigerated temperatures. We usually place the jar into a large mug half-full of hot water for a few minutes and then shake.

Pecan Crusted Chicken and Apple Salad

This nourishing salad can be served for as a main dish. Use a head of lettuce or use a bag of mixed organic greens. Serve with roasted winter squash and the Rosemary Sea Salt Breadsticks, page 133, for a complete meal. Our children like to have the chicken on the side of their salad so I keep it all separate and assemble each plate individually.

Chicken:
2 large organic chicken breasts, pounded
1 ½ cups pecans, finely ground
¼ teaspoon sea salt
¼ teaspoon freshly ground black pepper
¼ cup arrowroot powder
¼ cup water
olive oil for cooking

Salad:
1 head red leaf lettuce, rinsed and spun dry
1 tart apple, cored and thinly sliced
½ small red onion, thinly sliced
½ cup dried cranberries

Dressing:
¼ cup extra virgin olive oil
3 tablespoons balsamic vinegar
1 tablespoon maple syrup
1 teaspoon Dijon mustard
¼ teaspoon sea salt

Preheat oven to 400 degrees F. Rinse the chicken breasts, pound and set aside. Place the pecans, salt, and pepper in a food processor and process until finely ground, stopping before they turn into nut butter. Pour into a shallow, wide bowl. In another shallow bowl, whisk together the arrowroot and water. Dip each chicken breast in the arrowroot mixture so it is well coated. Then dip each breast into the ground pecans, coating completely. Set chicken breasts onto a plate.

Heat a large, heavy-bottom skillet over medium heat. Once it has heated for a few minutes, add about 3 tablespoons of olive oil. Then add the chicken breasts. Cook for 2 minutes on each side, any longer and the pecans will begin to burn. Transfer chicken to an 8 x 8-inch baking dish and cook for 15 to 20 minutes or until done. Cool for at least 5 minutes before slicing.

Add all salad ingredients to a large bowl. To make the dressing, add all ingredients to a small jar; cover and shake. Slice the chicken breasts into strips and place over the salad. Drizzle with the dressing and serve immediately.

Yield: 4 servings

Picnic Coleslaw

Crunchy cabbage coleslaw is always needed in the summertime to serve with barbecued chicken or fish, corn on the cob, roasted potatoes, and raw fruit pies! In this recipe I've made my own mock vegan mayo and the results are quite satisfying. If you have red cabbage then use a mix of red and green for a more colorful salad.

8 cups shredded green cabbage
2 large carrots, shredded
¼ cup chopped chives

Dressing:
½ cup raw cashews
½ cup water
¼ cup extra virgin olive oil
2 tablespoons apple cider vinegar
½ teaspoon Herbabamre
small handful fresh parsley

Place the shredded cabbage, carrots, and chives into a large bowl, set aside.

Place the cashews and water into a high-powered blender; blend until smooth. Then add the olive oil, vinegar, Herbamare, and parsley; blend again until the ingredients are just incorporated. If you blend it too long the parsley will completely break down, creating a green dressing.

Pour dressing over cabbage and toss together. Taste and add more salt if necessary. Refrigerate until ready to serve.

Yield: 6 servings

Kitchen Tip:

If you don't own a high powdered blender then place the cashews and water into your blender and let them soak for at least 3 hours. Then add the remaining ingredients and blend.

Nutrition Tip:

Cashews are lower in overall fat content than other nuts and are high in monounsaturated fats, specifically oleic acid—the same fat found in olive oil.

Purple Potato Salad with Radishes and Chives

This potato salad has a creamy dairy-free dressing made from shelled hemp seeds and raw cashews. It is incredibly nutritious, full of omega-3 fatty acids and magnesium. The dressing, once chilled in the fridge for a few hours, also makes a great dip for raw vegetables. If you cannot find purple potatoes, use red or yellow potatoes instead.

Salad:
2 ½ pounds purple potatoes
1 to 2 bunches radishes, thinly sliced
1 cup chopped parsley
½ cup snipped chives
freshly ground black pepper

Dressing:
¾ cup raw cashews
6 tablespoons hemp seeds
¾ cup water
3 tablespoons extra virgin olive oil
3 tablespoons apple cider vinegar
1 to 2 cloves garlic
½ to 1 teaspoon Herbamare
1 to 2 teaspoons dried dill

Place the whole purple potatoes in a pot of water. Bring to a boil and cook for about 15 minutes or until tender. Watch carefully as timing will depend on the size of your potatoes. You don't want to overcook potatoes or they will become waterlogged and mushy for the salad.

Once cooked place onto a plate to cool, then cut into chunks for the salad. I always leave the peels on. Place the potato chunks into a large bowl and add the remaining salad ingredients.

To make the dressing, add all ingredients, except dill, to a high-powered blender and blend until ultra smooth and creamy. Taste and add more Herbamare if necessary. Add the dried dill and turn the blender to low speed for a few seconds to incorporate it. Pour dressing over salad and gently toss together. Cover and refrigerate until ready to serve. The salad is best served at room temperature.

Yield: 6 servings

Raw Kale Avocado Salad

Serve this salad alone as a super food meal or serve it over cooked quinoa with a bean soup. If you plan to keep the salad for a few days in your refrigerator then wait to add the avocado until serving. Feel free to add other seasonal vegetables to the salad—grated carrots, grated beets, diced heirloom tomatoes, or chopped parsley are all delicious.

Salad:
1 large bunch curly kale
2 avocados, diced
1 cup sunflower seeds, soaked for 6 to 8 hours

Dressing:
3 to 4 tablespoons freshly squeezed lemon juice
3 to 4 tablespoons extra virgin olive oil
1 to 2 cloves garlic, crushed
½ teaspoon Herbamare or sea salt
freshly ground black pepper

Remove the tough stems from the bottom of the kale leaves, then chop the kale into small pieces. Place it into a colander and rinse it well. Drain and pat dry with a towel, then place it into a large bowl.

In a small bowl, whisk together the dressing. Add the dressing to the salad and gently massage it into the kale with your hands. This will soften it almost immediately. Add the diced avocado. Drain and rinse the sunflower seeds and add them to the salad as well. Gently toss together. Serve.

Yield: 4 to 6 servings

Nutrition Tip:

Kale's nutrient density is unparalleled. It is packed full of vitamin K, vitamin C, carotenoids, and antioxidants. The nutrients in kale provide immense protection against oxidative stress and chronic inflammation.

Raw Kale Salad with Lemon Tahini Dressing

When kale is tender and young it is best eaten raw. You'll find it is slightly sweeter and not very bitter. This salad pairs well with just about any meal. Serve it with a bean soup and dinner rolls or as part of a summer picnic. Our children think this kale salad is one of the best and will eat platefuls of it!

1 large bunch curly kale

Dressing:
¼ cup tahini
¼ cup extra virgin olive oil
¼ cup freshly squeezed lemon juice
1 to 2 cloves garlic, crushed
1 teaspoon Herbamare
freshly ground black pepper

Optional Additions:
shredded carrots
chopped parsley
snipped fresh chives
toasted sunflower seeds

Remove the tough stems from the bottom of the kale leaves, then chop the kale into small pieces. Place it into a colander and rinse it well. Drain and pat dry with a towel, then place it into a large bowl.

In a small bowl, whisk together the ingredients for the dressing. It will taste very lemony but once it is mixed with the kale the flavors will balance out.

Pour the dressing over the kale and toss it together. Use your hands to massage the dressing into the kale to soften it. Add any optional additions and serve.

Salad will keep in the fridge for up to 3 days. Serve at room temperature.

Yield: 4 to 6 servings

Roasted Beet Salad with Orange Vinaigrette

This salad is delicious as is and also works served over mixed baby greens. I like to serve this with Herb Roasted Halibut, page 319, and cooked quinoa for a balanced family meal. This salad also makes a great potluck dish. It can easily be made ahead of time. Just wait to add the walnuts until ready to serve.

6 large beets, trimmed
1 cup walnuts, roasted
½ cup chopped parsley

Dressing:
¼ cup freshly squeezed orange juice
¼ cup extra virgin olive oil
2 tablespoons champagne vinegar
½ teaspoon orange zest
sea salt and black pepper to taste

Optional:
crumbled feta cheese

Preheat oven to 350 degrees F.

Trim the greens off the beets and any root but don't peel them and place them in a casserole dish with a lid. Roast the beets in the preheated oven for approximately 1 ½ hours. Timing depends on the size of your beets. Smaller beets will take closer to an hour while very large beets can take up to 2 hours.

While the beets are cooking place the walnuts in a pie plate and roast for 10 to 12 minutes in the 350 degree oven. Once they are cool enough to handle, coarsely chop them.

After the beets are cooked and cool enough to handle, remove the skins; they should just slip off. Trim the ends then slice the beets in half lengthwise. Take each half and slice into ¼-inch thick half moons.

Place the beets, walnuts, and parsley into a large bowl and toss together.

In a smaller bowl, whisk together the ingredients for the dressing. Pour dressing over beets and toss together.

Yield: 6 servings

Smoked Salmon Salad with Honey Mustard Dressing

This salad and dressing was inspired by a salad served at a local, organic pizzeria called Seven Loaves. They serve their salad with organic shredded buffalo mozzarella on top, which is quite delicious. If you can tolerate dairy, try sprinkling shredded cheese over this salad.

Salad:
1 head red leaf lettuce, rinsed and spun dry
1 cup smoked salmon
1 small raw beet, peeled and very thinly sliced
½ small red onion, very thinly sliced
large handful alfalfa sprouts
½ to 1 cup sunflower seeds, toasted

Dressing:
¼ cup raw honey
¼ cup brown mustard
¼ cup extra virgin olive oil
1 to 2 tablespoons apple cider vinegar
¼ teaspoon sea salt

Place the lettuce into a large salad bowl, tear into pieces, and top with the smoked salmon, raw beet slices, red onion, sprouts, and toasted sunflower seeds. Set aside.

In a small jar, add the ingredients for the dressing. Screw a lid onto the jar and shake well until combined. If you are going to eat the entire salad in one sitting then dress the salad just before serving. If not, have each person serve themselves.

Store remaining dressing in the refrigerator for up to 3 weeks.

Yield: 4 to 6 servings

Spicy Green Salad with Blueberry Vinaigrette

We love to make this blueberry vinaigrette any time of year with the blueberries we harvested and froze during late summer. The flavors mingle very well with a spicy green salad mix and toasted hazelnuts. If you don't have access to a spicy salad mix then use whatever lettuce varieties are available.

Salad:
8 cups spicy mixed greens, rinsed and spun dry
2 to 3 carrots, sliced into rounds
1 to 2 green onions, thinly sliced
1 cup hazelnuts, roasted and chopped

Dressing:
⅓ cup fresh or frozen blueberries
⅓ cup champagne vinegar
½ cup extra virgin olive oil
1 tablespoon honey
½ teaspoon Herbamare or sea salt

Place all ingredients for the salad into a large bowl, toss together, and set aside.

To make the dressing, add all ingredients to a blender and puree for about 30 seconds until smooth. Pour into a jar for serving and storing.

Serve salad alongside the dressing. Store unused dressing in a sealed glass jar in the refrigerator for up to a week.

Yield: 4 to 6 servings

Ingredient Tip:

To toast hazelnuts, preheat the oven to 350 degrees F. Place hazelnuts into a pie plate and then toast them in the oven for about 15 to 20 minutes. Remove from oven and let them cool on a plate. Chop hazelnuts on a wooden cutting board and add them to the salad.

Spicy Summer Black Bean Salad

Nearly all of these ingredients can be purchased at our local Farmer's Market in the summertime. This fresh salad is full of antioxidants, vitamins (especially vitamin C), and live enzymes from the raw vegetables. It is low in fat and high in fiber—a perfect cholesterol lowering meal. Serve it for a party or bring it to a potluck. It can also be served in lettuce leaves as a wrap or taco.

Salad:
6 cups cooked black beans
4 cups chopped fresh heirloom tomatoes
3 ears raw corn, cut off the cob
3 spicy peppers such as jalapeno or banana peppers, diced finely
1 red bell pepper, diced
2 cups sliced green onions or chopped sweet onions
1 cup chopped cilantro

Dressing:
¼ cup extra virgin olive oil
2 limes, juiced
2 teaspoons Herbamare or sea salt
1 to 2 teaspoons ground cumin

Place all salad ingredients into a large glass bowl.

In a separate bowl, whisk together the ingredients for the dressing. Pour dressing over salad and gently toss together. Serve immediately or store in the fridge for later

Yield: 6 servings

Kitchen Tip:

To cut the corn from the cob, hold the corn upright over a plate. Use a serrated knife and a gentle sawing action to cut the corn away. To easily remove the seeds from hot peppers, hold the pepper upright on a cutting board and cut away the sides into fourths, leaving the "core." Rinse the pepper pieces under running water to remove any seeds.

Super Green Salad

This recipe is delicious anytime. Serve it with beans and rice or baked fish. Use it as part of the filling for the Sunflower Seed Pate and Collard Wraps, page 393.

Salad:
8 cups thinly sliced dark greens (kale, collards, chard)
¼ cup extra virgin olive oil
the juice of 1 lemon
2 to 3 cloves garlic, crushed
1 teaspoon sea salt

Optional Additions:
grated carrots
toasted sunflower seeds

Place all ingredients for the salad and any desired optional additions into a large bowl. Mix together well. Let rest for about 30 minutes before serving. Toss again.

Yield: 4 to 6 servings

Thai Cucumber Salad

We grow both Thai basil and cucumbers in our garden, both of which our children like to snack on all summer long. This salad has a little zing from the coconut vinegar and a little spice from the red chili flakes. Feel free to adjust amounts to your liking. Serve with the Thai Fish Curry, page 321, for a nutritious summer meal.

2 medium cucumbers, cut into thin slices
½ cup thinly sliced Thai basil
2 to 3 cloves garlic, chopped
½ to 1 teaspoon crushed red chili flakes
3 tablespoons coconut vinegar
1 tablespoon coconut nectar
sea salt to taste

In a medium-sized bowl toss together the sliced cucumbers, basil, garlic, and chili flakes. In a small separate bowl, whisk together the coconut vinegar and coconut nectar. Pour over cucumbers. Season with sea salt to taste. The salad is best served after the cucumbers have marinated for about an hour. Leftovers can be stored in the refrigerator for up to 4 days.

Yield: 4 to 6 servings

Coconut-Lime Cauliflower "Rice"

Using cauliflower is a fantastic grain-free option to rice. By grinding it up in the food processor you get the look and consistency of white rice but with many more nutrients and cancer-fighting compounds such as sulfurophane. Serve this "rice" dish along with baked fish or roasted chicken and a green salad.

1 medium head cauliflower
1 cup coconut milk
½ cup water or chicken stock
1 to 2 tablespoons freshly squeezed lime juice
2 cloves garlic, crushed
1 to 2 teaspoons grated ginger
½ to 1 teaspoon crushed red chili flakes
½ teaspoon Herbamare or sea salt

Garnishes:
sliced green onions
chopped cilantro
lime zest

Break or cut the cauliflower into smaller pieces and place them into a food processor fitted with the "s" blade. Pulse until the cauliflower is coarsely ground. It takes about two minutes of pulsing to accomplish this. Be careful not to over-process and turn the cauliflower to mush.

In a large skillet or wide pot, such as an 11-inch deep skillet, heat the coconut milk, water or stock, lime juice, garlic, ginger, chili flakes, and salt over medium heat. Once the mixture is simmering add the ground cauliflower.

Stir together and simmer uncovered for 10 to 15 minutes, stirring every few minutes, or until the cauliflower is cooked to your liking. Garnish with sliced green onions, chopped cilantro, and lime zest. Serve hot.

Yield: 4 to 6 servings

Creamed Kale

Serve this imple dairy-free recipe with cooked quinoa and black-eyed peas or grilled chicken. You might think that 10 to 12 cups of chopped kale is a lot, but remember that it cooks down considerably. We don't have any leftovers in our house when I make this recipe!

10 to 12 cups finely chopped kale

Sauce:
2 to 3 tablespoons extra virgin olive oil
1 small onion, chopped (about 1 heaping cup)
2 cloves garlic, chopped
½ cup raw cashews
2 cups water
½ jalapeno pepper, seeded
1 tablespoon freshly squeezed lemon juice
2 tablespoons nutritional yeast
1 to 2 teaspoons Herbamare

Heat an 11 or 12-inch skillet over medium heat. Add the olive oil, then add onions and garlic and sauté for about 5 minutes or until softened and beginning to change color. Add them to a high-powered blender along with the cashews, water, jalapeno pepper, lemon juice, nutritional yeast, and Herbamare. Blend until smooth and creamy.

Place the sauce and chopped kale into your large skillet and simmer for 10 to 15 minutes or until kale has softened and sauce has thickened. Taste and adjust salt and seasonings if necessary.

Yield: 4 to 6 servings

Variation:

In the summertime, when fresh organic sweet corn is in season, I like to cut the kernals off of 2 to 3 ears of corn and add it to the cooking kale. It provides a nice color contrast and a slight crunch.

Curried Root Vegetables

This savory root vegetable dish can be adjusted to the number of people you are serving. I have a large family and we like leftovers so I cook larger batches. If you are cooking only for one, two, or three, I suggest you cut this recipe in half. Also, make sure to cut all of your vegetables so they are about the same size, otherwise some will turn to mush while others may still be underdone at the end of cooking time. Serve over quinoa and garnish with chopped cilantro if desired.

2 to 4 tablespoons extra virgin olive oil or coconut oil
1 teaspoon whole cumin seeds
1 large onion, chopped
2 cloves garlic, crushed
4 teaspoons mild curry powder
1 teaspoon ground cumin
½ teaspoon turmeric
pinch or two cayenne pepper
2 to 3 teaspoons sea salt
3 medium parsnips, peeled and cut into chunks
3 large carrots, peeled and cut into chunks
2 medium yams, peeled and cut into chunks
6 small yellow or red potatoes, cut into chunks
4 cups chopped fresh tomatoes
2 cups water

Heat a cast iron dutch oven or 6-quart pot over medium heat. Add the oil, then add the cumin seeds and cook for about 30 to 60 seconds or until fragrant. Add the onions and sauté for about 10 minutes until softened and beginning to change color. Add the spices and sauté for another 60 seconds.

Next add the root vegetables and sauté for a few minutes to coat with the spices and oil, then add the tomatoes and water. Partially cover the pot with a lid, and simmer on medium heat, stirring occasionally for 25 to 30 minutes or until vegetables are tender. Cooking time will vary depending on what size you cut your vegetables.

Store leftovers in a tightly sealed container in the refrigerator for up to a week.

Yield: 8 servings

Lemon Garlic Sautéed Chard

This is one of our favorite methods of preparing fresh chard. The fresh lemon juice and crushed garlic pair perfectly with the tender chard. Serve this recipe with baked fish and roasted potatoes or a bean soup and a cooked whole grain.

2 tablespoons extra virgin olive oil
3 to 5 cloves garlic, crushed
2 bunches chard, rinsed and chopped
1 to 2 tablespoons freshly squeezed lemon juice
Herbamare or sea salt to taste

Heat an 11 or 12-inch skillet over medium heat. Add the oil and then the garlic; sauté for about 30 seconds. Quickly add the chard (it cooks best if it is still wet from rinsing); sauté for 5 minutes or until tender. Turn off heat, add the lemon juice and season to taste with sea salt or Herbamare. Serve immediately.

Yield: 4 to 6 servings

Sautéed Winter Greens with Caramelized Onions

With just a few ingredients, this recipe can be prepared in a snap. Kale and collards are great for breakfast, lunch, or dinner. I like to serve sautéed greens over cooked quinoa with two fried pastured eggs for breakfast. For dinner, serve this recipe with beans and rice or roasted chicken.

1 to 2 tablespoons extra virgin olive oil or coconut oil
1 large red onion, cut into crescent moons
1 large bunch kale, thinly sliced
1 large bunch collard greens, thinly sliced
Herbamare or sea salt to taste

Heat a large skillet over medium-low heat. Add the oil and then the onions. I like to also add a few dashes of sea salt to help draw out moisture from the onions. Sauté onions for 15 to 20 minutes or until caramelized and very fragrant. Keep the temperature steady and on the lower side so they don't cook too quickly and burn.

Add the kale and collards; sauté for 5 to 10 minutes, depending on the tenderness of the kale and desired doneness. You can add a few tablespoons of water to quickly finish the cooking by steaming if desired. Season with Herbamare or sea salt to taste. Serve warm.

Yield: 4 to 6 servings

Sautéed Snow Peas and Patty Pan Squash

This is a great quick recipe to make in summertime when the summer vegetables are in abundance! By doing a quick sauté the vegetables stay crispy and bright with all of their vibrant flavors intact. Serve with barbecued chicken or the Herb Roasted Halibut, page 319.

1 tablespoon extra virgin olive oil
3 small patty pan squash, quartered then sliced into ¼-inch thick slices
½ pound fresh snow peas
¼ teaspoon sea salt
1 to 2 teaspoons fresh thyme leaves

Heat a large skillet over medium-high heat. Add olive oil, then add the sliced patty pan squash and snow peas; sauté for about 5 to 7 minutes, stirring frequently. Turn heat down if they start to brown. You will want to have your burner set at a temp that will quickly cook but not brown or burn the vegetables.

Turn off heat and sprinkle with sea salt and fresh thyme leaves. Serve immediately.

Yield: 4 to 6 servings

Sautéed Brussels Sprouts with Shallots and Cranberries

This recipe is very quick to prepare. If you are planning on making this for your Thanksgiving meal, have all ingredients prepared ahead of time and about 20 minutes before you are ready to sit down begin sautéing the shallots. The recipe takes about 12 minutes from start to finish. If you don't have slivered almonds then try using chopped pecans instead.

2 tablespoons extra virgin olive oil
4 shallots, thinly sliced
½ cup slivered almonds
2 pounds brussels sprouts, trimmed and halved lengthwise
1 teaspoon Herbamare or sea salt
½ cup dried fruit juice sweetened cranberries
½ cup water
freshly ground black pepper

Heat an 11 or 12-inch skillet over medium heat. Add oil, then shallots; sauté for about 2 minutes then add slivered almonds, brussels sprouts, and Herbamare; sauté for about 5 minutes.

Add the dried cranberries and water. Cover pan and cook, stirring occasionally, for 5 to 10 minutes. Smaller brussels sprouts will take closer to 5 minutes, while large ones will take closer to 10 minutes. Cook until desired tenderness is reached. Season with freshly ground black pepper to taste.

Yield: 6 servings

Roasted Brussels Sprouts

This recipe is so easy and simple. Once you try it, I am sure you will make it again and again like we do! When brussels sprouts are in season during late autumn and winter, we literally make this recipe at least three times a week.

1 to 1 ½ pounds brussels sprouts, ends trimmed and sliced in half
1 to 2 tablespoons extra virgin olive oil
a few dashes of sea salt or Herbamare
freshly ground black pepper

Preheat oven to 425 degrees F.

Place halved brussels sprouts into a 9 x 13-inch glass baking dish and toss with olive oil, salt, and pepper.

Roast for 10 to 20 minutes depending on the size. Smaller brussels sprouts will take about 10 minutes while very large ones can take up to 25 minutes.

Yield: 4 servings

Nutrition Tip:

Sulphur compounds in brussels sprouts have been shown to benefit the liver by altering the function of liver enzymes. These enzymes allow for the metabolism of hormones and other fat-soluble substances that the liver may otherwise perceive as toxic. Sulphur compounds also up-regulate the gene expression of antioxidants in our bodies. Cancer researchers have determined these substances to be so important that they recommend at least 2 to 3 servings of cruciferous vegetables per week and some suggest as much as 1 to 2 servings per day.

Roasted Cauliflower

For those who aren't a fan of cauliflower, you'll probably love it prepared this way. When our twin boys were young toddlers they would literally fight over the serving dish of roasted cauliflower on the dinner table. Sometimes I add a little freshly grated lemon zest to the roasted cauliflower, which adds a nice touch.

1 head cauliflower, cut into florets
2 tablespoons extra virgin olive oil
¼ teaspoon Herbamare
freshly ground black pepper

Preheat oven to 425 degrees F. Place the cauliflower florets into a 9 x 13-inch baking dish or large, rimmed cookie sheet. Toss with the olive oil, salt, and pepper.

Roast for 20 to 25 minutes or until tender. It works best to turn them once during baking though it isn't necessary.

Yield: 4 servings

Roasted Golden Beets

This is one of my favorite ways to prepare beets. The first roasting slowly cooks the beets to perfection and then the second roasting brings out their flavor while slightly caramelizing them. Roasted beets can be used to top any salad or eaten as a simple side dish. Use any variety of beets you have on hand. Top a plate of baby arugula with these roasted beets and toss with the Champagne Vinaigrette, page 344.

4 medium golden beets, end trimmed
2 tablespoons coconut oil or extra virgin olive oil
¼ teaspoon sea salt
freshly ground black pepper

Preheat oven to 350 degrees F.

Place the beets into a small baking dish with a lid. Cover and bake for 2 hours. Once cool enough to handle, remove the skins. They should just slip right off, if not, use a small paring knife to remove them.

Turn the oven temperature up to 400 degrees F. Cut the beets into 1-inch cubes. Place into a rectangular glass baking dish. Toss with the olive oil, salt, and pepper.

Roast for about 40 to 45 minutes, turning once. Be careful not to overcook them as they can burn easily.

Yield: 4 servings

Chipotle Yam Fries

Yam fries are completely addicting, especially with the spice from the chipotle pepper! I've made these using Russet potatoes before with equally delicious results. Serve them with the Spicy Black-Eyed Pea Soup, page 194, or the Chipotle Lime Roasted Chicken, page 327.

2 medium yams, peeled
2 to 3 tablespoons extra virgin olive oil, ghee, or coconut oil
¼ to ½ teaspoon chipotle chili pepper
2 teaspoons smoked paprika
¼ to ½ teaspoon Herbamare or sea salt

Cut the yams lengthwise into ¼-inch cubed strips. I take the yam and cut it lengthwise first into ¼-inch thick slices then cut each slice into ¼-inch fries.

Place the yam fries into a square baking pan and cover with water and sprinkle with about 1 tablespoon of sea salt. Soak for about 30 minutes. This helps remove excess moisture and starch so the fries cook properly. Once soaked drain the fries well, rinse, and pat dry using a towel. Make sure to dry them well!

Preheat oven to 400 degrees F.

Place yam fries onto a large cookie sheet and toss with the oil, spices, and salt. Spread out evenly onto the pan. Place into preheated oven and bake for 20 minutes. Use a spatula to carefully turn the fries over. Bake for another 20 minutes. Check for doneness at this time by trying one. Bake them for a few minutes longer if they are not quite done.

Let cool slightly then serve!

Yield: 4 to 6 servings

Rutabaga Fries

Practically any starchy vegetable can replace potatoes when making fries. I've used parsnips, celery root, and sweet potatoes, but my favorite is the humble rutabaga. You can keep it simple and season them with sea salt, or for more flavor, try adding freshly ground black pepper, curry powder, or dried thyme.

2 medium rutabagas, peeled
2 tablespoons extra virgin olive oil, ghee, or coconut oil
Herbamare or sea salt

Preheat the oven to 400 degrees F.

Slice the rutabagas into ¼-inch rounds then cut into strips, about ¼-inch wide so they look like French fries. Place them onto one large cookie sheet. Add the olive oil and a few dashes of Herbamare or sea salt and toss together. Make sure they are not too close together on the pan otherwise they will not be able to steam off some of their liquid and will get rather mushy. Use two cookie sheets if needed.

Bake for about 20 to 25 minutes, then take a spatula and flip them over. Bake for another 10 minutes or so or until cooked though and lightly golden.

Yield: 4 servings

Mashed Cauliflower with Chives

This is a low-glycemic alternative to mashed potatoes. While I love potatoes, sometimes I can feel a little "weighed down" after eating them. This is diabetic-friendly, so go ahead and enjoy them with roast chicken and gravy! I've also made this recipe before into a "cheesy" casserole by adding a few tablespoons of nutritional yeast to the food processor along with the cauliflower.

2 small heads cauliflower or 1 large one
3 to 4 tablespoons organic butter or olive oil
2 tablespoons snipped fresh chives
Herbamare and freshly ground black pepper

Cut the stems off of the cauliflower. Chop into florets. Place the cauliflower into a pot fitted with a steamer basket. Add a few inches of water, cover, and steam for about 7 to 10 minutes or until tender.

Drain the cauliflower completely and place it into a food processor fitted with the "s" blade. Add the butter and process until creamy and smooth. Add the chives, Herbamare, and black pepper, pulse until combined. Taste and add more Herbamare if necessary. You can either serve this as is or put it into a buttered casserole dish and bake at 450 degrees until lightly browned on top.

Yield: 6 servings

Olive Oil Garlic Mashed Potatoes

This dairy-free recipe is just as creamy and flavorful as one made with milk and butter. Although you might think that using six cloves of garlic could be overpowering, the garlic flavor is actually quite subtle. Draining the cooked potatoes and reserving the liquid to help mash the potatoes is a great alternative to using any type of milk. I find that using dairy-free milk gives too much sweetness to mashed potatoes.

6 medium russet potatoes, cut into chunks
6 cloves garlic, peeled
½ cup reserved cooking liquid
6 tablespoons extra virgin olive oil
½ to ¾ teaspoon Herbamare

Wash or scrub the potatoes and cut them into 1 to 2-inch chunks. I like to leave the peels on, which keeps valuable nutrients in you meal.

Place potato chunks and whole garlic cloves into a 6-quart pot and cover with an inch or two of water. Boil at medium-high heat for 15 to 20 minutes or until potatoes are tender.

Drain off all of the liquid into a bowl or liquid glass measure. Measure ½ cup and add it back into the pot. Add the olive oil and Herbamare. Use a hand-held electric mixer to whip the potatoes. Beat for one to two minutes or until light and fluffy. Taste and add more Herbamare if necessary.

Yield: 4 to 6 servings

Whipped Sweet Potatoes with Cardamom

This is one of our favorite ways to enjoy sweet potatoes. Serve with roasted chicken, gravy, and sautéed kale for a balanced meal. You can use any milk of your choice but I prefer to use Raw Almond Milk, page 481. I normally use dark orange sweet potatoes but white sweet potatoes work as well.

2 to 3 pounds sweet potatoes, about 5 medium
½ cup almond milk
¼ to ½ teaspoon cardamom

Peel the sweet potatoes and cut them into chunks. Place them into a 3-quart pot and add an inch or two of water. Cover and cook over medium heat until tender, about 10 minutes.

Drain off the cooking water. Add milk and cardamom and beat with an electric mixer until light and fluffy. Serve warm.

Yield: 6 to 8 servings

Zucchini Almond Bake

My children like to call this recipe "Cheesy Zucchini Bake" because the flavors are reminiscent of cheese! Greek seasoning can be made by combining sea salt, dried oregano, garlic, dried lemon peel, ground black pepper, and dried marjoram together in a small jar. Serve with roasted chicken or a fresh bean and vegetable salad.

2 to 3 medium zucchini, sliced
1 large sweet onion, cut into crescent moons
½ cup blanched almond flour
2 to 3 tablespoons extra virgin olive oil
1 tablespoon Greek seasoning or Italian seasoning
½ teaspoon Herbamare

Preheat your oven to 375 degrees F.

Add about 1 tablespoon of olive oil to the bottom of a 10-inch deep dish pie plate. Add a layer of zucchini, next add a few onion slices, then sprinkle with a little Herbamare and Greek seasoning. Add about 3 tablespoons blanched almond flour.

Repeat by starting with a layer of zucchini again. Continue until you are out of ingredients. End with a layer of zucchini. Top with a few tablespoons blanched almond flour, Herbamare, and a drizzle of olive oil.

Bake uncovered for 40 to 45 minutes or until the desired doneness of the zucchini.

Yield: 6 servings

Whole Grains and Noodles

As you walk down a supermarket isle these days, "made with whole grains" or "whole grain goodness" are common labeling techniques used to promote the purchase of products. However, labels like these can be very misleading. In fact, just because a label says it is made with whole grains, doesn't make it a nourishing food. These products may contain some whole grain flour, but they are also filled with many other refined ingredients that are not beneficial for health.

What is a Whole Grain?

So, what exactly *is* a whole grain? Whole grains are the entire seeds of a plant. If you soak them in water for a period of time, they could germinate because they contain the bran, endosperm, and germ all intact. The bran forms a protective sheath around the grain holding all of the nutrients inside until it is ready to grow into a plant. The endosperm is the starchy part, the energy storehouse of the grain that is used for growing a plant. The germ is the embryo of the grain—the part that forms a new plant—where most of the healthy fats, vitamin E, B-vitamins, and antioxidants reside. It's very important to understand that processing whole grains removes the germ and bran leaving only the starchy endosperm. White rice and white flour are examples of refined grains or grain products. Refining grains removes about 25% of their protein and over seventeen nutrients that the body needs to properly assimilate the starchy part of the grain.

Gluten-Free Whole Grains

Gluten-free whole grains, which are the seeds of grasses, include brown rice, millet, teff, and sorghum. Pseudo-grains, which behave much like other whole grains but are actually the seeds of broad-leafed plants, include quinoa, amaranth, and buckwheat. Wild rice is not a grain nor the seed of a broad-leafed plant, but actually a seed of an aquatic grass native to North America.

Health Benefits of Grains

Whole grains are an excellent source of a wide variety of phenolic compounds, such as ferulic acid, vanillic acid, p-coumaric acid, anthocyanidins, quinines, and flavones. These compounds act in the body as antioxidants by donating hydrogen atoms to free radicals. In fact, certain whole grains such as corn, oats, and brown rice have a similar antioxidant capacity to that of berries and plums! Whole grains are also an excellent source of plant lignans, which have been shown to have strong antioxidant and phytoestrogenic effects.

They may provide protection against chronic diseases such as hormone-related cancers, diabetes, and heart disease. Actually, a plant-based diet rich in vegetables, whole grains, fish, and olive oil—such as the Mediterranean diet—has been found to significantly lower the risk of cardiovascular disease. Additionally, certain anti-nutrients present in whole grains such as phytic acid, lectins, protease inhibitors, amylase inhibitors, and saponins have been shown to lower plasma glucose, insulin, and cholesterol levels, and also lower the risk of certain cancers, such as colon cancer and breast cancer.

Whole Grains Promote Gut Health

Whole grains also contain some starches that are indigestible in the small intestine. They are then broken down—or fermented—by bacteria in the colon. These resistant starches and oligosaccharides actually promote GI health by acting as prebiotics, feeding beneficial bacteria in the colon, thereby decreasing pathogens and increasing short-chain fatty acid production, especially butyrate. Did you know that butyrate is the primary fuel for the cells that line the colon? Butyrate lowers inflammation and oxidative stress, while increasing mineral absorption and detoxifying enzymes!

The Phytic Acid Story

A hot topic surrounding whole grains is phytic acid. So let's delve into this subject in order to gain a better understanding of it. In order for a grain to sprout it must be soaked in water. In nature, you sow your seeds in the springtime so the rains can soak them and keep them moist in order for germination to happen. There is a compound in whole grains, legumes, nuts, seeds, and some tubers called phytic acid, otherwise known as inositol hexaphosphate or IP6. This very important compound stores phosphorus and other nutrients until exposed to water. Soaking the grain signals an enzyme, called phytase, to wake up. Phytase partially breaks down phytic acid, which frees nutrients allowing the grains to sprout and grow into plants. By soaking whole grains overnight in filtered water you can increase mineral availability as well as the digestibility of the proteins and carbohydrates in the grain. This is especially important for those who are dealing with mineral deficiencies and the symptoms associated with them, such as osteoporosis, iron-deficiency anemia, lowered immune function, learning disabilities, lack of taste/picky eating, muscle cramping, infertility, and dental carries. The minerals that have the most affinity for phytic acid are iron, calcium, magnesium, manganese, zinc, and copper—zinc and iron being the most influenced. Phytic acid can depress the bioavailability of dietary zinc, meaning that eating zinc-rich foods with phytate-rich foods at the same time can cause the two to bind together into insoluble complexes. Phytic acid can also substantially reduce the reabsorption of intestinal endogenous zinc.

Phytic Acid in Grains

Interestingly, phytic acid is found in higher amounts in oats, corn, and gluten grains such as wheat, barley, and rye. Soaking rolled oats doesn't break down much of the phytic acid because they do not contain enough phytase to break it down. The phytic acid in corn can be broken down through a traditional preparation called *nixtamalization*, a process in which the corn is soaked and cooked in limewater, an alkaline solution. If you eat corn chips, corn tortillas, tamales, or anything made from masa harina, it has undergone this process. Teff, buckwheat, amaranth, and sorghum grains contain the lowest amount of phytic acid. Additionally, buckwheat contains a high amount of phytase, the enzyme responsible for breaking down phytic acid. Soaking rolled oats with raw buckwheat groats overnight in water with the addition of a few tablespoons of cultured coconut water, yogurt, kefir, or apple cider vinegar can help break down the phytic acid in the rolled oats before cooking both grains into a porridge.

Mineral Deficiencies in Developing Countries

People in developing countries where grains make up most of the diet often have major mineral deficiencies, notably iron-deficiency anemia, zinc deficiency, and iodine deficiency. This is because they are not absorbing most of the minerals in the grains due to phytic acid and a low fruit intake (vitamin C is needed to absorb iron), and not eating other foods like meat, seafood, and vegetables in a great enough quantity to obtain enough available minerals. Higher intakes of phytic acid from whole grains are not always associated with mineral deficiencies and poor health. Those who eat a balanced diet and who have excellent digestive health may have no issues with unsoaked grains. Adequate stomach acid begins to break apart phytic acid and certain strains of beneficial bacteria in the gut produce phytase that helps to further break it down.

The Benefit of Phytic Acid

While phytic acid, or IP6, can cause some problems with mineral absorption, it has also been found to be a potent chelator of heavy metals and reduce the risk for numerous forms of cancer, type II diabetes, and kidney stone formation. The research on phytic acid reducing cancer cell growth is widespread. It seems that phytic acid stimulates the immune system by increasing the activity of natural killer cells. Directly, IP6 from rice bran reduces cell proliferation and increases the differentiation of cancer cells. Phytic acid can also suppress the oxidant damage associated with the oxygen radicals produced by the colonic bacteria, thereby protecting the intestinal epithelium.

It's All About Balance

In nature, there are always two sides to every story. For some people, whole grains may be part to blame for certain health issues and nutrient deficiencies, while for others they can be a miraculous healing food. Phytic acid is important to be aware of but nearly impossible to remove completely from the diet. The most important times to keep dietary phytic acid to a minimum are during pregnancy and early childhood when bone formation and growth are at their highest, and neuro-cognitive development is at its peak. Remember that unfermented soy products (fake meats, soy flour, and soy milk) are also very high in phytic acid; so are nuts, seeds, and beans. See the Getting Started chapter, page 51, for information on preparing these foods. We soak most of our grains before cooking them but still use unsoaked whole grain flours on occasion for cookies, muffins, and pancakes. Most of the homemade bread we make is from our gluten-free sourdough starter (see page 124). We also like to use sprouted gluten-free flours in place of regular stone-ground gluten-free flours for some of our recipes. I also make sure that some of our meals are grain-free and contain mineral-rich meat or poultry combined with non-starchy green vegetables for optimal mineral absorption. If your gut is in good shape, you are eating a diet full of fresh vegetables and fruits, and you don't rely on grain-based products with every meal and snack, you'll most likely have a good mineral status. And let's not forget about stress—chronic stress can cause more mineral depletion in the body than phytic acid! As with anything, you'll need to decide on a balance that works best for you.

How to Cook Whole Grains

Following these basic steps for cooking whole grains you can prepare highly nourishing, plant-rich meals for your family. We cook a few pots of whole grains every week to use in salads, soups, and as part of our main meals.

Sort

Sort through your grains for tiny rocks. Dry quinoa often contains small stones. Millet and buckwheat can be cross-contaminated with gluten grains if not certified gluten-free. Remove them from the rest of the grains before cooking. You can do this by pouring a third cup grain at a time onto a plate. Simply sort through them with your fingers and pick out the rocks or foreign material. This can be a very exciting job for young children to participate with!

Rinse

Some grains need to be rinsed prior to cooking to remove chaff, dust, or other debris. These include millet, quinoa, amaranth, and sometimes brown rice. Quinoa also has a bitter saponin coating that repels insects and birds and if not rinsed off, may cause digestive upset when consumed. To rinse grains, place them in a fine mesh strainer and run warm water through them until the water runs clear. You may also place them into a pot with water and swirl the grains around using your hand. Then pour off the water through a fine mesh strainer.

Soak

To soak grains, measure the desired amount and place into a bowl. Cover with at least one inch of warm water and add about 1 to 2 tablespoons of raw apple cider vinegar or raw coconut vinegar to each cup of grain. Soak, uncovered, on your kitchen counter for 12 to 24 hours. Then drain and rinse through a fine mesh strainer. Follow the guidelines on the next page for water requirements and cooking times.

Add Salt

Adding sea salt brings out the sweetness in grains and helps the grain to open up. Grains cooked without salt will taste flat. We generally use $\frac{1}{8}$ to $\frac{1}{4}$ teaspoon sea salt per one cup of dry grain.

Cook

To cook a whole grain you will need to first bring the pot of grain and water to a boil. Once boiling, immediately lower the heat to a simmer. Start timing when you turn down the heat to a simmer. Grains that have been boiled for too long may turn out tough and chewy. If your grains turn out mushy or clumped together, you may have added too much water or not brought the heat to a high enough temperature initially. It is also very important to use the proper cookware when cooking whole grains. A stainless steel pot with a thick bottom that contains an aluminum core will distribute the heat evenly and prevent the bottom layer of grains from getting burned. Use a 1-quart pot for cooking 1 cup of grain, a 2-quart pot for cooking 2 cups of grain, or a 3-quart pot for cooking 3 cups of grain.

No Stirring!

Remember to never stir a pot of cooking grains. Whole grains create their own steam holes so the top layer of grains cooks as evenly as the bottom layer of grains. When you stir a pot of cooking whole grains, the steam holes are destroyed, which causes some of your grain to never fully cook.

Cooking Chart for Soaked Whole Grains

Grains (1 cup dry)	Water (cups)	Cooking Times (minutes)	Yield (cups)
Short Grain Brown Rice	1 ½	50	3 ½
Long Grain Brown Rice	1 ¼ to 1 ½	45	3
Sweet Brown Rice	1 ½	50	2 ½
Wild Rice	1 ¾	75	4
Buckwheat	1	15	2
Millet	1 ½	25 to 30	3 ½
Quinoa	1 ¼ to 1 ½	12 to 15	3
Teff	-	-	-
Amaranth	-	-	-

Cooking Chart for Unsoaked Whole Grains

Grains (1 cup dry)	Water (cups)	Cooking Times (minutes)	Yield (cups)
Short Grain Brown Rice	2	55 to 60	3 ½
Long Grain Brown Rice	1 ¾	50	3
Sweet Brown Rice	2	55 to 60	2 ½
Wild Rice	2 ½	75	4
Buckwheat	1 ½	15 to 20	2
Millet	2 to 2 ½	30 to 35	3 ½
Quinoa	1 ¾	15 to 20	3
Teff	3	15 to 20	2 ½
Amaranth	2 ½	20 to 25	2

Grains

10 Steps to Creating Great Whole Grain Dishes

1.   **Make sure to follow the cooking chart on the previous page for cooking soaked grains**. Grains cooked with too much water will be too mushy to use for grain salads.

2.   **Use part homemade chicken stock and part water to cook your whole grains**. This adds more nutrients and flavor!

3.   **Make sure the cooked grain has cooled off to room temperature before using**. Hot grains can become mushy when stirred together.

4.   **Add olive oil to grain salads to not only add flavor and nutrients**, but also to help keep the grains from sticking together.

5.   **Add an acid such as lemon juice or vinegar to cold whole grain salads to make the flavors pop**! I typically use ⅓ to ½ cup per six cups of cooked grain.

6.   **Add cold or room temperature legumes to whole grain salads**. Hot, freshly cooked legumes can break apart when you mix the salad together.

7.   **Just before serving add toasted nuts or seeds to your whole grain salad**. Crispy toasted nuts or seeds become soft and soggy as they sit in the salad.

8.   **Use completely cooled grains for stir-fries**. Stir-frying hot grains causes them to lump together.

9.   **Allow refrigerated whole grain salads to warm to room temperature before serving**. Both olive oil and whole grains become hard in cold temperatures.

10.   **To reheat a grain casserole**, add to a small pot with a few tablespoons of water, cover, and warm on low heat. Grain dishes become harder when cold.

Lean, Mean, and Green Rice Salad

I've been making this salad for years without a recipe. It's our go-to salad when we have too much produce in our refrigerator that needs to be used up. Try adding fresh corn off the cob, cherry tomatoes, sliced baby zucchini, fresh peas, cooked beans, chopped mustard greens, and any chopped fresh herbs. The dressing is bright green, which turns the rice a beautiful green hue once all tossed together.

Salad:
6 cups cooked brown basmati rice
4 cups thinly sliced fresh kale
2 large carrots, grated

Dressing:
⅓ cup raw apple cider vinegar
⅓ cup extra virgin olive oil
large handful fresh parsley
small handful fresh basil
2 to 4 cloves garlic
1 teaspoon sea salt

Place the rice, kale, and carrots into a large bowl and toss together.

Place all of the ingredients for the dressing into a blender and blend on high for about 60 seconds, or until smooth and creamy. Pour over salad and toss together. Serve.

Salad will last in the refrigerator for up to 4 days.

Yield: 8 servings

Variation:

Replace the apple cider vinegar with freshly squeezed lemon juice.

Brown Rice, Black Bean, and Avocado Salad

Black beans, avocado, spicy peppers, and lime juice is one of our family's favorite combinations. Our children devour this salad. If you plan on storing this salad in the fridge then leave the avocado out. Simply place a little chopped avocado on top of each bowl at serving time. Serve this salad with the Chipotle Yam Fries, page 246, and the Cilantro Cabbage Slaw, page 213, for a balanced meal.

Salad:
6 to 7 cups cooked short grain brown rice
4 cups cooked black beans
4 green onions, sliced into thin rounds
1 cup chopped cilantro
2 jalapeno peppers, seeded and finely diced
2 avocados, diced

Dressing:
½ cup freshly squeezed lime juice
6 tablespoons extra virgin olive oil
1 teaspoon ground cumin
1 to 2 teaspoons Herbamare

Make sure your rice is completely cool, or better yet, a day old, before making this salad.

Place the rice into a large bowl and add the black beans, onions, cilantro, and jalapeno peppers. Add the ingredients for the dressing and toss together well. Taste and add more salt and seasonings if necessary. Top with the diced avocado and serve. Garnish with lime wedges if desired.

Yield: 8 servings

Coconut Rice

Coconut milk jazzes up plain brown rice to complement cooked beans, fish, or chicken. Serve it plain or with lime wedges, mint, cilantro, chopped hot peppers, chopped ginger, and chopped roasted peanuts for a Thai-style meal!

2 cups short grain brown rice
3 to 3 ½ cups water
1 cup coconut milk
¼ teaspoon sea salt

Place all ingredients into a 2-quart heavy-bottomed pot. Bring to a boil, cover, then reduce heat to low; cook for about 50 minutes. Remove pot from heat and let stand for at least 10 to 15 minutes before serving.

Yield: 6 to 8 servings

Kitchen Tip:

If using unsoaked brown rice, use 3 ½ cups water; if using soaked brown rice, use 3 cups water.

Nutrition Tip:

Rice has a high affinity for arsenic and is more likely to have higher levels than most other grains. The arsenic may come from the soil or water that the rice is grown in. Arsenic is likely to be higher in areas with arsenic laden herbicide use, oil refineries, or chemical plants. Jasmine and Basmati varieties of rice may come from India or Thailand where chemical use is not as regulated as in the US. In general, California grown rice has a lower risk of arsenic contamination. When rice is concentrated into either rice syrup or rice syrup solids, the potential for elevated arsenic levels increases tremendously. A recent study found that baby formulas with Organic Brown Rice Syrup (OBRS) had 20 times the amount of arsenic than formals not sweetened with OBRS. Similar elevations were found in energy bars and athletic energy "shots" that contained OBRS.

Dilled Adzuki Bean and Rice Salad

Any chopped raw vegetable can be added to this salad to liven the flavors and boost nutrition. Try diced cucumbers, red bell peppers, or broccoli. Serve this salad over fresh lettuce leaves and garnish each serving with toasted sunflower seeds and avocado slices.

Salad:
4 cups cooked long grain brown rice
3 cups cooked adzuki beans
4 large carrots, diced
4 green onions, sliced into rounds
small handful of fresh dill, finely chopped
butterhead lettuce leaves

Dressing:
4 tablespoons extra virgin olive oil
3 tablespoons raw apple cider vinegar
2 to 3 teaspoons fresh honey
1 teaspoon Herbamare
1 large garlic clove, crushed

Garnish:
toasted sunflower seeds
avocado slices

Place all ingredients for the salad, except for the lettuce leaves, into a large bowl. Set aside.

To make the dressing, place all ingredients into a glass jar with a tight fitting lid and shake well. Pour dressing over salad and toss together. Serve over lettuce leaves and garnish with toasted sunflower seeds and avocado slices if desired. Salad can be stored in an airtight container in the refrigerator for up to 5 days.

Yield: 4 to 6 servings

Everyday Rice Salad

This simple salad can be used as a base recipe to create many variations according to what you have on hand. In the springtime, try replacing the chicken with chopped hardboiled egg, diced radishes, and fresh dill. Use sea salt in place of the tamari. In the summertime when an abundance of fresh vegetables are available, add diced red bell peppers, blanched green beans, chopped kale, and chopped sugar snap peas. If you are vegan, replace the chicken with sautéed tofu or your favorite cooked bean. If you have a citrus sensitivity, replace the lemon juice with 1 to 2 tablespoons brown rice vinegar. Sometimes I like to sprinkle the salad with toasted sunflower seeds just before serving.

Chicken:

1 chicken breast, cut into 1-inch cubes

2 tablespoons wheat-free tamari or coconut aminos

2 to 3 teaspoons extra virgin olive oil or coconut oil

Salad:

5 cups cooked short grain brown rice

1 cup fresh or frozen peas

2 large carrots, diced

2 to 3 green onions, sliced into thin rounds

½ cup chopped parsley

2 tablespoons freshly squeezed lemon juice

2 tablespoons extra virgin olive oil

2 tablespoons wheat-free tamari or coconut aminos

To cook the chicken, first toss it with tamari or coconut aminos and let it marinate while you prepare the other ingredients. Heat a large skillet over medium-high heat, then add olive oil or coconut oil to the pan. Add the chicken and sauté until cooked through, about 5 minutes. You can cut through the largest piece to test for doneness. It should be opaque throughout.

Place the rice into a large bowl, add the chicken and salad ingredients. If the chicken and the rice are somewhat warm, the frozen peas will gently cook. If not, you can quickly blanch them in hot water for a minute or two, then drain and add to the salad. Toss everything together and serve.

Yield: 4 to 6 servings

Rice and Garbanzo Bean Salad with Kale

This super nutritious salad is even better on the second day after the kale has been softened from the olive oil and lemon juice! This salad makes an excellent quick lunch on the go and can also be packed in your child's lunchbox.

Salad:
4 cups cooked long grain brown rice
1 to 2 cups cooked garbanzo beans
2 cups chopped raw kale
2 large carrots, diced
3 green onions, thinly sliced
handful of fresh basil leaves, thinly sliced

Dressing:
¼ cup extra virgin olive oil
1 lemon, juiced
½ teaspoon Herbamare or sea salt
freshly ground black pepper

Place all ingredients for the salad into a large bowl and toss together. Add the dressing ingredients and toss again. Taste and adjust salt and pepper if needed.

Yield: 4 servings

Variation:

If you have chives growing in your garden then replace the green onions with a handful of snipped fresh chives.

Vegetable Fried Rice

This dish can easily be a meal by itself but with the addition of sautéed tofu, tempeh, chicken, or fish, you'll boost the protein content even more. You can vary the vegetables to what is in season. We like to add a lot of green vegetables to the mix, such as bok choy, kale, mustard greens, and spinach. Garnish with toasted sesame seeds for a beautiful presentation.

2 to 3 tablespoons coconut oil or sesame oil
½ cup raw cashews (optional)
5 green onions, cut diagonally into 2-inch pieces
1 cup broccoli florets
1 cup cauliflower florets
1 large carrot, peeled and sliced into diagonals
2 stalks celery, sliced into diagonals
4 cloves garlic, crushed
1 to 2 teaspoons grated fresh ginger
6 cups cooked brown basmati rice
2 to 3 cups chopped spinach, chard, cabbage, or bok choy
3 tablespoons tamari or coconut aminos
1 tablespoon brown rice vinegar or coconut vinegar

Heat a deep 11-inch or 12-inch skillet over medium-high heat. Add the oil and then the cashews; sauté for about 30 seconds or until golden. Quickly add the green onions, broccoli, cauliflower, carrot, and celery. Sauté for 5 to 7 minutes or until vegetables are crisp-tender. Add the garlic and ginger; sauté 30 seconds more.

Then add in the rice, adding more oil if necessary. Keep everything moving in the pan. Next add the chopped spinach. Sauté for a minute then add the tamari and vinegar. Taste and adjust seasonings if necessary. Serve immediately.

Yield: 6 to 8 servings

Ingredient Tip:

You will need to cook two cups of long grain, jasmine, or brown basmati rice for this recipe. Make sure it is completely cool before adding it to the vegetables. It is best to use rice that is at least a day old and straight from the refrigerator for fried rice. Warm, fresh rice will clump together and become mushy when fried.

Wild Rice Stuffing

This recipe is a delicious, savory addition to your holiday table or can enjoyed anytime! It makes enough to stuff one turkey and fill one medium casserole dish. I have also successfully made this using all wild rice instead of half wild rice and half brown rice.

1 cup wild rice
1 cup long grain brown rice
4 cups vegetable or chicken stock
¼ cup extra virgin olive oil
3 cups chopped red onion
1 tablespoon dried thyme
1 to 2 teaspoons dried sage
1 teaspoon ground black pepper
3 to 4 cups chopped mushrooms
2 to 3 cups chopped celery
1 cup pecans
½ to 1 cup unsweetened dried cranberries
1 apple, diced
1 cup chopped fresh parsley
Herbamare or sea salt, to taste

In a medium pot with a tight-fitting lid add the wild rice, brown rice, and stock. Cover, bring to a boil, then reduce heat to low and simmer for 45 minutes. Then let stand in the pot for at least 15 minutes.

In a large skillet, heat olive oil over medium heat. Add onions and sauté for about 5 or 6 minutes until softened. Then add herbs, mushrooms, and celery; sauté 5 minutes more. Turn off heat and add the pecans, cranberries, apple, and parsley. Stir in cooked rice. Add salt to taste.

Place some of the stuffing in the cavity of the turkey and the remaining into a covered casserole dish. Bake stuffing in a 350 degree F oven for 35 to 40 minutes.

Yield: 8 servings

Wild Rice, Kale, and Apple Salad

This festive autumn salad pairs well with roasted turkey breast, chicken, or a hearty vegetable bean soup. You will need to cook 1 ½ cups of wild rice to equal 6 cups cooked.

Salad:
6 cups cooked wild rice
½ small red onion, finely diced
1 tart apple, diced
4 to 5 large kale leaves, rinsed and thinly sliced
1 to 1 ½ almonds, roasted and chopped
½ cup currants (optional)

Dressing:
⅓ cup balsamic vinegar
⅓ cup extra virgin olive oil
1 tablespoon maple syrup
1 to 1 ½ teaspoons Herbamare or sea salt
freshly ground black pepper

Place all salad ingredients into a large bowl. In a small bowl, whisk together the ingredients for the dressing. Pour dressing over salad and toss together. Taste and add more sea salt and pepper if needed. Serve.

Store extra rice salad in a glass container in the refrigerator for up to 5 days.

Yield: 6 to 8 servings

Kitchen Tip:

To roast the almonds, place them into a shallow baking dish and roast in the oven at 350 degrees F for 15 to 20 minutes. Cool on a plate, then chop on a cutting board.

Chicken and Wild Rice Salad

Serve this scrumptious salad over mixed organic greens for a balanced meal. This salad is best served at room temperature. You will need to cook 1 ½ cups of wild rice to equal 6 cups cooked.

Salad:
6 cups cooked wild rice
2 cups cooked, diced chicken
1 cup hazelnuts, roasted and chopped
4 mandarins, peeled and segmented
4 green onions, sliced into rounds
¼ to ½ cup currants
large handful of fresh parsley, chopped

Dressing:
⅓ cup freshly squeezed orange juice
⅓ cup extra virgin olive oil
2 tablespoons white wine vinegar
1 to 1 ½ teaspoons Herbamare
freshly ground black pepper

Add the cooked rice, chicken, hazelnuts, mandarins, green onions, currants, and parsley to the bowl. In a small bowl, whisk together the dressing ingredients. Pour dressing over salad and toss together. Taste and add more sea salt and pepper if needed. Serve.

Store extra rice salad in a glass container in the refrigerator for up to 5 days.

Yield: 6 to 8 servings

Kitchen Tip:

To roast the hazelnuts, place them into a shallow baking dish and roast in the oven at 350 degrees F for 15 to 20 minutes. Cool on a plate then chop on a cutting board.

Millet Salad with White Beans and Chard

This salad is perfect served in the summertime when the large sweet heirloom tomatoes are in season. If fresh chard is unavailable use fresh spinach or kale as a replacement. You can also replace the millet with cooked quinoa. I like to use cooked cannellini beans because of their large size and soft creamy texture. If you tolerate dairy, garnish each serving with shaved Parmesan cheese.

Salad:
6 to 7 cups cooked millet
3 cups cooked white beans
4 cups thinly sliced fresh chard
1 large fresh tomato, chopped
handful fresh parsley, chopped fine

Dressing:
½ cup freshly squeezed lemon juice
6 tablespoons extra virgin olive oil
1 to 2 cloves garlic
1 to 2 teaspoons Herbamare or sea salt
freshly ground black pepper

Cool the cooked millet completely then add to a large bowl; fluff with a fork. Add the cooked white beans, chard, chopped tomato, and parsley. In a small separate bowl, whisk together the ingredients for the dressing. Pour dressing over salad and gently toss it all together. Serve immediately or store in the refrigerator for up to 4 days.

Yield: About 8 servings

Ingredient Tip:

Millet can be cross-contaminated with gluten grains. Be sure to purchase certified gluten-free millet.

Millet Salad with Roasted Pistachios and Dried Cranberries

This nutritious whole grain salad is perfect served as part of a big Thanksgiving or Christmas dinner with family and friends. It also makes a nice light lunch anytime of year. If you are cooking for one or two I suggest making a half batch of this recipe.

Salad:
6 to 7 cups cooked millet
1 cup raw pistachios
1 cup fruit juice sweetened dried cranberries
1 cup chopped flat-leaf parsley

Dressing:
½ cup freshly squeezed orange juice
½ cup extra virgin olive oil
2 to 3 tablespoons champagne vinegar
1 teaspoon Herbamare or to taste
1 teaspoon ground coriander

Preheat oven to 350 degrees F. Place pistachios into a small baking dish or glass pie plate. Roast in the oven for about 10 minutes.

Cool the cooked millet completely then add to a large bowl; fluff with a fork. Add the roasted pistachios, dried cranberries, and chopped flat-leaf parsley into a large bowl. Add dressing ingredients to bowl and toss together. The millet will absorb some of the dressing as it sits. Taste and adjust salt and seasonings if necessary.

Yield: About 8 servings

Mushroom Millet Risotto

I usually use half homemade chicken stock and half water for this recipe. If using a salted stock you may want to omit the Herbamare so the risotto doesn't get over salted. Serve this savory whole grain dish with the Poached Salmon with Spring Onions and White Wine, page 316, and the Arugula Salad with Shaved Fennel, page 207, for a balanced, nutritious meal.

3 tablespoons extra virgin olive oil
1 large leek, cut in half lengthwise then sliced thin
½ pound button mushrooms, sliced
3 cloves garlic, crushed
½ teaspoon Herbamare
1 ½ cups millet, rinsed and drained
6 cups chicken stock or water
¼ cup white wine
freshly ground black pepper

Heat a wide pot or deep 11-inch skillet over medium heat. Add oil and leeks; sauté for a few minutes or until soft. Then add mushrooms and sauté 5 to 10 minutes more. Add garlic and Herbamare; sauté a minute more. Add millet and 2 cups of the stock or water plus the white wine. Cover, bring to a boil, then reduce heat to a simmer and cook for 15 to 20 minutes.

Remove lid and add 2 more cups of liquid, stir for a minute, then cover and cook 10 minutes more. Add the remaining 2 cups of liquid, stir, cover and cook for 15 to 20 more minutes. Add more liquid for a thinner consistency.

Taste and add more Herbamare if needed. If your stock is salted, you probably won't need to add any. Add freshly ground black pepper to taste. The risotto should cook for a total of 40 to 50 minutes.

Yield: About 6 servings

Kitchen Tip:

When purchasing your mushrooms for this recipe, weigh them in the store to get the ½ pound requirement. Or you can always just toss in your desired amount.

Dilled Quinoa with Peas

Fresh herbs, peas, and greens are plants that are abundant during the months of spring. Serve this lively quinoa salad with poached salmon, hardboiled eggs, or baked chicken for a light springtime meal. You will need to cook 2 cups of quinoa to equal 6 cups cooked.

Salad:
6 cups cooked quinoa
2 cups fresh or frozen peas
½ cup chopped fresh dill

Dressing:
½ cup fresh lemon juice
⅓ cup extra virgin olive oil
2 cloves garlic, crushed
1 teaspoon Herbamare

Scoop the quinoa to a large bowl. Add chopped dill and peas. It is best if the quinoa is still slightly warm so the peas gently cook when they get tossed with the quinoa.

In a small bowl, whisk together the ingredients for the dressing. Pour dressing over quinoa and vegetables. Toss together. Serve. Store any leftovers in a covered container in the refrigerator for up to 5 days.

Yield: 6 to 8 servings

Ingredient Tip:

Higher lysine, methionine, and cysteine levels assist quinoa in having one of the best amino acid profiles compared to all other grains. Lysine is an amino acid that helps with tissue repair—helpful for repairing a damaged gut.

Quinoa Salad with Arame and Daikon

Although this ingredient list looks long the recipe is quick to prepare. Arame is a sea vegetable that is very high in trace minerals. Daikon radishes are long, white vegetables that look somewhat like a large carrot. You can find both of these ingredients at your local health food store.

Seaweed:
¼ cup arame
2 cups water

Salad:
6 cups cooked quinoa
2 medium daikon radishes, peeled and sliced
2 large carrots, peeled and sliced
3 to 4 green onions, sliced into thin rounds
1 to 2 cups thinly sliced red cabbage
3 to 4 cups thinly sliced kale
1 cup sunflower seeds, toasted

Dressing:
½ cup freshly squeezed lemon juice
⅓ cup wheat-free tamari or coconut aminos
⅓ cup extra virgin olive oil
1 clove garlic, crushed

Cook the arame by first rinsing it. Then place it in a small saucepan, cover with the 2 cups of water and simmer for 10 to 15 minutes, uncovered. Drain through a fine mesh strainer.

To assemble the salad, placed the cooled quinoa into a large bowl, add the cooked arame, sliced daikon and carrots, green onions, cabbage, kale, and toasted sunflower seeds. In a small bowl, whisk together the ingredients for the dressing and pour over the quinoa and vegetables. Toss everything together and serve. Quinoa salad will last up to 5 days in the refrigerator.

Yield: 6 to 8 servings

Kitchen Tip:

To toast sunflower seeds, add them to a 10-inch skillet over medium heat; keep them moving in the pan until light golden brown and fragrant, about 5 to 6 minutes.

Nutrition Tip:

Sea vegetables are an excellent source of iodine—a mineral needed to make thyroid hormones. Those without sufficient thyroid hormone production can experience weight loss resistance, hair loss, constipation, chronic fatigue, have cold hands and feet, and may have difficulty becoming pregnant.

Spring Radish Quinoa Salad

Serve this light and lively spring grain salad as a light lunch or with grilled salmon or chicken for dinner. We grow French sorrel in our garden and usually by mid-march it is up and ready to be harvested. Sorrel is a tangy green with a slight lemon flavor. It is also delicious added to green smoothies. If you can't find sorrel then substitute it with napa cabbage.

Salad:
6 cups cooked quinoa
2 to 3 cups thinly sliced sorrel
1 large bunch radishes, sliced into thin rounds
1 cup chopped parsley
4 to 5 green onions, sliced into rounds

Dressing:
½ cup freshly squeezed lemon juice
6 tablespoons extra virgin olive oil
2 cloves garlic, crushed
1 ½ teaspoons Herbamare or sea salt
1 to 2 teaspoons lemon zest (optional)

Scoop cool, cooked quinoa to a large bowl. Add the sorrel, radishes, parsley, and green onions to the bowl.

In a small bowl, whisk together the dressing ingredients. Pour dressing over quinoa. Toss together and serve at room temp.

Yield: 6 to 8 servings

Quinoa Tabouli

We make this recipe quite often during mid to late summer when cucumbers, tomatoes, and mint are at their peak. Combined with some homemade energy bars, this salad makes a great picnic lunch during a day hike on the trails. We pack it in small stainless steel lunch containers for each child.

Salad:
6 cups cooked quinoa
1 large cucumber, diced (about 2 to 3 cups)
2 cups diced fresh tomatoes
½ cup finely chopped fresh mint
½ cup finely chopped parsley

Dressing:
½ cup fresh lemon juice
⅓ cup extra virgin olive oil
2 cloves garlic, crushed
1 teaspoon Herbamare

Scoop cool, cooked quinoa into a large bowl. Add diced cucumber, tomatoes, fresh mint, and parsley.

In a small bowl whisk together the ingredients for the dressing. Pour dressing over quinoa and vegetables. Toss together. Serve.

Store any leftovers in a covered container in the refrigerator for up to 5 days.

Yield: 6 to 8 servings

Quinoa and Lentil Salad with Caramelized Onions

This salad is a favorite for summertime picnic potlucks. People who are new to quinoa usually enjoy this recipe very much. Black beluga lentils are very small and hold their shape well in salads. You can find them at your local health food store or order them online. I often cook a large pot and then store some in the freezer to use in salads like this.

Caramelized Onions:
2 tablespoons extra virgin olive oil
2 to 3 medium red onions, cut into crescent moons
1 teaspoon Herbamare or sea salt

Salad:
6 cups cooked quinoa
2 cups cooked baby beluga lentils
2 to 3 Roma tomatoes, chopped
large handful fresh basil, thinly sliced
3 tablespoons balsamic vinegar
2 tablespoons extra virgin olive oil
sea salt and freshly ground black pepper to taste

Optional Additions:
crumbled feta cheese
chopped flat-leaf parsley

Heat an 11 or 12-inch skillet over medium heat. Add the 2 tablespoons of oil, then add the onions and salt; sauté for a few minutes or until the onions begin to release some of their moisture, then reduce heat to low and cook for 25 to 30 minutes or until onions are caramelized.

Scoop the quinoa to a large bowl. Add the caramelized onions, cooked lentils, chopped tomatoes, basil, vinegar, oil, salt, and pepper; toss together. Taste and adjust salt and pepper if necessary. Sprinkle with crumbled feta and parsley if desired.

Yield: 6 to 8 servings

Buckwheat Chia Tortillas, page 386

Chocolate Banana Bread, page 159

Adzuki Bean and Yam Hash, page 93

Apple Almond Muffins, page 146

Orange Creamsicle Smoothie, page 69

Mexican Quinoa

This is a great way to jazz up plain quinoa. I like to serve it with cooked black beans, roasted yams, and sautéed collard greens for a quick, balanced weeknight meal. You can also add salsa and diced avocado on top. Sometimes we will also serve this with the Cumin Spiced Pinto Beans, page 296, and a shredded napa cabbage salad tossed in fresh lime juice and sea salt.

2 tablespoons extra virgin olive oil or coconut oil
1 small onion, finely diced
1 small green or red bell pepper, finely diced
1 jalapeno pepper, seeded and finely diced
2 to 3 cloves garlic, crushed
1 to 2 teaspoons ground cumin
1 teaspoon paprika
¼ teaspoon chipotle chili powder
1 teaspoon Herbamare
2 cups quinoa, rinsed
3 ½ cups water
4 to 5 tablespoons tomato paste

Heat a heavy-bottomed 3-quart pot over medium heat. Add the oil, then add the onions, peppers, and garlic; sauté for a few minutes to soften. Then add the spices and Herbamare; sauté a minute more. Add quinoa, water, and tomato paste. Stir, cover, and bring to a boil.

Once boiling immediately reduce heat to low and simmer for about 25 minutes. Then remove the pot from the heat and let rest for about 10 minutes. Fluff with a fork and serve.

Yield: 6 to 8 servings

Moroccan Quinoa Pilaf

This recipe can be made ahead of time and then reheated in a pan. To reheat add a few tablespoons of water to the pan before adding the pilaf and sauté until warmed. You will need to cook 2 cups of quinoa for this recipe. It works best if your quinoa is completely cooled before using it in this recipe. Serve with roasted chicken and sautéed kale for a balanced meal.

2 to 4 tablespoons extra virgin olive oil
1 medium onion, diced
4 carrots, sliced into rounds
1 cup raw almonds, chopped
½ cup currants
1 ½ to 2 teaspoons mild curry powder
½ teaspoon turmeric
½ teaspoon ground cardamom
1 teaspoon Herbamare
4 cups chopped kale
4 to 5 cups cooked and cooled quinoa
1 small lemon, juiced
freshly ground black pepper

Heat an 11 or 12-inch deep skillet or wide pot over medium heat. Add olive oil, then add chopped onions; sauté for 4 to 5 minutes. Add sliced carrots and sauté about 10 minutes more. Adjust temperature to keep the heat at medium to allow the onions to cook but not brown.

Add almonds, currants, spices, and salt; sauté 5 minutes more. Add the kale and sauté about 5 more minutes, or until kale is tender. Then add cooked quinoa and stir together over low heat. Add a few tablespoons of water if the pilaf seems dry. An extra tablespoon of oil will also help prevent the quinoa from sticking to the pan.

Remove from heat and add the juice of the lemon. Stir together, taste, and adjust salt and seasonings if needed. I also like to add a generous amount of freshly ground black pepper at this point.

Yield: 6 to 8 servings

Ingredient Tip:

It is best if your kale is still dripping wet from rinsing when adding it to the pot. The extra water will help it to cook properly.

Variation:

Replace the currants with chopped dried apricots and the quinoa with cooked brown basmati rice.

Red Quinoa Masala

This recipe was inspired by my friend Sea and her blog, www.BookofYum.com. I've put my own spin on it but the original idea is hers. We like to serve this with the Red Lentil Dal, page 184, along with a yogurt-cucumber sauce or the Raw Cilantro Lime Chutney, page 378.

Quinoa:
2 cups red quinoa
3 ½ cups water
pinch sea salt

Masala:
3 to 4 tablespoons extra virgin olive oil or coconut oil
1 teaspoon whole cumin seeds
1 teaspoon brown or black mustard seeds
2 tablespoons finely chopped fresh ginger
1 large onion, cut into crescent moons
½ teaspoon turmeric
2 to 3 plum tomatoes, chopped
1 to 1 ½ teaspoons Herbamare or sea salt
½ to 1 cup chopped cilantro

Rinse the quinoa in a fine mesh strainer under running water. Drain well. Place quinoa into a 2-quart pot, add water and salt; cover and bring to a boil. Then reduce heat to low and simmer for about 15 to 20 minutes. Remove pot from heat and let cool for about 30 minutes before using.

To make the masala, first heat a 6-quart stainless steel or cast iron pot (a 12-inch skillet also works). Add the oil, let it heat for 10 to 20 seconds, then add the cumin and mustard seeds; sauté 30 to 60 seconds until they begin to pop. Immediately add the ginger and onions; sauté for about 10 minutes or until the onions are very soft and beginning to change color.

Add the turmeric, tomatoes, and salt. Sauté a minute more and then add the cooked red quinoa. Gently stir, then cover the pot and cook for 5 to 10 minutes over medium-low heat. Turn off heat, add cilantro, and fluff with a fork. Serve hot.

Yield: 6 to 8 servings

Spicy Coconut Quinoa Amaranth Casserole

This recipe is great on its own or serve it with baked fish and steamed broccoli for a heartier meal. It also pairs well with sautéed tempeh and greens. Portions can be frozen in serving-sized containers and then reheated in a small covered pot on the stove as needed.

2 tablespoons coconut oil
1 large onion, chopped
2 to 3 jalapeno peppers, seeded and diced
3 cloves garlic, crushed
1 teaspoon crushed red chili flakes, optional
1 ½ cups quinoa, rinsed and drained
½ cup amaranth, drained and rinsed
6 cups water
1 can coconut milk
1 to 2 teaspoons sea salt or Herbamare
1 large red bell pepper, seeded and diced
2 to 3 green onions
large handful fresh cilantro

Heat a 6-quart pot over medium heat. Add the oil, then add onions; sauté for about 5 to 10 minutes or until soft. Then add the jalapeno, garlic, and chili flakes. Sauté a few minutes more. Add the rinsed and drained quinoa and amaranth to the pot. Cover with the water; stir together. Cover and bring to a boil, then reduce heat to a simmer and cook for 30 minutes.

Preheat oven to 350 degrees F. Coat a 9 x 13-inch glass baking dish with coconut oil.

Add the coconut milk, Herbamare, diced red bell pepper, and green onions to the pot of quinoa and amaranth; stir. Scoop mixture into pan, spread evenly with the back of a spoon, and bake for about 30 minutes or until bubbly. Sprinkle with cilantro and serve.

Yield: About 8 servings

Grains

Cold Spaghetti Salad

Serve this noodle salad at a summer picnic or as a main meal paired with a large garden salad and our Everyday Salad Dressing, page 347.

two 12-ounce packages brown rice spaghetti noodles

Sauce:
1 to 2 tablespoons extra virgin olive oil
1 large onion, chopped
2 tablespoons minced garlic
4 medium tomatoes, chopped
1 cup chopped fresh parsley
½ cup pine nuts, lightly toasted
1 cup pitted kalamata olives
6 tablespoons extra virgin olive oil
4 tablespoons red wine vinegar
sea salt or Herbamare and freshly ground black pepper

Cook the noodles al dente according to the package directions. Rinse with cold water in a colander to stop cooking. Set aside.

Heat a skillet over medium heat. Add the 1 to 2 tablespoons of olive oil and chopped onions; sauté for about 10 to 15 minutes being careful not to brown too much. Keep the heat low enough to cook the onions until completely soft and flavorful. Add garlic and cook for a minute more. Remove from heat.

Add the noodles to a large bowl. Then add in the cooked onions and garlic, and all of the remaining ingredients. Toss well. Add sea salt and pepper to taste. I prefer to use quite a bit of freshly ground pepper.

Yield: 6 to 8 servings

Kitchen Tip:

To toast the pine nuts use a dry skillet and place over medium heat. Add the pine nuts and keep them moving in the pan for a few minutes until lightly browned. Watch them closely as they can burn easily!

Dairy-Free Macaroni and Cheese

This "cheese" sauce has a lovely yellow color very similar to traditional mac and cheese. It gets its color from the turmeric powder and red pepper. The nutritional yeast gives a cheesy flavor while the cashews create a creamy sauce.

one 16-ounce package brown rice elbow macaroni

Cheese Sauce:
1 cup raw cashews
2 cups water
1 very small red bell pepper, seeded and chopped
¼ cup sweet rice flour
¼ cup nutritional yeast
2 tablespoons minced fresh onion
1 clove garlic, peeled
2 tablespoons freshly squeezed lemon juice
1 teaspoon Dijon mustard
1 ½ teaspoons Herbamare
½ teaspoon turmeric

Cook pasta according to package directs. Drain and set aside.

To make the sauce, place the cashews and water into a high-powered blender. Blend until very smooth and creamy. Add the remaining sauce ingredients; blend again until smooth.

Pour sauce into a medium-sized pot. Simmer over low heat until thickened and warm. If the sauce seems too thick, add a little extra water. Taste and add more salt if necessary. Add noodles and stir to coat, heating until warmed. Serve.

Yield: 4 to 6 servings

Dairy-Free Fettuccini Alfredo

We like to boost the nutrition of this meal by adding in sautéed zucchini, carrots, cauliflower, peas, and a sprinkling of fresh garden herbs to the finished dish. Try the grain-free variation below using zucchini noodles and serve with roasted chicken.

one 16-ounce package brown rice fettuccini noodles

Sauce:
½ cup raw cashews
1 cup water
½ cup white wine
¼ cup extra virgin olive oil
1 small shallot, peeled and chopped
2 cloves garlic, peeled
2 tablespoons nutritional yeast
1 tablespoon sweet rice flour
1 teaspoon Herbamare
pinch nutmeg

Garnish:
finely chopped flat-leaf parsley
freshly ground black pepper

Bring a large pot of water to a boil and cook the noodles according to the package directions. Rinse and drain in a colander. Set aside.

To make the sauce, place all ingredients into a high-powered blender and blend until ultra smooth and creamy. Pour sauce into a 2-quart saucepan and simmer for 10 minutes until thickened.

Toss warm sauce and noodles together in a large bowl, sprinkle with the chopped parsley and ground black pepper. Serve immediately.

Yield: 4 to 6 servings

Variation:

Grain-Free: Replace the rice noodles with zucchini noodles. To make zucchini noodles, trim the ends from 3 to 4 medium zucchini, peel them, and then use a spiralizer to create long, thin "noodles." Cook them in the sauce for 2 to 3 minutes to soften, but don't overcook! Also, replace the sweet rice flour in the sauce with 2 tablespoons of arrowroot powder.

Main Meals

At our house, the main meal is what brings us all together. Little hands help with the chopping, peeling, stirring, and sautéing. The table gets set with colorful napkins and a vase of freshly picked flowers. We hear words of gratefulness such as "mmm this is good" and "yummy, thanks for the meal mommy." Mostly it's a time to relax and be thankful for such nourishing food, though like most families, mealtimes can also be very busy.

Creating Balanced Family Meals

How do I create a balanced meal for my family and how do I implement feeding my family nourishing meals each and every day? Many of us are trying to juggle work, school, after-school activities, and have young children. Life can be harried and crazy, and sometimes it may be easier just to go out to eat. Yet with eating out, you run the risk of getting unintentional gluten, other potential food allergens, and genetically engineered food, not to mention the drain on your bank account. With a little thought and a well-stocked kitchen, you can make simple meals for your family every day.

Whole and Unprocessed
When putting together meals for your family use whole, unprocessed foods—both raw and cooked, more raw in the summer and less in the winter. Revolving meals around whole foods that are naturally gluten-free makes meals simpler and easier to implement. Consider incorporating a lot of color to your meals. The wide array of beautiful colors you see in fresh fruits, vegetables, nuts, beans, and whole grains are actually disease-protective phytochemicals that change the way in which our genes are read!

Carbohydrates for Energy
Does my meal contain some form of unprocessed carbohydrates for fuel? As the energy of the sun falls to the earth, it is captured in leaves of plants and combined with air (CO_2), and water (H_2O) to become carbohydrates like glucose (CH_2O_6). It is no wonder that our cells are designed to use glucose as their primary source of energy. "Time-released" glucose can be found in foods that are rich in complex carbohydrates. These are often chains of glucose molecules stuck together that need to be broken down over time in the body. Examples of unrefined complex carbohydrates include lightly steamed starchy vegetables such as root vegetables and winter squash, and cooked whole grains and beans. Non-starchy vegetables also contain a smaller amount of sugars beneficial for the human body. These include, lettuce, kale, green beans, broccoli, radishes, and mushrooms.

Healthy Fats

Does my meal have some type of healthy fat? Fats are essential for all cell membranes in our bodies, especially the brain cells of a growing baby and child. They help our cells communicate properly, contributing to a healthy, functioning nervous system. Avoiding trans fats and focusing on healthy fats also contributes to increased fertility in women. Fat is needed to absorb the fat-soluble nutrients A, D, E, and K. Healthy fats, like conjugated linoleic acid and omega-3 fatty acids, can also be found in the fats from animals raised on their natural diet of grasses and other foliage. You may, however, consider limiting the amounts of animal fats in your family's diet because persistent organic pollutants (POPs) bioaccumulate in animals and are stored in fatty tissues. Sources of healthy fats include extra virgin olive oil, virgin coconut oil, nuts, seeds, avocados, wild fish, and pastured eggs.

Enough Protein?

Is there an adequate amount of protein in my meals? Proteins are the building blocks for all cells and are needed for tissue repair. Sedentary people require less protein, while athletes and pregnant women require more. We often think of protein and meat simultaneously; however, proteins are found in dark leafy greens, beans, whole grains, seeds, and nuts. We would need to eat a lot of greens to match the protein content in a small piece of fish, but it is possible. Three ounces of steak has about 24 grams of protein. Two cups of cooked quinoa has about 16 grams. One quarter cup of almonds has about 6 grams of protein and one cup of cooked beans has about 20 grams. Daily protein requirements easily add up when consuming a whole foods diet.

Vitamins and Minerals

What about vitamins and minerals? Using vegetables as the basis for at least one meal a day while incorporating them into other meals and snacks will greatly contribute to your overall nutrient requirements. Vitamin C, potassium, folate, B2, B6, magnesium, beta-carotenes, polyphenols, and flavonoids are all found abundantly in fruits and vegetables. Be sure to incorporate both raw and fermented foods daily as cooking may destroy certain vitamins—but not minerals—present in vegetables and fruits. Whole carbohydrate and protein foods also contain a vast amount of the necessary vitamins and minerals required for humans. To incorporate enough iodine and trace minerals, use sea vegetables several times a week, kelp granules as a condiment, and unrefined sea salt daily.

10 Steps to Creating Balanced Meals

1. **What is in season right now**? We have a number of garden beds on our lot. In the summer and fall we can make a lot of meals that revolve around food harvested from our yard. In the winter we eat a lot of stored root vegetables, cabbage, and preserved or fermented foods. Shopping at your local Farmer's Market can provide a lot of inspiration for seasonal dishes as well.

2. **Use what you have before buying more**. Are there any grains or beans in the pantry that need be used before buying anything new? Grains and beans don't last that long so it is important to use them up within about six to nine months of purchasing them. What about meat in the freezer? Meat should be used within a year of freezing it so I like to check and see if there is any available that needs to be thawed out before shopping for anything new.

3. **In the morning make a plan for the day**. When I wake up, I think about what I will make for dinner and calculate if anything needs to be done earlier in the afternoon or if I can simply toss it all together at 5pm.

4. **How do the meals fit into the bigger nutrition picture**? What was the composition of the other meals we had that day? I like to recall what we ate for breakfast or lunch before prepping dinner. For example, if we had homemade gluten-free bread for breakfast I don't want to serve bread or a starchy meal for dinner. On that same token, if we had eggs and kale for breakfast and a green salad topped with salmon for lunch, I will serve something starchy for dinner, such as roasted yams with rice and beans.

5. **Plan Meals Ahead**. Before I go grocery shopping, I like to plan at least three to four main meals and buy what I need. The remainder of our meals I create from what is left in the refrigerator or pantry as well as using up leftovers.

6. **Use the weekends to prep food for the week**. Saturday mornings we head off to the Farmer's Market to load up on seasonal organic produce. We also like to fit in a grocery shopping day on the weekend. With a plan of action in hand I will use Sunday afternoon to prep a few things for the week, such as cooking one pot of beans and two pots of grains, in order to quickly make soup or grain-bean salads for dinner later in the week. Cutting celery and carrot sticks and placing them in a container filled with a small amount of water makes a handy snack for school lunches. We also like to make raw energy bars, individually wrap them in waxed paper, and store them in the refrigerator for quick snacks on-the-go.

7. **Make large batches of certain recipes**. This way you can have nutritious home-cooked meals on evenings when you are too busy to cook. Or cook a double batch of soup to make packing lunches for kids a breeze. Just make sure you have a few child-sized stainless steel thermoses on hand. Big pots of rice or quinoa can be divided into individual Pyrex dishes and topped with chopped veggies, beans, or soup for a grab-and-go meal as you run out the door to school or work.

Meals

8. **What meals do other members of the household**, including the children, enjoy eating? Have they requested anything for the week? If not, then how about involving them in a quick meal brainstorming session before heading to the market? Even better, have them help you pick out the items at the market in anticipation for the meal. With our children, we are never ceased to be amazed at what they will eat when they are involved in the preparation process of a meal.

9. **Include the children in meal preparation**. At least one night a week, plan to have your children make a meal. You'd be amazed at how much cutting a three-year-old can do or that an eight or nine-year-old can cook a whole meal. Plus, they learn so much in the process. Reading skills are enhanced through following recipes, math skills are enhanced when needing to double or halve a recipe. Communication skills are enhanced when needing to work with siblings.

10. **Bring baby into the kitchen**. If you have a baby, use a wrap or sling to be able to get things done. Once my babies were about 5 months old we could put them on our backs in either a backpack or Ergo carrier. Newborns can ride snug up against your chest in a Moby wrap while dinner is being made. Just think of the brain stimulation happening as baby smells the food cooking and hears all of the chopping and cooking noises!

Meals

Balanced Sample Menu Plan

Day 1:
Moroccan Roasted Chicken, page 326
Cooked Millet, page 257
Sauteed Winter Greens with Caramelized Onions, page 240

Day 2:
Apple Cider Baked Beans, page 290
Roasted Delicata Squash
Kohlrabi Apple Slaw, page 220

Day 3:
Garlic Ginger Salmon, page 314
Whipped Sweet Potatoes with Cardamom, page 250
Lemon Walnut Green Bean Salad, page 221

Day 4:
Zucchini Lasagna with Pine Nut Ricotta, page 308
Arugula Salad with Shaved Fennel, page 207

Day 5:
Black Bean and Yam Casserole, page 291
Cooked Basmati Rice, page 257
Jalapeno-Lime Kale Slaw, page 218

Day 6:
Red Lentil Dal, page 184
Red Quinoa Masala, page 279
Cilantro Cabbage Slaw, page 213

Day 7:
Halibut and Potato Chowder, page 200
Sourdough Teff Bread, page 124
Dilly Radishes, page 506

Apple Cider Baked Beans

Baked beans have always been part of our summer family picnics. We like to serve them with a cabbage slaw such as the Picnic Coleslaw, page 226, and a potato salad such as the Purple Potato Salad, page 227. Baked beans freeze well, so if you have leftovers you cannot finish within a few days, freeze the remainder in portion-sized containers. Just reheat in a small, covered saucepan on the stove.

5 to 6 cups cooked cannellini beans, drained and rinsed

Sauce:
2 to 3 tablespoons extra virgin olive oil
1 medium onion, chopped
4 to 6 cloves garlic, crushed
1 ½ cups organic apple cider
1 cup tomato sauce
½ cup coconut sugar
¼ cup apple cider vinegar
2 tablespoons blackstrap molasses
1 to 2 teaspoons dry yellow mustard powder
1 tablespoon smoked paprika
2 teaspoons Herbamare

Preheat the oven to 375 degrees F. Place the drained and rinsed cannellini beans into a large casserole dish.

Heat a 10-inch skillet over medium heat. Add the olive oil and onions; sauté for 5 to 10 minutes until very soft and beginning to change color. Add the garlic and sauté a minute more. Scrape onions, garlic, and oil from pan into the casserole dish with the beans. Add the remaining ingredients for the sauce to the casserole dish. Gently stir together.

Bake covered for about 1 hour. Then remove the lid, stir, and bake uncovered for another 30 to 45 minutes. Taste and adjust salt and seasonings if necessary. Serve warm.

Yield: 8 to 10 servings

Black Bean and Yam Casserole

Casseroles are oh-so comforting to serve on a cold winter evening. I like to serve this over cooked quinoa with sautéed dark leafy greens in the wintertime or with an arugula salad in early autumn.

2 tablespoons extra virgin olive oil
1 large onion, chopped
2 teaspoons Herbamare or sea salt
1 to 3 small jalapeno peppers, seeded and diced
3 to 4 cloves garlic, crushed
2 teaspoons ground cumin
2 teaspoons smoked paprika
1 teaspoon dried oregano
½ teaspoon chipotle chili powder
2 large yams, peeled and diced
1 large red bell pepper, chopped
4 cups cooked black beans
1 cup water
1 cup tomato sauce
1 tablespoon honey, agave nectar, or coconut nectar
3 tablespoons arrowroot powder

Preheat oven to 350 degrees F.

Heat a 10-inch skillet over medium heat. Add the olive oil, onions, and Herbamare; sauté for about 5 to 10 minutes or until tender. Place the onions into a large casserole dish. Add the jalapeno peppers, garlic, and spices. Stir together. Then add the yams, red bell pepper, and cooked black beans; toss together.

In a separate bowl, whisk together the water, tomato sauce, sweetener, and arrowroot powder. Pour mixture over black beans and vegetables. Stir together.

Cover casserole dish and bake for 30 minutes, then remove lid and bake uncovered for about another 30 minutes.

Yield: 6 servings

Ingredient Tip:

Any type of spicy pepper is suitable for this recipe. For the tomato sauce, I use Bionaturae Strained Tomatoes, which come in tall glass jars.

Butternut Squash and Pinto Bean Enchiladas

This is a great child-friendly recipe. The sauce isn't too spicy, so even the youngest of children can enjoy it. Our children like to help with the entire process of making this recipe. One evening, when I made this using steamed yams instead of butternut squash, I asked my 3-year old son to remove the peels from the steamed yam slices and mash them. After a few minutes I looked over to see if he had finished peeling the yams so I could hand him a fork to mash them. He had taken those peels off so fast that mashing was already in full swing by the time I looked over. All I saw were yams oozing through little fingers and a huge smile splitting the sweetest cheeks on the planet! Then of course comes the fun part of filling and rolling the tortillas. You can really get creative here and use just about any type of filling you would like.

Sauce:
2 tablespoons extra virgin olive oil
1 small onion, chopped
3 to 4 cloves garlic, peeled and chopped
1 tablespoon ground cumin
1 ½ to 2 teaspoons Herbamare or sea salt
2 dried ancho chiles, seeded
1 ½ to 2 cups water
2 cups tomato sauce
¼ cup arrowroot powder

Enchiladas:
12 to 16 corn tortillas or collard greens
2 cups cooked mashed butternut squash
3 cups cooked pinto beans
2 cups baby spinach leaves
grated raw organic jack cheese (optional)

Preheat oven to 400 degrees F. Oil one 9 x 13-inch glass baking dish.

To make the sauce, heat a 3-quart saucepan over medium heat. Add the oil and onions; sauté for 5 to 10 minutes or until softened. Add the garlic, cumin, and salt; sauté a few minutes more. Then add seeded ancho chiles, water, and tomato sauce. Cover and simmer for about 20 minutes. Pour sauce into a blender, add arrowroot powder; blend until smooth.

To assemble the enchiladas, first be sure to heat each tortilla so they won't crack after you fill them. The easiest way to do this is to add a little oil to a hot skillet and heat each tortilla in the oil for about 10 seconds on each side. You can fill one while the next one is heating in the pan. If you are using collard greens, just cut the bottom part of the stem off and blanch them before using. Add a few small spoonfuls of mashed squash, then beans, and a small handful of spinach leaves. Roll tightly and place the filled tortilla seam-side down in your oiled baking dish. Repeat with remaining ingredients, pushing the filled tortillas closely together. Top with the sauce. Sprinkle cheese on top if using. Cover and bake for 30 to 35 minutes.

Yield: 4 cups of sauce, and about 6 servings of enchiladas

Cajun Red Beans and Quinoa

This is a spin off the classic Southern red beans and rice. Here I use cooked quinoa and cooked beans for a meal than can be made in about 15 minutes. If desired, you can add about two organic chopped andouille sausages to the onion and pepper mixture. Serve with braised collard greens or steamed broccoli for a balanced meal. If you don't have any cooked quinoa on hand already, you'll need to cook one cup for this recipe. See page 257 for directions on cooking quinoa.

2 to 3 tablespoons extra virgin olive oil
1 medium onion, diced
1 large red bell pepper, seeded and diced
1 teaspoon Herbamare or sea salt
1 teaspoon smoked paprika
½ teaspoon freshly ground black pepper
pinch cayenne pepper
2 cups cooked red beans
3 cups cooked quinoa

Garnish:
chopped parsley
thinly sliced green onions

Heat a large 11-inch skillet or 3-quart pot over medium heat. Add the oil and onion; sauté for 10 to 15 minutes or until beginning to caramelize. Add the diced pepper and cook for about 5 minutes more or until softened. Add the Herbamare and spices; sauté a minute more.

Then add the cooked red beans and cooked quinoa; sauté 3 to 5 minutes more. Remove from heat, taste and adjust salt and seasonings if necessary.

Garnish with parsley and green onions.

Yield: 4 to 6 servings

Chana Masala

Chana Masala is a very common North Indian dish typically served over basmati rice topped with a yogurt-cucumber sauce. My version might not be authentic, but it is still lip-smackin' good! Sometimes we add two to three chopped red potatoes and spinach to this recipe too. We usually serve it over brown basmati rice with a slew of other Indian dishes.

3 tablespoons extra virgin olive oil or coconut oil
3 cups minced yellow onion
3 jalapeno peppers (or another spicy pepper), seeded
1-inch piece of fresh ginger, peeled
4 cloves garlic
1 tablespoon ground cumin
1 tablespoon ground coriander
1 teaspoon turmeric
1 teaspoon garam masala
3 cups fresh tomato puree
3 to 4 cups cooked garbanzo beans
2 teaspoons Herbamare or to taste
1 to 2 tablespoons freshly squeezed lemon or lime juice

Heat an 11-inch deep skillet over medium heat. If you don't own one then use a wide pot instead. Add the oil and minced onions; sauté for about 10 minutes.

While the onions are sautéing place the spicy peppers, ginger, and garlic in a food processor fitted with the "s" blade and process until ingredients are minced. Add mixture to the onions and sauté for a few minutes more. Then add spices.

Next add the tomato puree, cooked garbanzo beans, Herbamare, and lemon or lime juice. If you would like to add diced potatoes then add them now along with about ½ to 1 cup of water. Simmer for 25 to 30 minutes. Taste and adjust seasonings and salt if necessary.

Yield: 4 to 6 Servings

Ingredient Tip:

To make the fresh tomato puree, place 1 ½ to 2 pounds of fresh tomatoes into a food processor fitted with the "s" blade and process until you get a slightly chunky, but mainly smooth, puree.

Coconut Cashew Curry

Curry is a staple in our house. Our children will eat anything flavored with curry spices. Use any vegetables you have on hand, just keep in mind the total amounts. You may need to add extra coconut milk, water, and spices to compensate for any additional ingredients. We like to serve it over quinoa with a generous amount of fresh cilantro on top. This recipe doesn't freeze very well so I have kept it on the smaller size. I need to double this recipe to feed our family.

1 tablespoon coconut oil or extra virgin olive oil
1 teaspoon brown or black mustard seeds
1 teaspoon whole cumin seeds
1 tablespoon curry powder
pinch crushed red chili flakes
1 can coconut milk
1 cup water
2 to 3 tablespoons cashew butter
1-inch piece fresh ginger, peeled and finely grated
3 large carrots, peeled and sliced into diagonals
3 small red potatoes or one yam, cut into cubes
¼ pound fresh green beans, trimmed and cut in half
1 to 2 cups cauliflower florets
1 to 2 cups chopped savoy or napa cabbage
1 tablespoon freshly squeezed lemon juice
1 teaspoon Herbamare or sea salt

Garnish:
fresh cilantro, chopped
1 cup raw cashews, roasted

Heat a large pot or 11-inch skillet over medium heat. Add the oil, mustard and cumin seeds; sauté for about 30 seconds or until they begin to pop. Add the curry powder and chili flakes; stir in with the oil. Then immediately (so the spices don't burn) pour in the coconut milk and water. Add the cashew butter and stir it in. Grate the ginger, using a microplane, right into the pot. Add the carrots and potatoes. Cover and simmer for about 5 to 10 minutes, depending on the size of your veggies.

Then add the green beans and simmer 5 minutes more. Add the cauliflower and simmer about 5 minutes more. Add the cabbage, lemon juice, and salt; cover and simmer a few more minutes or until vegetables are tender but not overcooked. Total cooking time should be around 25 to 30 minutes.

Serve curry in individual bowls over cooked quinoa. Garnish each bowl with chopped cilantro and roasted cashews.

Yield: 4 servings

Kitchen Tip:

To roast cashews, place them into a small glass baking dish and roast in a preheated 350 degree F oven for about 12 minutes, or until just slightly golden.

Cumin Spiced Pinto Beans

This is one of our family's favorite weekday meals. We serve the beans over cooked brown basmati rice and then offer a variety of toppings such as Salsa Fresca, page 382, sliced avocados, thinly sliced romaine lettuce, sliced black olives, and fresh lime wedges.

3 cups dry pinto beans, soaked overnight
2 tablespoons extra virgin olive oil
1 large onion, chopped
6 cloves garlic, crushed
1 to 2 jalapeno peppers, seeded and finely diced
2 tablespoons ground cumin
8 to 10 cups water
3 teaspoons Herbamare or sea salt

Rinse the dry beans and sort through them to pick out any old, shriveled beans or clumps of dirt. Rinse again and place into a large bowl. Cover with a few inches of water and soak overnight or up to 24 hours. When ready to cook, drain beans and set aside.

Heat an 8-quart pot over medium heat. Add the oil and onions; sauté onions for about 10 minutes or until very soft and beginning to change color. Add the crushed garlic, diced peppers, and cumin; sauté a few minutes more. Then add the soaked and drained beans. Cover with the water. Bring to a boil, reduce heat to a simmer, partially cover, and cook for about 1 hour.

Once the beans are tender and cooked through remove the lid, add the salt, and continue to cook uncovered until most of the water has evaporated, about another 30 to 40 minutes.

Serve hot or puree in a food processor to make "refried beans." These beans can also be frozen in small containers once cooled.

Yield: 8 to 10 servings

Nutrition Tip:

Pinto beans contain certain phytochemicals—such as cinnamic acid, secoisolariciresinol, and coumestrol—that have been shown to be beneficial in the prevention of stomach cancer.

Curried Lentil and Rice Casserole

Lentils have been consumed since prehistoric times and are one of the first foods to have ever been cultivated. They have been found in archeological dig sites dating back 8,000 years! If you work during the week, try making this recipe on the weekend to have available for the week. This dish has a long baking time and is not suitable for a quick weeknight meal. I use a stone casserole dish for this recipe, though a 9 x 13-inch glass baking dish also works well. Portions can be frozen into small containers for future use.

2 tablespoons extra virgin olive oil or coconut oil
1 medium onion, chopped
2 tablespoons finely chopped fresh ginger
1 tablespoon finely chopped fresh turmeric, or 1 teaspoon dried
2 teaspoons curry powder
1 teaspoon ground cumin
1 teaspoon ground coriander
½ teaspoon cinnamon
2 teaspoons sea salt
4 carrots, chopped
1 ½ cups French lentils or black beluga lentils
1 cup long grain brown rice
5 cups water
1 can coconut milk

Preheat oven to 350 degrees F.

Heat a 10-inch skillet over medium heat. Add the olive oil and onions; sauté for 5 to 6 minutes. Add ginger, turmeric, spices, and salt. Continue to sauté for another 2 minutes until fragrant.

Place onion-spice mixture into a large casserole dish. Add carrots, lentils, rice, water, and coconut milk. Mix together well. Cover and bake for 2 hours.

After 2 hours, turn oven temp up to 425 degrees F. Remove cover and cook for another 20 to 30 minutes to let excess liquid cook off. Stir and serve.

Yield: 4 to 6 servings

Nutrition Tip:

Lentils are high in both soluble and insoluble fiber. Soluble fiber binds to bile laden with cholesterol and allows it to be pulled from the body thus lowering cholesterol levels. Insoluble fiber helps to keep you regular while preventing digestive disorders like IBS and diverticulitis.

Eggplant and White Bean Ragout

This stew is more like a thick nutritious sauce that can be served over cooked quinoa, brown rice noodles, or spaghetti squash. You can also omit the white beans and serve it over grilled fish or chicken. I usually use navy beans in this dish but great northern or cannellini would also work. I prefer to cut the onions and vegetables in this stew into larger chunks so everything doesn't just turn to mush.

2 to 4 tablespoons extra virgin olive oil
1 medium red onion, chopped
4 to 5 cloves garlic, crushed
1 medium eggplant, cut into cubes
2 medium zucchini, chopped
8 to 10 cremini mushrooms
3 cups cooked white beans
2 to 3 cups tomato sauce or pureed tomatoes
1 tablespoon Italian seasoning
1 teaspoon sea salt
½ teaspoon crushed red chili flakes (optional)

Heat an 11 or 12-inch skillet over medium heat. Add oil and onion; sauté for about 5 minutes or until soft. Add the garlic, eggplant, zucchini, and mushrooms; sauté for 5 to 10 minutes more or until the vegetables have softened, adding more olive oil if necessary. Timing will depend on the size you cut your vegetables.

Next add the white beans, tomato sauce or puree, Italian seasoning, salt and chili flakes. Simmer for about 8 to 10 more minutes or until sauce has thickened slightly. Taste and add more salt if necessary. Extra sauce can be frozen if necessary.

Yield: About 8 servings

Nutrition Tip:

The beautiful purple hue you see on the skin of eggplants comes from the potent antioxidant chemical called anthocyanin. This amazing phtyochemical has been found to be protective against cardiovascular disease, diabetes, and age-related macular degeneration.

Fresh Vegetable Curry

This delectable vegan curry recipe uses cooked chickpeas for added protein. It can also be made with chunks of salmon, halibut, or chicken breast. Try adding any vegetable you have on hand. I often make this with diced sweet potatoes or squash in autumn. Chopped fresh spinach is another fantastic addition. Since spinach cooks so quickly so you'll want to toss it in when you take the pan off the stove. Serve curry over cooked long grain brown rice or quinoa.

2 to 3 tablespoons virgin coconut oil
1 teaspoon black mustard seeds
2 to 3 teaspoons finely chopped fresh ginger
4 medium red potatoes, cut into cubes
3 carrots, peeled and sliced
2 teaspoons curry powder
1 teaspoon ground cumin
1 teaspoon ground coriander
½ teaspoon ground turmeric
dash cayenne pepper
1 ½ to 2 teaspoons Herbamare or sea salt
6 Roma tomatoes, diced
1 cup water
1 tablespoon arrowroot powder
½ pound green beans, trimmed and cut into pieces
¾ pound cauliflower, cut into florets
½ pound mushrooms, cut in half
3 cloves garlic, crushed
2 cups cooked chickpeas or 1 can

Garnish:
chopped cilantro

Heat a deep 11-inch skillet over medium to medium-high heat for a few minutes. Add the coconut oil, mustard seeds, and ginger; sauté for about 30 seconds until the seeds begin to pop. Add the potatoes and carrots; sauté for about 10 to 15 minutes on moderate heat so they don't brown too much. Add the spices and Herbamare; stir well and sauté for about a minute more. Sautéing the spices in oil is key to a good curry!

Add the diced tomatoes and sauté for about 2 minutes. Mix the cup of water with the arrowroot in a small bowl. I use a fork to whisk it together. Add this mixture to the cooking veggies.

Then add the green beans, cauliflower, mushrooms, garlic, and chickpeas. Stir gently. Cover and cook for about 15 minutes, stirring occasionally, or until vegetables are fork-tender.

Garnish with chopped cilantro.

Yield: 4 to 6 servings

Lentil and Kale Dal

I add kale to everything because we grow it in our backyard green garden and because we love the flavor and nutrition it imparts. Of course, you could add spinach, chard, broccoli leaves, or any other green you have on hand. You can also add whatever vegetables you like to this. I like to keep it simple so I can prepare it in 10 minutes or less then walk away while it is simmering on the stove. Serve over cooked brown basmati rice with a dollop of Spicy Peach Chutney, page 380.

2 tablespoons extra virgin olive oil or coconut oil
1 small onion, finely diced
2 tablespoons finely chopped fresh ginger
2 teaspoons ground cumin
2 teaspoons turmeric
1 ½ teaspoons garam masala
⅛ to ¼ teaspoon cayenne pepper
2 ½ cups French lentils or black beluga lentils, rinsed
6 cups water
4 cups chopped kale
1 ½ teaspoons sea salt
handful cilantro, chopped

Heat a 6-quart pot over medium heat. Add the olive oil and onion; sauté for 6 to 7 minutes. Add the ginger and spices; sauté a minute more. Add the lentils and water; cover and simmer for 40 minutes.

Then add the kale and the salt; stir and simmer uncovered for about 10 minutes to cook the kale and reduce the liquid. Continue cooking if you like your dal thicker. Turn off heat and add the cilantro. Serve over rice or quinoa.

Yield: 6 servings

Ingredient Tip:

Remember to sort through your lentils and pick out any gluten grains, then rinse very well before proceeding with this recipe.

Mung Bean Dal

This recipe is very quick to prepare and requires few ingredients. Mung beans don't require any soaking so you can easily get dinner on the table with little thought beforehand. This recipe is very versatile. Add different vegetables towards the end of cooking, such as chopped zucchini, chopped tomatoes, diced hot peppers, fresh or frozen peas, chopped cauliflower, or whatever you have on hand that needs to be used up! Serve this nutritious and easy to digest dal over cooked long grain brown rice.

3 to 4 tablespoons virgin coconut oil or extra virgin olive oil
2 tablespoons finely chopped ginger
1 tablespoon cumin seeds
2 teaspoons turmeric
1 large onion, diced
2 cups mung beans
8 cups water
1 large yam, peeled and diced
½ cup chopped cilantro
2 to 3 teaspoons Herbamare or sea salt

Heat a large pot over medium heat. Add the oil, ginger, cumin seeds, and turmeric; sauté for a few minutes until you smell a very fragrant aroma. Add onion and sauté for 5 minutes until softened.

Add the mung beans, water, and yams; cover and cook for about 35 to 40 minutes. Uncover and cook off water until desired consistency is reached, about 5 to 10 more minutes. Add chopped cilantro. Stir in salt to taste.

Yield: 6 to 8 servings

Nutrition Tip:

Although mung beans don't need to soak in order to cook properly, it is still best to soak them for 12 to 24 hours to make the nutrients contained in the beans more bioavailable.

Quick Curried Chickpeas and Potatoes

This recipe is one of our children's favorite meals. It is very quick to put together if you don't have a lot for time to prepare dinner. About once a month I cook a very large pot of chickpeas. Some of the cooked beans get made into hummus, some into bean soups and stews such as this one, and the rest I freeze in 2-cup containers to have on hand for busy weeknight meals. Feel free to add about 4 cups of chopped greens to this recipe near the end of cooking. Spinach, kale, and chard are our favorites.

2 to 3 tablespoons extra virgin olive oil or coconut oil
1 small onion or 1 large shallot, finely diced
1 small jalapeno pepper, seeded and finely diced
2 teaspoons Herbamare or sea salt
2 teaspoons curry powder
½ teaspoon ground cumin
½ teaspoon ground coriander
⅛ teaspoon cinnamon
3 yellow or red potatoes, diced (about 4 cups)
3 to 4 cups cooked chickpeas
2 cups tomato sauce
1 cup water
handful chopped cilantro

Heat a 4-quart pot or a deep 11-inch skillet over medium heat. Add oil and add onions or shallots; sauté for 5 to 10 minutes until very soft and beginning to change color. Add the diced jalapeno pepper and sauté a minute more. Add the spices and salt; sauté about 30 seconds more being careful not to burn the spices.

Immediately add the potatoes and stir to coat with the oil and spices. Then add the cooked chickpeas, tomato sauce, and water; stir then cover and simmer over medium or medium-low heat for 25 to 30 minutes or until the potatoes are fork-tender.

Garnish with chopped cilantro. Serve over cooked brown rice or quinoa.

Yield: 6 servings

Summer Vegetable Kitcheree

Kitcheree is a highly nourishing, easy-to-digest, hypoallergenic Indian stew made from mung beans and brown rice. Spices and vegetables make up the remaining ingredients, which can vary widely. The spices and summer vegetables create a luscious stew that can be made in just minutes using a pressure cooker, though you don't need one to make this.

2 tablespoons virgin coconut oil or olive oil
2 tablespoons finely chopped fresh ginger
1 tablespoon black mustard seeds
1 tablespoon cumin seeds
pinch or two of crushed red chili flakes
2 cups dry mung beans, rinsed
2 cups brown jasmine or basmati rice, rinsed
3 to 4 large carrots, cut into large chunks
1 ½ teaspoons turmeric
½ teaspoon ground coriander
8 to 10 cups water
4 cups finely chopped kale or spinach
1 to 2 cups fresh or frozen peas
3 medium tomatoes, chopped
½ cup chopped cilantro
2 to 3 teaspoons sea salt or Herbamare
dollop of chilled coconut milk, for garnish

Heat an 8-quart pot or pressure cooker over medium heat. Add the oil, ginger, mustard seeds, cumin seeds, and chili flakes; sauté for about 60 seconds or until the seeds begin to pop. Add the mung beans, rice, carrots, turmeric, and coriander; stir together a bit so the spices evenly coat the rice and beans. Then add the water (start with 8 cups and add more after the stew is cooked if necessary).

If you're using a pressure cooker lock the lid into place and bring to high pressure, cook for about 10 minutes, then use the quick release method to bring the pressure down. If the stew needs more time, bring to high pressure again and cook for 1 to 2 more minutes. Add more water if necessary.

If you don't have a pressure cooker bring the stew to a boil, cover, and simmer on low for about 45 minutes, adding more water if necessary.

Then add in the chopped kale, tomatoes, peas, cilantro, and salt. Stir until just mixed. Turn off heat, cover, and let stand for about 5 minutes. The vegetables will quickly become tender in the hot stew. Add more salt to taste if necessary.

Yield: About 8 servings

Spicy Lentils and Rice in Cabbage Leaves

This is one of our family's favorite meals. Our children adore cabbage, especially with a spicy lentil filling! They prefer raw cabbage to nearly any other vegetable. Napa cabbage is quite mild and slightly sweet, so start with this variety if your children are not accustomed to eating cabbage. Elevate this recipe to the next level with Spicy Coconut Cream, page 373, or the Raw Mango Chutney, page 379.

3 cups French lentils or black beluga lentils
8 cups water
1 bunch chard
2 large shallots
1 jalapeño pepper, seeded
3 cloves garlic
1-inch piece fresh ginger, peeled
1 tablespoon coconut oil
2 teaspoons black mustard seeds
2 teaspoons curry powder
1 teaspoon garam masala

Other Ingredients
cooked long grain brown rice
napa cabbage leaves

Add lentils and water to a large pot and bring to a boil. Reduce heat to a simmer, cover, and cook for 40 to 45 minutes. Drain lentils through a fine mesh colander once cooked.

Place the chard, shallots, jalapeno pepper, garlic, and ginger into a food processor fitted with the "s" blade. Process until all of the ingredients are minced. Set aside.

Heat a large 11-inch deep skillet over medium heat. Add the oil and mustard seeds; sauté for about 20 to 30 seconds or until they begin to pop. Add the curry powder and garam masala; sauté another 10 seconds or so. Quickly add the processed chard mixture to the skillet and sauté for a few minutes stirring frequently. Add cooked lentils into the skillet; gently stir together. Add salt to taste.

To serve, add a small scoop of brown rice and the lentil-chard mixture to each cabbage leaf. Serve with your favorite sauces and chutneys.

Yield: 6 to 8 servings

Sautéed Tempeh and Spinach

I like to make this quick meal for lunch on occasion. It is great served over leftover cooked quinoa or brown rice. If I have more time and want to make this meal more elaborate I will serve it with the Ginger Plum Sauce, page 364, or the Garlic Ginger Peanut Sauce, page 363.

two 8-ounce packages tempeh, cut into cubes
6 tablespoons wheat-free tamari
3 tablespoons coconut oil or sesame oil
8 cups chopped fresh spinach

Garnish:
¼ cup sesame seeds, toasted

Place the tempeh and tamari into a shallow bowl or pie plate and marinate for about 15 minutes, turning once to make sure all sides get soaked in the tamari.

Heat an 11 or 12-inch skillet over medium-high heat. Add the oil. Drain the tamari off of the tempeh and it to the hot oil; be careful it doesn't splatter. Sauté for 4 to 5 minutes, turning the tempeh, until lightly browned and slightly crispy. Then add the spinach and sauté a minute more until spinach is wilted.

While the tempeh is cooking, toast sesame seeds in a small skillet over medium heat. Keep them moving in the pan until they begin to turn golden and give off a rich aroma. It only takes about 3 minutes.

Remove tempeh and spinach from heat and serve over a bed of rice or quinoa with toasted sesame seeds sprinkled on top.

Yield: 4 servings

Ingredient Tip:

Be sure to always purchase organic tempeh. Over 90% of soybeans are now genetically engineered. Food labeled organic cannot be genetically engineered.

Nutrition Tip:

Consuming a lot of unfermented soy products, such as soy flour and soy milk, can contribute to mineral deficiencies in some people. For example, zinc has a great affinity for phytic acid found in unfermented soy. Zinc is needed to make active thyroid hormones. Without sufficient thyroid hormones some people tend gain weight and have a lowered metabolic rate. Tempeh, miso, natto, and naturally brewed soy sauce are examples of fermented soy products. Constituents in them that can bind to minerals have been neutralized through fermentation.

Raw Burritos with a Spicy Raw Mole Sauce

Blanching large collard leaves for 60 seconds creates a beautiful, bright green, and pliable wrap. These burritos are very filling, especially when you load them up with your favorite fixings! Use the raw mole sauce to either drizzle over the platter of rolled burritos or as a sauce for dipping. If you don't have time to make the sauce, skip it—the burritos are still very flavorful on their own. Store leftover burritos in a glass container in the refrigerator for up to 3 days.

6 large collard greens

Burrito Filling:
3 cups raw walnuts, soaked for 6 hours
1 cup fresh cilantro
3 to 4 green onions, coarsely chopped
1 to 2 cloves garlic, crushed
2 teaspoons ground cumin
2 teaspoons smoked paprika
1 teaspoon Herbamare
¼ cup freshly squeezed lime juice

Sauce:
2 ancho chilies, seeded
3 medjool dates, pitted
1 cup warm water
1 medium tomato, chopped
¼ cup raw pumpkin seeds
2 tablespoons raw cacao powder
1 teaspoon ground cumin
¾ teaspoon Herbamare or sea salt

Optional Additions:
fresh salsa
guacamole
sliced avocado
thinly sliced napa cabbage

Fill an 8-quart pot ¾ full with water and bring to a boil. Trim the ends off of the collard greens. Once boiling, place the 6 large collard greens into the pot all at once and blanch for 60 seconds. Remove from water immediately and place onto a plate or a towel to cool.

Place all of the ingredients for the burrito filling into a food processor fitted with the "s' blade and process until everything is finely ground and sticking together. Set aside.

To make the sauce, first place the ancho chilies and pitted dates into a small bowl and cover with warm water. Let soak for 15 to 30 minutes or until softened. Drain off soaking water and reserve. Place the soaked chilies and dates, tomato, pumpkin seeds, cacao powder, cumin, and salt into a blender and blend until you have a smooth sauce. Add the reserved soaking water as needed to thin out the sauce enough for it to be able to blend properly.

To assemble the burritos, lay one collard leaf on a plate, place a scoop or two of the burrito filling in the middle of the bottom of the leaf. Add any other filling ingredients such as salsa, avocado slices, or thinly sliced napa cabbage. First fold the left and right side edges in and then roll from the side closest to you (where the filling is) to the top. Repeat with remaining collard greens and filling. Use the mole sauce for dipping or drizzle on top of the platter of rolled burritos.

Yield: 6 servings

Nutrition Tip:

Compared to all other nuts, walnuts have the highest omega-3 content, the greatest amount of antioxidant polyphenols, and contain unique compounds such as juglone that are showing promising effects in combatting cancer.

Zucchini Lasagna with Pine Nut Ricotta

Cut flat, thin, long strips from large zucchinis to create simple, nutritious gluten-free lasagna noodles. You can sauté about one pound of grass-fed ground beef and add it to the pasta sauce for a heartier main dish if desired. The Pine Nut Ricotta recipe is also great dolloped atop the Almond Herb Pizza Crust, page 135, spread with freshly made pesto.

2 to 3 medium zucchinis

Ricotta:
1 cup pine nuts, soaked for 4 to 6 hours
1 cup blanched almond flour
2 to 3 tablespoons freshly squeezed lemon juice
1 to 2 tablespoons water
½ teaspoon Herbamare or sea salt

Other Ingredients:
3 to 4 cups pasta sauce
sautéed sliced mushrooms
fresh baby spinach
fresh basil leaves

Preheat oven to 350 degrees F. Lightly oil a 9 x 13-inch pan with olive oil.

Make your zucchini noodles by cutting long, thin, flat strips about 1/8 to ¼-inch in thickness.

To make the ricotta, drain the pine nuts and add them to a food processor fitted with the "s" blade along with the remaining ingredients; process until pasty.

To assemble the lasagna, first pour about one cup pasta sauce into the bottom of your pan and spread out evenly. Place a layer of zucchini noodles over the sauce. Take half of the ricotta and spread it over the noodles. Add any other ingredients you like such as spinach, sautéed mushrooms, or fresh basil. Add another cup of pasta sauce and repeat the layering process. Then add the rest of the sauce and the final layer of noodles. Drizzle olive oil over the noodles and sprinkle with Italian herbs and a few tablespoons of blanched almond flour.

Bake uncovered for 40 to 45 minutes. Let the lasagna rest for about 10 minutes and then slice and serve.

Yield: 8 to 10 servings

Walnut Rice Loaf

We like to serve this delicious vegan alternative to meat loaf with baked potatoes or baked sweet potatoes and a large green salad. Make sure your rice is completely cooled before making this recipe; in fact, one day old rice is better to use than freshly cooked.

2 cups raw walnuts
½ small red onion
1 to 2 small carrots
2 teaspoons poultry seasoning
1 teaspoon sea salt
½ teaspoon black pepper
¼ cup ground golden flaxseeds
4 cups cooked brown basmati rice
¼ cup ketchup
1 to 2 tablespoons coconut sugar

Preheat oven to 350 degrees F. Oil a 9 x 5-inch glass bread loaf pan.

Place the walnuts into a food processor fitted with the "s" blade. Process until finely ground. Add onion and carrots; process again until ground. Then add poultry seasoning, salt, black pepper, and ground flax; pulse a few times to combine.

Add cooked and completely cooled brown rice; process until rice breaks down and the mixture begins to form a ball. Press mixture evenly into pan. Spread with a thin layer of ketchup and sprinkle with coconut sugar.

Bake for approximately 1 ½ hours. Cool for about 10 minutes before slicing. Nut loaf is done when it slices easily without falling apart. If you cut into it and it still has a whitish color then it is not done. Place it back into the oven and cook until the internal color darkens slightly.

Yield: About 6 servings

Sweet Potato Falafels

I like to serve these easy falafels on a weeknight when my cooking time is limited. As long as I have cooked sweet potatoes in the fridge, this recipe can be made in about 10 minutes. Serve over a bed of lettuce and cooked quinoa with the Mint Tahini Dressing, page 352. To mince the green onions and parsley, I just process them in my food processor for about 30 seconds. You will need 1 large or 2 small sweet potatoes for this recipe.

1 ½ cups mashed cooked sweet potatoes
1 ½ cups garbanzo bean flour
3 to 4 green onions, minced
large handful fresh parsley or cilantro, minced
1 teaspoon lemon zest
½ to ¾ teaspoon Herbamare or sea salt
¼ teaspoon baking soda
2 to 4 tablespoons coconut oil or olive oil for cooking

To cook the sweet potatoes, slice them with the skin on into 1 to 2-inch thick slices. Place them into a steamer basket, cover, and cook until soft, about 15 minutes. You can also bake the whole sweet potato in a 350 degree oven for about an hour. Let them cool completely before mashing and measuring.

Place all of the ingredients, except the oil, into a medium-sized mixing bowl and use a fork to mix and mash the ingredients together. Once they are evenly mixed, heat a large skillet over medium heat. I prefer to use a cast iron skillet for this recipe. Use wet hands to roll 1 to 2-inch sized balls, then place them onto a plate. Lightly flatten each of the balls into a thick burger shape. This will allow them to cook properly since we are not deep-frying them.

Add 2 to 4 tablespoons of oil to the skillet. If the skillet is too hot, turn it to medium-low. Place half of the falafels into the skillet and cook for 1 to 2 minutes on each side. Set onto a plate to cool. Cook the second batch, adding more oil to the pan if necessary. Serve hot or cold.

Yield: 4 to 6 servings

Garbanzo Bean Burgers

If you have brown rice and garbanzo beans already cooked, these burgers can be made in a snap, you just need a food processor. We like to use either a romaine lettuce leaf or a napa cabbage leaf for a "bun." Add a dollop of dairy or non-dairy plain yogurt and a few fresh mint leaves; or mustard and ketchup on your burger. We like to serve these with a side of Rutabaga Fries, page 247, or Chipotle Yam Fries, page 246.

2 small carrots, chopped
2 to 3 green onions, chopped
handful fresh parsley
1 teaspoon Herbamare
2 cups cooked short grain brown rice
1 heaping cup cooked garbanzo beans, drained well
1 to 2 tablespoons ground golden flaxseeds
olive oil for cooking

Place the carrots, green onions, parsley, and Herbamare into a food processor fitted with the "s" blade; process until finely minced. Add the rice, garbanzo beans, and ground flax; pulse until the ingredients are combined and begin to form a doughy ball. Using either wet or lightly oiled hands, form the mixture into 5 or 6 patties and set onto a plate.

Heat an 11 or 12-inch skillet over medium to medium-high heat. Add about 1 to 2 tablespoons olive oil. Place the burgers on the skillet and cook for a few minutes on each side or until light golden brown.

Yield: 5 to 6 burgers

> **Kitchen Tip:**
>
> Make sure both your beans and rice are completely cooled, or better yet, straight out of the refrigerator. It is best to cook the short grain brown rice with a little less water than usual—moist rice will create very moist burgers.

Spicy Thai Mung Bean Burgers

Mung beans take about 45 to 60 minutes to cook on the stovetop and about 10 minutes to cook in the pressure-cooker. Make sure you drain them very well before using in this recipe. The burgers won't stick together if there is too much liquid added. To help the burgers hold together, use less water to cook the quinoa: 1 cup quinoa to 1 ¼ to 1 ½ cups of water. Lastly, be sure all of your ingredients are either cool or at room temp before making this recipe. Serve burgers in a Napa cabbage leaf with sliced avocado and a dollop of Spicy Pepper Coconut Cream, page 373.

small handful fresh cilantro
4 green onions, ends trimmed
2 fresh hot peppers, seeded
3 cloves garlic
1-inch piece fresh ginger, peeled
2 teaspoons lime zest
1 teaspoon sea salt
2 cups cooked mung beans, drained well
2 cups cooked quinoa

Using a food processor fitted with the "s" blade process all ingredients, except the mung beans and quinoa, until finely minced. Add mung beans and quinoa and process again until mixture comes together and forms a ball.

With slightly oiled hands, shape into six patties. Heat a heavy-bottomed skillet over medium to medium-high heat. Add a tablespoon of olive oil or coconut oil. Cook patties for about 3 to 5 minutes on each side.

Serve each burger inside two napa cabbage leaves with your favorite toppings.

Yield: 6 burgers

Quinoa Salmon Burgers

This is one of the most popular recipes on our blog. I like to serve these burgers with a raw green salad and homemade parsnip fries. I have found that using wild King salmon instead of sockeye is easiest for removing the bones; the bones are larger and there seems to be less of them in the King. Use your hands or tweezers to pull the bones out. If you don't want to bother removing the skin, have it done when you purchase the fish. Once you have the patties formed you can refrigerate them in between pieces of waxed paper for a few days or freeze them the same way.

3 to 4 green onions, ends trimmed
1 large handful fresh cilantro
1 to 2 teaspoons lemon zest (optional)
1 teaspoon Herbamare
freshly ground black pepper
1 to 1 ½ pounds wild salmon, skinned and deboned
1 cup cooked quinoa
olive oil or coconut oil for cooking

Place the green onions, cilantro, lemon zest, Herbamare, and black pepper into a food processor fitted with the "s" blade. Process until it is finely minced. Add the salmon and quinoa and process again until desired consistency. I like to have a few little chunks of salmon in the patties. Form into patties and place onto a plate.

Heat a large skillet over medium to medium-high heat. Add a tablespoon or so of oil and place a few patties in the skillet. I cook only three at a time in a 10-inch skillet. If your pan is hot it should only take 2 to 3 minutes per side to cook. If your pan is not quite heated it will take about 5 minutes per side and they may stick a little. Remove patties from skillet and set onto a plate. They will continue to cook once off the stove so be sure not to overcook them.

Yield: 6 Burgers

Variation:

Try fresh dill and parsley in place of the cilantro. You could also add about ½ teaspoon chipotle chili powder and use lime zest in place of the lemon zest.

Garlic Ginger Salmon

The following soy-free marinade recipe works as a sauce for steamed veggies and rice, or as a marinade for other types of fish and chicken. Add about a tablespoon of arrowroot powder or kudzu, whisk together, and simmer over low heat to create a thicker sauce. Serve salmon over mashed sweet potatoes and top with sautéed mustard greens and oyster mushrooms that have been seasoned with coconut aminos and brown rice vinegar.

1 ½ to 2 pounds wild salmon

Marinade:
¼ cup coconut aminos or wheat-free tamari
1 to 2 tablespoons brown rice vinegar or coconut vinegar
1 tablespoon maple syrup
1 tablespoon toasted sesame oil
2 cloves garlic, peeled
1-inch piece fresh ginger, peeled

Rinse the salmon fillet and place it skin-side up in a glass baking dish. Place all of the ingredients for the marinade into a blender and blend until smooth. Pour marinade over fish, cover, and refrigerate for 3 hours or until ready to use.

Preheat oven to 400 degrees. Pour off marinade and flip salmon fillet so the skin is down.

Bake for approximately 10 minutes per inch of thickness. The fish will continue to cook after it comes out of the oven so it is best to take it out when still a little undercooked.

Yield: 4 to 6 servings

Nutrition Tip:

The positive effects from eating salmon start at four ounces of salmon per week. Research has demonstrated that the consumption of omega-3 fatty acids can provide protection from cardiovascular disease, improve mood, decrease joint pain, increase eye health, and decrease ADD/ADHD symptoms. Consuming twelve ounces of salmon a week has been shown to raise the anti-inflammatory omega-3 fatty acids in red blood cells from 4 to 6 percent in four months.

Orange Pepper Salmon

Since we live in the Pacific Northwest, we have access to fresh, wild salmon. In autumn we take our children to local rivers and watch the salmon run while the bald eagles fly above us. If you don't live in a place with access to wild salmon, use this recipe with another variety of fish that is local to your area. Remember to always avoid using farmed salmon or Atlantic salmon, which are high in accumulated toxic chemicals. Serve this salmon recipe with cranberry sauce in place of turkey at your Thanksgiving table.

2 pounds wild salmon
zest of one orange
¼ cup freshly squeezed orange juice
½ teaspoon Herbamare or sea salt
freshly ground black pepper
extra virgin olive oil
or coconut oil

Preheat your oven to 400 degrees F.

Rinse your salmon fillet and pat dry with a paper towel. Cut it into 6 fillets. Arrange fillets on a baking sheet or large glass baking dish.

First grate the orange for zest, then juice. Drizzle orange juice over salmon fillets and sprinkle with zest, Herbamare, and plenty of freshly ground black pepper. Drizzle each fillet with a little olive oil or dot with coconut oil.

Bake for about 8 minutes for sockeye, 10 minutes for coho, and usually about 20 minutes for king, depending on the thickness.

Yield: 6 servings

Kitchen Tip:

It works best to zest the orange before you juice it. I use my microplane fine grater to do this.

Poached Salmon with Spring Onions and White Wine

I use a stainless steel fish-poaching pan for this recipe, which, along with the salmon and spring onions, creates a gorgeous presentation. You could also use a 10-inch skillet though you would need to cut the fish fillet in half to make it fit correctly. I prefer using coho salmon for all poached recipes because it is thin and cooks evenly in the poaching liquid. Serve this recipe with the Mushroom Millet Risotto, page 271, and the Arugula and Shaved Fennel Salad, page 207.

one 2-pound wild salmon fillet
2 spring onions
3 to 4 sprigs fresh thyme
3 tablespoons extra virgin olive oil
½ cup white wine
Herbamare and freshly ground black pepper

Rinse and the fish fillet and pat dry. Place into pan skin-side down.

Trim the ends off of the onions and cut in half lengthwise; run under cool water to remove any dirt and sand. Place the spring onions and fresh thyme on top of the salmon. Drizzle with olive oil. Add the white wine to the pan and then season the fillet with Herbamare and freshly ground black pepper.

Cover and poach over medium to medium-low heat for 10 to 12 minutes. Serve immediately.

Yield: 4 to 6 servings

Tandoori Salmon

Tandoori food is traditionally cooked in extremely hot clay ovens throughout India. Here I use traditional tandoori seasonings, but bake the salmon in a regular oven. The tandoori seasoning I use is made from ground coriander, cumin, sweet paprika, garlic, ginger, cardamom, and saffron. Combined with a little coconut milk and lemon juice, this salmon recipe is very fresh and flavorful! Serve with whipped sweet potatoes and a crunchy romaine, cucumber, and tomato salad for a balanced meal.

1 ½ to 2 pounds wild salmon
¼ teaspoon sea salt
1 small lemon, juiced
1 to 2 teaspoons tandoori seasoning
½ cup coconut milk

Preheat oven to 400 degrees F. Take out a small enough baking dish to just fit the salmon. You will want it small so the coconut milk can surround the salmon while cooking. Place a little coconut oil on the bottom of the baking dish.

Rinse the salmon and place it skin-side down into your baking dish. Sprinkle salt and lemon juice over the salmon, then evenly scatter the tandoori seasoning over the fillet. Lastly, pour the coconut milk over the salmon.

Bake for about 10 minutes per inch of thickness of your fillet: sockeye needs about 8 minutes, cook coho for about 12 to 15 minutes, and king usually takes about 20 to 25 minutes. The fish will continue to cook once it is out of the oven.

Yield: About 4 to 6 servings

Meals

Fish Tacos

You can use any "safe" local fish for this recipe. Be sure to use a variety that is on the firmer side, such as salmon or halibut. We like to serve fish tacos with Homemade Corn Tortillas, page 387, fresh salsa, sprouts, thinly sliced napa cabbage, and homemade guacamole. If you don't want to use a tortilla to hold your fillings, try using a napa cabbage leaf!

1 ½ to 2 pounds fish, skinned
2 large limes, juiced
2 to 3 cloves garlic, peeled
1 to 2 jalapenos, seeded
1 to 2 teaspoons cumin
1 to 2 teaspoons Herbamare
coconut oil for sautéing

Cut the fish with a very sharp knife into 1 to 2-inch cubes and place into a shallow baking dish, such as an 8 x 8-inch pan. Combine the lime juice, garlic, jalapenos, cumin, and Herbamare in a blender and blend for 30 to 60 seconds. Pour marinade over fish. Marinate for about an hour.

To cook the fish, heat a large heavy-bottomed, stainless steel skillet over medium-high heat. Let the pan heat up for a few minutes, then add about 2 tablespoons of coconut oil. Add the fish, start with ⅓ to ½ of the fish if your skillet is smaller (say 10-inches). If you add too much fish at once to a skillet, it is not able to sear and retain its liquid, therefore drying out quickly. You'll notice a bit of water at the bottom of the pan if you add too much at once. Sauté for 3 to 4 minutes, depending on the size of the pieces. Remove from the skillet, add a little more oil, and then cook the remaining fish.

Serve with corn tortillas, salsa, guacamole, sprouts, and thinly sliced napa cabbage or your favorite taco ingredients.

Yield: 4 to 6 servings

Nutrition Tip:

Mercury, a heavy metal commonly found in fish, has the potential to damage tissues of the body. The rapidly growing brain tissue of developing fetuses, infants, and young children is particularly susceptible to mercury's adverse effects. Mercury is also capable of damaging heart tissue in adults, male reproductive organs, and sperm. Two-thirds of mercury in our environment comes from coal-burning power plants, and a significant amount comes from medical and municipal waste. Microorganisms convert elemental mercury to methylmercury, a toxic form of mercury that our bodies cannot get rid of. It first accumulates in microorganisms at the bottom of the food chain and then moves up the food chain ultimately reaching the highest levels in predatory fish. For more information on "safe" fish and to download regional Seafood Watch pocket guides, visit **MontereyBayAquarium.org**.

Herb Roasted Halibut

This is one of our favorite ways to prepare fish in spring and summertime, when halibut is in season. Our garden beds are blossoming with fresh herbs and this is a perfect way to use them up. Serve this fish with a variety of sautéed summer vegetables, such as the Sautéed Snow Peas and Patty Pan Squash, page 241, along with a large garden salad.

Fish:
1 ½ to 2 pounds fresh halibut fillets
¼ teaspoon sea salt
freshly ground black pepper
2 tablespoons extra virgin olive oil

Herb Topping:
½ cup packed fresh basil
½ cup packed fresh chives
2 to 3 tablespoons fresh oregano leaves
1 tablespoon thyme leaves
3 cloves garlic, peeled
the zest from ½ of a lemon

Preheat oven to 400 degrees F.

Rinse and pat dry the fish. Place into a rectangular baking dish skin side down. Sprinkle with sea salt and freshly ground black pepper. Drizzle with olive oil.

Place all topping ingredients into a mini food processor and process until minced. You can also place all ingredients onto a wooden cutting board and mince using a large, sharp knife.

Using your fingers, rub the herb topping evenly over the top of the fish. Place in the oven and roast for 10 minutes per inch of fish thickness. It doesn't take long to cook, usually about 15 minutes. The fish will continue to cook after it comes out of the oven so it is best to take it out when still a little undercooked.

Yield: 4 to 6 servings

Thai Coconut Fish Sticks

Fish cooks very fast and will dry out if overcooked so watch these carefully. Since I am not great at cutting off the skin, I have it done when I am purchasing the fish; it is so much easier this way. If you decide to do it yourself, just make sure your knife is very sharp. Serve with the Garlic Ginger Peanut Sauce, page 363, or the Ginger Plum Sauce, page 364.

1 ½ to 2 pounds halibut, skin removed
¼ cup sweet rice flour or arrowroot powder
4 to 6 tablespoons water
1 teaspoon red curry paste
1 teaspoon Herbamare
2 cups unsweetened shredded coconut
3 to 4 tablespoons coconut oil for cooking

Rinse the halibut, then cut into "sticks" about ½-inch wide and 3 inches long. In a separate bowl whisk together the sweet rice flour, water, red curry paste, and Herbamare. Place the shredded coconut into a separate bowl.

Begin heating a large 11 or 12-inch skillet over medium-high heat. Your skillet needs to be hot before adding the fish.

While your skillet is heating, place the fish into the rice flour-water mixture and coat evenly. Then dip the fish sticks into the shredded coconut to coat using your hands to press the coconut into the fish sticks.

Add the coconut oil to your skillet. Make sure the oil spreads out quickly. This means your pan is hot enough. Add the fish sticks in batches so they don't overcrowd the pan. Cook for 2 to 3 minutes on each side. Timing may differ depending on the thickness of the fish. Use tongs to flip them. The fish sticks will continue to cook after you remove them from the pan. Check doneness by breaking apart the thickest one with a fork. Add more coconut oil and cook the remaining fish sticks.

Yield: 4 to 6 servings

Variation:

In place of the sweet rice flour and water you can use one beaten large egg. Whisk the curry paste and Herbamare into the beaten egg, then dip your fish sticks into the egg and proceed with the rest of the recipe.

Thai Fish Curry with Garden Veggies

Any variety of garden vegetables will work in this simple curry; try walla walla onions, cauliflower, cabbage, green beans, or mushrooms. Kaffir lime leaves, which give curried dishes an authentic Thai flavor, can be found at your local Asian market. I keep a few small bags in my freezer and then take them out as I need them. Remember fish only takes a few minutes to cook, so be sure to add it last! Serve curry over cooked brown jasmine rice for a satisfying meal.

1 tablespoon coconut oil or olive oil
1 medium onion, cut into crescent moons
4 medium carrots, sliced diagonally
4 to 5 cloves garlic, crushed
1 teaspoon ground turmeric
1 can coconut milk
1 cup water, chicken stock, or fish stock
4 kaffir lime leaves
4 teaspoons red curry paste
2 tablespoons fish sauce or coconut aminos
½ to 1 teaspoon Herbamare
2 medium zucchini, sliced in half lengthwise and then cut into rounds
2 small red bell peppers, cut into 1-inch pieces
2 medium ripe garden tomatoes, diced
1 ½ to 2 pounds Alaskan halibut, skin removed and cut into cubes
large handful of fresh Thai Basil leaves, thinly sliced

In an 11-inch skillet or other large pan, heat the oil over medium-high heat. Add the onions and sauté for about 5 minutes. Add the carrots and garlic; sauté a few minutes more. Add the turmeric, coconut milk, water, lime leaves, red curry paste, fish sauce, and Herbamare. Stir to incorporate the curry paste. Simmer for about 5 to 7 minutes or until carrots are partway cooked.

Then add the zucchini and bell peppers; simmer until the veggies are crisp-tender. Add the tomatoes and fish; simmer for an additional 3 minutes or so or until the fish is cooked through. Be careful not to stir too much otherwise the fish will fall apart.

Sprinkle with Thai basil and serve hot!

Yield: 4 to 6 servings

Apricot Glazed Chicken

This chicken recipe can made ahead of time and set in the fridge, covered, to marinate while you are at work. When you get home, drain off the marinade and pop the pan in the oven. Serve with the Cabbage Salad with Mung Bean Sprouts, page 211, and cooked brown rice.

4 organic bone-in, skin-on chicken thighs

Marinade:
¼ cup fruit-sweetened apricot jam
¼ cup wheat-free tamari or coconut aminos
2 tablespoons extra virgin olive oil or toasted sesame oil
1 to 2 teaspoons grated fresh ginger

Rinse the chicken thighs and place them into an 8 x 8-inch or 7 x 11-inch baking dish. In a separate bowl, whisk together the ingredients for the marinade. Pour marinade over chicken. Marinate for 30 minutes or cover pan and place in the refrigerator to marinate for up to 8 hours.

Preheat oven to 400 degrees F. Pour off excess marinade from pan. Place pan in the oven and bake chicken for about 25 to 30 minutes.

Yield: 4 to 6 servings

Ingredient Tip:

I use Bionaturae sugar-free organic apricot jam in this recipe.

Nutrition Tip:

Be sure to always purchase organic chicken. Non-organic chicken, including "free-range" and "naturally raised" often contains high levels of arsenic. This heavy metal can easily get absorbed into the body where it causes certain nutrient deficiencies such as zinc and thiamin.

Balsamic Roasted Chicken with Figs and Sweet Onions

This recipe is very simple and kid-friendly. My kids don't eat the roasted figs or onions but they love the chicken over cooked brown rice. It is delicious even as leftovers! Be sure to serve the chicken with a large, raw green salad, which helps to digest the protein.

1 whole organic chicken (about 3 ½ to 4 pounds)
Herbamare and freshly ground black pepper
1 large sweet onion, chopped
8 to 10 fresh figs
¼ cup balsamic vinegar
¼ cup extra virgin olive oil
1 tablespoon maple syrup
fresh rosemary sprigs
water

Preheat oven to 450 degrees F.

Rinse chicken under cold running water. Place it into a 9 x 13-inch baking dish or other roasting pan. Generously sprinkle with Herbamare and freshly ground black pepper. Put the chopped onion inside the cavity of the chicken and on the bottom of the pan. Place the figs around the chicken.

Whisk together the balsamic vinegar, olive oil, and maple syrup in a small bowl or cup. Pour over the chicken. Place a few fresh rosemary springs on and around the chicken.

Add about ½ cup of water to the bottom of the pan. Roast chicken for about 20 minutes to seal in the juices. Then reduce heat to 325 degrees and continue to cook until juices run clear, about another 1 ½ hours.

Remove chicken from pan and place onto a platter or large plate. Wait 10 minutes before carving to let the juices return to the meat. Place the cooked figs and sweet onions on the platter with the sliced chicken. Drizzle pan juices over chicken and serve.

Yield: 6 to 8 servings

Roasted Whole Chicken with Root Vegetables

In autumn, when root vegetables are in abundance, I try to add them to just about everything I cook. By late afternoon the days are growing darker and I usually begin preparing dinner just after the children arrive home from school. It is comforting to see the beautiful array of orange and yellow vegetables surrounding the chicken before going in the oven. Once in the oven, I have about two hours to be with my children before dinner is ready. We usually serve a simple blanched kale salad with this meal and possibly some Chia Dinner Rolls, page 134.

Chicken:
1 whole organic chicken (about 3 ½ to 4 pounds)
½ cup Madeira wine
½ cup water
½ cup chopped celery
½ cup finely chopped shallot or red onion
sea salt and freshly ground black pepper

Vegetables:
1 medium yam, peeled and cut into chunks
2 Yukon gold potatoes, cut into chunks
2 large carrots, cut into ½-inch rounds
2 parsnips, peeled and cut into ½-inch rounds
1 medium red onion, cut into chunks
¼ cup extra virgin olive oil
½ teaspoon sea salt

Herbs:
5 sprigs fresh thyme
1 tablespoon chopped fresh sage
1 tablespoon chopped fresh rosemary
2 tablespoons fresh marjoram leaves

Preheat oven to 450 degrees F.

Rinse chicken under cold running water. Place it into a 9 x 13-inch baking dish or other roasting pan. Pour the Madeira wine and water over the chicken. Place the chopped celery and shallots or onions into the cavity of the chicken. Drizzle a little olive oil and generously sprinkle sea salt and freshly ground black pepper over the chicken.

Place the vegetables, olive oil, and salt into a large bowl and toss together. Place them in the pan around the chicken. Sprinkle the chicken and vegetables with the fresh herbs.

Roast chicken for about 20 minutes to seal in the juices. Then reduce heat to 325 degrees and continue to cook until juices run clear, about another 1 ½ hours. Remove chicken from pan and place onto a platter or large plate. Wait 10 minutes before carving to let the juices return to the meat. Place root vegetables into a serving bowl. Pour pan juices into a gravy boat and serve alongside chicken and root vegetables.

Yield: 6 to 8 servings

Ingredient Tip:

In autumn all of the herbs used in this recipe are right there at my fingertips in my front garden. Feel free to use what you have on hand or use a few tablespoons of dried poultry seasoning in place of the fresh herbs.

Kitchen Tip:

Be sure to cut your root vegetables into larger chunks. If they are too small they will get quite mushy during the long roasting time.

Moroccan Roasted Chicken

This is an easy weeknight meal that I can make in 10 minutes. Some days are so busy with afterschool activities and other events that I need to be able to come home at 5:30pm and put together a balanced meal quickly. I serve this over cooked millet with a green salad, sautéed kale, or steamed green beans.

3 to 4 split organic chicken breasts, bone-in and skin-on
1 small red onion, cut into large chunks
1 Meyer lemon, cut into wedges
½ to 1 cup dried apricots
1 teaspoon Herbamare or sea salt
1 teaspoon ground cumin
1 teaspoon ground coriander
1 teaspoon ground cardamom
1 teaspoon ground black pepper
½ teaspoon turmeric
pinch cayenne pepper
2 to 3 tablespoons organic butter or coconut oil

Garnishes:
chopped cilantro
green onion slices

Preheat the oven to 425 degrees F.

Rinse the chicken breasts and place them into a casserole dish or 9 x 13-inch pan in a single layer. Place the onion chunks, lemon wedges, and dried apricots around the chicken.

In a small bowl, mix together the salt and spices. Sprinkle spice mixture over the chicken. Dot with butter or coconut oil. Roast for 30 to 40 minutes, depending on the size of the breasts, or until the juices run clear. Slice chicken from the bone and serve it with the apricots, red onions, and juices at the bottom of the roasting dish. Garnish with chopped parsley or cilantro.

Yield: 6 to 8 servings

Nutrition Tip:

Be sure to purchase organic, sulfite-free apricots. Sulfite is a preservative that reduces discoloration and oxidation. You'll notice that organic apricots are a dark brownish-orange color because they don't have any sulfites added. The FDA estimates that 1 out of 100 people have a reaction to sulfites. A sensitivity to sulfites may lead to a difficulty with breathing, hives, excessive sneezing, or swelling of the throat. This may be exacerbated by a deficiency in molybdenum, a mineral commonly found in legumes. Sulfites listed on a food label could appear as sulfur dioxide, sodium sulfite, sodium bisulfite, potassium bisulfite, sodium metabisulfite, or potassium metabisulfite.

Chipotle-Lime Roasted Chicken

This is another one of those easy meals that can be prepared in minutes. I use the leftover chicken to make variations of chicken salads such as wild rice and chicken, or my Chicken Salad Lettuce Wraps, page 395. When I put the chicken in the oven I like to also place four or five small yams on the oven to bake too. Serve chicken with baked yams, cooked quinoa, and a green salad.

3 to 4 split organic chicken breasts, bone-in and skin-on
2 teaspoons coarse sea salt
1 to 2 teaspoons chipotle chili powder
2 to 3 tablespoons organic butter or coconut oil
1 lime, cut into wedges

Garnishes:
chopped cilantro
green onion slices

Preheat oven to 425 degrees F.

Rinse the chicken breasts and place them into a casserole dish or 9 x 13-inch pan in a single layer. Sprinkle with the coarse sea salt. If you only have fine sea salt then use just one teaspoon instead of two. Then sprinkle with chipotle chili powder. Dot each chicken breast with butter or coconut oil.

Gently squeeze lime wedges over the chicken and then add them to the pan. Roast for 30 to 40 minutes, depending on the size of the breasts, or until the juices run clear. Garnish with cilantro and green onions.

Yield: 6 to 8 servings

Variation:

Slow-Cooked Variation: If you have more time, you can slow cook the chicken in the oven to create more flavorful, tender chicken, which is also more digestible. Heat oven to 325 degrees F and cook for 60 to 75 minutes or until juices run clear.

Chicken Pot Pie

Chicken pot pie is a timeless classic that never gets boring. Our children love this meal and always ask for seconds. This recipe is delicious served on a cold winter's evening along side the Sautéed Winter Greens with Caramelized Onions, page 240, or a fresh green salad. If you are avoiding grains, simply replace the crust in this recipe with a half recipe of the Coconut Flour Biscuits, page 143.

Crust:
½ cup superfine brown rice flour
½ cup superfine sweet rice flour
¼ cup quinoa flour or millet flour
½ teaspoon sea salt
8 tablespoons organic palm shortening or organic butter
4 to 6 tablespoons ice cold water

Filling:
1 to 2 tablespoons extra virgin olive oil
1 medium onion, diced
1 ½ cups diced carrots
1 ½ cups diced celery
1 ½ cups diced red potatoes
2 cups chicken stock
2 to 3 tablespoons sweet rice flour or arrowroot powder
2 cups chopped cooked chicken
1 teaspoon dried thyme
1 teaspoon dried marjoram
1 cup frozen peas
½ cup chopped parsley
Herbamare and black pepper to taste

Preheat oven to 350 degrees F. Set out a 9.5-inch deep-dish pie plate.

To make the crust, whisk together the flours and salt. Cut in the shortening with your fingers or a pastry cutter until small crumbs form. Freeze the bowl of flour and shortening for about 10 to 15 minutes. If you use butter then freeze the butter-flour mixture for closer to 20 minutes to create a flakey crust. You can also add half butter and half shortening which will give the crust a good flavor while keeping it flakey.

Add the water, beginning with the lesser amount. Use a spoon or fork to mix the dough together until it forms a ball. If necessary, knead together ever so slightly to form a ball. Roll out crust in between two pieces of waxed paper into a circle the size of the pie plate. Set aside.

To make the filling, heat a large skillet over medium heat. Add oil and onion; sauté until soft, about 5 to 6 minutes. Then add carrots, celery, and potatoes; sauté for about 10 minutes more, being careful not to brown.

Whisk together chicken stock and sweet rice flour or arrowroot powder; pour into pan with vegetables. Add the cooked chicken and dried herbs; simmer uncovered for about 5 to

10 minutes or until thickened. Turn off heat. Add peas and parsley. Season with sea salt or Herbamare and black pepper to taste. Pour filling into a 9.5-inch deep-dish pie plate.

Carefully remove the top layer of waxed paper from the rolled out pie dough. Pick up the crust and flip over onto the pie filling. Remove the second layer of waxed paper. Tuck any edges in or cut them off with a knife.

Bake on a cookie sheet (to catch any drips from the filling) for 45 to 60 minutes or until filling is bubbling up around the edges of the crust and the crust is cooked.

Yield: 6 servings

Kitchen Tip:

I always use homemade chicken stock made from leftover roasted whole organic chickens. After I pull the meat from the bones, I save it and store it in a container (to be used in a pie like this). Then I take the skin and bones and simmer them with onions, carrots, celery, herbs, Herbamare, and a dash of apple cider vinegar to create a rich, healing chicken stock. After it is strained, I store the stock in quart jars in my freezer. See page 170 for more details.

Crispy Chicken Fingers

This is a great transition recipe if you or your child are just beginning a gluten-free, casein-free diet and are accustomed to fast food versions of chicken fingers. We use Erewhon Crispy Brown Rice Cereal, which can be found in the cereal isle of your local food co-op or health food store. Serve with the Honey Mustard Dressing, page 351, steamed broccoli, and the Dilled Quinoa with Peas, page 272, for a balanced meal.

2 large organic chicken breasts, cut into ½-inch thick strips
½ cup sweet rice flour
1 to 2 teaspoons poultry seasoning
1 teaspoon Herbamare
freshly ground black pepper
¾ cup water
5 cups Crispy Brown Rice Cereal, crushed
coconut oil for cooking

Rinse and cut the chicken breasts, set aside on a plate. In a shallow bowl, whisk together the sweet rice flour, poultry seasoning, Herbamare, and black pepper. Add the water and whisk together; set aside.

To crush the cereal, either place it into a Ziploc bag and roll with a rolling pin (your child may want to do this) or give it a whirl in a food processor fitted with the "s" blade. Pour into a separate shallow bowl.

Dip each piece of chicken into the rice flour slurry then dredge in the crushed cereal. Set each piece on a separate plate until you are ready to cook them all.

Heat a large skillet over medium-high heat. Heat about 2 to 3 tablespoons of oil in the skillet. Be sure the skillet is hot before adding the oil. Quickly add ½ of the chicken fingers being careful not to overcrowd them in the pan. Cook for 3 minutes on each side. Add more oil in between batches. Place onto a warmed platter to serve.

Yield: 4 to 6 servings

Ingredient Tip:

Poultry seasoning can easily be blended from dried herbs in your pantry. I like to use a combination of 2 tablespoons dried sage, 2 tablespoons dried marjoram, 2 tablespoons dried thyme, 1 tablespoon dried rosemary, and 2 teaspoons ground black pepper. Just place all of the ingredients into a coffee grinder, small electric grinder, or mortar and pestle and pulverize to a powder. Store in a small glass spice jar.

Grain-Free Chicken Nuggets

This is the healthiest take on a chicken nugget that I've been able to create. Using low-glycemic almond flour, organic chicken breasts, and heat-stable coconut oil are what makes them so nutritious. Serve nuggets with the Honey Mustard Dressing, page 351, for dipping and a green salad. For optimal digestion, serve the meal with a few spoons full of raw sauerkraut or cultured vegetables.

2 large organic chicken breasts (about 1 ½ pounds)
2 to 3 teaspoons poultry seasoning
½ to 1 teaspoon Herbamare or sea salt
4 tablespoons arrowroot powder
4 tablespoons water
1 ½ cups almond flour
6 tablespoons coconut oil

Set out two shallow, wide bowls. In one bowl mix together the poultry seasoning, Herbamare, arrowroot powder, and water. In the other bowl, add the almond flour.

Rinse the chicken breasts and cut them into small chunks. Make sure to keep the size of each piece relatively even. Place the chicken breast chunks into the arrowroot slurry and mix them around to coat evenly. Then toss a few of them at a time in the almond flour. The almond flour will feel moist. You can press some of it into each nugget to help coat them.

Heat a deep 11 or 12-inch skillet over medium heat. Add 3 tablespoons of coconut oil. Once the oil has heated for 30 to 60 seconds, place half of the chicken nuggets into the pan. Cook for about 3 minutes on each side. Add the remaining coconut oil to the pan and cook the rest of the chicken nuggets.

Yield: 4 to 6 servings

Minty Chicken-Zucchini Kebobs

We have a little herb garden outside our front door. I planted spearmint in it the year we bought the house. Then a month later I began pulling it all out as it soon began to take over the garden. I thought I had eradicated it from the garden but apparently my efforts did not work as it began to creep back the next year. Mint is impossible to get rid of. I learned later that I was supposed to plant it in a bottomless bucket to contain the roots. Now I know, and now I have mint every summer that needs to be made into recipes like this. You can add more vegetables to the kebabs to make the meat go further. Try adding mushrooms, peppers, onions, or tomatoes. Serve with a large garden salad and cooked quinoa for a balanced meal.

1 recipe Pepper-Mint Dressing (page 354)
2 to 3 organic chicken breasts, cut into chunks
4 to 5 small zucchini, cut into thick rounds
bamboo skewers

Prepare the Pepper-Mint Dressing. Set out a 9 x 13-inch or 10 x 14-inch glass baking dish for marinating the kebobs.

Alternately stick the chunks of chicken and zucchini rounds onto the bamboo skewers. Place skewers into the glass pan and pour the mint marinade over them. Turn them a few times to coat evenly. Cover, refrigerate, and let marinate for 30 minutes to 4 hours.

Heat your grill to medium-high. Cook for 10 to 15 minutes, turning two or three times during cooking.

Yield: 6 to 8 servings

> **Nutrition Tip:**
>
> Chicken is an excellent source of B vitamins, particularly niacin. A deficiency of niacin in the diet has been linked to DNA damage. In the 1950's, Linus Pauling and others found that a niacin deficiency may be associated with neuro-psychiatric disorders. Tryptophan is the precursor to the neurotransmitters serotonin and melatonin. When your body is deficient in niacin, it will use *sixty* tryptophan molecules to make *one* niacin molecule leading to a decrease in available tryptophan to make these vital neurotransmitters responsible for regulating mood and sleep.

Slow Cooked Chicken Tacos

This recipe can be made ahead of time, refrigerated or frozen, and then reheated when needed. This recipe will also work using a crockpot. This taco filling can be used to fill corn or gluten-free flour tortillas, a lettuce leaf, cabbage leaf, or even a collard green. Add in brown rice, avocado, a squeeze of lime, and cherry tomato halves for a complete, balanced meal.

1 Ancho chili, seeded
1 cup boiling water
4 cloves garlic
½ teaspoon chipotle chili powder (add more for a kick)
1 to 2 tablespoons ground cumin
3 teaspoons sea salt or Herbamare
3 pounds organic chicken breast or thigh meat
1 medium onion, diced
3 cups tomato puree
2 to 3 tablespoons extra virgin olive oil

Preheat oven to 325 degrees.

Place the ancho chili in a small bowl and pour the boiling water over it; let soak for 5 to 10 minutes. Add the chili and soaking water to a blender with the garlic, chipotle chili powder, cumin, and salt. Blend on high until pureed.

Place the pureed chili mixture into a large casserole dish with the remaining ingredients. Cover and bake for one hour. Remove cover, stir, and bake uncovered for an additional hour.

After it is done, use the back of a large spoon to mash the chicken until it begins to fall apart. Taste and add any extra salt or seasonings to bring it up to flavor. Serve as a taco filling or over cooked quinoa. Store leftovers in the refrigerator for up to 5 days or freeze in portion sizes.

Yield: 8 to 10 servings

Ingredient Tip:

I use Bionaturae Strained Tomatoes. Ancho chilies are dried poblano peppers. I buy mine in the bulk spice section at my local co-op.

Herb Roasted Turkey Breast

If you have ever felt intimidated by roasting a whole turkey, try a turkey breast instead. You can make the marinade the night before and actually let the turkey breast marinate for 12 to 24 hours in the refrigerator. Then just pop it into the oven and walk away. Serve with baked potatoes, roasted winter squash, or the Millet Mushroom Risotto, page 271, and a green salad.

one 3 ½ to 4-pound bone-in turkey breast

Marinade:
½ cup white wine
¼ cup extra virgin olive oil
¼ cup fresh sage leaves
¼ cup fresh rosemary leaves
¼ cup fresh thyme
¼ cup fresh oregano
2 small shallots, peeled
2 teaspoons Herbamare
1 teaspoon whole black peppercorns

Rinse the turkey breast and place into the smallest sized roasting pan that will fit. I use a stone roasting dish with a lid which works perfectly.

To make the marinade, place all ingredients into a blender and blend until smooth and creamy. Pour marinade over turkey breast, cover the pan, and let marinate in the refrigerator for at least 3 hours or for up to 24 hours. For longer marinating you may want to place the turkey breast and marinade into a large Ziploc bag.

Preheat oven to 325 degrees F. Place the roasting pan with turkey and marinade into the oven with the lid on. Cook with the lid on for about 1 hour then remove the lid, baste the turkey with some of the marinade at the bottom of the pan and return it to the oven to cook uncovered for another 1 to 1 ½ hours or meat thermometer inserted reads 170 degrees F.

Yield: 8 servings

Turkey Quinoa Meatballs

These meatballs freeze amazingly well. I like to freeze them in serving sized containers to have a quick lunch ready to go when needed. It is the food processor that helps bind these together without using eggs. I use a 14-cup sized processor but an 11-cup will work as well. Serve meatballs and sauce over cooked brown rice noodles, cooked quinoa, or baked spaghetti squash with a large green salad.

Meatballs:
1 to 2 tablespoons extra virgin olive oil
1 medium onion, diced
3 to 4 cloves garlic, crushed
2 pounds ground turkey
2 cups cooked quinoa
1 tablespoon Italian seasoning
1 teaspoon paprika
1 to 2 teaspoons Herbamare
½ to 1 teaspoon freshly ground black pepper
large handful fresh parsley

Sauce:
2 cups chicken or turkey stock
2 tablespoons arrowroot powder
½ to 1 cup pasta sauce

Heat a 10-inch skillet over medium-high heat. Add the oil and onions; sauté for 5 to 10 minutes or until softened and beginning to change color. Add the garlic and sauté for another minute or so. Remove pan from heat.

Place the ground turkey, cooked quinoa, Italian seasoning, paprika, Herbamare, pepper, and parsley into a food processor fitted with the "s" blade. Add the sautéed onions and garlic. Process until combined and ingredients are broken down (such as the parsley and cooked onions). You may need to pulse the mixture a few times and scrape down the sides. Roll mixture into equal sized meatballs. Set them all onto plates as you roll them.

Preheat oven to 325 degrees F. Heat a large skillet over medium to medium-high heat for a minute or two. Add a few tablespoons extra virgin olive oil. Place enough meatballs into the pan so they have still some room to move. Sauté for about 5 minutes moving the meatballs around a little so they cook on all sides. They won't be all the way cooked at this point so don't eat them. Add more oil in between batches.

Place sautéed meatballs into a 9 x 13-inch pan as they come off the stove. While meatballs are cooling, combine the stock, arrowroot powder, and pasta sauce into a bowl and whisk together to dissolve the arrowroot. Once you have sautéed all of the meatballs, pour the stock-sauce mixture into the pan you cooked the meatballs in and simmer for about 2 minutes. Pour sauce over meatballs in baking dish. Cover, and bake for about 45 minutes. Remove cover and bake for another 15 to 20 minutes.

Yield: 8 servings

Sloppy Joes

Try serving this recipe with the Sourdough Buckwheat Burger Buns, page 125, and a side of Beet Sauerkraut, page 503, for a balanced, nourishing meal. Cultured vegetables, like sauerkraut, contain enzymes that help break down other parts of your meal and are especially helpful in digesting meat.

1 tablespoon extra virgin olive oil or organic butter
1 small onion, finely diced
1 small green bell pepper, finely chopped
1 to 2 cloves garlic, crushed
½ to 1 teaspoon Herbamare or sea salt
½ teaspoon paprika
¼ teaspoon celery salt
¼ teaspoon yellow mustard powder
pinch ground cloves
freshly ground black pepper
1 pound grass-fed ground beef
one 7-ounce jar tomato paste (about ½ cup)
½ cup water
2 tablespoons coconut sugar
1 tablespoon coconut vinegar

Heat a 10-inch skillet over medium heat. Add the oil, onions, and green bell peppers; sauté until softened, about 5 minutes. Then add the garlic, Herbamare, paprika, celery salt, mustard powder, ground cloves, and black pepper; sauté a minute more.

Next add the ground beef and cook, breaking it up with a spatula as it cooks. Do this for a few minutes until it is no longer pink. Add the tomato paste, water, coconut sugar, and vinegar; cover a simmer over low heat for about 7 to 10 minutes, adding more water if necessary. Taste and add more salt and black pepper if needed. Serve.

Yield: 4 to 5 servings

Variation:

Replace the ground beef with 2 to 3 cups of cooked lentils for a vegan version. Three of our children don't like beef but love this recipe made with lentils.

Nutrition Tip:

Why Grass-Fed Beef? Grass-fed or "pasture finished" beef has a higher levels of essential omega-3 fatty acids, lower antibiotic and pesticide residues, and no growth hormones. This type of cattle husbandry reduces the use of tractor fuel, pesticides, herbicides, fertilizers, and GMO feed crops. Cattle farming is responsible for 28% of global methane emissions that contribute to global warming. When cows are exclusively fed grasses for their entire lives, they are found to reduce their production of these greenhouse gases.

Slow Cooked Beef Stew

During the deepest, coldest part of winter I crave warming, hearty stews such as this one. Using a crockpot can make getting dinner on the table an easy task, especially on very busy days. This stew can be started in the morning before you go to work or started just after lunchtime. I like to serve it over mashed potatoes with a raw cabbage slaw. Sometimes I sauté the onion first, before adding it to the crockpot, in order to give the stew more flavor.

1 medium onion, diced
3 to 4 large carrots, cut into ¼-inch rounds
½ pound mushrooms, quartered
1 pound grass-fed beef stew meat
½ cup water
¼ cup dry red wine
¼ cup tomato puree or sauce
2 tablespoons arrowroot or sweet rice flour
1 ½ teaspoons sea salt or Herbamare
½ teaspoon ground black pepper

Place the onion, carrots, mushrooms, and stew meat into a 3-quart slow cooker. In a small bowl whisk together the water, red wine, tomato puree, and arrowroot. Pour into the slow cooker. Add the salt and pepper. Mix all ingredients together. There won't be enough liquid to cover the ingredients. This is how it should be so don't be tempted to add more liquid.

Cook on high for 4 hours or on low for 8 hours. Sometimes I crack the lid for the last 45 minutes or so in order to cook off some of the liquid to create a thicker stew.

Yield: 4 servings

Slow Cooked Mexican Beef Roast

This easy, flavorful roast can be used to make shredded beef tacos, quesadillas, or simply served with mashed yams and sautéed dark leafy greens. I like to store whole tomatoes from the summer harvest in my freezer and thaw a few on my counter before using them in my recipes—a great alternative to canned tomatoes! If fresh chili peppers are unavailable, use 2 to 3 teaspoons of chili powder.

one 2 to 3-pound grass-fed beef roast
1 small onion, peeled
2 to 4 cloves garlic, peeled
2 to 3 cups diced tomatoes
2 to 3 jalapeno or serrano peppers
1 tablespoon ground cumin
2 teaspoons sea salt
1 cup water

Preheat oven to 325 degrees F.

Place the roast into a small roasting pan that has a lid. The smaller and taller the pan, the better. This keeps the liquid up around the roast, which keeps it from drying out.

Place the remaining ingredients into a blender and blend on high until smooth and pureed. Pour the liquid over the roast, cover, and cook for about 4 hours or until meat is very tender and can shred easily.

For tacos, serve with corn tortillas, shredded cabbage, and salsa.

Yield: 8 servings

Variation:

You can also make this recipe using a slow cooker. For best results, cook on low for about 8 hours.

Dressings, Dips, and Sauces

C reate simple nutritious meals without much effort using a variety of homemade salad dressings, dips, salsas, and sauces. Store-bought condiments often have many ingredients that are unnecessary for our bodies, but by preparing your own, you know exactly what is in your food. Homemade condiments add flavor and depth to any meal whether used to dress greens, dip vegetables or crackers, as a sauce over meat and grains, or in a sandwich or wrap. Steamed greens straight from the garden over cooked quinoa with grilled salmon is rather plain, but add a drizzle of a peanut-ginger sauce, fresh plum sauce, or mango chutney and your meal is elevated to the next level!

Salad Dressings

It's our habit to have at least two different homemade salad dressings in our refrigerator every week. Have you ever looked at the labels on commercial salad dressings, including natural and organic brands? Most have gums and stabilizers, sugars, highly processed vegetable oils, and a list of ingredients too long for us to feel comfortable using them. Since a homemade dressing can be whipped up in two minutes or less, there really isn't a need to rely on commercial salad dressings.

We like to reuse small jam jars for salad dressings. Just add all of your ingredients and shake! Store any unused portions in a glass jar in the refrigerator.

Dips and Spreads

You'll find a variety of dips and spreads in this chapter, from homemade egg-free mayonnaise to herbed hummus and raw vegetable-seed dips—there is something for everyone.

We like to make large batches of bean dips and then freeze in small containers. This way we can take out a small amount when we need it for school lunches or a healthy snack when nothing else is readily available. Generally, recipes using nuts and seeds don't freeze well; instead store them in your refrigerator for up to a week in covered glass containers.

Spread bean or raw vegetable-seed dips on a tortilla, then add shredded carrots, strips of cucumbers, sprouts, and lettuce to create a nutritious wrap. Or set out the dip in a small bowl surrounded by a variety of raw vegetables. Carrots and celery are always a crowd pleaser, but consider trying thinly sliced kohlrabi or homemade kale chips.

Fresh Salsas and Chutneys

In the summertime, fresh tomatoes and peppers are in abundance and it is our favorite time to serve a simple meal of cooked beans, quinoa or rice, chopped salad greens from our garden, and a fresh salsa. Chutneys complement Indian flavors quite nicely, such as the spicy curries and main dish recipes found in this book. While cooked chutneys freeze well, fresh, raw salsas and chutneys do not and should be kept in the refrigerator for only a few days. Use a small glass jar or glass container to store them in.

Sauces

Sauces have been around for centuries. During Roman times sauces made from a variety of seasonings were used to disguise the taste of meat that wasn't very fresh. Now, they continue to be used to marinate meat, fish, or vegetables and can be used to drizzle over the final meal. Sauces are made with a liquid base such as vegetable juice, stock, milk, nut butters mixed with water, or blended tomatoes. They are generally thickened with heat or sometimes a starch such as arrowroot powder, though we've also created some very thick raw sauces in the blender using soaked nuts, garlic, spices, and soft dates. Sauces can literally be made in a matter of minutes, though those that require cooking need constant attention and whisking to take care not to burn. Many of the sauces in this chapter freeze very well, check the headnotes of each recipe for storage tips.

10 Tips for Dressings, Dips, Salsas, and Sauces:

1. **Store salad dressings in small glass jars** in your refrigerator.

2. **Remember to bring the dressing to room temperature before serving as olive oil partially solidifies in the refrigerator**. You can place your jar of dressing into a bowl of hot water to quickly warm before serving.

3. **Salad dressings made with an acid—vinegar or citrus—can also be used as a marinade** for meat, fish, or vegetables.

4. **Leftover salad tossed in dressing won't keep**, so unless you are serving a salad to a large crowd it is best to let each person dress their own salad. You can easily store the undressed leftover salad greens in the refrigerator for days and take a serving out when needed.

5. **Most sauces, especially those thickened with a starch, will firm up once chilled** in the refrigerator. To reheat and serve, simply place the sauce into a small pot, add one to two tablespoons water and gently reheat over low heat, whisking occasionally.

6. **Sauces made with tomatoes freeze well**, such as pizza sauce or barbecue sauce.

7. **Bean dips freeze very well**. When ready to use, remove them from the freezer and let them thaw in the refrigerator.

8. **Use dips to add extra flavor and protein** in sandwiches and wraps.

9. **Salsas and chutneys actually taste better the day after they are made**. The more time the ingredients have to mingle, the better the flavors.

10. **Store freshly made salsa in the refrigerator** for up to 3 to 4 days.

Apple Cider Vinaigrette

This is one of our children's favorite salad dressings. They like it tossed with thinly sliced napa cabbage and peeled mandarins. We also use this dressing for making impromptu grain and bean salads. For example, combining cooked quinoa, white beans, parsley, and green onions with this dressing creates a delicious, nutritious quick lunch.

½ cup raw apple cider vinegar
½ cup extra virgin olive oil
1 to 2 tablespoons honey
2 teaspoons Dijon mustard
¾ teaspoon Herbamare
1 teaspoon dried dill

Place all ingredients into a pint-sized glass jar, cover, and shake. Store in the refrigerator for up to 3 weeks.

Yield: About 1 cup

Blueberry Vinaigrette

You can use either fresh or frozen blueberries for this recipe but if they are frozen you will need to let them thaw before making this dressing. If you don't have champagne vinegar, replace it with either white wine vinegar or raw apple cider vinegar.

½ cup extra virgin olive oil
⅓ cup fresh or frozen blueberries
⅓ cup champagne vinegar
1 tablespoon honey
½ teaspoon Herbamare or sea salt

Add all ingredients to a blender and puree for about 30 seconds until smooth. Pour into a jar for serving.

Dressing will last in the refrigerator for up to a week.

Yield: About 1 cup

Champagne Vinaigrette

This dressing is so simple it can be made in less than 30 seconds! I never even measure the ingredients anymore.

3 tablespoons extra virgin olive oil
3 tablespoons champagne vinegar
1 teaspoon Dijon mustard
sea salt and freshly ground black pepper to taste

In a small bowl, whisk together the ingredients for the dressing. Just before serving, pour the dressing over the salad and toss together. Serve immediately.

Store any unused dressing in the refrigerator for up to 2 weeks.

Yield: About ⅓ cup

Cherry Balsamic Vinaigrette

Adding fruit to your homemade salad dressings gives them an antioxidant boost, not to mention a ton of flavor. I make this dressing a few times a week during cherry season!

½ cup fresh or frozen pitted cherries
½ cup extra virgin olive oil
5 to 6 tablespoons balsamic vinegar
1 tablespoon maple syrup
¼ teaspoon sea salt

Place all ingredients for the dressing into a blender and blend until smooth and creamy. Pour into a glass jar and serve immediately.

Store leftover dressing in the refrigerator for up to a week.

Yield: About 1 ¼ cups

Creamy Herb Salad Dressing

This dressing recipe is so nutritious and flavorful that it might become a family favorite. Walnuts are an excellent source of healthy fats and recent research shows that eating walnuts can improve brain function and memory. Soaking walnuts overnight makes them more digestible and also creates a creamy white salad dressing!

½ cup raw walnuts, soaked 6 to 8 hours
½ cup water
¼ cup extra virgin olive oil
1 large lemon, juiced
1 clove garlic
½ teaspoon Herbamare
2 to 3 tablespoons chopped fresh chives
1 to 2 tablespoons fresh oregano leaves
1 tablespoon fresh rosemary
1 tablespoon fresh thyme

Place the raw walnuts in a small bowl and cover with purified water. Soak for 6 to 8 hours.

Rinse and drain the soaked walnuts. Add them to a blender with the water, oil, lemon juice, garlic, and Herbamare. Blend until smooth and creamy. Add herbs and blend on a low speed until just combined.

Yield: About 1 cup

Kitchen Tip:

If you blend everything at once you will create a greenish colored dressing. Adding the herbs at the end creates a white dressing with little flecks of green.

Everyday Salad Dressing

I like to store this dressing in the refrigerator to have on hand for all of the fabulous greens my children pick from our garden during the spring and summer. It can also be used as a marinade for grilled chicken or fish. You can use your favorite combination of fresh herbs in this recipe. Our favorite combination is oregano and basil.

¾ cup extra virgin olive oil
¼ cup red wine vinegar
2 tablespoons balsamic vinegar
2 tablespoons honey
1 small lemon, juiced
6 cloves garlic, crushed
2 to 3 tablespoons minced red bell pepper
2 to 3 tablespoons minced fresh herbs
¾ teaspoon sea salt
½ teaspoon freshly ground black pepper

Place all ingredients into a glass jar, cover, and shake. Taste and adjust salt and seasonings if necessary. Store in a sealed glass jar in the refrigerator for up to 2 weeks.

Yield: 1 ½ cups

Fig-Balsamic Vinaigrette

I love to find ways to use up all of the beautiful figs available in late summer and early autumn. We like to use this dressing to top a crisp apple and green salad. It is also good as a chicken marinade.

5 fresh figs, stems removed
6 tablespoons balsamic vinegar
1 to 2 tablespoons maple syrup
½ teaspoon sea salt or Herbamare
½ cup extra virgin olive oil
freshly ground black pepper, to taste

Place the figs, balsamic vinegar, maple syrup, and salt in a blender and blend on medium speed until combined and the figs are lightly pureed. With the motor running on a low speed, slowly pour in the olive oil. Add black pepper if desired and blend on low speed, slightly, to incorporate.

Store dressing in a glass jar in the refrigerator for 7 to 10 days.

Yield: About 1 ½ cups

Green Apple Dressing

The green apple in this dressing offers enough acidity that vinegar is not needed. You can vary the recipe a little and add green onions and cilantro in place of the garlic.

1 medium Granny Smith apple, cored and chopped
½ cup water
⅓ cup extra virgin olive oil
1 to 2 cloves garlic
1-inch piece of fresh ginger, peeled
Herbamare or sea salt to taste

Add all ingredients to a blender and blend about 60 seconds, until smooth and creamy. Taste and add a little salt, blend again.

Store leftover dressing in a sealed glass jar in the fridge for up to a week.

Yield: About 1 cup

Greek Dressing

I like to serve this dressing over a salad of chopped crisp romaine lettuce, tomatoes, cucumbers, and feta cheese. It is also good tossed with garbanzo beans, brown rice, chopped cucumbers, and mint.

½ cup extra virgin olive oil
6 tablespoons freshly squeezed lemon juice
1 to 2 cloves garlic
2 tablespoons fresh oregano leaves
½ teaspoon sea salt
freshly ground black pepper

Place all ingredients for the dressing into a blender and blend until smooth. Store dressing in the refrigerator for up to 10 days.

Yield: About ¾ cup

Condiments

Honey Mustard Dressing

Use this recipe as a dip for chicken nuggets or to top your favorite green salad.

¼ cup honey
¼ cup brown mustard
¼ cup extra virgin olive oil
1 to 2 tablespoons apple cider vinegar
¼ teaspoon sea salt

In a small jar add the ingredients for the dressing. Put a top on the jar and shake well until combined.

Dressing will last in the refrigerator for up to 3 weeks.

Yield: About ¾ cup

Mint Tahini Dressing

Tahini is made from ground sesame seeds and is very high in calcium. You can reduce the water called for in this recipe to make a sauce. Serve the sauce over the Sweet Potato Falafels, page 310.

½ cup sesame tahini
½ cup freshly squeezed lemon juice
¼ cup extra virgin olive oil
6 to 8 tablespoons water
handful fresh mint leaves
2 cloves garlic, crushed
½ to 1 teaspoon sea salt, or to taste

Place all ingredients into a blender and blend until smooth and combined. Taste and add more salt if necessary. Store dressing in the refrigerator for up to 10 days.

Yield: About 1 ½ cups

Orange Vinaigrette

I like to make this salad dressing for the holidays. It pairs well with dried cranberries, toasted nuts, and greens.

¼ cup extra virgin olive oil
2 tablespoons freshly squeezed orange juice
2 tablespoons apple cider vinegar
½ teaspoon Herbamare or sea salt
¼ teaspoon freshly grated orange peel
pinch cinnamon

Place all ingredients into a glass jar with a lid and shake well. Serve.

Store in a glass jar in the refrigerator for up to 10 days.

Pepper-Mint Dressing

This lemony, peppery, garlicky, minty salad dressing is fantastic over a crisp romaine lettuce salad topped with toasted pine nuts, green onions, and shredded carrots. It also works as a marinade for grilled meat or vegetables. I usually only use the shallot if I am using this recipe as a marinade for fish or chicken.

½ cup packed fresh spearmint leaves
½ cup freshly squeezed lemon juice
4 to 5 garlic cloves, peeled
1 small shallot (optional)
1 teaspoon whole black peppercorns
1 teaspoon sea salt
¾ cup extra virgin olive oil

Add all ingredients except for olive oil to a blender. Blend on high until very smooth, 1 to 2 minutes. Add the olive oil, blend on low speed until just incorporated. Store dressing in the refrigerator for up to 10 days.

Yield: About 1 ¼ cups

Ranch Dressing

This dairy-free dressing is better after the flavors have had time to meld. Give it about a day and the tartness from the lemon juice will lessen. Use this as a salad dressing over crispy greens or as a dip for carrot and celery sticks.

1 cup raw cashews, soaked for 3 hours
1 cup water
2 cloves garlic
½ cup extra virgin olive oil
¼ cup freshly squeezed lemon juice
2 tablespoons apple cider vinegar
1 to 1 ½ teaspoons Herbamare
1 tablespoon dried dill
1 teaspoon dried thyme
1 teaspoon dried basil
1 to 2 teaspoons cracked black pepper

Place the raw cashews in a small bowl and cover with purified water and let soak for 3 hours.

Rinse and drain the soaked cashews. Place the cashews, water, and garlic into a Vita-mix or blender fitted with a sharp blade. Blend until very smooth and creamy, then add the remaining ingredients and blend until just combined.

Pour into a glass jar and refrigerate overnight. Dressing will thicken up in the refrigerator. Shake and pour over your favorite salad or use as a dip for raw vegetable sticks. Store dressing in the refrigerator for up to 10 days.

Yield: About 2 cups

Variation:

Replace the dried herbs with fresh herbs. I like to add a handful of fresh parsley and dill if I have them available.

Sesame Ginger Dressing

In addition to drizzling over fresh greens, this dressing tastes great tossed with kelp noodles or rice noodles along with shredded carrots, green onions, and thinly sliced red cabbage.

¼ cup sesame seeds, lightly toasted
¼ cup extra virgin olive oil
3 tablespoons brown rice vinegar or coconut vinegar
1 to 2 tablespoons wheat-free tamari or coconut aminos
1 tablespoon toasted sesame oil
2 tablespoons chopped celery
1-inch piece of fresh ginger, peeled
1 to 2 cloves garlic

Place all ingredients into a blender and blend on high until smooth and creamy.

Store leftover dressing in the refrigerator for up to 10 days.

Yield: About ¾ cup

Soy-Free Asian Dressing

I use this dressing for my Asian Chicken Salad, page 206. It is also good tossed with noodles, shredded carrots, and green onions. If you tolerate soy, then you can replace the coconut aminos with wheat-free tamari.

4 tablespoons extra virgin olive oil
3 tablespoons coconut vinegar or brown rice vinegar
3 tablespoons coconut aminos
1 tablespoon sesame oil
2 to 3 teaspoons honey
1 clove garlic
1-inch piece of fresh ginger, peeled

To make the dressing, place all ingredients into a blender and blend on high until combined.

Store in a glass jar in the refrigerator for up to 10 days.

Yield: ¾ cup

Zucchini Lime Dressing

In the summertime our garden is overflowing with summer squash that I need to use up in creative ways. This dressing is an inconspicuous way to serve raw zucchini to your children.

⅓ cup finely diced zucchini
⅓ cup freshly squeezed lime juice
⅓ cup extra virgin olive oil
⅛ to ¼ teaspoon ground cumin
¼ teaspoon Herbamare

Add all ingredients to a blender and blend until smooth. Taste and adjust salt and seasonings if necessary.

Store in a glass jar in the refrigerator for up to 5 days.

Yield: About 1 cup

Chipotle Barbecue Sauce

Use this sauce to marinate chicken for the grill or to simmer with cooked beans. It is also a great dipping sauce for the Crispy Chicken Fingers, page 330.

¼ cup extra virgin olive oil
½ cup diced onion
6 to 8 cloves garlic, peeled and coarsely chopped
one 24-ounce jar strained tomatoes
½ cup maple syrup
½ cup apple cider vinegar
1 tablespoon blackstrap molasses
2 teaspoons Herbamare or sea salt
1 to 2 teaspoons chipotle chili powder
1 to 2 teaspoons smoked paprika
½ to 1 teaspoon ground black pepper

Heat a 3-quart pot over medium heat. Add olive oil and let it heat up for a minute before adding the onions. Sauté onions in the oil for about 10 minutes, or until they are very soft and golden brown. Add garlic and sauté a minute more.

Add the remaining ingredients, stir, cover, and simmer on medium-low heat for about 15 to 20 minutes, stirring occasionally.

Remove from heat and transfer sauce to a blender and blend until smooth. If you would like a thinner sauce then add a little water. Taste and adjust salt and seasonings to your liking.

Store any unused sauce in a glass jar in the refrigerator for up to 10 days or freeze for longer storage.

Yield: About 4 cups

Ingredient Tip:

I use organic strained tomatoes from the company Bionaturae. I like this product because it comes in a glass container thereby eliminating the use of the BPA-lined cans so often used for tomato products. Their strained tomatoes are similar to tomato sauce, so feel free to use 24 ounces of organic tomato sauce if you cannot locate these strained tomatoes.

Easy Homemade Pizza Sauce

Use one batch of this sauce for a 12-inch pizza. I use a rectangular stone baking sheet which is 12 x 15 inches. The 7-ounce jars of Bionaturae tomato paste can be found at most food co-ops and health food stores. Once the jars are empty I soak them in hot water to remove the labels, wash them, and use them to store dried herbs. They also make great cups for smoothies when we are out and about.

one 7-ounce jar tomato paste
2 tablespoons extra virgin olive oil
2 teaspoons honey
2 teaspoons dried Italian herbs
1 teaspoon onion powder
½ teaspoon garlic powder
½ teaspoon Herbamare or sea salt
2 to 3 tablespoons water

Place all ingredients into a bowl and mix together well. Add water to desired consistency. Spread onto your favorite pizza crust and top with your favorite toppings. Bake pizza as directed.

Store unused sauce in the refrigerator for up to 10 days.

Yield: About ¾ cup

Oven Roasted Pizza Sauce

Use this fabulous sauce to top the Whole Grain Pizza Crust recipe, page 137, or as a dip for the Rosemary Sea Salt Breadsticks, page 133. If you have an abundance of tomatoes in your garden you can make a few batches of this sauce and freeze it in glass jars once cool.

2 to 3 pounds roma tomatoes, chopped
½ cup diced shallots or onions
4 to 6 cloves garlic, coarsely chopped
½ cup chopped fresh basil
1 teaspoon honey or coconut sugar
1 teaspoon sea salt
¼ to ½ teaspoon crushed red chili flakes
4 to 6 tablespoons olive oil

Preheat oven to 450 degrees F. Place all ingredients into a 9 x 13-inch or 10 x 14-inch pan and toss well. Roast for about 60 to 70 minutes, stirring the sauce occasionally. When done, lightly mash with the back of a spoon.

Yield: About 2 cups

Fresh Thai Green Curry Sauce

This delicious Thai style sauce can be made in about 20 minutes from start to finish. My favorite way to use this sauce is to sauté a variety of fresh vegetables in a little coconut oil until crisp-tender, then add this sauce to the pan and simmer for a minute or two. Serve over cooked basmati rice. I've also used this sauce to poach salmon and halibut. I serve the fish over a bed of steamed spinach and cooked basmati rice. Garnish with Thai basil leaves. In the summer when the cilantro is taking over our garden and fresh chilies are available at the market I will freeze the blended sauce before cooking it in glass mason jars to use during the winter months.

1 can coconut milk
2 handfuls fresh cilantro (leaves and stems)
2 small shallots
4 cloves garlic
1 to 2 jalapeno peppers, seeded
1-inch piece of fresh ginger, peeled
2 teaspoons coconut sugar
1 teaspoon sea salt, or to taste
½ teaspoon lime zest
¼ to ½ cup water

Place all ingredients into a blender and blend until smooth. Pour into a small pot and simmer for about 10 to 15 minutes, uncovered. Or pour over sautéed vegetables in the pan and then simmer.

Yield: About 2 ½ cups

Variation:

For a spicier sauce, use 2 to 4 whole Thai chilies (with the seeds) in place of the jalapenos.

Garlic Ginger Peanut Sauce

We love to make this sauce to top sautéed dark leafy greens and cooked quinoa, or use it as a dip for the Thai Salad Wraps, page 392. You can thin it out with a small amount of water and use it as a salad dressing. If you are allergic to peanuts replace the peanut butter with sunflower seed butter.

½ cup creamy organic peanut butter
½ cup water
2 tablespoons toasted sesame oil
1 ½ tablespoons wheat-free tamari or coconut aminos
1 tablespoon brown rice vinegar or coconut vinegar
1 to 2 cloves garlic, peeled
1-inch piece of ginger, peeled
pinch red chili flakes

Place all ingredients into a blender and blend until smooth. Pour into small serving dishes to use as a dip or add a little more water and use it as a salad dressing. Store in a covered glass container for up to 5 days in the refrigerator.

Yield: About 1 cup

Ginger Plum Sauce

This recipe creates a beautiful purple-hued sauce, reminiscent of sweet and sour sauce! In the summertime here in the Pacific Northwest we go around town and pick boxes full of fresh Italian plums. I pit and freeze many of them to use for sauces like this throughout the year. Use this sauce to dip nori rolls into or drizzle over sautéed vegetables and rice. We love it over grilled salmon too!

1 tablespoon kudzu
½ cup water
4 to 6 Italian plums, pitted
1 cup apple juice
4 cloves garlic, peeled
1 to 2-inch piece of ginger
1 teaspoon sea salt

Place water and kudzu into a small pan and whisk together to dissolve the kudzu.

Place all other ingredients into a blender and blend until smooth. Pour into pot with kudzu, whisk together. Turn heat to medium and simmer for about 10 minutes or until thickened and clear.

Store any unused sauce in a covered glass container in the refrigerator for up to a week.

Yield: 2 cups

Cranberry-Pear Sauce

This flavorful cranberry sauce can be served over turkey, roasted salmon, and even on top of oatmeal for breakfast! The pears sweeten up the tart and tangy cranberries thereby reducing the need for a ton of sugar. I always use ¼ cup of coconut sugar, which is just enough to sweeten it up a little but still keep it tart. You could add more if you like.

2 ½ cups fresh or frozen cranberries (about 10 ounces)
2 small ripe pears, peeled, cored, and diced
½ cup freshly squeezed orange juice or apple cider
¼ cup coconut sugar
¼ teaspoon ground allspice
1 whole cinnamon stick

Place all ingredients into a 2-quart saucepan and bring to a boil, reduce heat to medium-low and simmer for about 10 to 15 minutes. After about 7 minutes of cooking, use a large spoon to begin mashing the pears and cranberries. Continue to do this until the sauce begins to thicken. It will thicken more once it cools. Remove the cinnamon stick.

Cover and refrigerate until ready to serve. Serve cold or heat on low to warm it up.

Yield: About 2 ½ cups

Holiday Cranberry Sauce

Spoon some of this warm sauce over servings of Orange Pepper Salmon, page 315. It is also delicious over Herb Roasted Turkey Breast, page 334.

4 cups fresh cranberries
1 cup coconut nectar or 1 ½ cups apple juice concentrate
1 cup freshly squeezed orange juice
1 to 2 teaspoons orange zest

Place all ingredients into a medium-sized pot and bring to a boil, then reduce heat to a simmer. Cook for about 10 minutes while using a large spoon to mash the berries as they cook. The sauce will begin to thicken as the berries cook.

Remove from heat after the sauce is thickened and the berries are mashed. Pour into a serving bowl or store in the refrigerator for future use.

This sauce will stay fresh in a tightly sealed container for about a week in the fridge.

Yield: 2 ¾ cups

Almond Mayonnaise

This egg-free, vegan mayo recipe will satisfy your craving for mayonnaise in sandwiches, noodle dishes, and potato salads. I use this recipe for my Chicken Salad Lettuce Wraps, page 395. Even those who can tolerate eggs enjoy this recipe.

1 cup raw almonds, simmered in a few cups of water
½ cup water
¼ cup raw apple cider vinegar
2 tablespoons freshly squeezed lemon juice
1 teaspoon Herbamare
½ teaspoon yellow mustard powder
½ cup avocado oil

Place almonds into a medium-sized pot. Cover with a few cups of water. Simmer for about 45 minutes or until very soft and cooked through. Drain water off and rinse almonds with cold running water. Once they are cool enough to handle, pinch each almond to remove the skin. It should pop right off.

Place cooked, skinned almonds into a high-powered blender. Add the ½ cup water, apple cider vinegar, lemon juice, Herbamare, and mustard powder. Blend until very smooth, as smooth as you can get the mixture. Then, with the motor running on low speed, pour in the oil. Blend for another 30 seconds.

Scoop out mayo and place into a covered glass container. Chill for a few hours before using. It will firm up in the fridge. Mayonnaise will keep in the refrigerator for a few weeks.

Yield: Approximately 2 cups

Variation:

You can make "raw" mayonnaise by soaking the almonds for 8 to 10 hours in warm water instead of cooking them. Drain and rinse almonds before adding to the blender. The overall consistency is better when they are cooked, but the raw version is still quite good.

Condiments

Avocado Mayonnaise

When making this recipe, I usually just add ingredients until the mayonnaise reaches the right consistency and flavor. Use this mayo for your favorite sandwich or to make salmon, tuna, or chicken salads.

2 small avocados, pitted
2 to 3 tablespoons fresh lemon juice
2 to 3 tablespoons extra virgin olive oil
2 to 3 tablespoons water
sea salt or Herbamare to taste

Place all ingredients into a bowl or large mug and blend with an immersion blender. You can also use a blender or food processor, but given the small quantity of mayo you will be making it is much easier and more efficient to use a hand blender.

Leftovers can be stored for up to 3 days in the refrigerator.

Yield: About 1 ¼ cups

Nutrition Tip:

Avocados are a rich source of monounsaturated fats, specifically oleic acid that helps to lower LDL cholesterol while increasing the good HDL cholesterol. Some research has indicated that oleic acid may provide protection against breast cancer. Avocados are also a rich source of the carotenoid lutein and vitamins E and K, all of which are lipid soluble, meaning you need to eat these nutrients with fat for them to be absorbed. That is why eating the "whole food"—the avocado—works, as nature intended of course.

Cashew Sour Cream

It is so easy to make your own cultured dairy-free sour cream once you get the hang of the different times required for soaking and culturing. Once your sour cream is done you can create a fabulous dip for vegetables, serve with beans and rice, or in an egg and salsa burrito. Use it anywhere you would use regular cow's milk sour cream. We use a high quality dairy-free probiotic powder from Klaire Labs called Ther-Biotic Complete Powder for this recipe, which is the same powder we feed our children daily.

2 cups raw cashews or macadamia nuts, soaked for 8 hours
1 cup water
½ to 1 teaspoon probiotic powder
pinch sea salt
raw apple cider vinegar

Place the nuts into a bowl and cover with filtered water, soak for about 8 hours or overnight. Then drain and rinse. Place the nuts into a high-powered blender, such as a Vita-Mix, and add the water. Puree until ultra smooth, stopping the machine to scrape down the sides if necessary. It will take a few minutes to do this. Add a small amount of water if necessary. Then add the probiotic powder and blend again to incorporate it.

Place a medium-sized fine mesh strainer over a bowl and insert a piece of cheesecloth or thin clean dishtowel into the strainer. Pour the sour cream into the towel. Cover the strainer with the edges of the towel and let sit on your kitchen counter for about 24 hours.

Finally, stir in a pinch or two of salt and a dash of apple cider vinegar to balance the flavors if necessary.

Store in your refrigerator in a sealed glass container for up to 10 days.

Yield: About 2 cups

Cashew Roasted Red Pepper Dip

Serve this cheese-like dip with a platter of crackers and vegetables such as cauliflower florets, raw green beans, celery sticks, and cucumber slices. It is also very tasty served with the Sesame Thins, page 165.

1 cup raw cashews
½ cup water
2 large roasted red bell peppers or 4 small ones
¼ cup extra virgin olive oil
2 tablespoons freshly squeezed lemon juice
2 tablespoons nutritional yeast
1 clove garlic
1 teaspoon Herbamare or to taste

If you don't have a high-powered blender then place the cashews in water and soak for about 3 hours. Then add cashews and remaining ingredients to blender and blend.

If you have a high-powered blender, place all ingredients into the blender and blend until smooth and creamy. Put in a container and place in the refrigerator to chill before serving. Dip will thicken slightly as it chills.

Place into a bowl and sprinkle with chopped chives if desired.

Store in a covered glass container in the refrigerator for up to a week.

Yield: About 1 ½ cups

Macadamia Nut Cheese

You'll need a high-powered blender to get this spreadable "cheese" ultra creamy. When purchasing the macadamia nuts be sure to buy the raw, unsalted variety. This vegan nut cheese recipe is perfect for topping homemade gluten-free pizza or for using in between layers of lasagna noodles, vegetables, and sauce. I find the flavors of this cheese are best balanced with the acidity of tomatoes, such as my Homemade Pizza Sauce recipe, page 360.

1 cup raw macadamia nuts
½ cup hot water
1 roasted red bell pepper (optional)
2 tablespoons extra virgin olive oil
1 to 2 tablespoons nutritional yeast
½ teaspoon onion powder
¼ teaspoon garlic powder
½ to 1 teaspoon Herbamare

Place all ingredients into a high-powered blender and blend for 1 to 2 minutes or until smooth and creamy.

Store in a covered glass container in the refrigerator for up to a week.

Yield: About 1 ¾ cup

Sunny Raw Zucchini Dip

This dip is perfect to make during the summertime when there is an abundance of fresh garden zucchini! You can use this recipe as a spread in a veggie wrap, thinned out with a little water as a salad dressing, or as a dip for vegetables. Try serving this dip with more unusual vegetables, such as kohlrabi, cauliflower, bok choy stems, or radishes.

1 cup raw sunflower seeds, soaked 6 to 8 hours
1 medium zucchini, chopped (about 1 heaping cup)
¼ to ½ cup chopped fresh parsley
1 to 2 cloves garlic, peeled
¼ cup freshly squeezed lemon juice
¼ cup extra virgin olive oil
¼ cup water
1 teaspoon Herbamare
few pinches crushed red chili flakes (optional)

Rinse and drain the soaked sunflower seeds. Place them into a high-powered blender or food processor fitted with the "s" blade along with the chopped zucchini, fresh parsley, garlic, lemon juice, olive oil, water, Herbamare, and chili flakes.

Blend or process until you reach a creamy consistency. A high-powered blender will create a luscious, creamy dip, which is what we prefer, though a food processor works well too.

Store in a covered glass container until ready to serve.

Yield: 2 cups

Spicy Pepper Coconut Cream

The trick to making this recipe is to chill one can of coconut milk overnight. When you open the can, the cream will have hardened and separated at the top and the watery part is left behind on the bottom of the can. We use this thick, luscious cream to dollop on top of the Spicy Mung Bean Burgers, page 312, or over the Spicy Lentils and Rice in Cabbage Leaves, page 304. It is also delicious over cooked quinoa and beans with chopped avocado and cilantro on top

½ cup coconut cream
2 cherry bomb peppers, seeded
1 to 2 cloves garlic, peeled
½ to 1 teaspoon lime zest
sea salt or Herbamare to taste

Chill one can of coconut milk overnight. The next day scoop out the coconut cream on top and measure about ½ cup, it doesn't need to be exact, I usually just take what is there. It will be very hard and white.

Place the coconut cream in a blender or mini food processor along with the cherry bomb peppers, garlic, lime zest, and salt.

Blend until a smooth puree forms. Taste and adjust salt if necessary. You can also add a squeeze of lime juice of desired.

Place the pepper-cream in a small, covered container in the refrigerator until ready to serve. It will keep in the fridge for up to 10 days.

Yield: ½ cup

> **Ingredient Tip:**
>
> Be sure to use a can of full fat coconut milk. Light coconut milk does not contain enough fat to create a layer of "cream" when refrigerated.

Garlic Rosemary White Bean Dip

This recipe can be prepared in just minutes once you have your beans cooked. I use cannellini beans but great northern or navy beans would also work. My kids love to dip carrots and celery into this dip. It makes a delicious wrap when used as a filling for tortillas, lettuce leaves, or collard greens.

3 cups cooked white beans
¼ cup extra virgin olive oil
1 large lemon, juiced (about ¼ cup)
1 to 2 cloves garlic, peeled and coarsely chopped
1 tablespoon chopped fresh rosemary
1 teaspoon Herbamare or sea salt
reserved bean cooking liquid as needed

Place all ingredients, except bean-cooking liquid, into a food processor fitted with the "s" blade. Process until very smooth and creamy adding bean cooking liquid as necessary to reach desired consistency (start by adding a tablespoon or so at a time).

Chill until ready to serve. The flavors become deeper and more pronounced as the bean dip sits in the refrigerator.

Yield: About 3 ½ cup

Herb and Olive Oil Hummus

Hummus is a traditional Middle-Eastern dish made from garbanzo beans, also called chickpeas, and tahini. I've added fresh herbs and a drizzling of extra virgin olive oil for a more sophisticated dip. Use it to spread onto the Herbed Sunflower Seed Crackers on page 164, or as a filling for a wrap using either a tortilla or a blanched collard green.

3 cups cooked garbanzo beans, or 2 cans drained
¼ cup bean cooking liquid or water
½ cup sesame tahini
½ cup freshly squeezed lemon juice
¼ cup extra virgin olive oil
2 to 3 cloves garlic, crushed
1 teaspoon ground cumin
1 to 2 teaspoons sea salt or Herbamare, or to taste
small handful fresh parsley
2 to 3 tablespoons fresh oregano leaves
1 to 2 tablespoon fresh marjoram leaves

Place all ingredients except for the fresh herbs into a food processor fitted with the "s" blade and process until smooth and creamy. You will want to taste the hummus to see if it needs more lemon, tahini, garlic, or salt. Also, add more water if needed for a thinner consistency and process again.

Add the fresh herbs and pulse until combined, but not completely pureed. Place the hummus into small serving dishes and sprinkle with extra chopped herbs and a drizzle of extra virgin olive oil if desired.

Store in a covered glass container in the refrigerator for up to a week.

Yield: 4 cups

Nutrition Tip:

We have all heard that the Mediterranean diet has protective effects on our hearts. Some researchers are now attributing that to the beneficial phenolic compounds found in the fruits, vegetables, and the high quality olive oil frequently used in the Mediterranean diet. One study found that when people used olive oil exclusively in their food preparation, they could reduce their likelihood of coronary heart disease by 47%. If saturated fat was replaced with olive oil, total cholesterol dropped by 13.4%, and LDL by 18%.

Red Pepper Chickpea Spread

Roasting your own red peppers is very easy, it only takes about 10 minutes. This spread is used in the Roasted Cauliflower and Arugla Wrap, page 389, and is also quite good spread onto a piece of Sourdough Teff Bread, page 124. I know for our family, having ready-made bean spreads is indispensable.

1 to 2 small red bell peppers, roasted
2 cups cooked chickpeas
4 tablespoons almond butter
3 tablespoons extra virgin olive oil
2 cloves garlic, crushed
1 to 2 teaspoons Herbamare or sea salt

Preheat oven to broil.

Place peppers on a baking sheet and cook on the center rack of the oven until the skin is charred, turning occasionally, about 8 to 10 minutes.

Remove peppers from pan and place them into a paper bag or a covered glass bowl, let stand at room temperature for about 10 minutes. Remove peppers and peel off charred skin, then cut and remove seeds.

Place the peppers and the rest of the ingredients into a food processor and process until smooth and creamy. Taste and add more salt, pepper, and garlic if needed.

Store in the refrigerator for up to a week.

Yield: About 2 ½ cups

Variation:

Nut-Free Variation: If you are nut-free or have a toddler who is not yet eating nuts then replace the almond butter with sunflower seed butter or pumpkin seed butter.

Mexican Bean Dip

This flavorful bean dip can be served with crackers or corn chips. Our children prefer to dip carrot sticks in it. I also like to double this recipe and make a layered bean dip with shredded lettuce, chopped tomatoes, olives, and guacamole, and Cashew Sour Cream, page 369.

1 to 2 tablespoons olive oil
1 shallot, diced
1 carrot, diced
1 stalk celery, diced
2 teaspoons ground cumin
½ teaspoon chili powder
½ teaspoon smoked paprika (optional)
2 cups kidney beans, drained
squeeze of lime or dash of apple cider vinegar
sea salt to taste

Heat a small skillet over medium-low heat. Add the oil, then add the shallot, carrot, and celery and sauté for about 5 to 10 minutes or until vegetables are tender. Add the spices and sauté for 30 seconds more.

Place the sautéed vegetables, beans, lime juice, and sea salt into a food processor fitted with the "s" blade. Process until smooth and combined.

Store in a covered glass container in the refrigerator for up to a week.

Yield: About 2 ½ cups

Raw Cilantro Lime Chutney

Serve this chutney with a spicy lentil dal or curried vegetable dish. You can use my measurements below or just toss the ingredients into the food processor with wild abandon and see what comes of it. Most likely it will be delicious!

2 large jalapeno peppers, seeded
2-inch piece of peeled ginger
4 large cloves of garlic
zest from 1 large lime
½ teaspoon sea salt
2 large bunches cilantro (stems and leaves)
juice from 1 large lime
½ cup shredded coconut

Place the jalapeno peppers, ginger, garlic, lime zest, and salt into a food processor fitted with the "s" blade and process until minced. Add the cilantro, lime juice, and shredded coconut and pulse until combined.

Store in a small covered glass container in your refrigerator for up to a week.

Yield: About 1 cup

Raw Mango Chutney

This chutney recipe can be spooned over lentil dal and rice. We like to serve it along side a slew of Indian dishes. Or try serving it over baked halibut and basmati rice for a simple dinner. It tastes great with just about anything.

2 large ripe mangos, peeled and diced small
½ cup raisins or dates, soaked in warm water
½ small red onion
1 jalapeno pepper, seeded
large handful fresh cilantro
1 tablespoon coconut oil
½ to 1 teaspoon whole cumin seeds
½ to 1 teaspoon brown or black mustard seeds
¼ teaspoon turmeric
2 small limes, juiced
¼ teaspoon sea salt or Herbamare, or to taste

Place the diced mangos into a mixing bowl. Let the raisins or dates soak in warm water in a smaller, separate bowl for about 30 minutes. Drain, and then place into a food processor fitted with the "s" blade. Add the onion, pepper, and cilantro. Process until minced. Scoop out and add to the bowl with the mango.

Heat a small skillet over medium heat, add the oil and then the seeds. Sauté for about 30 seconds or until the seeds begin to pop; add the turmeric. Scrape out the oil and spices from the pan and add them to the mixing bowl. Add the lime juice and sea salt. Toss all ingredients together, cover, and refrigerate for a few hours so the flavors can meld. Place into small serving dishes to serve with your meal.

Store in a small covered glass container in your refrigerator for up to a week.

Yield: About 2 cups

Spicy Peach Chutney

Serve this flavorful, fresh chutney recipe over dal and rice or your favorite curry recipe. We like to make extra during peach season and then freeze small jars of it to enjoy during the winter. If you would like a milder chutney, omit the habanero peppers. If you don't have coconut sugar on hand use another granulated sugar such as raw cane sugar or Sucanat.

8 medium-sized ripe peaches, peeled and diced
2 limes, juiced
3 habanero peppers, seeded and finely diced
2 to 3 jalapeno peppers, seeded and finely diced
1 ½ tablespoons grated fresh ginger
4 to 6 cloves garlic, crushed
½ cup coconut sugar
few dashes sea salt or Herbamare

Place all of the ingredients into a medium-sized saucepan and set heat to medium. Simmer covered for about 20 minutes over medium to medium-low heat then remove the cover and simmer for about 10 minutes more to let some of the liquid evaporate. Serve warm or chill and serve the next day. The flavors will definitely improve with age.

Store in small glass jars in the refrigerator for up to 3 weeks. Chutney can also be frozen for longer storage.

Yield: About 3 cups

Fresh Apple Salsa

I like making this salsa in autumn when apple season is in full swing. The best apples to use for this salsa are crisp, firm apples such as Honeycrisp. Soft, sweet apples are better for sauce and baking. Use whatever hot peppers you have on hand—serrano, jalapeno, or cherry bomb peppers are good choices. Use this recipe to top grilled fish, fish tacos, or over a bowl of cooked quinoa.

2 large apples
½ cup chopped cilantro
¼ cup finely diced red onion
1 to 4 hot peppers, finely diced
1 tablespoon extra virgin olive oil
1 tablespoon apple cider vinegar
sea salt or Herbamare to taste

Place all of the ingredients into a bowl and mix together. Cover and place in the refrigerator for up to an hour before serving to let the flavors meld.

This salsa will keep in the refrigerator for about 3 days.

Yield: About 3 cups

Variation:

Replace the apple cider vinegar with 2 tablespoons of freshly squeezed lime juice.

Salsa Fresca

Use this quick and easy recipe to serve with tacos or to top homemade enchiladas. This recipe is especially good with the Raw Burritos, page 307. If you don't own a food processor you can finely chop all of the ingredients, though using a food processor cuts preparation time in half. I like to dice the tomatoes—if they are processed along with the rest of the ingredients the salsa gets very watery.

4 cups finely diced plum tomatoes
1 small orange or yellow bell pepper, seeded
½ small red onion, ends trimmed and peeled
large handful fresh cilantro
2 to 4 jalapeno peppers, seeded
2 to 3 cloves garlic
½ teaspoon cumin
1 tablespoon apple cider vinegar
1 teaspoon sea salt or Herbamare

Place the diced tomatoes into a mixing bowl. Place the remaining ingredients into a food processor fitted with the "s" blade. Process until coarsely ground or a bit smaller than they would be if you had diced them.

Add the ingredients from the food processor to the bowl of tomatoes. Gently stir together then chill in the refrigerator for at least an hour before serving. This gives the flavors a chance to meld.

This salsa will keep in the refrigerator for about 3 days.

Yield: About 5 cups

Ingredient Tip:

Two jalapeno peppers creates a mild salsa. Four jalapeno peppers creates a spicier salsa. We use two peppers so our children will eat it though we prefer the flavor and heat of four peppers.

Wraps and Rolls

Wraps and rolls are simple to assemble and make for a nutritious snack or meal. Use homemade tortillas, collard greens, cabbage leaves, or sheets of nori as your wrap. Fill with any combination of marinated vegetables, spicy greens, leftover fish or meat, cooked beans, raw nut and seed pâtés, or cooked whole grains.

Creating a Quick Lunch

Although we have a number of recipes in this chapter for homemade tortillas, we've found that the best wraps come from nature—plants! If you are like most people and have little time in the morning to prepare breakfast, let alone lunch, consider using plants as a wrap or roll for a quick option. Nori rolls can easily be made the night before and stored in a glass container ready to take to school or work. Napa cabbage or romaine lettuce leaves can be used as a "taco" and filled with a scoop of leftover grain and bean salad, cooked fish or chicken, fermented vegetables, or fresh garden herbs. Collard greens make the best replacement for tortillas—just blanch, drain, and use!

Here are a few options for using plants as your wrap:
- Nori sheets
- Lettuce leaves
- Napa cabbage leaves
- Collard greens
- Lacinato kale leaves
- Grape leaves
- Long thin strips of raw zucchini

10 Tips for Using Wraps and Rolls:

1. **Use a tortilla press to make homemade tortillas**. We have an 8-inch cast iron press that comes in handy for making both corn and almond tortillas, though having one is not necessary to be able to make the recipes in this book.

2. **Store homemade gluten-fee tortillas in between pieces of waxed paper** in a sealed plastic bag or glass container. If stored properly, the gluten-free tortillas made from the recipes in this chapter will remain soft enough for wraps.

3. **Save the bag and papers from store-bought gluten-free tortillas** to use for storing your homemade wraps.

4. **Steam gluten-free tortillas one at a time** on a wire rack placed over a pot of boiling water.

5. **Heat corn tortillas in a little olive or coconut oil** in a hot skillet for 30 seconds on each side.

6. **Blanch collard greens for 30 to 60 seconds in boiling water and then drain**. When our garden is overflowing with collard greens we use them in place of any other type of tortilla. For example, collard greens can be used in place of corn tortillas in enchiladas, they can be used for bean and rice burritos, and also as a wrapper for pates and vegetables.

7. **Soak cabbage leaves in a pot of boiled water and for 5 to 10 minutes**. Use them to replace corn tortillas in enchiladas or for cabbage roll casseroles.

8. **When using nori**, be sure that some of your ingredients are moist. This will naturally moisten the nori sheet making it easy to slice. Sticky brown rice or a moist pate will do the trick.

9. **When using Asian rice or tapioca wrappers**, place them into a 10-inch skillet filled with hot water for about 1 to 2 minutes to soften.

10. **For a packed lunch**, lay a wet paper towel or cloth napkin over an assembled gluten-free tortilla wrap and place in a tightly sealed container.

Wraps

Almond Flax Tortillas

The ground flax in these tortillas gives them flexibility and the almond flour gives them body. For these tortillas to remain flexible it is important to keep close watch to avoid overcooking otherwise you might get some very tasty, crispy crackers! In order for these tortillas to work, be sure to use finely ground blanched almond flour.

½ cup ground golden flax seeds
½ cup warm water
1 cup blanched almond flour
¼ cup arrowroot powder
¼ teaspoon sea salt

Preheat oven to 350 degrees. Tear four pieces of parchment paper into four large squares. Get out two cookie sheets and set aside.

Add the ground flax seeds to a large bowl, and slowly whisk in the warm water. Let rest for about 3 to 4 minutes so the flax can form its gel. Add the remaining ingredients and stir with a large spoon until combined and thickened. Form dough into 4 to 5 equally sized balls.

Place a square of parchment onto a cookie sheet. Place one of the dough balls onto the center of it. Cover with the other sheet. Roll dough into a large circle using a rolling pin. Try to get them fairly thin and keep the batter evenly distributed.

Leave tortillas in between parchment paper for baking. You may be able to bake two tortillas at once on the same cookie sheet, depending on size. Bake each tortilla for 5 to 7 minutes then flip, parchment and all, and bake for another 3 to 4 minutes. Watch carefully as overcooking will lead to a dry tortilla that can crack easily. Take out of the oven and remove the parchment paper, it should easily peel off when done. Repeat with remaining tortillas. Stack on a plate to cool.

Store in between pieces of waxed paper in a plastic bag or sealed glass container for up to 5 days in the refrigerator.

Yield: 4 to 5 tortillas

Buckwheat Chia Tortillas

These tortillas are soft, pliable, and full of flavor. I grind my own buckwheat flour from raw buckwheat groats in my Vita-Mix and grind chia seeds to a fine meal in my Vita-Mix, though a coffee grinder works too.

½ cup ground chia seeds
2 cups warm water
2 tablespoons extra virgin olive oil
1 ¾ cup freshly ground buckwheat flour
1 teaspoon sea salt

Preheat oven to 350 degrees. Tear four pieces of parchment paper into four large squares. Get out two cookie sheets and set aside.

In a large bowl add the ground chia seeds. Slowly whisk in the warm water. Let rest for about 3 to 4 minutes so the chia can form its gel. Then whisk in the olive oil. Add the buckwheat flour and salt and stir with a large spoon until combined and thickened. Dough will be sticky.

Place a square of parchment onto a cookie sheet. Drop dough by the ½-cup onto the center of the parchment paper. Cover with another sheet. Using your hands gently spread the batter into a large circle. Try to get them fairly thin and the batter evenly distributed. After a few tries you'll get the hang of it.

Leave the tortilla in between the parchment paper for baking. You may be able to bake two tortillas at once on the same cookie sheet, depending on size. Bake for 6 to 7 minutes, then flip tortilla, parchment and all, and bake for another 3 to 4 minutes. Watch carefully as overcooking will lead to a dry tortilla that can crack easily. Take them out of the oven and remove the parchment paper, it should easily peel off when done. Repeat with remaining tortillas. Stack on a plate to cool.

Store in between pieces of waxed paper in a plastic bag or sealed glass container for up to 5 days in the refrigerator.

Yield: 4 to 6 tortillas

Homemade Corn Tortillas

Making our own corn tortillas is a fun family activity. Our twin boys like to mix the masa and water together while our girls like to press the dough into tortillas and cook them. Use homemade tortillas for chicken fajitas, black bean tacos, or Fish Tacos, page 318. Be sure to purchase <u>organic</u> masa harina to avoid consuming genetically engineered food.

4 cups white, blue or yellow masa harina
1 teaspoon sea salt
3 to 4 cups boiling water
coconut oil for cooking

Place the masa harina and salt into a large glass bowl; whisk together. Slowly pour in the boiling water, stirring with a large spoon, until it reaches "play-dough" consistency. The dough should not be too dry or too wet. If you added too much water just add more masa. Knead the dough a few times with your hands (it will be hot so work fast).

Form the dough into 10 equal-sized balls. Place each ball into a tortilla press and press into a thin disk.

Heat a cast iron skillet over medium heat on the stove. Add about 1 tablespoon of coconut oil to the pan and one tortilla; cook each side for about 2 minutes. Place onto a plate to cool. Add a little coconut oil in between cooking each tortilla. Continue until each tortilla is cooked.

Yield: 10 tortillas

Kitchen Tip:

We use an 8-inch cast iron tortilla press. You can easily find and purchase these on-line. Be sure to use two pieces of parchment paper in the tortilla press otherwise the dough will stick to the press.

Teff Tortillas

Our children like to make almond butter and jam quesadillas with these tortillas. Spread one tortilla with almond butter and the other with jam, then put them together like a sandwich and slice into triangles using a pizza cutter. This is one of their favorite quick lunches for school.

½ cup ground golden flax seeds
2 cups warm water
2 tablespoons extra virgin olive oil
1 cup teff flour
¾ cup brown rice flour
½ cup tapioca flour
1 teaspoon sea salt

Preheat oven to 350 degrees. Tear four pieces of parchment paper into four large squares. Get out two cookie sheets and set aside.

In a large bowl add the ground flax seeds. Slowly whisk in the warm water. Let rest for about 3 to 4 minutes so the flax can form its gel. Then whisk in the olive oil. Add the dry ingredients and stir with a large spoon until combined and thickened. Dough will be sticky.

Place a square of parchment onto a cookie sheet. Drop batter by the ½-cup onto the center of the parchment paper. Cover with another piece of parchment paper. Using your hands gently spread the batter into a large circle. Try to get them fairly thin and keep the batter evenly distributed.

Leave the tortilla in between the parchment paper for baking. You may be able to bake two tortillas at once on the same cookie sheet, depending on size. Bake for 6 to 7 minutes, then flip tortilla, parchment and all, and bake for another 3 to 4 minutes. Watch carefully as overcooking will lead to a dry tortilla that can crack easily. Take them out of the oven and remove the parchment paper, it should easily peel off when done. Repeat with remaining tortillas. Stack on a plate to cool.

Store in between pieces of waxed paper in a plastic bag or sealed glass container for up to 5 days in the refrigerator.

Yield: 4 to 6 tortillas

Roasted Cauliflower and Arugula Wraps with Red Pepper Chickpea Spread

Once the ingredients for this recipe are prepped, you will have tasty meals or snacks for days to come—just store all of the finished parts of this meal separately in the fridge. When ready to assemble another wrap, steam another tortilla and fill it with the pre-made fillings.

Red Pepper Chickpea Spread (page 376)
2 tablespoons extra virgin olive oil
1 small red onion, cut into chunks
1 small head cauliflower, cut into florets
⅛ teaspoon sea salt
fresh arugula
gluten-free tortillas

Make the roasted red pepper spread.

To roast the cauliflower, preheat oven to 425 degrees. Place onions and cauliflower pieces on a baking sheet and toss in the 2 tablespoons of olive oil. Sprinkle with sea salt. Roast for about 15 to 20 minutes.

To assemble the wrap, steam and warm the tortillas. Spread the entire tortilla with a thin layer of the red pepper spread, add veggies and arugula on one side, tightly roll from the veggie side. Cut in half and serve immediately.

Store all parts separately in the refrigerator for up to 5 days.

Yield: 6 wraps

Nori Rolls with Pumpkin Seed-Parsley Pâté

This nutrient dense lunch or snack will keep you energized all day. Soaked pumpkin seeds are more digestible and also easy to blend down into a paste. Add your favorite veggies to the nori rolls along with the pâté. Try sliced cucumbers, red bell peppers, shredded carrots, or spinach leaves.

Pâté
1 cup raw pumpkin seeds, soaked for 8 hours
1 lemon, juiced
1 tablespoon extra virgin olive oil
1 clove garlic, crushed
¾ teaspoon Herbamare
large handful fresh parsley
water

Other Ingredients:
4 nori sheets
sliced avocado
micro greens

Rinse and drain the soaked pumpkin seeds. Add them to a food processor fitted with the "s" blade. Add the lemon juice, olive oil, garlic, and Herbamare. Process until smooth, scraping down the sides if necessary. Add the parsley and process again. Add water, a tablespoon at a time, until you get the desired consistency.

Spread pâté onto nori. Add the avocado and micro greens to one end of the nori sheet, then roll. Let rest for a few minutes before slicing. Repeat with remaining ingredients.

Yield: 4 nori rolls

Nutrition Tip:

Pumpkin seeds are high in minerals such as manganese, magnesium, phosphorus, copper, and zinc. Soaking the seeds enables these minerals to become more available. Manganese, for example, is needed to help maintain normal blood sugar levels, keep your thyroid functioning properly, and to help build strong bones. One quarter cup of pumpkin seeds provides about 1.5mg of manganese. Considering we need anywhere from 1.2mg (if you are a toddler) to 2.3mg (if you are a man), pumpkin seeds are a great source of this mineral!

Nori Rolls with Salmon and Mustard Greens

One of our favorite on-the-go meals is a nori roll filled with our favorite vegetables. This one combines spicy mustard greens, creamy avocado, and cooked salmon for a flavorful, nutritious meal or snack. If you pack these in your lunch remember to bring a small bottle of coconut aminos or wheat-free tamari for dipping!

Sticky Brown Rice:
2 cups sweet brown rice
1 cup short grain brown rice
6 cups water
¼ teaspoon sea salt

Other Ingredients:
6 to 8 toasted nori sheets
1 avocado, sliced
2 green onions, cut into thirds, then sliced into thin strips
2 large mustard greens, cut into strips
½ pound cooked salmon

Optional:
toasted black sesame seeds
wheat-free tamari or coconut aminos
wasabi

To make the rice, place both types of rice, the water, and sea salt into a 3-quart pot. Cover and bring to a boil. Immediately turn heat to low or medium-low and simmer for about 45 minutes. Remove pot from heat and let stand about 30 minutes or more before using.

To make the nori rolls, place one sheet of nori, shiny side down, onto a large plate or wooden cutting board. Spread a thin layer of the rice onto the nori leaving about 1 to 2 inches free of rice on the top of the nori sheet—this is needed so the nori can adhere to itself and hold together after you roll it up.

On the bottom of the nori roll, place a thin strip of avocado slices, green onions, mustard greens, and salmon. Begin to tightly roll from the bottom. To seal the nori together, dip your finger in water and place a little water along the seam-side of the roll.

After you have made all of your rolls, take a clean serrated knife and slice the rolls into rounds. Dip in wasabi and tamari, then black mustard seeds if desired.

Yield: 6 to 8 rolls

Ingredient Tip:

If you have soaked your rice overnight, then drain and rinse it and use 4 ½ to 5 cups of fresh water for cooking.

Thai Salad Wraps

If you are craving a lot of vegetables but don't want a traditional salad, try these wraps! They are delicious dipped in the Garlic Ginger Peanut Sauce, on page 363. These are not very filling but highly nutritious, so go ahead and eat five or more at a time! We use tapioca flour paper wrappers that can be found at your local Asian market or health food store. They are paper thin and translucent once softened in warm water. These are used in fresh spring rolls at Thai restaurants.

15 to 20 tapioca or rice paper wrappers
1 small head leaf lettuce, rinsed and spun dry
2 cups thinly sliced red cabbage
1 large red bell pepper, seeded and sliced very thin
1 cucumber, sliced into very thin strips
2 to 3 carrots, shredded
large handful fresh basil leaves
large handful cilantro, chopped
large handful sprouts of any kind (alfalfa, mung bean, broccoli)
small handful fresh spearmint leaves

To soften the wraps, fill a 10-inch skillet filled with hot water, and place each wrap in the hot water to soften for about 30 to 60 seconds If you leave them in the water for too long they will begin to break apart. You will need to change the water about 3 times during this process to keep it fresh and hot.

For the filling, tear the lettuce into small pieces and place into a large bowl. Add the remaining ingredients to the bowl and toss together.

To assemble the wraps, place a softened tapioca paper onto a plate. Add a handful of filling to the bottom of the wrapper. Facing the wrapper think of a north, south, east, west orientation, your vegetables would be on the south end, fold the west and east end in, then tightly roll up towards the north.

Repeat this process with remaining filling and wrappers. To store leftovers, place into a container, layered between wet paper towels. Cover the top layer with a wet paper towel.

Yield: 6 servings

Collard Wraps with Raw Sunflower Pâté

The first few times I made this I used red chili flakes in place of the black pepper. Go ahead and get creative by using whatever ingredients you would like. These wraps can be stored in a glass storage container in your refrigerator for a grab-an-go meal.

1 bunch large collard greens

Sunflower Pate:
2 cups raw sunflower seeds, soaked for 6 to 8 hours
1 cup chopped celery
¼ cup finely diced shallots
2 to 3 tablespoons freshly squeezed lemon juice
1 teaspoon dried thyme
½ to 1 teaspoon Herbamare or sea salt
½ teaspoon freshly ground black pepper

Filling:
1 recipe Super Green Salad (page 234)
grated carrots
sprouts
sliced avocados

Cut the stems off of the bottom of each collard green. Put on a large pot of water to a boil.

While the water in coming to a boil, drain and rinse the sunflower seeds in a fine mesh strainer. Place all pate ingredients into a food processor fitted with the "s" blade and pulse until desired consistency. I like mine processed until the pate is fairly smooth. Set aside.

Then blanch the collard greens by placing them into the boiling water for approximately 60 seconds. Gently remove with tongs and set on a plate to cool.

To assemble the wrap, place a green onto a large plate or cutting board. Place a few spoonfuls of the pâté on the bottom (stem-end) of the green. Add your other filling ingredients on top of the pâté. Fold the long ends in slightly (about an inch on each side) and then tightly roll. Refrigerate right away or cut in half and serve.

Store prepared wraps in the refrigerator for up to 3 days.

Yield: Approximately 8 wraps

Turkey and Avocado Wraps with Honey Mustard

Use this recipe for a simple lunch on the run. You can blanch a bunch of collard greens and then store them in your refrigerator in a covered glass container for a few days. This recipe also works with any gluten-free tortilla of course. You can use the Honey Mustard Dressing on page 351 or use your favorite store-bought organic variety.

3 large collard greens
6 slices organic turkey breast
1 small avocado, sliced
honey mustard

Optional Additions:
grated carrot
grated apple
baby greens

To blanch the collard greens, bring a pot of water to a boil. Trim the stems off of the collards and then place them into the pot of boiling water for 60 seconds. Carefully remove from the pot and place on a towel or plate to cool.

Lay one collard green on a plate or cutting board. Roll two turkey slices up and place them on the bottom, or stem end, of the collard green. Top with sliced avocado, and drizzle with honey mustard. Add any optional additions if desired.

To roll, start by folding in the long sides of the collard green. Then begin to roll from the stem end, where the turkey is until the wrap is rolled. Place seam-side down on a plate or into a container and repeat with remaining ingredients.

Store wraps in a covered container in the refrigerator for a day.

Yield: 3 wraps

Chicken Salad Lettuce Wraps

Sometimes I like lunches to be loaded with vegetables and some lean protein. I find I have plenty of energy for the rest of the day with a lunch like this. Use the Almond Mayonnaise, page 367, or your favorite brand of mayonnaise. If I don't have any almond mayo in the fridge I will use Soy-Free Veganaise. For the chicken in this recipe, I like to use leftover chicken breast from a whole organic chicken I have previously roasted.

1 cup cooked chopped chicken breast
½ cup diced celery
¼ cup diced carrots
¼ cup finely chopped fresh parsley
1 to 2 green onions, sliced into thin rounds
1 tablespoon capers
2 to 4 tablespoons mayonnaise
Herbamare and freshly ground black pepper to taste
lettuce leaves, rinsed and patted dry

Place all of the ingredients except the lettuce leaves into a bowl and mix together. Season with salt and pepper to taste.

Place a few scoops of chicken salad into a large piece of lettuce. Repeat until you are out of chicken salad. You can also use the salad to top a bed of mixed greens. Either way it is delicious.

Store leftover salad in the refrigerator for up to 3 days.

Yield: 2 servings

Snacks and Treats

The healthiest, freshest, and easiest foods for snacking are—you guessed it—plants! Fresh fruits, vegetables, nuts and seeds are ready-made snacks that require little preparation. The billion-dollar snack industry has perpetuated the idea that children need and want processed snack foods on a daily basis. These highly processed foods have created many health problems in our population. Packaged "healthy" snacks from the health food store may not be much better either.

Healthy Snacking

Imagine if we did not have a food industry and every food that we consumed we grew, hunted, or bought from a local farmer. We would probably stick to consuming foods that required the least amount of energy to prepare. If we approach food this way, fresh fruits and vegetables become the cornerstone of our diet.

When you are hungry and needing something to snack on, look to plants to fill the need. Carrots and apples can be purchased from the grocery store instead of chips; fruit and greens can be blended into a green smoothie; nuts and seeds store well and can be packed as a traveling food; a bunch of kale can be turned into addictive chips; and fresh fruit can be made into popsicles.

10 Quick Snack Ideas:

1. **Celery sticks** dipped in sunflower butter or almond butter.
2. **Carrot sticks** dipped in hummus.
3. **Raw cauliflower** dipped in pesto.
4. **Sliced kohlrabi** dipped in your favorite creamy salad dressing.
5. **Sliced hardboiled** egg wrapped in a lettuce leaf and drizzled with honey mustard.
6. **Green smoothie**!
7. **Nut and fruit smoothie** made from soaked nuts and frozen fruit.
8. **Handful of raw almonds** and dried apricots
9. **Bowl of frozen blueberries**, cherries, and raspberries
10. **Banana dipped in almond butter** and shredded coconut

Snacks

Lemon Tahini Kale Chips

Kale chips are a nutritious way to satisfy the need for something crunchy and salty without sacrificing your health. They can either be baked at a very low temperature in the oven or dehydrated using a food dehydrator. If using a dehydrator, set the temp to 115 degrees and dehydrate for about 8 hours or until crisp. The oven method is obviously the fastest but you need to watch them closely as the kale can begin to burn. Fresh lemon juice and sesame tahini is one of our favorite ingredient combinations.

2 bunches curly kale, inner stems removed
¼ cup tahini
2 to 4 tablespoons water
2 tablespoons nutritional yeast
2 tablespoons extra virgin olive oil
2 tablespoons freshly squeezed lemon juice
2 cloves garlic, crushed
¼ teaspoon sea salt

Preheat oven to 250 degrees F.

Rinse the kale and pat dry. Remove the tough inner stem that runs lengthwise through the center of each kale leaf, then tear or chop into large pieces. In a small bowl add the rest of the ingredients. Whisk together well.

Place kale pieces onto a large cookie sheet and toss with the tahini-lemon mixture. Gently massage the mixture into the kale so it is evenly coated. Spread the leaves out on the cookie sheet.

Bake for about 30 to 35 minutes, turning once. Remove from oven, let cool a little, and enjoy! Extra kale chips can be stored in an airtight container for a few days on the counter.

Yield: 4 small servings

Snacks

Nutrition Tip:

Isothiocyanates from kale have been found to regulate the body's detoxification mechanisms at a genetic level, and have been found to lower the risk of developing certain forms of cancer including breast, bladder, colon, prostate, and ovarian.

Sweet and Spicy Kale Chips

Once out of the oven these kale chips disappear fast in our house! I like to use the full teaspoon of chili flakes to create a medium-spiciness. Use ½ teaspoon for a mild spiciness. Baking kale chips at a temperature over 250 degrees causes them to burn—it may take longer at a lower temp, but the flavor and crisp are worth it.

2 large bunches kale, inner stems removed
1 small lime, juiced
2 tablespoons extra virgin olive oil
2 tablespoons creamy almond butter
1 tablespoon maple syrup or honey
½ to 1 teaspoon crushed red chili flakes
½ teaspoon Herbamare or sea salt

Preheat oven to 250 degrees F.

Rinse the kale and pat dry. Use a knife to cut out the tough inner stem that runs lengthwise through the center of each kale leaf, then tear or cut into large pieces.

In a small bowl, whisk together the remaining ingredients. Place the kale into a large bowl and add the mixture. Use your hands to gently massage the mixture in, coating each leaf.

Use one very large cookie sheet, or two medium-sized sheets, and distribute the kale evenly in one layer. Bake for about 40 minutes, stir and flip the leaves 2 or 3 times. If they are not crisp and dry at the end of cooking time just pop them back in until they crisp up. Once done, let them cool on the cookie sheets then transfer to a bowl to serve. Extra kale chips can be stored in an airtight container for a few days on the counter.

Yield: 4 small servings

Variation:

Nut-Free Variation: Replace the almond butter with sesame tahini or sunflower seed butter.

Snacks

Chipotle Lime Kale Chips

I prefer to use black kale, also called lacinato kale, for this recipe though any variety of kale will work fine. Once the kale chips are completely cool, you can tuck some away in a small stainless steel container for your child's lunchbox.

2 bunches kale, inner stems removed
2 tablespoons extra virgin olive oil
1 to 2 tablespoons freshly squeezed lime juice
¼ teaspoon chipotle chili powder
¼ teaspoon sea salt

Preheat oven to 250 degrees F.

Rinse the kale and pat dry. Remove the tough inner stem from the middle of each kale leaf, then tear or chop into large pieces.

Place kale pieces onto a large cookie sheet and toss with the olive oil, lime juice, chipotle, and salt. Gently massage the oil mixture into the kale so it is evenly coated. Spread the leaves out on the cookie sheet.

Bake for 25 to 30 minutes, turning once. Remove from oven, let cool a little and enjoy! Extra kale chips can be stored in an airtight container for a few days or the counter.

Yield: 4 small servings

Ingredient Tip:

The kale needs to be completely dry after rinsing it otherwise it won't crisp up into chips in the oven.

Toasted Sunflower Seeds with Coconut Aminos

Coconut aminos can be used to replace tamari in any recipe. They are a great soy-free soy sauce! When I use Coconut aminos I sometimes add a pinch or two of sea salt, as they aren't as salty as tamari. This recipe is so easy, it only takes about five minutes to prepare, and it's one of our children's favorite snacks! They are also delicious sprinkled on a green salad.

1 cup raw sunflower seeds
1 tablespoon coconut aminos
pinch sea salt

Heat an 11-inch skillet over medium heat for a few minutes, or until the pan is hot. Add the sunflower seeds; use a spatula to keep them moving in the pan. Toast them for about 1 ½ to 2 minutes. Turn off heat and add coconut aminos and sea salt. Immediately stir the mixture to coat the seeds evenly. Let cool on a plate then transfer to a glass jar for storage.

Yield: 1 cup

Nutrition Tip:

Sunflower seeds are a good source of magnesium. Magnesium is nature's nerve calmer. It helps to relax tight muscles, prevent migraines, and lower high blood pressure. One-quarter cup of sunflower seeds provides about 200 calories and 115 mg magnesium.

Smokey Tamari Roasted Nuts

Smoked Spanish paprika is what gives these nuts a hint of smoke flavor. Make sure you follow the directions and roast the nuts first, then add the tamari, and roast again for a few minutes. You'll have a burned mess if you roast them all at once. These nuts make a fabulous appetizer for a holiday gathering or a great afterschool snack for your kids.

1 cup raw cashews
1 cup raw almonds
2 to 3 tablespoons tamari or coconut aminos
1 to 2 teaspoons smoked paprika

Preheat oven to 350 degrees F.

Place nuts into a 9 x 13-inch glass baking dish. Roast in the oven for 12 to 15 minutes (watch timing as oven temps vary). Remove pan from oven and quickly add the tamari and smoked paprika. Toss together with a spatula.

Return pan to oven and roast for about 3 minutes more. Remove pan from oven and let the nuts cool. They will become crispy once completely cooled. Store in an airtight container.

Yield: 2 cups

Variation:

Omit the paprika and add crushed dried rosemary for a savory flavor, or try chipotle chili powder for a kick.

Candied Walnuts

These nuts make a fantastic appetizer, especially during the holidays. I like to use wide-mouth pint-size jars to package these nuts. This recipe also works with other nuts such as pecans. Each year we like to make a few batches of candied nuts to give out as holiday gifts.

2 cups walnut halves
3 tablespoons maple syrup
1 tablespoon coconut oil or extra virgin olive oil
1 teaspoon cinnamon
pinch or two of sea salt

Preheat oven to 375 degrees F.

Place all ingredients into a baking dish (I use a 7 x 11-inch glass baking dish). Stir well with a spoon. Bake for 12 to 15 minutes, watching carefully so they don't burn.

As soon as they come out of the oven, stir them so the syrup sticks to the nuts and not the pan. Immediately transfer them to a plate to cool.

Yield: 2 cups

Cinnamon Sunflower Truffles

You'll need a food processor to make these and other date-based snack balls. You may try using different nuts or seeds. Pecans, almonds, or cashews can be used in place of the sunflower seeds for variation. I have found that these truffles are even better on the second day, if they last that long!

2 cups raw sunflower seeds
2 tablespoons ground cinnamon
⅛ teaspoon sea salt
1 cup pitted medjool dates
2 tablespoons extra virgin olive oil
2 tablespoons maple syrup (if needed)
unsweetened shredded coconut

Place the sunflower seeds, cinnamon, and sea salt into a food processor fitted with the "s" blade. Process until seeds are very finely ground; about a minute.

Then add the pitted dates and olive oil. Process again until combined and sticky. Only add the maple syrup if needed; your dates may be moist enough and not require extra sweetener. Check to see if you can form a truffle by rolling some of the mixture in your hands, if it falls apart then add the sweetener and process again.

Scoop out the sunflower mixture by the large spoonful and roll into balls. Then roll in shredded coconut. Store in the fridge for up to 2 weeks.

Yield: 1 dozen balls

Nutrition Tip:

Sunflower seeds are an excellent source of Vitamin E. Each quarter cup of sunflower seeds contains about 12 milligrams of Vitamin E. This fat-soluble vitamin is used in the body as an antioxidant, preventing cholesterol, and fat found in cell membranes and brain tissue from free radical damage. Inflammation from free radical damage is a root cause of conditions such as arthritis and asthma. Vitamin E has shown significant anti-inflammatory effects with these diseases.

Cranberry Pecan Energy Balls

These little fruit-nut balls are a great snack to take hiking or packed in a school lunch. I roll them in hemp seeds for extra nutrition, but you could also use shredded coconut.

2 cups raw pecans
¼ teaspoon ground nutmeg
pinch sea salt
1 cup medjool dates, pitted
¾ cup dried cranberries
½ to 1 cup hemp seeds

Place the pecans, nutmeg, and salt into a food processor fitted with the "s" blade. Process until a very fine meal forms.

Add the dates and dried cranberries; process again, stopping the machine and pulsing as needed to break down the dates. It will take a minute or two for the mixture to become fine enough to form into balls

Roll tightly into small one-inch balls then roll each truffle in hemp seeds. Place truffles into a glass storage container and store in the refrigerator for up to 2 weeks.

Yield: 1 dozen balls

Ingredient Tip:

Use fruit juice sweetened dried cranberries to avoid consuming refined white sugar.

Cashew Orange Date Balls

If you are in the mood for a sweet snack, this recipe can be whipped up within 10 minutes! I like to have a container of some sort of nut-date ball in the refrigerator for my children to pack in their school lunches. One ball serves as a sweet treat and also a good dose of protein and healthy fat.

1 ½ cups raw cashews
1 cup medjool dates, pitted
2 tablespoons coconut oil, melted
1 teaspoon orange zest
pinch sea salt
unsweetened shredded coconut

Place the cashews into a food processor fitted with the "s" blade. Process until very finely ground, then add the dates, melted coconut oil, orange zest, and salt. Process again until the dates are very finely ground and the mixture begins to form a ball.

Take small handfuls of the cashew-date mixture and form small balls. Roll each ball in the shredded coconut. Transfer to a glass storage container and place into the refrigerator for up to 2 weeks.

Yield: 1 dozen balls

Ginger Macadamia Nut Energy Bars

Having nut-date energy bars in our refrigerator is indispensable for our family. I can serve them for breakfast with a green smoothie and bring them along on hikes or outings with my children. I prefer to make a double batch of this recipe when making it, which makes thicker bars. If you don't have macadamia nuts, try pecans.

1 ½ cups raw macadamia nuts
1 cup pitted medjool dates (about 10)
1 teaspoon cinnamon
½ teaspoon ground ginger
¼ teaspoon ground cardamom
pinch sea salt

Place the nuts into a food processor fitted with the "s" blade and process for about 60 to 90 seconds or until finely ground. Then add the dates, spices, and salt. Process again for another 60 to 90 seconds or until the dates are completely ground and the mixture is starting to form a ball.

Press mixture into an 8 x 8-inch pan and refrigerate for 4 to 5 hours. Then cut into bar shapes and individually wrap in waxed paper. You can also roll the mixture into balls and then roll in shredded coconut.

Yield: 12 bars

Variation:

For chocolate energy bars, omit spices and add 4 tablespoons raw cacao powder along with 2 tablespoons melted coconut oil.

Snacks

Herbed Popcorn

Popcorn wins over sweet treats any day in our house. Our children adore this and can polish off a large bowl in a matter of minutes. Popcorn makes a great snack for outings and can be used as part of a healthy school lunch. For more flavor, try adding ¼ teaspoon each of garlic powder and onion powder to the topping mixture.

Popcorn:
4 tablespoons coconut oil
½ teaspoon sea salt
1 cup organic popcorn kernels

Topping:
1 tablespoon dried thyme
1 tablespoon dried rosemary
2 to 3 tablespoons nutritional yeast
½ teaspoon Herbamare
2 to 4 tablespoons coconut oil, melted

Heat a large, 6 to 8-quart heavy-bottomed pot over high heat. It is really important that you use a high quality stainless steel pot with a thick bottom, otherwise the popcorn with burn.

Add the coconut oil and salt to the pot. Once the oil has melted add the popcorn kernels. Cover and cook for a few minutes, moving the pot vigorously, until the popping has subsided. Immediately pour the popcorn into a large bowl.

Place the dry topping ingredients into a coffee grinder or blender and grind until you have a somewhat coarse powder. Drizzle the popcorn with the melted coconut oil and then toss with the herb mixture.

Yield: About 5 quarts

Maple Caramel Corn

Serve a large bowl of this tasty popcorn at your holiday party. It also makes a great gift for a teacher. If you want to double the recipe, make it in batches—popping one cup of popcorn will nearly fill an 8-quart stockpot!

Popcorn:
2 to 3 tablespoons virgin coconut oil
¼ teaspoon sea salt
1 cup organic popcorn kernels

Caramel:
½ cup coconut oil or organic butter
1 cup maple syrup
few dashes sea salt

Preheat oven to 325 degrees F.

Heat an 8-quart stockpot over high heat for a minute or so. Add oil and salt, then popcorn. Cover and cook for a few minutes, moving the pot vigorously, until the popping has subsided. Immediately remove from heat to prevent burning and pour popcorn into two large bowls.

In a medium saucepan heat the coconut oil or butter, maple syrup, and a few dashes sea salt over medium heat. Once small bubbles form, cook for 4 to 5 minutes whisking occasionally until thickened and foamy. Quickly pour half of the caramel over each bowl of popcorn and toss together using two large spoons. Spread into two shallow baking pans or cookie sheets and place in the oven.

Bake for 10 minutes stirring half way through. Let cool completely. Caramel corn will crisp up as it cools. Once completely cooled, store in a tightly sealed container to keep crisp.

Yield: About 4 quarts

Honeydew-Cucumber-Mint Popsicles

I like to use a very ripe honeydew melon for this recipe. You could also add the juice from one to two limes to add a refreshing, tart flavor. If you don't have very many popsicle molds, I would suggest using either a small melon or half a melon and a medium cucumber. You can also add ice cubes to any leftovers that won't fit into the molds and make a smoothie.

1 medium to large honeydew melon, seeded
1 large cucumber, chopped
1 large handful fresh spearmint leaves

Cut the melon in half, remove the seeds, and scoop the flesh into a bowl to catch the juices. Add the melon and juices to a blender or Vita-Mix, then add the chopped cucumber and fresh mint. Blend until smooth. Pour into popsicle molds and freeze overnight.

Yield: 8 to 12 popsicles

Nutrition Tip:

Cucumbers contain lignans, or polyphenols found in plants, that can help to reduce the risk of developing breast, uterine, ovarian, and prostate cancer, as well as cardio-vascular disease.

Blueberry-Orange-Coconut Swirl Popsicles

I like to make a few batches of these just after we go blueberry picking. Making popsicles with freshly picked fruit is an effective way to help preserve the harvest! Sometimes I will use apple juice in place of the orange juice and other times I will simply blend up the blueberries with a little water, or coconut water, and liquid stevia.

1 cup fresh blueberries
1 cup freshly squeezed orange juice
¼ to ½ cup full fat coconut milk

Place the blueberries and juice into a blender or Vita-Mix; blend until smooth. Pour into popsicle molds leaving a little room at the top of each one. Top each off with a tablespoon or so of coconut milk, then take a chopstick and lightly swirl it into the blueberry mix. Freeze overnight.

Yield: 4 to 8 popsicles

Desserts

Our take on dessert is to keep it as simple and wholesome as possible. Natural sweeteners are used in place of refined sugars. Whole grain gluten-free flours and grain-free flours are used instead of refined flours. Organic fruit and nuts are used as the base for many desserts and avocados are added for healthy fats in some recipes. You'll find that when your diet consists of real, whole foods, with plenty of vegetables and enough protein, you may not even crave sugar! Dessert will naturally become something to be savored and eaten in moderation.

When we consume dessert in our home, it is usually a scoop of coconut milk ice cream topped with frozen organic berries. Cookies are baked occasionally, only about twice a month. Baked pies are enjoyed a few times a year on special occasions, and fruit crisps are made when there is too much fruit to process in the summertime. By consuming dessert on occasion instead of everyday, your children will learn to develop a healthy relationship with the sweet flavor.

Alternatives to Refined Sugar

Eliminating refined sugars from your family's diet can help improve everyone's health. When consuming white sugar, the body needs to tap into its stores of B vitamins and minerals, such as calcium and magnesium, to be able to properly digest it. A child who is a picky eater and is not consuming a well-balanced diet; who has damaged upper intestine from gluten and is therefore not absorbing sufficient magnesium and calcium; and who already consumes a high amount of refined foods will suffer the most from sugar consumption. Consuming sugar overtime can lead to nutrient deficiencies, yeast overgrowth, inflammation, weight gain, dental carries, insulin resistance, hypoglycemia, lowered immunity, erratic behavior, poor concentration, learning disabilities, and cancer cell growth. Sugar is a main ingredient in many processed foods so working to eliminate those will drastically cut down on total daily intake.

Natural sweeteners contain all of the vitamins, minerals, and phytochemicals originally found in the plant they came from. They often digest slower than refined white sugar and actually have some nutritional value. But remember, natural sweeteners are still sugar so use them wisely and sparingly!

10 Tips for Using Natural Sweeteners:

1. **Coconut Nectar is the sap from the coconut palm tree**. It is very thick and rich with a low glycemic index of about 35, meaning it won't spike blood sugar as quickly as other sweeteners. It contains very little glucose and fructose, a small percentage of sucrose, and a high percentage of fructooligosaccharides (FOS). These indigestible sugars, or prebiotics, feed beneficial bacteria in the gut! Use coconut nectar anywhere a liquid sweetener is called for.

2. **Local Honey is a simple sugar made up of mostly glucose and fructose**. It is easily digested and can be used anywhere a liquid sweetener is called for. Raw honey has a much lower glycemic index than pasteurized honey, so always read labels or talk to your local beekeepers to find a source of raw honey. When combined with eggs in a baked good honey can cause a lot of browning, which is why I prefer to use as little as possible in my recipes. You can replace part of the honey called for in a recipe with unsweetened applesauce and add in liquid stevia to boost sweetness if desired.

3. **Maple Syrup is made up of mostly sucrose**. Because of this it doesn't cause a lot of browning when baked but will offer a distinct maple flavor. Use it anywhere a liquid sweetener is called for. Remember to always purchase pure maple syrup made from the sap of the sugar maple tree. We prefer to use Grade B, which is cheaper and richer in flavor. Imitation maple syrup is made of non-food chemicals like caramel color, flavorings, and high-fructose corn syrup.

4. **Coconut Sugar is basically dried and granulated coconut nectar and comes with the same low-glycemic properties**. It is light brown in color and the flavor is rich and caramel-like. Use it anywhere a granulated sugar is called for.

5. **Maple Sugar is simply dried and granulated pure maple syrup**. It is quite expensive but very tasty. It will give your dessert a distinct maple flavor. Use it anywhere a granulated sugar is called for.

6. **Whole Cane Sugar is the dried juice of the sugar cane plant**. It is dark brown in color and rich in flavor. It has a much higher glycemic index compared to coconut sugar but is less expensive and easier to come by. You can use it in place of coconut sugar if desired.

7. **Medjool Dates can be soaked in hot water and pureed into a paste to be used in cakes**, muffins, or cookies. You can use dates as a primary sweetener in many recipes, but you will need to lessen other liquids in the recipe if you use date paste to replace a granulated sweetener.

8. **Mashed Ripe Bananas are such a perfect natural sweetener**! The riper your bananas, the sweeter they will be. You can puree bananas in a blender and use the puree to replace any liquid sweetener.

9. **Prunes work in a similar fashion to dates but are less sweet and higher in fiber**. They can be used to thicken, bind, and sweetened most baked treats.

To make prune puree, place 1 cup of prunes into a bowl and cover with 1 cup of boiling water. Soak for 20 minutes then pour the soaked prunes and water into a blender and puree. You can use this in place of applesauce or other liquid sweeteners in most recipes.

10. **Stevia has zero calories and a glycemic index of zero.** It can be used to sweeten treats without adding sugar. Stevia is a green plant that grows in warm climates. We've been able to successfully grow it in our garden in the Northwest but it doesn't survive our cool winters. We prefer to use liquid stevia over powered stevia because it is less processed. If you are using ingredients in a recipe that are naturally sweet such as applesauce, mashed banana, or coconut flour then you can add about ¼ teaspoon of liquid stevia to boost sweetness if desired.

Maple Sunbutter Candy

I use organic Sunbutter, which is made from roasted sunflower seeds (the non-organic versions have sugar and other stuff added). I also prefer to use grade B maple syrup over grade A because it has a richer flavor. This candy easily burns if it is not tended to or if the heat is too high, so watch it carefully. Add one of these candies to your child's lunchbox as a sweet treat. They are also fun to make for Halloween or as a Christmas stocking stuffer.

1 cup maple syrup
½ cup organic Sunbutter
⅛ teaspoon sea salt

Place all ingredients into a 2-quart stainless steel pot with a thick, heavy bottom. Whisk together.

Then turn heat to high and bring to a boil, whisking constantly. Once it is boiling, immediately turn heat to medium or medium-high, whichever maintains a steady, low boil. Whisk continuously for about 8 minutes or until the candy thickens and begins to stick to the bottom of the pan. Remove pan from heat and remove the whisk (otherwise the candy will get stuck inside of the wires as it cools).

Let it cool until the temperature is low enough to handle, about 5 to 10 minutes; any longer and the candy will get too hard to work with.

Place a piece of parchment paper down on a clean work surface. Roll warm candy into 5 thin, long logs then slice into 1 to 2-inch pieces. Wrap each piece in unbleached parchment or waxed paper. Let cool completely before serving.

Yield: About 3 dozen candies

Variation:

This candy can be made with other nut butters if you desire. Almond butter is particularly delicious! You can also add a few dashes of vanilla extract or a little cocoa powder to make it extra special.

Almond Fig Truffles

These truffles are so nutritious you could eat them for breakfast along with a green smoothie! Keep them in the refrigerator in a glass container to have a healthy treat on hand for those infamous chocolate cravings. I use Dagoba Organic Chocodrops, which are gluten-free.

Filling:
1 cup raw almonds, soaked overnight
1 cup dried black mission figs
2 to 3 tablespoons coconut nectar or maple syrup

Chocolate Coating:
1 cup dark chocolate chips
1 tablespoon coconut oil
¼ teaspoon orange flavoring

Rinse and drain the soaked almonds. Place them into a food processor fitted with the "s" blade. Add the figs and coconut nectar or maple syrup. Process until a smooth paste forms. You will need to stop the food processor occasionally and scrape down the sides then process again. Roll filling into 1-inch balls and set onto a plate.

Prepare a large plate for your finished truffles by covering it with a piece of parchment paper. Set aside.

In a double boiler, add the ingredients for the chocolate coating. You can also use a stainless steel bowl over a pot filled with a few inches of water, just don't let the bowl touch the water. If you don't do this, the chocolate with burn and become unusable. Melt over low heat, stirring, until the chocolate is completely melted.

Turn off heat and immediately drop the first truffle into the chocolate, gently swirl the melted chocolate over it using a spoon. Lift up and place onto the prepared plate with parchment paper. Repeat with remaining truffles.

Once you are finished, place the plate with the truffles into the freezer for about 30 minutes to set the chocolate. Once set, place truffles into a sealed glass container and store in your refrigerator for up to a week.

Yield: About 1 dozen truffles

Desserts

Almond Goji Berry Truffles

These beautiful truffles contain a flavorful red filling and a rich chocolate exterior, making them a special treat for Valentine's Day.

Filling:
1 cup dried goji berries
½ cup creamy almond butter
¼ cup coconut nectar or maple syrup
1 teaspoon almond flavoring

Chocolate Coating:
1 cup dark chocolate chips
1 tablespoon virgin coconut oil
1 teaspoon vanilla extract

Place all filling ingredients in a food processor fitted with the "s" blade; process/pulse for a few minutes until ground and sticky. Roll filling into small balls and set onto a plate.

Prepare a large plate for your finished truffles by covering it with a piece of parchment paper. Set aside.

In a double boiler, add the ingredients for the chocolate coating. You can also use a stainless steel bowl over a pot filled with a few inches of water, just don't let the bowl touch the water. If you don't do this, the chocolate with burn and become unusable. Melt over low heat, stirring, until the chocolate is completely melted.

Remove pan or bowl from heat and immediately drop the first truffle into the chocolate, gently swirl the melted chocolate over it using a spoon. Lift up and place onto the prepared plate with parchment paper. Repeat with remaining truffles.

Once you are finished, place the plate with the truffles into the freezer for about 30 minutes to set the chocolate. Once set, place truffles into a sealed glass container and store in your refrigerator for up to a week.

Yield: About 1 dozen truffles

Nutrition Tip:

Goji berries are a truly remarkable superfood. Ounce for ounce goji berries contain more vitamin C than oranges, more beta-carotene than carrots, and more iron than spinach. They also contain over 20 trace minerals and 18 amino acids!

Fresh Strawberries with Lemon Avocado Custard

This slightly sweet, creamy custard is bright green! The flavor is lemony, just perfect for spooning over fresh berries in the spring or summer. The coconut milk helps to thicken it once it chills.

Avocado Custard:
2 small ripe avocados, pitted
¼ cup freshly squeezed lemon juice
¼ cup raw coconut nectar
¼ cup coconut milk
½ teaspoon lemon flavoring

Other Ingredients:
1 to 2 pints fresh organic strawberries, rinsed, hulled, and halved
unsweetened shredded coconut

Place all custard ingredients into a blender and blend for 60 seconds, scraping down sides and blending again if necessary, until thick and creamy. Scrape out the custard into a glass container with a lid to chill. Chill in the refrigerator for at least an hour, though six hours works better.

Place strawberries into individual serving bowls or small, clear juice glasses.

Place a large dollop of the avocado custard over the berries in each serving dish and sprinkle with a little shredded coconut if desired.

Yield: 4 to 6 servings

Nutrition Tip:

Avocados are a rich source of phytosterols and carotenoids, both which help keep inflammation in check. Additionally, avocados are a rich source of oleic acid, a fatty acid that helps to prevent heart disease.

Berry Parfaits with Orange Cashew Cream

This is a favorite recipe to make during the summer months when the berries are in abundance. Serve it for breakfast, a healthy snack, or dessert. Use any berries that are fresh and available. Try blueberries, strawberries, blackberries, and raspberries.

Cashew Cream:
1 cup raw cashews, soaked for 3 hours
½ cup freshly squeezed orange juice
2 medjool dates, pitted
½ teaspoon orange zest
pinch sea salt
dash maple syrup (optional)

Other Ingredients:
4 cups fresh organic berries
hemp seeds

To make the cashew cream, drain and rinse the cashews, place them into a blender along with the orange juice, dates, orange zest, and salt. Blend on high until very smooth and creamy. You might need to turn off your blender, scrape down the sides, and blend again a few times. Taste and add a dash of maple syrup for a sweeter cream and blend again if needed.

Set out 4 to 6 parfait cups or clear juice glasses. Add a layer of berries to the bottom of each. Then a thin layer of the cashew cream, then another layer of berries, then a final layer of cashew cream. Sprinkle the top layer with hemp seeds.

Yield: 4 to 6 servings

Nutrition Tip:

Making your own orange juice from fresh oranges is much more nutritious than buying store-bought pasteurized orange juice. Pasteurization kills harmful bacteria to be able to prolong shelf life, but it also destroys live enzymes and certain vitamins. Freshly squeezed orange juice contains all of the enzymes, vitamin C, and antioxidants present in the orange, which makes the juice far more digestible and easier to assimilate.

Desserts

Dark Chocolate Coconut Custard

This thick and rich custard can help to alleviate any chocolate cravings you might be having! It's really not designed for children—ours think it is far too rich. You'll need six small ramekins for this recipe, which can be purchased at most kitchen stores or online. I use Dagoba organic bittersweet chocolate, though any brand of chocolate will do—just make sure it's organic and gluten-free. Serve with a dollop of Whipped Coconut Cream, page 476, and sliced fresh strawberries.

1 can coconut milk
4 ounces bittersweet chocolate
½ to ¾ cup coconut sugar
2 teaspoons vanilla
pinch sea salt
2 large organic eggs

Preheat oven to 350 degrees F. Fill a 9 x 13-inch pan halfway with water. Set out 6 small ramekins.

Heat the coconut milk, chocolate, and coconut sugar in a small saucepan over very low heat. Whisk continuously until the chocolate has melted. Add the vanilla and salt; whisk again. Remove from heat and let cool for about 10 minutes.

Add eggs and vigorously whisk to incorporate. Evenly pour into the ramekins. Carefully place each ramekin into the pan with water. Place pan into oven and bake for approximately 30 minutes.

Remove each ramekin from the pan and let cool completely before serving. Cover and refrigerate any leftover custard for up to a week.

Yield: 6 servings

Ingredient Tip:

We use Native Forest organic coconut milk which comes in BPA-free cans.

Sweet Potato Custard

This custard recipe can be baked in a 10-inch deep pie plate or in individual ramekins. Serve with Whipped Coconut Cream, page 476, and a dusting of cinnamon.

2 pounds orange sweet potatoes or yams
1 cup coconut milk
6 large organic egg yolks
¼ cup honey
1 teaspoon vanilla
1 to 2 teaspoons cinnamon
½ to 1 teaspoon ground ginger
pinch sea salt

Bake whole sweet potatoes, with their skins on, in a 350 degree F oven for about an hour, or until tender. Let cool. Sweet potatoes can be baked 1 to 2 days in advance.

Remove the skins from the sweet potatoes and place flesh into a food processor fitted with the "s" blade. You should have about 3 cups mashed. Add remaining ingredients and process until smooth.

Pour mixture into a greased 10-inch deep pie plate or 6 individual ramekins. Bake for about an hour for the pie plate or 40 to 45 minutes for the ramekins. Serve warm or cold. Store leftover custard in the refrigerator for up to a week.

Yield: 6 to 8 servings

Variation:

If you tolerate dairy products you may replace the coconut milk with organic heavy cream, preferably raw.

Mango Coconut Pudding

You can use either fresh or frozen mangos in this recipe. You'll need about 5 large fresh mangos or two 10-ounce bags of frozen, plus another fresh one for the topping. This recipe can be used in lieu of a cake for a child's first birthday party.

4 to 6 tablespoons kudzu
½ cup water
4 cups diced fresh or frozen mango
1 can coconut milk
¼ cup honey or coconut nectar
2 teaspoons vanilla

Topping:
diced fresh mango
shredded, unsweetened coconut

Place the kudzu and water in a 3-quart saucepan. Use less kudzu if you like a softer pudding or use the full six tablespoons if you like it firmer. Whisk together so that the kudzu dissolves. The kudzu needs to be dissolved before heating so whisk again just before adding the remaining ingredients.

In a blender, add the mango, coconut milk, and sweetener. Blend on high until very smooth and creamy. Pour into the saucepan with the dissolved kudzu.

Turn heat to medium-high. Whisk constantly until it boils then reduce heat to low and simmer while whisking for 6 to 10 minutes. You'll notice the color change from a creamy yellow to an egg-yolk yellow indicating that it is about ready to be removed from the heat. Whisk in vanilla and remove from heat.

Pour or ladle into six small bowls and place into the refrigerator to set. Chill for 1 to 2 hours. Top with diced fresh mango and shredded coconut.

Yield: 6 servings

Desserts

Raspberry Almond Pudding

This is one of our children's favorite desserts to pack in their school lunches. I pour the hot pudding into half-pint wide-mouthed mason jars and let them cool in the refrigerator overnight. In the morning, they will top the pudding with whatever fresh fruit we have, such as diced peaches or fresh berries, screw a lid on, and put it into their lunch baskets. You can use other fruits if desired, but you will need to blend them up with the milk before cooking. I don't like blending the raspberries because their seeds make the pudding gritty. I like to use the Quick Rich Almond Milk, page 480, in this recipe but you could use any type of milk, such as coconut milk, fresh goat's milk, or hazelnut milk.

3 cups almond milk
4 tablespoons kudzu
4 tablespoons honey
1 cup fresh or frozen raspberries
1 teaspoon vanilla
½ teaspoon almond flavoring
pinch sea salt

Place the almond milk into a 2-quart pot and whisk in the kudzu. Make sure it is dissolved before turning on the heat. Then add the honey and whisk in. Turn heat to medium. Once simmering, cook pudding for 5 to 7 minutes or until thickened.

Then add the raspberries, vanilla, almond flavoring, and salt; keep whisking and cook for another 3 to 4 minutes. The raspberries will break down and turn the pudding a lovely pink color.

Pour into 6 to 8 small serving dishes or jars. Pudding will seem thin but will solidify once completely chilled. Place into the refrigerator and chill for at least 4 hours.

Yield: About 3 ½ cups or seven ½-cup servings

Desserts

Vanilla Chia Pudding

This raw pudding is similar to tapioca pudding. The chia seeds expand and release their gelatinous substance when soaked in a liquid. Serve pudding in small bowls topped with fresh raspberries or sliced fresh strawberries. If you do not own a high-powered blender then you will want to soak the cashews for about 3 hours before blending them. Also, if using a regular blender the whole vanilla bean may not completely blend, therefore use 1 tablespoon of non-alcoholic vanilla in place of it.

½ cup raw cashews
1 ½ cups water
¼ cup coconut nectar or maple syrup
1 whole vanilla bean
pinch sea salt
5 tablespoons whole chia seeds

Place the cashews, water, coconut nectar or maple syrup, vanilla bean, and salt into a high-powered blender and blend until smooth and ultra-creamy. Pour into a medium-sized bowl or glass container.

Add the chia seeds, whisk together. Let soak on the counter at room temp for about 1 hour. Then cover and transfer to the refrigerator to soak and thicken for at least 2 more hours.

Scoop into serving bowls and top with fresh berries.

Yield: 4 to 6 servings

Avocado Fudgesicles

This recipe is quite a treat for anyone, young or old. I think you'll like how healthy they are too! I like to use a raw Ecuadorian cacao powder that makes them extra tasty. I also like Dagoba chocolate products, which are all gluten-free though not raw. After blending all of the ingredients together you can immediately serve this as pudding or pour it into your Popsicle molds for fudgesicles.

8 medjool dates, pitted
½ cup water
3 medium avocados, pitted
1 cup coconut milk
¼ cup honey
5 to 7 tablespoons cacao or cocoa powder
2 teaspoons vanilla
pinch sea salt

Place the dates into your blender and cover with the ½ cup water. Pack the dates down if needed so they are covered, for the most part, in the water. Let soak for about 30 minutes.

Then add in the remaining ingredients and blend until very smooth and creamy. Depending on your blender, you may need to add a little extra coconut milk or water.

Pour into small bowls and serve as pudding or pour into popsicle molds and freeze for at least 6 hours. Run under hot water to release.

Yield: 8 servings

Dark Chocolate Ice Cream

Having an ice cream maker to make your own fresh dairy-free and sugar-free ice cream is such a treat! The avocado makes this recipe extra rich and creamy yet doesn't detract from the chocolate flavor. We often add frozen, pitted cherries that I chop into small pieces. Chilling the coconut milk prior to making this recipe helps the mixture form "ice cream" once in the ice cream maker.

2 cans coconut milk, chilled
1 medium avocado (optional)
½ cup honey, maple syrup, or coconut nectar
¾ cup cocoa powder
2 to 3 teaspoons vanilla extract
½ teaspoon almond flavoring

Optional Additions:
finely chopped dark chocolate bar
sliced almonds
chopped frozen cherries

Chill the coconut milk cans in your refrigerator for at least 3 hours or overnight.

Once chilled, open the cans and pour the coconut milk into a blender. Add the avocado, honey, cocoa powder, vanilla, and almond flavoring; blend until smooth, about 30 seconds.

Pour blender contents into your ice cream maker and process for about 25 minutes or longer if needed. After about 15 minutes of running the ice cream maker add any optional additions, continue to run until thick and creamy.

The ice cream will be the consistency of soft serve ice cream just out of the ice cream maker. To harden it up, scoop it out and place the ice cream into a large container. Freeze for about 2 hours. Remove from freezer and let stand for about 10 minutes before serving.

Yield: 8 servings

Desserts

Mint Chocolate Chip Ice Cream

Our children love the combination of mint and chocolate chips and I feel good serving them this ice cream knowing that it is providing them with healthy fats and a slew of anti-oxidants. The avocado gives the ice cream a light green color and helps to make it very creamy. Our oldest daughter strongly dislikes avocado, but she likes this recipe because she cannot detect an avocado flavor. Be sure to use a high-powered blender as the avocado and coconut milk thicken up immediately after you start the blender.

2 cans coconut milk, chilled
2 medium avocados
¼ to ½ cup honey or coconut nectar
1 to 2 teaspoons organic peppermint flavoring
½ cup mini chocolate chips or cocoa nibs

Chill the coconut milk cans in your refrigerator for at least 3 hours or overnight.

Place the coconut milk, avocados, honey or coconut nectar, and peppermint flavoring into a high-powered blender and blend on medium to high, until smooth and creamy. Be careful about blending it too long or the mixture will heat up and will have difficulty turning into ice cream.

Pour blender contents into your ice cream maker and process for about 25 minutes or longer if needed. After about 15 minutes pour in the chocolate chips.

The ice cream will be the consistency of soft serve ice cream just out of the ice cream maker. To harden it up, scoop it out and place the ice cream into a large container. Freeze for about 2 hours. Remove from freezer and let stand for about 10 minutes before serving.

Yield: 8 servings

Strawberry Coconut Ice Cream

This ice cream needs to be made in an ice cream maker. You may have a little extra that won't fit into your ice cream machine, depending on its size. Simply pour the extra pureed strawberry-coconut milk mixture into popsicle molds and freeze. Serve ice cream with sliced fresh strawberries and fresh mint leaves for a cooling summer dessert.

2 cans coconut milk, chilled
2 to 2 ½ cups frozen strawberries (about 1 pound)
¼ to ½ cup honey or coconut nectar
1 tablespoon vanilla
½ teaspoon lemon flavoring

Chill the coconut milk cans in your refrigerator for at least 3 hours or overnight.

Once chilled, open the cans and pour the coconut milk into a blender. Place the remaining ingredients into a blender or Vita-Mix and blend until smooth and creamy.

Pour blender contents into your ice cream maker and process for about 25 to 30 minutes or longer if needed.

The ice cream will be the consistency of soft serve ice cream just out of the ice cream maker. To harden it up, scoop it out and place the ice cream into a large container. Freeze for about 2 hours. Remove from freezer and let stand for about 10 minutes before serving.

Yield: 8 servings

Ingredient Tip:

Adding a tablespoon or two of alcohol to the ice cream, such as an alcoholic vanilla extract or brandy, helps to keep the ice cream from crystalizing once in the freezer.

White Nectarine Ice Cream

This off-white ice cream is flecked with little bits pink from the diced nectarine. It is sweet, rich, and scoops perfectly. Definitely a crowd pleaser! I use my Cuisinart Ice Cream Maker, which can be found at most kitchen supply stores or online. For the ice cream, you can use either fresh or frozen nectarines. If using frozen, your blended cream with turn into "ice cream" much quicker.

¾ cup raw cashews
5 medjool dates, pitted
1 can coconut milk, chilled
2 large white nectarines, pitted
¼ to ½ cup honey or coconut nectar
1 tablespoon vanilla extract
1 to 2 teaspoons almond flavoring

Other Ingredients:
1 large white nectarine, diced
½ cup slivered almonds (optional)

Chill the coconut milk cans in your refrigerator for at least 3 hours or overnight. Place the cashews and dates into a small bowl and cover with water. Let soak for about 3 hours.

Drain and rinse the cashews and place into a high-powered blender along with the dates, coconut milk, 2 pitted nectarines, honey, vanilla, and almond flavoring. Blend on high until very smooth and creamy.

Pour blender contents into your ice cream maker and process for about 25 minutes or longer if needed. After about 15 minutes add the 1 large diced nectarine and slivered almonds if using.

The ice cream will be the consistency of soft serve ice cream just out of the ice cream maker. To harden it up, scoop it out and place the ice cream into a large container. Freeze for about 2 hours. Remove from freezer and let stand for about 10 minutes before serving.

Yield: 6 servings

Ingredient Tip:

If you cannot find large nectarines, use five small ones in place of the three used in the recipe. Use three for blending into the cream and the remaining two for dicing.

Peach Blackberry Sorbet

Making your own sugar-free sorbet is easy! We like to pick hundreds of pounds of local fruit in the summertime and then store it in an extra freezer so we can have special fruit treats all year round! This is one of our favorites, created by our daughter, Lily, and her friend, Kaia, when they were eight years old.

2 large frozen peaches, chopped
2 cups frozen blackberries
1 lemon, juiced
2 to 4 tablespoons honey or coconut nectar
10 drops liquid stevia

Place all ingredients into a food processor fitted with the "s" blade. Process/pulse until all of the fruit is broken down and a smooth sorbet has formed. You may need to stop the food processor to scrape down the sides. The pulsing is really the trick here to help break down the fruit chunks.

You can serve it right away or scoop it out and freeze for a few hours in a container. Use an ice cream scoop to serve.

Yield: 6 to 8 servings

Variation:

Use frozen blueberries in place of the blackberries.

Watermelon Sorbet

This is the perfect refreshing dessert or snack on a hot summer's afternoon. The lycopenes in the watermelon give this sorbet a beautiful pink hue that is very attractive to children. To make this recipe at a moment's notice, have your freezer already stocked with chopped watermelon. Then all you need to do is toss everything into the food processor in order to have a healthy, refreshing dessert in minutes! Just be sure you are using <u>seedless</u> watermelon.

4 to 5 cups frozen watermelon chunks
4 to 6 tablespoons honey or coconut nectar
1 lime, juiced

Place all ingredients into a food processor fitted with the "s" blade and pulse. Process/pulse until all of the fruit is broken down and a smooth sorbet has formed. You may need to stop the food processor to scrape down the sides. The pulsing is really the trick here to help break down the watermelon chunks. Taste and add more sweetener if necessary. Pulse again.

You can serve it right away or scoop it out and freeze for a few hours in a container. Use an ice cream scoop to serve.

Yield: 6 servings

Frozen Banana Coconut Cream Pie

This luscious pie gets its sweetness mainly from the bananas. I find that it is nutritious enough to have a slice for breakfast along with a green smoothie! Serve each slice with a warm chocolate sauce for a divine dessert! To make coconut cream, first chill a can of full fat coconut milk in the refrigerator overnight. When you open the can, the layer of fat will have separated to the top. Scoop it off and measure out ½ cup.

Chocolate Cookie Crumb Crust:
1 ½ cups almond flour
¼ cup arrowroot powder
¼ cup coconut sugar
3 tablespoons cocoa powder
¼ teaspoon sea salt
¼ cup coconut oil
1 to 2 tablespoons water

Coconut Cream Filling:
4 medium frozen bananas
½ cup coconut cream
2 to 4 tablespoons honey or coconut nectar
1 to 2 teaspoons non-alcoholic vanilla

To make the crust, first preheat the oven to 350 degrees F. Place the almond flour, arrowroot, coconut sugar, cocoa powder, and salt into a food processor fitted with the "s" blade. Pulse a few times to mix the ingredients together.

Add the coconut oil and process again until crumbly. While the motor is running slowly add the water starting with 1 tablespoon. Continue to process until dough begins to form a ball. Add a tad bit more water if necessary. Press into a 9-inch deep-dish pie plate. Bake for 15 to 20 minutes. Cool completely or freeze before adding the filling.

To make the filling, place all ingredients into a food processor fitted with the "s" blade. Process/pulse to break down the bananas; continue to process until you have a smooth creamy filling. Scoop into chilled crust.

Freeze for 2 to 4 hours or until firm. Slice and serve.

Yield: 8 servings

Lime Avocado Tart with a Macadamia Nut Crust

This is one of our favorite raw desserts. I love giving my children a slice knowing it is full of healthy fats, antioxidants, and protein. Serve it with candles in lieu of a birthday cake.

Macadamia Nut Crust:
1 cup raw macadamia nuts
½ cup unsweetened shredded coconut
4 medjool dates, pitted
pinch sea salt

Filling:
4 small ripe avocados
6 tablespoons melted coconut oil
6 tablespoons freshly squeezed lime juice
4 tablespoons honey
1 to 2 teaspoons lime zest

You will need a 9-inch spring form pan to make this. Cut out a 9-inch circle of parchment or waxed paper to line the bottom of the pan.

Place the macadamia nuts into a food processor fitted with the "s" blade. Process until finely ground. Then add the shredded coconut, dates, and salt; process again until the dates are ground and the mixture is combined. Press into an even layer on the bottom of the pan.

Rinse out the food processor and then place all of the ingredients for the filling in it. Process until smooth and creamy. Pour into springform pan and spread with a spatula or the back of a spoon to get an even layer. If you would like to add another layer to this you can do so now. Use a freshly made ice cream or soften a frozen ice cream and spread evenly on top of the avocado layer. Garnish with lime zest.

Freeze for 2 hours or until set. If the whole pie isn't eaten in one sitting then return it to the freezer for storage. Once it is frozen solid you will need to remove it from the freezer 30 minutes before you would like to serve it.

Yield: 8 servings

Raw Blueberry Cheesecake

This raw cheesecake is dairy-free and still ever so rich and creamy! The combination of raw soaked cashews and coconut oil is what makes the "cheese" filling. I use hazelnuts and almonds for the crust but just about any nut will work. If you would like to savor this cheesecake then slice it up and freeze each piece in serving-sized containers. When ready to serve, put a container of frozen cheesecake in the fridge to thaw for a day before serving.

Crust:
¾ cup raw hazelnuts
¾ cup raw almonds
pinch sea salt
6 to 8 medjool dates, pitted
1 tablespoon coconut oil

Filling:
1 ½ cups raw cashews, soaked in water for 3 hours
¾ cup melted coconut oil
¼ cup freshly squeezed lemon juice
4 to 6 tablespoons coconut nectar or honey
2 teaspoons non-alcoholic vanilla
½ teaspoon almond flavoring
1 cup fresh blueberries (thawed if frozen)

To make the crust, place the hazelnuts, almonds, and sea salt into a food processor fitted with the "s" blade. Pulse until finely ground. Add the dates and coconut oil; process until combined and finely ground.

Line a 9-inch springform pan with parchment paper. Add the crust mixture and press it firmly and evenly into the bottom of the pan. Chill in the refrigerator or freezer while preparing the filling.

To make the filling, first drain and rinse the soaked cashews. Place them into a high-powered blender along with the melted coconut oil, lemon juice, coconut nectar, vanilla and almond flavoring. Blend on high, stopping to scrape the sides down, until very smooth and creamy. Mixture will be somewhat thick so you may need to stop the blender, stir, and continue to blend. Then add the blueberries and blend until combined.

Pour filling into crust. Chill in the freezer for about 1 hour then transfer to the refrigerator and chill until set and firm, 2 to 3 more hours. To serve, unlatch the springform pan to remove the edges, then slice and serve.

Yield: 8 servings

Raw Chocolate Pie

This pie requires a food processor; a blender will not work, nor a Vita-Mix. Top each slice with a simple Raspberry Sauce made by combining 2 tablespoons arrowroot, ½ cup water, 1 cup fresh raspberries, and 1 to 3 tablespoons honey or coconut nectar; whisk together and simmer over low heat until translucent. This pie makes a lovely treat for Valentine's Day or a birthday party.

Crust:
2 cups raw pecans
8 to 10 medjool dates, pitted
1 tablespoon virgin coconut oil
1 tablespoon cinnamon
1 pinch ground cardamom (optional)

Filling:
1 cup raw cashew butter
1 small avocado
½ cup + 2 tablespoons raw cacao powder
½ cup coconut nectar or honey
½ cup barely melted coconut butter
¼ cup water
1 tablespoon non-alcoholic vanilla

Place nuts into food processor and pulse until finely ground. Add remaining ingredients for crust and pulse until thoroughly ground and mixed. Press crust into the bottom of a 9 ½-inch deep-dish pie plate. Place into refrigerator to chill.

Place all ingredients for filling into food processor and process until smooth and creamy. Add a little more water for a thinner filling, one tablespoon at a time. (It will take longer to set if you do this). If you do not like a strong chocolate flavor then start with less cacao powder and gradually add more as your taste suggests.

Pour chocolate filling into pie plate. Spread out evenly with a rubber spatula and place back into the refrigerator to chill. Chill for 3 to 4 hours. Slice and serve with fresh berries if desired. Pie can also be frozen for longer storage.

Yield: 8 to 12 servings

> **Ingredient Tip:**
>
> Coconut butter is different from coconut oil. It is made from the whole coconut—the flesh and the oil. Be sure to just barely warm the coconut butter on very low heat as it can quickly burn.

Deep Dish Apple Pie

Enjoy a little slice of autumn with this fresh apple pie. My favorite baking apple for pie is McIntosh, though Granny Smiths work well too. I core them and slice them as thin as possible for a perfect pie. A faster way to do this is to use the slicing disc on your food processor and you'll have all the apples sliced in about 60 seconds

Double Pie Crust:
1 cup superfine brown rice flour
1 cup superfine sweet rice flour
½ cup quinoa flour or millet flour
1 teaspoon sea salt
16 tablespoons organic palm shortening or organic butter
8 to 10 tablespoons ice cold water

Filling:
6 to 8 medium baking apples, cored and sliced very thin
½ cup coconut sugar
2 tablespoons arrowroot powder
1 tablespoon lemon juice
2 teaspoons cinnamon
½ teaspoon nutmeg

Preheat oven to 425 degrees F. Set out a 9-inch deep-dish pie plate.

To make the crust, whisk together the flours and salt. Cut in the shortening with your fingers or a pastry cutter until small crumbs form. Freeze the bowl of flour and shortening for about 10 to 15 minutes. If you use butter then freeze the butter-flour mixture for closer to 20 minutes to create a flakey crust. You can also add half butter and half shortening which will give the crust a good flavor while keeping it flakey.

Add the water, beginning with the lesser amount. Use a spoon or fork to mix the dough together until it forms a ball. If necessary, knead together ever so slightly to form a ball, then cut the dough in half, forming two balls. Roll out each ball between two pieces of waxed paper. Set aside.

To make the filling, place all filling ingredients into a large bowl and toss together well.

Take one rolled out crust and remove the top layer of waxed paper, flip over and place into a 9-inch deep-dish pie plate, and remove the second piece of waxed paper. Add the filling to the pie plate, then add the top crust. Flute the edges, cut steam vents, and brush the top of the crust with hemp milk and sprinkle with sugar if desired.

Bake pie on a cookie sheet (to catch any drips) for about 15 minutes, then reduce heat to 350 degrees F and bake for about 45 more minutes. Cool for about an hour before serving.

Yield: 8 servings

Pumpkin Pie with a Pecan Crust

I love pumpkin pie, whether for a bedtime snack or a quick breakfast. In autumn, we like to harvest sugar pie pumpkins from our own garden or local farms. I store the pumpkins, along with a variety of other winter squashes in cardboard boxes in our garage. They last for many months this way. You can use any variety of winter squash in this recipe if you don't happen to have a sugar pie pumpkin sitting around.

Crust:
1 cup raw pecans, finely ground
1 cup superfine sorghum flour
¼ cup arrowroot powder
1 tablespoon ground chia seeds
½ teaspoon sea salt
6 tablespoons cold butter or organic palm shortening
4 to 6 tablespoons icy cold water

Filling:
1 ¾ cup cooked and mashed sugar pie pumpkin or 1 can
½ cup maple syrup
½ cup milk
2 large organic eggs
¼ cup arrowroot powder
1 tablespoon pumpkin pie spice

Preheat oven to 350 degrees F. Set out a 9-inch deep-dish pie plate.

To make the crust, place the finely ground pecans (I use my Vita-Mix to grind them), sorghum flour, arrowroot powder, ground chia seeds, and salt into a small mixing bowl and whisk together. Add the cold butter or shortening. Use a pastry cutter or your fingers to combine the flour mixture with the fat until pea-sized crumbs form. Add the cold water and quickly mix together using a fork.

Use your hands to form a ball. The dough may be a little sticky; if it is, cover the bowl and put it in the fridge for 20 to 30 minutes. Roll out dough in between two pieces of waxed paper, then remove the top layer of waxed paper, flip over and place into the pie plate, and remove the second piece of waxed paper. Flute edges and prick bottom of crust with a fork a few times. Prebake for 10 to 12 minutes.

To make the filling, place all ingredients into a blender and blend until smooth. Pour filling into partially baked crust. Bake for about 50 to 60 minutes. Chill at room temp for about an hour and then place pie into the refrigerator and chill until set, about 3 hours.

Yield: 8 servings

Ingredient Tip:

I prefer to use homemade cashew milk in this recipe. For best results, use a rich, fatty milk.

Maple Pecan Pie

Pecan pie is a delicacy around the holidays. It is always the first to go on the dessert table and nobody ever knows that it is egg-free and made with natural sweeteners!

Crust:
1 cup raw pecans, finely ground
1 cup superfine sorghum flour
¼ cup arrowroot powder
1 tablespoon ground chia seeds
½ teaspoon sea salt
6 tablespoons cold organic butter or organic palm shortening
4 to 6 tablespoons icy cold water

Filling:
3 cups pecans, divided
¼ cup arrowroot powder
1 ½ teaspoons cinnamon
⅛ teaspoon baking soda
¼ teaspoon sea salt
½ cup maple syrup
¼ cup brown rice syrup
¼ cup unsweetened applesauce
¼ cup melted coconut oil or butter

Preheat oven to 350 degrees F. Set out a 9-inch pie plate.

To make the crust, place the finely ground pecans (I use my Vita-Mix to grind them), sorghum flour, arrowroot powder, ground chia seeds, and salt into a small mixing bowl and whisk together. Add the cold butter or shortening. Use a pastry cutter or your fingers to combine the flour mixture with the fat until pea-sized crumbs form. Add the cold water and quickly mix together using a fork.

Use your hands to form a ball. The dough may be a little sticky; if it is, cover the bowl and put it in the fridge for 20 to 30 minutes. Roll out dough in between two pieces of waxed paper, then remove the top layer of waxed paper, flip over and place into the pie plate, and remove the second piece of waxed paper. Flute edges and prick bottom of crust with a fork a few times. Prebake for 10 to 12 minutes.

To make the filling, place 2 cups of the pecans into a food processor fitted with the "s" blade. Process until a coarse meal is formed. Place the ground pecans into a large mixing bowl and add the arrowroot, cinnamon, baking soda, and sea salt. Mix together well. Then add the maple syrup, brown rice syrup, applesauce, and oil. Mix again until combined.

Pour filling into partially baked pie crust and spread out. Place the remaining one cup of pecans on the top of the filling in your own pattern. Bake for about 45 minutes. Filling will set when cooled. Let cool completely in the refrigerator before serving. You can bring it to room temperature before slicing and serving.

Yield: 8 servings

Fig-Pear Tart with a Hazelnut Crust

This scrumptious, nutritious grain-free dessert can be served as an elegant dessert or a healthy after-school snack. I like to serve it during the winter holidays. Everyone always enjoys it no matter their food preferences. I prefer to use Bob's Red Mill hazelnut flour, but you can also grind your own from raw hazelnuts and then sift it to remove the large chunks.

Filling:
2 cups dried black mission figs
1 cup orange juice
½ cup port wine
2 tablespoons honey (optional)
2 ripe pears, sliced

Crust:
2 cups hazelnut flour
½ cup arrowroot flour
¼ cup coconut sugar
½ teaspoon sea salt
¼ cup unsalted butter or coconut oil, chilled
2 tablespoons hemp milk or coconut milk

Chocolate Sauce:
½ cup dark chocolate chips
2 to 3 tablespoons honey or maple syrup
2 to 3 tablespoons hemp milk or coconut milk
1 teaspoon orange flavoring

Place the figs, orange juice and port wine into a quart jar and soak for 12 to 24 hours at room temp. Wait to slice the pear until the next day when you assemble the tart.

Preheat oven to 325 degrees F.

To make the crust, place the hazelnut flour, arrowroot, sugar, and salt into a food processor fitted with the "s" blade. Pulse a few times to combine. Add the butter or coconut oil and process until completely combined. Then add milk and process until the dough forms a ball. Lightly grease an 8 x 8-inch tart pan. Press dough into the tart pan on both the bottom and sides. Bake on a cookie sheet for about 20 to 25 minutes. Let cool completely before filling.

Drain the figs, but reserve soaking liquid. Place soaked figs into a food processor fitted with the "s" blade. Add a few tablespoons of the reserved soaking liquid and about 2 tablespoons honey if you think the fig paste needs to be a little sweeter. Process until a smooth paste forms. Spread evenly into the crust. Arrange pear slices on top.

To make the chocolate sauce, heat a small pan over low heat. Add all ingredients and whisk together until just melted being careful so the chocolate doesn't burn. Drizzle over pear slices. Cut into squares. Serve at room temperature with small glasses of port wine.

Yield: 16 servings

Apple Plum Crisp

In late August through early September here in the Pacific Northwest the plum trees are drooping with their succulent purple fruit. We often have so many boxes of Italian plums sitting around at that time of year that I cannot process them fast enough. I slice the plums in half, pit, and freeze them so we can use them all year round. This recipe combines plums with fresh apples. Early season baking apples and plums are in season at the same time. This recipe can be made entirely of apples or a mix of other fruits if desired.

Filling:
2 apples, cored and chopped
2 to 3 cups halved Italian plums
3 to 4 tablespoons arrowroot powder
3 to 4 tablespoons maple syrup or honey
1 tablespoon freshly squeezed lemon juice (optional)

Topping:
1 ½ cups gluten-free rolled oats
½ cup sweet rice flour
½ to ¾ cup coconut sugar or Sucanat
1 teaspoon cinnamon
½ teaspoon cardamom
¼ teaspoon sea salt
½ cup melted coconut oil or organic butter
1 teaspoon vanilla extract

Preheat oven to 375 degrees F.

Place all ingredients for the filling into a 7 x 11-inch baking pan. Gently stir together with a large spoon. A good gauge for sufficient fruit is to fill your pan almost to the top with sliced fruit. It will cook down quite a bit.

To make the topping, in a small mixing bowl, stir together the oats, rice flour, sugar, cinnamon, cardamom, and sea salt. Add oil and vanilla; stir together with a fork. If the topping seems a little dry, try adding a few more tablespoons melted oil or butter. Using your hands, crumble the topping evenly over the filling.

Bake for about 40 minutes or until the juices are bubbling up and the topping is lightly browned.

Yield: 8 to 10 servings

Variation:

Try adding one cup of coarsely chopped pecans, almonds, or hazelnuts to the topping for added flavor and nutrition.

Blueberry Peach Crisp

Blueberries and peaches are the highlight of the summer, available from mid-July through September, though if fresh fruit is unavailable then frozen berries and peaches work just fine. This oat-free crisp is easy to make and is always a crowd pleaser!

Filling:
2 cups blueberries
2 ripe peaches, sliced thin
2 tablespoons lemon juice
2 tablespoons arrowroot powder
2 tablespoons maple syrup
¼ teaspoon nutmeg

Topping:
1 cup almond flour
¾ cup brown rice flour
¼ cup tapioca flour
¼ teaspoon sea salt
¼ cup organic butter, palm shortening, or coconut oil
¼ cup maple syrup
½ teaspoon almond extract

Preheat oven to 375 degrees F.

Place all filling ingredients into an 8 x 8-inch baking pan. Stir together with a large spoon.

In a medium sized bowl, add the almond flour, rice flour, tapioca flour, and salt. Whisk together well. Then add the butter or shortening and maple syrup. Begin to mix the topping with a fork and then finish the mixing with your fingers. After it is evenly mixed, use your fingers to crumble it over the filling.

Bake for 30 to 35 minutes or until the juices are bubbling up and the topping is lightly browned.

Yield: 6 to 8 servings

Ingredient Tip:

I prefer to use Authentic Foods Superfine Brown Rice Flour in this recipe. Regular brown rice flour can be somewhat gritty when not combined with sufficient liquids such as in a crisp or pie crust.

Desserts

Pear Almond Crumble

This sweet fruit dessert reminds me of crisp fall evenings, candlelight dinners, and picking boxes of apples and pears with my children. Be sure to use pears that are ripe but still firm. I like to use Bartlett pears in crisps and crumbles.

Topping:
1 ½ cups almond flour
¼ cup arrowroot powder
1 cup packed medjool dates, pitted
¼ cup coconut oil
1 teaspoon cinnamon
½ teaspoon ground ginger
⅛ teaspoon sea salt

Filling:
4 large firm pears, cored and sliced thin
2 tablespoons coconut sugar or honey
2 tablespoons arrowroot powder

Preheat oven to 350 degrees. Set out an 8 x 8-inch glass pan.

To make the topping, place all ingredients into a food processor fitted with the "s" blade. Process until dates are ground and topping is crumbly.

For the filling, place all ingredients into the pan and gently toss together. Crumble the topping over the filling evenly.

Bake for 35 to 45 minutes or until the fruit is bubbling up the sides of the pan.

Yield: 6 to 8 servings

Banana Coconut Cookies

These cookies are crisp on the outside and soft on the inside. They are only slightly sweet and high in protein, making them a nutritious after school snack served alongside carrot and celery sticks. You can add mini chocolate chips to some of them if desired though this will add a little bit of cane sugar.

Wet Ingredients:
⅓ cup mashed ripe banana (about 1 medium)
⅓ cup melted coconut oil
2 tablespoons maple syrup
1 teaspoon vanilla
½ teaspoon almond flavoring

Dry Ingredients:
2 cups blanched almond flour
1 cup unsweetened shredded coconut
½ teaspoon baking soda
¼ teaspoon sea salt

In a medium-sized mixing bowl whisk together the wet ingredients. Add the dry ingredients and mix together using a fork. Form dough into a ball and refrigerate for 30 to 60 minutes.

Preheat oven to 350 degrees F. Form dough into small balls (about 15) and place onto an ungreased cookie sheet. Flatten each cookie ball with the palm of your hand. Bake for about 15 minutes. Cookies will be soft straight out of the oven but will firm up once completely cool. You can place them onto a wire rack to cool and then place the rack into your freezer for quick cooling.

Yield: About 15 two-inch cookies

Ingredient Tip:

Be sure to use the very finely ground blanched almond flour in this recipe. It can be found at Benefit Your Life or Lucy's Kitchen Shop.

Cashew Ginger Cookies

This grain-free cookie recipe doesn't require any flour. The cookies are high in protein, and can be used as a healthy after-school snack for children or packed in their school lunchboxes.

1 cup roasted cashew butter
2 large organic eggs
2 tablespoons blackstrap molasses
¾ cup coconut sugar
2 teaspoons ground ginger
1 teaspoon cinnamon
½ teaspoon baking soda
¼ teaspoon sea salt

Preheat oven to 350 degrees F. Lightly grease a cookie sheet with coconut oil.

Place all ingredients into a medium-sized mixing bowl. Beat together using an electric mixer. Drop by the tablespoon onto a greased cookie sheet.

Bake for approximately 15 minutes. Use a thin spatula to remove from the cookie sheet. They will be slightly fragile while hot. Cool on a wire rack.

Yield: About 1 ½ dozen cookies

Chewy Oatmeal Raisin Cookies

My children absolutely love these cookies. I have no problem giving them one for breakfast with a green smoothie. They are packed with protein and fiber. For new moms, omit the chocolate and serve these as a lactation-promoting cookie!

Wet Ingredients:
¼ cup ground chia seeds
½ cup hot water
½ cup melted coconut oil
½ cup unsweetened applesauce
1 cup almond butter
1 cup coconut sugar
1 tablespoon vanilla

Dry Ingredients:
5 cups gluten-free rolled oats
¾ teaspoon baking soda
¾ teaspoon sea salt
1 tablespoon cinnamon

Other Ingredients:
½ to 1 cup raisins, chopped
chopped dark chocolate bar (optional)

Preheat oven to 325 degrees F.

Place the chia seeds into a large bowl and pour the hot water over them; immediately whisk together (otherwise it will clump up). Let rest for a few minutes, then add the oil, almond butter, sugar, and vanilla. Whisk well.

Add the oats, baking soda, salt, and cinnamon. Stir well with a large wooden spoon. Add the raisins and optional chocolate. Stir again.

Drop by the large spoonful onto a lightly greased cookie sheet. Gently press each cookie down with the palm of your hand. Bake for 12 to 15 minutes. Cool on a wire rack.

Yield: 2 dozen cookies

Chocolate Chip Cookies

These cookies are high-protein, low-sugar, and vegan. With no grainy gluter-free flours, you'll find that these cookies stay moist and gooey in the center for days. Be sure to use roasted almond butter as raw almond butter is too runny for this recipe. I use Ancient Harvest Quinoa Flakes, which can be found in the breakfast cereal isle at your local health food store.

½ cup packed pitted medjool dates (about 5 to 6 dates)
¼ cup hot water
¼ cup coconut oil
¼ cup honey
¼ cup ground flax seeds
2 teaspoons vanilla
1 cup almond butter
1 cup quinoa flakes
½ cup almond flour
¾ teaspoon baking soda
¼ teaspoon sea salt
¼ to ½ cup mini chocolate chips

Preheat oven to 350 degrees F. Lightly grease a large cookie sheet with coconut oil.

Place the pitted dates and water in a blender and let them soak for about 5 minutes. Then add the coconut oil and honey. Blend until very smooth, about a minute.

Transfer date-oil mixture to a medium-sized mixing bowl (scooping out every last bit) and add ground flax seeds and vanilla; beat on high with an electric mixture until combined. Add almond butter and beat again.

Sprinkle the quinoa flakes, almond flour, baking soda, salt, and chocolate chips over the almond butter mixture; beat again until well combined.

Drop dough by the large spoonful onto the greased cookie sheet. Lightly press each cookie down with the palm of your hand. Bake for about 10 to 12 minutes. Remove gently with a thin spatula and transfer to a wire rack to cool. The cookies will be slightly fragile when hot but will hold together very well after about 5 minutes of cooling. Enjoy with a glass of fresh, raw almond milk!

Yield: 18 cookies

Variation:

Nut-Free: Replace the almond butter with organic Sunbutter (made from roasted sunflower seeds) and the almond flour with finely ground raw sunflower seeds.

Chocolate Sunbutter Cookies

I love being able to serve these cookies to my children knowing they are getting some good nutrition out of every bite! Sunbutter is made from ground roasted sunflower seeds. It is a great high-protein alternative to nut butters. Serve these grain-free, vegan cookies with a glass of raw almond milk or a green smoothie for a healthy afternoon treat!

Wet Ingredients:
1 cup organic Sunbutter
⅓ cup coconut nectar
1 tablespoon ground chia seeds
3 tablespoons water
1 teaspoon vanilla

Dry Ingredients:
¼ cup cocoa powder
½ teaspoon baking soda
¼ teaspoon sea salt

Optional Additions:
½ cup mini chocolate chips

Preheat oven to 350 F. Lightly grease a cookie sheet with coconut oil.

In a medium-sized mixing bowl, using an electric mixer, beat together the wet ingredients until light and fluffy. Add the dry ingredients. Beat together until thickened and combined. Mix in the chocolate chips if using..

Roll equal-sized balls of dough in your hands. You should have between 12 and 15 cookies. Then press each cookie dough ball down using the tongs of a fork into a crisscross pattern.

Bake for approximately 12 to 15 minutes. Cool on a wire rack. Cookies will be fragile and crumbly when hot so be careful when you remove them from the pan. They will firm up once completely cooled.

Yield: 12 to 15 cookies

Coconut Almond Sugar Cookies

These flakey, flavorful low-glycemic cut-out cookies are sweetened with stevia and can be used for just about any holiday. Ice with the Simple Icing recipe, page 475. Once the cookies are baked and iced, they are best frozen until ready to serve. This keeps them crisp and flakey, and the icing set in place. They will thaw out in a matter of minutes. You can store these cookies in the freezer in a sealed container for months. Be sure to use a finely ground blanched almond flour for this recipe or else they won't work.

Dry Ingredients:
1 ¼ cups almond flour
1 cup unsweetened shredded coconut
½ cup arrowroot powder
½ teaspoon baking powder
¼ teaspoon baking soda
¼ teaspoon sea salt

Wet Ingredients:
6 tablespoons virgin coconut oil
4 tablespoons unsweetened applesauce
1 teaspoon vanilla
½ teaspoon lemon flavoring
30 to 35 drops liquid stevia

Place the dry ingredients into a food processor fitted with the "s" blade. Pulse the ingredients until combined and ground fine, about 60 to 90 seconds. Add the wet ingredients and process until a dough ball forms. It will be soft but you should be able to form it into a ball. Place the dough into a bowl sprinkled with a little arrowroot powder. Chill for one hour in the refrigerator.

Preheat oven to 350 degrees F.

Remove dough from refrigerator and roll it out in between 2 pieces of wax paper or parchment paper to about ⅛ inch of thickness. Use your favorite cookie cutters to cute shapes in the dough (they should all be fairly equal in size).

Bake for 10 minutes. Watch carefully as timing and temperature may need to be adjusted. If they are cooking too fast and browning, turn oven temp down to just over 325 degrees. Cool on a wire rack. Ice cookies once completely cooled.

Yield: 2 dozen cookies

Variation:

For a honey-sweetened variation, replace the applesauce with honey and omit stevia. The honey can cause them to burn, so watch them carefully in the oven.

Gingerbread Hazelnut Cut-Out Cookies

Use currents, raisins, sliced almonds, natural sprinkles or anything else you can imagine to decorate these lovely cut-out cookies. I find the dough is best if it is refrigerated overnight.

Dry Ingredients:
2 cups hazelnut flour
1 cup sweet rice flour
½ teaspoon baking soda
½ teaspoon sea salt
2 teaspoons cinnamon
1 teaspoon ground ginger
⅛ teaspoon ground nutmeg

Wet Ingredients:
1 cup coconut sugar
½ cup softened butter
¼ cup blackstrap molasses
1 large organic egg
2 teaspoons vanilla

Icing:
½ cup powdered coconut sugar
2 to 3 teaspoons milk
½ teaspoon vanilla

Whisk together the dry ingredients in a large mixing bowl. In a separate smaller bowl, add the wet ingredients and beat with an electric mixer, or vigorously whisk together. Add the wet to the dry and mix together until combined. Form dough into a ball, cover, and place into the refrigerator for a couple of hours or overnight.

When the dough is firm and chilled, preheat your oven to 350 degrees F.

Place a large piece of parchment or waxed paper down onto a clean flat work surface. Lightly flour the paper with sweet rice flour. Take part of the dough and roll it out to a little less than ¼ inch of thickness. Put the remaining dough back in the fridge to keep it chilled. Cut the dough out using your favorite holiday cookie cutters. Carefully peel away the dough around the cut-outs. Then take a thin spatula and lift the cookies onto a lightly greased cookie sheet.

Bake for 12 to 15 minutes depending on how crisp you like them. Just watch them so they don't overcook. Transfer cookies to a wire rack to cool. Then repeat with remaining dough. Let cool completely before frosting.

Yield: 2 dozen cookies

Kitchen Tip:

To make powdered coconut sugar, place 1 cup of coconut sugar and 1 tablespoon arrowroot powder into a high-powered blender and blend for 60 to 90 seconds or until light and powdery. Leave the blender lid on until the sugar dust settles and then pour into a jar for storage.

Oatmeal Heart Cut-Out Cookies

My daughters like to cut these cookies out with heart-shaped cookie cutters and bring them to school on Valentine's Day to share with their friends. You can of course use any shaped cookie cutter and serve them for any holiday or special occasion. Decorate cookies with the Simple Icing, page 475, or the Chocolate Ganache, page 471.

Dry Ingredients:
3 cups gluten-free rolled oats
¾ to 1 cup coconut sugar or maple sugar
½ cup arrowroot powder
½ teaspoon baking soda
¼ teaspoon sea salt

Wet Ingredients:
½ cup virgin coconut oil
¼ cup unsweetened applesauce
2 teaspoons vanilla

Preheat oven to 350 degrees F.

Place the dry ingredients into a food processor fitted with the "s" blade. Process until very finely ground; not as fine as oat flour, but still a little coarse. Add wet ingredients, process until the mixture forms a cohesive ball. It may take a few minutes but it will happen. Pulse the processor if needed.

Remove dough from food processor and finish forming it into a ball with your hands. Chill the dough for 20 to 30 minutes if it is too soft. Then place onto a piece of parchment or waxed paper for rolling. Roll out dough to a little less than ¼-inch of thickness. Cut into shapes with a cookie cutter.

Place onto a parchment-lined baking sheet. Bake for approximately 15 to 16 minutes. Cool on a wire rack.

Yield: 2 dozen cookies

Orange Hazelnut Thumbprint Cookies

Hazelnuts grow all around the Pacific Northwest. Our children like to pick them up off the ground and use them in their play. You can make your own hazelnut meal by grinding whole hazelnuts in a food processor or you can buy it in the package from Bob's Red Mill. Be sure to store it in the freezer or refrigerator to keep it fresh. Any jam will work in the thumbprint. I make my own honey-sweetened jams from all of the fruit we harvest in the summertime. We also like the brand, Bionaturae, fruit juice-sweetened jam. Try apricot, raspberry, blackberry, or sour cherry.

Dry Ingredients:
2 ½ cups hazelnut flour
2 cups brown rice flour
½ cup tapioca flour
2 teaspoons baking powder
½ teaspoon sea salt

Wet Ingredients:
⅔ cup melted coconut oil
⅔ cup maple syrup
¼ cup orange juice
2 tablespoons ground flax seeds
2 teaspoons vanilla
1 to 2 teaspoons finely grated orange zest

Other Ingredients:
sugar-free jam

Preheat oven to 350 degrees F. Lightly grease a cookie sheet with coconut oil.

Mix the dry ingredients in a mixing bowl. In a separate small bowl, whisk together the wet ingredients. Add the wet ingredients to the dry and mix together with a fork or large spoon. Continue to mix for another 60 seconds or until the dough thickens.

Roll large spoonfuls of the dough into balls with the palms of your hands. Place evenly onto greased cookie sheet. Gently press your thumb into the middle of each cookie making a small indent. Place a small spoonful of jam into each indent.

Bake for about 15 to 20 minutes. Remove cookies and place onto a wire rack to cool.

Yield: 2 dozen cookies

Variation:

Replace the hazelnut flour with finely ground raw almonds or use Bob's Red Mill Almond Meal Flour. Replace the orange juice with unsweetened applesauce and omit orange zest. You can add a dash of almond flavoring if desired.

Peanut Butter Monster Cookies

These healthy, high-protein, flourless cookies make a great late afternoon snack. You can also pack them in your child's lunchbox as part of a balanced lunch.

1 cup creamy unsalted peanut butter
1 cup coconut sugar or Sucanat
2 large organic eggs
1 tablespoon vanilla
½ teaspoon baking soda
½ teaspoon sea salt
½ cup shredded coconut
½ cup raisins
½ cup dark chocolate chips

Preheat oven to 350 degrees F. Grease a large cookie sheet with a little coconut oil.

In a medium sized mixing bowl, beat together the peanut butter, coconut sugar, eggs, vanilla, baking soda, and sea salt. Add the shredded coconut, raisins, and chocolate chips. Stir together.

Drop by the spoonful onto the cookie sheet. Gently press each one down with the palm of your hand. They won't spread much at all so you can place them close together.

Bake for 10 to 15 minutes depending on the size of the cookie. Cool on a wire rack.

Yield: 1 ½ dozen cookies

Variation:

Dried cranberries can replace the raisins, chopped nuts can be added in, and cocoa nibs can replace the chocolate chips.

Pumpkin Oatmeal Drop Cookies

These cookies are best the day that they are made. They will begin to soften the next day but are still tasty. Make sure all of your ingredients are at room temp before mixing. Your coconut oil will be soft enough if your house is around 70 degrees F or above. Do not melt your coconut oil or use another liquid oil. I like to use homemade pumpkin or winter squash puree in this recipe. If you use canned pumpkin you will want to use the lesser amount of oat flour. Canned pumpkin generally contains less moisture than freshly baked winter squash.

Dry Ingredients:
2 to 2 ½ cups gluten-free oat flour
1 cup gluten-free rolled oats
¾ teaspoon baking soda
¾ teaspoon sea salt
3 to 4 teaspoons cinnamon
1 teaspoon ground ginger
½ teaspoon ground nutmeg

Wet Ingredients:
1 cup softened virgin coconut oil or unsalted butter
1 cup pumpkin puree
1 ½ cups coconut sugar, maple sugar, or brown sugar
¼ cup ground flax seeds
1 tablespoon vanilla extract

In a large bowl, whisk together the dry ingredients. In another large bowl, beat together the wet ingredients using an electric mixer. Add the dry ingredients to the wet and beat together again.

Preheat your oven to 350 degrees F. While your oven is preheating let your cookie dough rest on the counter for 10 to 15 minutes. The oat flour will absorb some of the liquid during this time, which helps the cookies hold their shape.

Drop by the spoonful onto an ungreased cookie sheet. Bake for 12 to 15 minutes or until slightly golden around the edges. Remove cookies and place them onto a wire rack to cool. Cookies are best after they have cooled.

Yield: 2 dozen cookies

Ingredient Tip:

I grind my own oat flour in my Vita-Mix from gluten-free rolled oats. I have not been able to find oat flour that isn't rancid. If you do use rancid flour these cookies will have a very "off" flavor. You can also use a regular blender or coffee grinder to make your own oat flour.

Desserts

Sunflower Seed Cookies

These cookies make the perfect nutritious toddler snack cookie. They are free from all major allergens so even a one year old can enjoy them. Be sure to use the Corn-Free Baking Powder recipe, page 57, if you are avoiding corn. To make these cookies more nutritious and easier to digest, use sprouted brown rice flour and make sure to soak and dehydrate the sunflower seeds before using them (see the Getting Started chapter, page 51).

Dry Ingredients:
1 cup raw sunflower seeds
1 cup brown rice flour
¼ cup tapioca flour
1 teaspoon cinnamon
1 teaspoon baking powder
¼ teaspoon sea salt

Wet Ingredients:
⅓ cup melted coconut oil
⅓ cup maple syrup
2 tablespoons applesauce
1 tablespoon ground flax seeds
1 teaspoon vanilla extract

Other Ingredients:
¼ to ½ cup chopped raisins

Preheat oven to 350 degrees F.

Grind the sunflower seeds in a food processor, coffee grinder, or the dry container of a Vita-Mix until finely ground. You should have 1 ¼ cups ground. Place them into a large bowl with the rest of the dry ingredients. Whisk together well.

In a separate bowl, or liquid glass measure, whisk together the wet ingredients.

Add the wet ingredients to the dry. Add the chopped raisins. Whisk together. Then continue to mix with a wooden spoon until the dough thickens, another 60 seconds or so.

Roll dough into 1-inch balls and place onto a greased cookie sheet. Gently flatten each ball with the bottom of an oiled glass.

Bake for 15 to 20 minutes. The cookies won't brown on top but will on the bottom. Cool on a wire rack.

Yield: 1 dozen cookies

Chocolate Chip Cookie Bars

I keep many jars of organic unsalted Sunbutter in my pantry for quick snacks and for use in healthy baking recipes such as this one. These bars make an excellent nut-free, vegan treat for your child's lunchbox!

Dry Ingredients:
1 cup brown rice flour
½ cup sorghum flour
¼ cup tapioca flour
½ teaspoon baking powder
½ teaspoon baking soda
¼ teaspoon sea salt

Wet ingredients:
2 tablespoons ground chia seeds
¼ cup hot water
½ cup softened coconut oil
½ cup sunflower seed butter
½ cup unsweetened applesauce
¾ cup coconut sugar
1 to 2 teaspoons vanilla

Other Ingredients:
¼ to ½ cup mini chocolate chips

Preheat oven to 350 degrees F. Grease an 8 x 8-inch or 8 x 10-inch baking dish with coconut oil.

Add the dry ingredients to a small mixing bowl; whisk together and set aside. In a medium-sized mixing bowl, whisk together the ground chia and hot water; let stand for 1 minute. Then add the remaining wet ingredients and beat together using an electric mixer. Add the dry ingredients to the wet and beat again until combined.

Stir in the chocolate chips. Scoop dough into prepared pan and press down evenly. Bake for approximately 30 minutes. Let cool completely before cutting into bars.

Yield: 12 bars

Variation:

Replace the sunflower seed butter with either unsalted peanut butter or almond butter. If you would like to omit the chocolate chips you can replace them with currants or raisins. Also, I've made this recipe with freshly ground buckwheat flour in place of the rice and sorghum flours. If you enjoy the flavor of buckwheat this might be a good option as it creates a more nutritious bar.

Chocolate Chip Teff Brownies

These brownies are designed for the gluten, dairy, and egg sensitive chocoholic, though your non gluten-free friends might agree that these brownies are quite divine. The fudge-like consistency from the pureed dates and coconut oil combined with the rich buttery flavor of the teff flour make these a real treat. Add extra chocolate chips for pure decadence!

Dry Ingredients:
1 cup teff flour
¼ cup tapioca flour
⅓ cup cocoa powder
1 teaspoon baking powder
½ teaspoon baking soda
¼ teaspoon sea salt

Wet Ingredients:
½ cup dates, pitted
¼ cup ground flaxseeds
1 ¼ cups boiling water
½ cup coconut oil
½ cup coconut sugar, Sucanat, or maple sugar
2 teaspoons vanilla

Other Ingredients:
½ cup dark chocolate chips

Preheat oven to 350 degrees F. Oil a 7 x 11-inch baking dish, an 8 x 8-inch baking dish works too though the brownie will be much thicker and more cake-like.

In a medium sized mixing bowl, whisk together the dry ingredients. Set aside.

Place the pitted dates and ground flax into a blender; pour the boiling water over them. Let them sit for about 5 to 10 minutes. Then add the rest of the wet ingredients and blend until smooth and creamy.

Add the wet ingredients to the dry and quickly whisk together. Add the chocolate chips and continue to whisk until the dry and wet ingredients are mixed together.

Pour batter into pan and bake for 20 to 25 minutes.

Yield: 12 servings

Chocolate Walnut Brownies

This grain-free brownie recipe can be whipped up in a snap! Only a food processor is needed, meaning not too many dishes to wash! There is no need to add any extra oil or butter because the ground walnuts provide plenty of fats—and heart healthy ones at that. Serve brownies with one of our coconut ice cream recipes for a decadent dessert treat.

Dry Ingredients:
2 cups raw walnuts
⅓ cup cocoa powder
½ teaspoon baking soda
¼ teaspoon sea salt

Wet Ingredients:
2 large organic eggs
½ cup maple syrup
1 tablespoon vanilla

Preheat oven to 350 degrees F. Grease an 8 x 8-inch glass baking dish with coconut oil.

Place the walnuts into a food processor fitted with the "s" blade. Process until very finely ground, stopping just before they turn into nut butter. Then add the remaining dry ingredients and pulse again to combine. Add the wet ingredients and process again until smooth. You will still have tiny chunks of walnuts visible and this is fine.

Pour batter into baking dish. Spread evenly into pan with a rubber spatula or spoon. Bake for 25 minutes. Cool for about 20 minutes before slicing.

Yield: 16 servings

Variation:

Replace the walnuts with raw pecans.

Gingerbread

I love making this healthy, high protein, grain-free treat for my children as an afterschool snack during the winter months. It is also the perfect holiday dessert served with a dollop of Whipped Coconut Cream, page 476. The smell is intoxicating while it is baking. Serve with apple or pear slices and warm spice tea.

1 ½ cups creamy almond butter
½ cup mashed cooked sweet potatoes
¼ cup blackstrap molasses
¼ cup maple syrup
2 large organic eggs
1 teaspoon baking soda
½ teaspoon sea salt
1 tablespoon cinnamon
1 to 2 teaspoons ground ginger
¼ teaspoon nutmeg

Preheat oven to 325 degrees F. Grease an 8 x 8-inch glass baking dish with coconut oil.

Place all ingredients into a food processor fitted with the "s" blade and process until smooth and combined. You can also use a hand held mixer but the food processor is easier and creates a smoother batter.

Pour batter into baking dish. Bake for about 35 minutes. Cool and slice. Gingerbread will be fragile hot out of the oven but will firm up once cooled.

Yield: About 8 servings

Carrot Orange Spice Cupcakes

These grain-free cupcakes are moist and light with a mild, natural sweetness from the carrots, honey, and coconut flour. Serving one for breakfast along with a green smoothie is actually quite nutritious! We like to top them with a dollop of Whipped Coconut Cream, page 476, or Coconut Orange Buttercream Frosting, page 473, and a sprinkling of finely chopped walnuts.

Dry Ingredients:
1 cup coconut flour
1 teaspoon baking soda
¼ teaspoon sea salt
2 teaspoons cinnamon
1 teaspoon ground ginger
½ teaspoon nutmeg

Wet Ingredients:
1 cup coconut milk
6 large organic eggs
⅓ cup honey
2 teaspoons vanilla
2 teaspoons orange zest

Other Ingredients:
2 cups grated carrots
½ cup currants or raisins

Preheat oven to 350 degrees F. Line a 12-cup muffin pan with paper liners.

Place the dry ingredients into a food processor fitted with the "s" blade. Pulse a few times to combine. Add the wet ingredients and process until combined. Add the carrots and currants and pulse just a few times to combine, being careful not to over process the batter.

Scoop batter (it will be rather thick) into muffin cups. You will fill each one to the top. Bake for 35 to 40 minutes or until toothpick inserted into center comes out clean.

Remove cupcakes from pan and cool on a wire rack. Serve warm or let cool completely before frosting.

Yield: 1 dozen cupcakes

Desserts

Chocolate Brownie Cupcakes

When making these, be sure to use a finely ground blanched almond flour. Coarser flour, such as Bob's Red Mill, will not work in this recipe. Once cooled, these cupcakes can be frosted with the Chocolate Ganache Frosting, page 471, and sprinkled with shredded coconut or chopped nuts for decoration.

Dry Ingredients:
3 cups blanched almond flour
½ cup cocoa powder
¼ cup arrowroot powder
2 teaspoons baking powder
½ teaspoon sea salt

Wet Ingredients:
1 cup coconut milk
½ cup honey or coconut nectar
¼ cup melted coconut oil
2 teaspoons vanilla
1 teaspoon almond flavoring

Preheat oven to 350 degrees. Line a 12-cup muffin pan with paper liners.

In a medium-sized mixing bowl whisk together the dry ingredients. Use your fingers to break up any lumps from the cocoa or almond flour. In a separate bowl, whisk together the wet ingredients. Add the wet to the dry and whisk together well.

Spoon batter into muffin cups. Bake for approximately 30 minutes. Let cool in the pan for 10 to 15 minutes before transferring to a wire rack to cool. Handle the cupcakes carefully, as they are very fragile when hot. They will firm up once completely cool.

Yield: 1 dozen cupcakes

Nutrition Tip:

Almonds are a great source of fiber, protein, and magnesium and have been studied to assist in lowering weight, cholesterol, and blood pressure. But did you know that eating almonds can also lower the rise in blood sugar from a meal? A study in the journal *Metabolism* demonstrated that eating two ounces of almonds with a high carbohydrate meal lessened the rise in blood sugar by over 40 percent!

Molasses Spice Cupcakes

This recipe uses unrefined ingredients to create a delicious, moist, gluten-free and vegan cupcake. Reduce the spices and use this recipe for your child's first birthday cake. I like to frost these with the Dairy-Free Cream Cheese Frosting, page 474, and decorate them with finely chopped walnuts.

Dry Ingredients:
1 ½ cups teff flour
¼ cup arrowroot powder
2 teaspoons baking powder
½ teaspoon baking soda
½ teaspoon sea salt
2 to 3 teaspoons cinnamon
1 to 2 teaspoons ground ginger
¼ to ½ teaspoon nutmeg

Wet Ingredients:
1 ½ cups boiling water
½ cup pitted medjool dates
½ cup pitted prunes
2 tablespoons ground chia seeds
½ cup + 2 tablespoons coconut oil
¼ cup maple syrup
¼ cup blackstrap molasses
2 teaspoons vanilla

Preheat oven to 350 degrees F. Line a 12-cup muffin pan with paper liners.

In a large bowl, whisk together the dry ingredients. Set aside.

In a medium-sized bowl, add the boiled water, dates, prunes, and chia seeds. Give it a little stir and then let it soak for 20 minutes. Pour into a high-powered blender and add the remaining wet ingredients. Blend on high until smooth.

Pour the wet ingredients into the dry and whisk together well. Spoon batter into muffin pan; you will fill each cup to the top. Bake for 30 to 35 minutes. Cool complexly on a wire rack before frosting.

Yield: 1 dozen cupcakes

Raspberry Cupcakes

My friend Kim Wilson of Simply Natural Health (www.SimplyNaturalHealth.com) inspired these beautiful, red-flecked vegan cupcakes made from soaked brown rice. They are perfect to serve for your child's first birthday because the rice has been soaked, which neutralizes mineral-binding phytates and makes the carbohydrates more digestible. Use any of the frosting recipes in this book on top of these cupcakes. My children particularly like the Whipped Coconut Cream, page 476, or Chocolate Ganache, page 471, topped with a fresh raspberry and shaved dark chocolate.

Day 1:
2 cups brown basmati rice
warm water to cover
2 tablespoons apple cider vinegar

Day 2:
1 cup coconut milk
½ cup water
⅓ cup melted coconut oil
⅓ cup honey
1 tablespoon vanilla
½ teaspoon almond flavoring
6 tablespoons ground golden flax seeds
2 ½ teaspoons baking powder
¾ teaspoon sea salt

Other Ingredients:
1 cup fresh raspberries

Place the rice into a medium-sized bowl and cover with water. Make sure the water rises above the rice by about two inches. Add the apple cider vinegar and give it a swirl with a spoon. Let the bowl sit out on your counter for 12 to 24 hours. I've even let the rice soak for up to 72 hours, changing the soaking water daily.

Preheat oven to 350 degrees F. Line a 12-cup muffin pan with paper liners.

Rinse and drain the rice through a fine mesh strainer. Place the soaked rice into a high-powered blender along with the coconut milk, oil, honey, vanilla, and almond flavoring. Blend on high until very smooth and creamy. Then add the ground flax seeds, baking powder, and salt; blend again on high for about 60 to 90 seconds to incorporate.

Pour the batter into the muffin cups; you will fill each one up all the way. Drop about 3 to 4 raspberries onto the top of each cupcake. Use a spoon or knife to press them into the batter. Bake for 25 to 30 minutes. Cool completely before frosting. Cupcakes are best served the day they are made, after that they begin to dry out.

Yield: 1 dozen cupcakes

Pumpkin Cupcakes

These moist and spicy grain-free cupcakes are made with coconut flour and sweetened only with medjool dates. You'll need a high-powered blender such as a Vita-Mix to make these. I use soft medjool dates that are not soaked first so a regular blender just wouldn't be able to puree them. Use fresh, homemade pumpkin puree or canned in this recipe. You can also use any type of winter squash puree if sugar pie pumpkins are unavailable. I like to bake and puree a lot of pumpkins in autumn and then freeze the puree in 2-cup containers to use throughout the year. Frost with the Dairy-Free Cream Cheese Frosting, page 474.

Dry Ingredients:
½ cup coconut flour
½ cup arrowroot powder
1 teaspoon baking soda
½ teaspoon sea salt
2 teaspoons cinnamon
1 teaspoon ground ginger
½ teaspoon nutmeg

Wet Ingredients:
1 ¼ cups pumpkin puree
1 cup soft medjool dates, pitted
½ cup melted coconut oil
4 large organic eggs
1 tablespoon apple cider vinegar

Preheat oven to 350 degrees F. Grease a 12-cup muffin pan or line with paper liners.

In a medium-sized mixing bowl, whisk together the dry ingredients. Add all of the wet ingredients to a high-powered lender, blend until smooth and creamy, pulsing if needed. Scoop out wet ingredients with a rubber spatula and whisk into the dry ingredients until combined.

Scoop batter into prepared muffin pan, filling each cup to the top. Gently smooth the top of each with your fingertips. Bake for 30 minutes. Remove cupcakes and cool on a wire rack. If you want to frost these, wait until they are completely cooled. Then top each cupcake with a little freshly grated nutmeg if desired.

Yield: 1 dozen cupcakes

Almond Apricot Snack Cake

Using only a few basic ingredients, and no sweeteners, this recipe tastes like a decadent cake rather than something nutritious. Be sure to use only organic, unsulphured dried apricots—they will be a dark orange-brown color, not bright orange like the sulphured version. Serve this cake for dessert topped with Whipped Coconut Cream, page 476. It is also makes a great afterschool snack for children along with apple slices and herbal tea.

1 cup dried apricots
1 cup creamy roasted almond butter
½ cup unsweetened applesauce
2 large organic eggs
2 teaspoons vanilla
½ to 1 teaspoon almond flavoring
½ teaspoon baking soda
½ teaspoon sea salt

Preheat your oven to 350 degrees F. Grease an 8 x 8-inch glass baking dish with coconut oil.

Place the dried apricots into a food processor fitted with the "s" blade. Process until finely chopped. Add all of the remaining ingredients and process until combined, about 20 seconds. Be careful not to over process the mixture; otherwise, the apricots will turn into a puree. You want the mixture to be a little chunky.

Pour into the baking dish and smooth the top with a rubber spatula. Bake for 25 to 30 minutes. Cool slightly before cutting.

Yield: 9 to 12 servings

Banana Layer Cake

This recipe can also be made into 24 cupcakes. Serve with the Cashew Date Frosting, page 470, or drizzled with the Blueberry Syrup, page 115. We like to decorate the top of the cake we banana slices and fresh, edible flowers.

Dry Ingredients:
2 cups sorghum flour
1 cup brown rice flour
¾ cup tapioca flour
1 tablespoon baking powder
1 ½ teaspoons baking soda
1 ½ teaspoons xanthan gum
¾ teaspoon sea salt

Wet Ingredients:
½ cup milk
¾ cup melted coconut oil
1 cup maple syrup
2 ½ cups mashed banana (about 5 bananas)
1 tablespoon vanilla

Preheat oven to 350 degrees. Grease a 9 x 13-inch pan or two 9-inch round cake pans.

In a large mixing bowl, whisk together the dry ingredients. Set aside. In a separate bowl, whisk the melted coconut oil and maple syrup together. Add the mashed banana, non-dairy milk, and vanilla; whisk again. Add the wet ingredients to the dry and beat with an electric mixer until all of the ingredients are well incorporated and the batter thickens slightly.

Pour batter into the prepared pan(s). Bake for 45 minutes for the 9 x 13-inch pan, or 25 to 30 minutes for the cake pans. Let cool completely before frosting. This cake will last for up to 3 days at room temperature.

Yield: 8 to 12 servings

Variation:

Xanthan-Free: Omit xanthan gum in the dry ingredients. Instead, add 6 tablespoons ground golden flax seeds and 3 tablespoons whole psyllium husks to the ½ cup milk in the wet ingredients and whisk together in a small bowl; let rest for 2 to 3 minutes and then whisk into the rest of the wet ingredients.

Desserts

Blackberry Buckwheat Cake

When the blackberries are in season, our children like to take small baskets on trail hikes or walks through the green spaces in our neighborhood, and fill them up with blackberries. Most of them get eaten right away, but sometimes there are enough leftover to bake with. Serve this healthy cake for a weekend brunch or after a light evening meal. For a more decadent cake, top with the Dairy-Free Cream Cheese Frosting, page 474, or the Coconut Orange Buttercream Frosting, page 473.

Dry Ingredients:
2 cups freshly ground buckwheat flour
2 teaspoons baking powder
½ teaspoon baking soda
¼ teaspoon sea salt
1 teaspoon cinnamon
¼ teaspoon ground allspice or cardamom

Wet Ingredients:
2 tablespoons ground chia seeds
½ cup hot water
¾ cup milk
¾ cup coconut sugar
½ cup melted coconut oil or olive oil
2 teaspoons vanilla

Other Ingredients:
1 cup fresh or frozen blackberries

Preheat oven to 350 degrees F. Grease an 8 x 8-inch baking dish with coconut oil.

In a medium-sized mixing bowl, whisk together the dry ingredients and set aside.

Place the ground chia seeds into a blender. Add the hot water and blend for a few seconds to combine. Let rest for about 2 minutes to form a gel. Then add the remaining wet ingredients and blend again to combine. Pour the wet ingredients into dry and whisk together. Fold in blackberries.

Pour batter into baking dish and bake for 35 to 40 minutes. Cool slightly before cutting into squares and serving. If you plan on frosting the cake you'll need to cool it completely before doing so.

Yield: 9 servings

Variation:

Use any variety of berries in place of the blackberries or a combination of a few.

Vanilla Coconut Cake

This moist, spongy grain and dairy-free cake is quick and easy to make. Make sure to use full-fat canned coconut milk for best results. You can double this recipe and make it into a beautiful layered cake. Frost with the Chocolate Avocado Frosting, page 472, or drizzle individual slices with Chocolate Ganache Frosting, page 471, and top with fresh berries.

Dry Ingredients:
1 cup coconut flour
1 teaspoon baking soda
¼ teaspoon sea salt

Wet Ingredients:
1 cup coconut milk
6 large organic eggs
⅓ cup honey
2 tablespoons unsweetened applesauce
1 tablespoon vanilla
1 teaspoon almond flavoring

Preheat oven to 350 degrees F. Grease a 9-inch cake pan and dust with coconut flour.

Place the dry ingredients into a food processor fitted with the "s" blade. Pulse a few times to combine. Add the wet ingredients and process until combined, immediately pour into the cake pan.

Bake for 35 to 45 minutes or until toothpick inserted into center comes out clean. Cool for at least 10 minutes before flipping out onto a wire rack to cool. Serve warm with Chocolate Ganache or let cool completely before frosting.

Yield: 8 servings

Variation:

To make a lemon cake, reduce vanilla to 1 teaspoon and add 1 to 2 teaspoons of lemon flavoring to the wet ingredients. Replace the applesauce with 2 tablespoons freshly squeezed lemon juice. Add ¼ teaspoon turmeric to the dry ingredients to give the cake a natural yellow tint. To make a spice cake, add 2 teaspoons cinnamon, 1 teaspoon ground ginger, ½ teaspoon allspice, and ½ teaspoon nutmeg to the dry ingredients. Replace the applesauce with 2 tablespoons blackstrap molasses.

Desserts

Warm Chocolate Cake

Decadent yet nutritious, this recipe will probably become a family favorite. Nobody will ever know that this cake is gluten-free! This cake is best served warm, about 20 to 30 minutes out of the oven. Any leftover cake will stay moist for days from the layer of frosting. I like to use Dagoba organic baking chocolate for this recipe because it comes in 6-ounce bars that are divided into 2-ounce squares.

Dry Ingredients:
1 cup sorghum flour
½ cup sweet rice flour
1 cup coconut sugar
¼ cup ground chia seeds
¼ cup cocoa powder
¾ teaspoon baking soda
½ teaspoon sea salt

Wet Ingredients:
¾ cup plain kefir (cow, goat, or coconut)
½ cup water
½ cup melted organic butter or coconut oil
2 large organic eggs
2 teaspoons vanilla

Frosting:
¼ cup organic butter or coconut oil
2 ounces bittersweet chocolate
½ cup coconut sugar
2 tablespoons arrowroot powder
¼ cup plain kefir (cow, goat, or coconut)

Preheat oven to 350 degrees F. Grease an 8 x 8-inch glass pan.

Whisk together the dry ingredients in a large bowl. In a smaller bowl, whisk together the wet ingredients. Pour the wet into the dry and whisk together well.

Pour batter into pan and spread out with the back of a spoon. Bake for 35 to 40 minutes. Remove from oven and let cool slightly while making the frosting.

In a small saucepan, add the butter, chocolate, and sugar. Whisk over very low heat until just melted. Whisk in the arrowroot powder. Pour into a blender and then add the kefir. Blend on high for about 60 seconds. Immediately pour over cake. Let cake rest for about 10 to 20 minutes then serve warm.

Yield: 12 servings

Cashew Date Frosting

This luscious frosting is actually nutritious too! You will need a high-powered blender such as a Vita-Mix to make this recipe. Use it to frost your favorite cupcakes or layered cake. It is delicious spread over the Banana Layer Cake, page 466. This recipe will frost one dozen cupcakes, but will need to be doubled for a layered cake.

1 cup raw cashews
½ cup medjool dates, pitted
¾ cup water
¾ cup melted coconut oil
1 tablespoon non-alcoholic vanilla
pinch sea salt

Place the cashews, dates, and water into your blender. Let them soak for about 3 hours. After soaking they will be soft and blend very easily into a creamy frosting.

Blend on high for 30 to 60 seconds or until very smooth. Add melted coconut oil, vanilla, and salt. Blend again until smooth, scraping down the sides if necessary. Frosting will seem a little thin but will solidify once chilled.

Pour frosting into a bowl and chill uncovered in the refrigerator for 6 hours or overnight before using. Once it is completely chilled, whip by hand using a spoon or beat with an electric beater. Make sure your cake or cupcakes are completely cooled before using this frosting.

Yield: About 2 cups

Desserts

Chocolate Ganache Frosting

This frosting is very easy to make, just be sure not to cook it at too high a temperature otherwise the chocolate will burn. Use it to drizzle over your favorite cake, cupcake, raw pie, ice cream, or fresh fruit.

½ cup dark chocolate chips (about 3 ounces)
¼ cup coconut milk
2 tablespoons maple syrup or honey

Place all ingredients into a small pot and heat over low heat. Stir continuously until melted and thickened, just about 2 minutes. Remove from heat and let cool for about 5 minutes. Do not chill! Then drizzle over a cake or cupcakes.

If you would like a thick, creamy, spreadable frosting then let the ganache thicken at room temperature for about 3 hours.

Yield: About ¾ cup

Chocolate Avocado Frosting

This heart-healthy frosting is full of monounsaturated fats from the avocado and is rich and creamy despite the lack of saturated fat. Avocados contain oleic acid, a monounsaturated fat that has been shown to lower cholesterol. Use this frosting recipe to frost your favorite cupcake or cookie. This recipe makes enough to frost one dozen cupcakes.

3 small ripe avocados, about 1 cup mashed
6 to 8 tablespoons honey or maple syrup
6 to 8 tablespoons cocoa powder
4 tablespoons melted virgin coconut oil
1 tablespoon vanilla
1 to 2 teaspoons almond flavoring
1 teaspoon lemon juice

Place all ingredients into a food processor fitted with the "s" blade. Process until very smooth and creamy.

Put frosting into a container and chill in the refrigerator for about 2 hours before using.

Yield: About 2 cups

Coconut Orange Buttercream Frosting

I like to use this nutritious dairy-free frosting to top just about anything from brownies to cupcakes. Make a double batch for a layered cake. To naturally color this frosting for a child's birthday party, add a few teaspoons of beet powder for pink, spirulina for green, or turmeric for yellow.

1 cup coconut butter
½ cup coconut oil
¼ cup honey or coconut nectar
¼ cup freshly squeezed orange juice
¼ to ½ teaspoon orange flavoring

Place all ingredients into a small saucepan. Warm over very low heat, whisking, until the coconut butter and oil have melted. The mixture will look thick and gelatinous. Pour it into a bowl and place the bowl into your freezer for no more than 20 minutes.

When you pull it out you'll notice some of the frosting hardened on the side of the bowl and the rest is still sort of gelatinous and clear. Use a whisk, fork, or electric beater to vigorously beat it up. It should quickly turn into a thick, creamy, cream-colored frosting. Use it immediately to frost your cupcakes or cake.

Yield: About 2 cups

Ingredient Tip:

Coconut butter is different from coconut oil in that it is made from pureed coconut meat, rather than pressing the meat to extract the oil. Our favorite brand of coconut butter is Artisana.

Variation:

For a vanilla frosting, replace orange juice with either coconut milk or almond milk and omit the orange flavoring and add 1 tablespoon of non-alcoholic vanilla.

Dairy-Free Cream Cheese Frosting

I like to drizzle this frosting, while it's still warm, over freshly baked cinnamon rolls. Once it is completely chilled it has the consistency of a spreadable cream cheese style frosting. Double this recipe to frost a cake or use a single batch for one dozen cupcakes. If you want your frosting to be white make sure to purchase sweet potatoes with white flesh and light tan-colored skin.

¾ cup cooked, mashed sweet potatoes (still warm)
6 tablespoons coconut oil
¼ cup maple syrup
2 tablespoons unsweetened applesauce
2 tablespoons arrowroot powder
2 teaspoons vanilla
pinch sea salt

To cook the sweet potatoes, leave the skins on and slice them into thick rounds. Place into a small pot and fill about ⅓ of the way with fresh water. Cover and cook over medium heat until tender. The skins will easily peel off after they are cooked. You can also place large pieces of sweet potatoes into a steamer basket and steam until tender.

Place all ingredients into a high-powered blender and blend until very smooth and creamy. Scrape frosting from blender and place into a container in the refrigerator and chill until firm. If you would like it to chill and firm up quickly you can place the container in your freezer for 30 to 40 minutes, stirring every so often, until firm. Then spread onto your favorite cupcake.

Yield: About 2 cups

Desserts

Simple Icing

This icing recipe works great for cookies or cupcakes. You can color the icing with natural food colorings. I have used turmeric powder to create yellow, beet juice for pink, and spirulina powder for green. I have also used Seelect brand plant-based food coloring in this icing, which works beautifully.

½ cup raw cashews
6 tablespoons melted coconut oil
¼ cup warm water
2 tablespoons coconut nectar or honey
1 tablespoon arrowroot powder
½ to 1 teaspoon vanilla
¼ teaspoon lemon flavoring
2 to 3 teaspoons fresh lemon juice

Place all ingredients for the icing into a high-powered blender and blend until ultra smooth, stopping the machine if necessary to scrape down the sides. Spoon icing into individual small bowls and add a tiny amount of natural food coloring if desired.

Ice cookies or cupcakes, and then sprinkle them with shredded coconut or natural sprinkles for decoration. To set the icing, freeze the iced cookies or cupcakes for 20 minutes before serving.

Yield: About 1 cup

Variation:

For an almond flavored icing, replace the lemon flavoring with 1 teaspoon almond flavoring and omit fresh lemon juice.

Whipped Coconut Cream

Use this simple recipe as a replacement for whipped heavy cream; dollop on top of fresh strawberries and blueberries, or use to frost cupcakes. The coconut cream will begin to soften as it sits at room temperature, and will soften quickly on a hot summer afternoon so be sure to keep it chilled. You can easily re-whip it after you remove the container from the refrigerator.

2 cans coconut milk, chilled for 12 hours
2 tablespoons coconut nectar, honey, or maple syrup
pinch sea salt

After the cans of coconut milk have chilled, open them up and scoop the thick white cream from the top. Pour the watery milk into a jar and use it for your favorite fruit smoothie at another time.

Place the coconut cream, coconut nectar, and salt into a mixing bowl. Use an electric mixer to whip the chilled cream into soft peaks. Serve immediately. Can be stored in a covered glass container in the refrigerator for up to a week.

Yield: About 1 cup

Desserts

Beverages

Homemade nut milks, teas, and sodas require simple ingredients and are easy to prepare. Nut milks are made using soaked nuts, water, and a touch of sweetener. Herbal teas are made using creative combinations of dried herbs—some of which we regularly harvest and dehydrate ourselves, such as nettles and spearmint. Natural sodas are made using sparkling mineral water and organic fruit juices.

Homemade Dairy-Free Milks

Homemade nut and seed milks can be used in place of cow's milk in all recipes calling for milk. Commercial dairy-free milks often have ingredients that our bodies don't need such as "natural" flavorings, stabilizers, and too much sugar. In making your own nut milks, you reduce and regulate ingredients while eliminating excess packaging from going to the landfill. Using homemade nut and seed milks will keep your diet be cleaner and greener.

Herbal Teas

Making dried herbal tea blends is a wonderful way to preserve the harvest and benefit your health. Herbs often work very efficiently on children to calm digestion, sooth anxiety, or aid in sleep. Our children love to come up with their own herb combinations for tea using the many different jars of dried herbs we have in kitchen our cabinet.

Natural Sodas

Drinking a lot of juice early on in childhood sets the stage for blood sugar imbalances leading to cravings for sugary, starchy foods. It's easy to never begin this vicious cycle with your child by only offering pure water, herbal teas, and homemade nut milks. Natural, homemade sodas can be used for special occasions or to wean your child off of a liquid sugar addiction. All commercial sodas, diet or otherwise, cause weight gain. Studies show that diet sodas actually cause more weight gain and obesity problems than sugar-laden sodas do! If this isn't enough, the phosphoric acid in soda leaches precious minerals from your bones. If you are craving something fizzy and sweet, consider gulping down some sort of fermented drink like kombucha or cultured coconut water, or try some of our homemade soda recipes in this chapter.

10 Tips for Making Homemade Beverages:

1. **Soak almonds, brazil nuts, and hazelnuts** for at least 8 hours, though they can be soaked for up to 24. If you live in a warm climate, or if your kitchen is very warm, you may need to drain and add new soaking water once or twice to keep the nuts from spoiling.

2. **Softer nuts—such as cashews—don't need to be soaked unless you are not using a powerful blender.** Then soaking these nuts for at least 3 hours will help them to blend properly.

3. **Seeds can also be blended with nuts** for added nutrition—pumpkin seed almond milk is a delicious combination.

4. **Nut and seed milks can be stored in a covered glass container**, such as a pitcher or mason jar, in the refrigerator for 3 to 4 days.

5. **Nut milks can be frozen in ice cube trays and then stored in a sealed container in the freezer.** Use to make a refreshing fruit smoothie.

6. **Use a nut milk bag to strain out the pulp** to make the process of creating your own nut milks very easy!

7. **Find a local herb store selling dried bulk organic and wild-crafted herbs.** Bring in your glass jars to fill up.

8. **Store dried herbs in labeled clean glass jars in a cool**, dark, dry location.

9. **Leftover herbal teas can be stored in glass jars in the refrigerator** and then reheated in a small pot when ready to drink.

10. **To make a quick and easy natural soda take any organic**, sugar-free fruit juice concentrate and stir it with sparkling mineral water in a large pitcher.Use a large glass bowl with a ladle and float thinly sliced oranges, lemons, and limes in the soda for a beautiful presentation.

Beverages

Homemade Coconut Kefir

I use the kefir starter from Body Ecology Diet (www.BodyEcology.com) to make this recipe. Use coconut kefir for smoothies, poured over homemade granola, or to soak whole grains in before baking. If you have an allergy to almonds you can use another seed milk, such as hemp milk, but the end result won't be as tasty. I use the Quick, Rich Almond Milk, page 480.

1 can coconut milk
2 cups almond milk
1 teaspoon honey
1 package kefir starter
quart jar

Optional Additions:
non-alcoholic vanilla
almond flavoring
stevia
honey

Pour the coconut milk, almond milk, and honey into a small saucepan. Heat on low to about 92 degrees F or until barely warm to the touch.

Pour the warm milk into a clean quart jar. Add package of kefir starter, cover, and gently shake. I like to use a plastic lid because metal can begin to corrode from the acids. Make sure the lid isn't screwed on too tightly, as this will prevent gasses formed during fermentation from escaping.

Place the jar into a warm, undisturbed place on your kitchen counter. Let it sit for 24 to 48 hours or until soured and slightly bubbly. If your house is very warm it should only take about 24 hours. If your house is cooler, fermentation could take 48 hours or longer. After it is done fermenting you can stir in flavorings such as vanilla, almond flavoring, stevia, or honey.

Store in the refrigerator for up to one week. The coconut fat will separate from the other liquids at refrigerated temperatures—just shake it vigorously before using.

Yield: 1 quart

Nutrition Tip:

Kefir contains trillions of probiotics. These beneficial bacteria line your digestive tract helping to break down and assimilate your food while keeping guard against pathogenic bacteria and toxins. Therefore, a balanced digestive tract full of beneficial bacteria is vital to modulate immune system function, improve digestion, heal food allergies, and reduce exposure to potentially toxic substances

Quick Rich Almond Milk

If I am in need of milk for baking muffins or making pancakes in the morning, I will make this milk because it does not require presoaked nuts. You can use either finely ground blanched almond flour or almond meal, such as Bob's Red Mill almond meal flour. Use less water or more almond flour for a richer, creamier milk.

½ cup almond flour
3 cups water
pinch sea salt

Place all ingredients into a blender, cover, and blend on high for 60 to 90 seconds.

Use a nut milk bag or cheesecloth to strain out the pulp. I like to put a nut milk bag into a quart mason jar or a 4-cup Pyrex glass measure and pour the milk through it and then squeeze out any remaining liquid.

Store in a covered glass jar or pitcher in the refrigerator for up to 4 days.

Yield: 3 cups

Raw Almond Milk

Raw almond milk can be used for fresh fruit smoothies or as a nutritious beverage with meals. Add it to tea in place of cow's milk or poured over chia seeds, hemp seeds, and fresh fruit for a morning "cereal." I usually make a double or triple batch of this at a time and store it in a glass pitcher with a lid in the refrigerator.

½ cup raw almonds, soaked overnight
3 cups water
1 to 2 tablespoons maple syrup
pinch sea salt

Place almonds into a small bowl and cover with purified water. Soak at room temperature for about 8 to 12, hours or overnight.

After the almonds have soaked, rinse them well under warm running water. Place them in a blender with the water, maple syrup, and sea salt. Blend on high for 2 to 3 minutes or until you have a very smooth milk.

Pour the milk through cheesecloth or a nut milk bag into a container and squeeze out the liquid. You can add the leftover pulp to muffins or pancakes for extra fiber and protein.

Store in a covered glass jar or pitcher in the refrigerator for up to 3 days.

Yield: 3 ½ cups

Hemp Milk

Use this dairy-free milk for baking, for pancakes, as a base for smoothies, over whole grain breakfast porridge, or just for drinking. I always strain my hemp milk using a nut milk bag, though it isn't completely necessary. You can add more or less water for thicker or thinner milk.

½ cup hulled hemp seeds
3 cups filtered water
1 tablespoon maple syrup
pinch sea salt

Place all ingredients into a high-powered blender and blend for 60 to 90 seconds or until ultra smooth.

Place a nut milk bag into a large jar or pitcher and pour hemp milk through the bag; squeeze out the milk, and leave the pulp behind. I compost the leftover pulp.

Store in a covered glass jar or pitcher in the refrigerator for up to 4 days.

Yield: About 3 ½ cups

Nutrition Tip:

Hemp is the second highest source of plant protein after soy. If you are needing additional protein in your diet, hemp is a fantastic vegan source.

Cashew Milk

Cashews are a softer nut and therefore do not need to be soaked overnight to be able to blend smoothly as almonds or hazelnuts do. Use fresh cashew milk over a cooked whole grain cereal for breakfast or use it to make fruit smoothies. I sometimes like to make this milk a little thicker by reducing the amount of water to one cup, to use like a creamer. I store it in a small glass pitcher in the refrigerator and add it to spice tea with a little coconut sugar for a late night warming drink.

½ cup raw cashews
2 cups water
2 tablespoons maple syrup
pinch sea salt

Place all ingredients into a high-powered blender. Blend on high until very smooth. Taste and adjust sweetness if necessary.

Store in a covered glass jar or pitcher in the refrigerator for up to 4 days.

Yield: 2 ½ cups

Kitchen Tip:

If you do not own a high-powered blender such as a Vita-Mix or Blendtec, you will need to soak the cashews in filtered water for about 3 hours. Then drain the nuts and follow the recipe above.

Creamy Macadamia Nut Milk

This recipe is such a treat as macadamia nuts can be a bit pricy. Pour over granola or drizzle over cooked brown rice cereal. I love to use this milk poured over a bowl of sliced bananas topped with a little ground golden flax seed as a calming bedtime snack.

1 cup raw macadamia nuts, soaked for 3 hours
3 to 4 cups water
1 to 2 tablespoons honey or maple syrup
pinch sea salt

Place macadamia nuts into a bowl and cover them with water. Let them soak for at least 3 hours then rinse and drain.

Place the soaked nuts into a blender with the 3 cups of water, honey, and salt. Blend on high for 1 to 2 minutes until ultra smooth and creamy. Add up to one more cup of water to desired consistency.

Store in a covered glass jar or pitcher in the refrigerator for up to 4 days.

Yield: About 4 cups

Nutrition Tip:

Tip: Although macadamia nuts are known to have a high fat content, around 80 percent of the fats are in a monounsaturated form. Having more monounsaturated and less polyunsaturated fats in your diet is healthier. One monounsaturated fat found in macadamia nuts is called palmitoleic acid, which helps lower cholesterol, curb appetite, and burn more body fat for fuel.

Beverages

Mineral Tea

Because of our modern diet and depleted soil, many people are deficient in essential minerals. This herbal tea blend can be used daily to naturally increase minerals in the diet. People often find that they sleep better, are less anxious, have greater clarity, and for women, have far less menstrual cramping when the diet has an adequate amount of minerals. This tea is also beneficial to drink all throughout pregnancy—growing a baby requires extra minerals!

½ cup dried oatstraw
½ cup dried nettles
½ cup dried red raspberry leaf
½ cup dried alfalfa
¼ cup dried peppermint
2 tablespoons dried horsetail

Optional Additions:
¼ cup dried chamomile
2 to 3 tablespoons dried rose petals
1 to 2 tablespoons dried licorice root

Place all of the dried herbs into a large glass jar. Cover with a lid and shake to blend the herbs. Store in a cool, dry place until ready to use.

To make the mineral tea, place 2 to 3 tablespoons of the herb mixture into a quart jar and pour four cups of boiling water over the herbs. Cover and steep for 20 to 30 minutes. You can also steep it overnight for best extraction of minerals and then reheat the tea in the morning.

Strain out herbs with a small fine mesh tea strainer and enjoy plain or with a touch of raw honey. Drink up to one quart a day.

Yield: About 2 ½ cups of dry tea blend

Fresh Spearmint Tea

We have loads of spearmint growing in our kitchen herb garden, just steps from our front door. After I planted it, Tom told me that we'd never get rid of it and that I should have planted it in a bottomless bucket to keep it contained in the ground. Oops! Now, every year we pull and pull that mint out of the garden, only to have it take over a month later. Instead of hate it, we make tea, lots of it. Use any mint you have on hand. Spearmint, cinnamon-mint, chocolate-mint, regular mint—whatever—it all works. In the summertime I let the tea cool and add a few cups of ice and fresh mint leaves to garnish.

large handful fresh mint leaves, chopped
3 cups boiling water
honey

Place the chopped mint into a French press or a glass quart jar. Pour boiling water over it. Cover and let steep for 5 to 7 minutes.

Strain with a small fine mesh tea strainer and serve with a touch of honey.

Yield: 3 cups

Nettle Mint Tea

Here in the Pacific Northwest, from February through April, we go out as a family and harvest nettles. All you need is a pair of gardening gloves, scissors, and a large paper bag. Nettles are best harvested when they are young, just a few inches high. This is the time when the energy and nutrients of the plant are going into the leaves, rather than later in the summer when energy is put forth into seed production. We dry our fresh nettles in a dehydrator and then place them into a food processor to break them down further. I store the pulverized, dried nettles in glass jars. We do the same thing with all of the mint growing in our garden in the summertime.

6 cups water
3 tablespoons dried nettles
3 tablespoons dried mint

Place the water into a medium-sized pot, cover, and bring to a boil. Once the water has boiled, turn off heat and add the dried herbs. Cover and steep for about 30 minutes.

Strain though a fine mesh strainer into mugs for serving.

Store leftover tea in glass jars in the refrigerator.

Yield: 6 cups

Nutrition Tip:

Nettles are a fabulous blood tonic and purifier, being especially helpful for those with anemia or women who have just given birth.

Tummy Comfort Tea

This tea is great for children who may have eaten food that hurts their stomach. We dilute this tea with water for our children; the younger they are, the more dilution. The licorice makes this tea naturally sweet but you could add a touch of fresh honey to each cup if desired.

6 cups water
2 to 4 tablespoons sliced fresh ginger
1 ½ tablespoons dandelion root
1 tablespoon licorice root
2 tablespoons dried spearmint
1 tablespoon dried chamomile

Place the 6 cups water, fresh ginger, dandelion root, and licorice root in a medium-sized pot. Cover and simmer for 20 to 25 minutes.

Remove from heat and add spearmint and chamomile. Cover and steep for about 10 to 15 more minutes.

Strain, pour into small tea cups and dilute each with water to desired taste.

Store in a large glass jar in the refrigerator for up to 5 days.

Yield: 6 cups

Nutrition Tip:

Chinese medicine appropriately lists ginger as a "warming food." This is obvious after consuming it as you can sense the heat in your mouth, esophagus, and stomach. It has long been known to calm seasickness and nausea of all types. Beyond calming the stomach, studies have also noted the amazing ability of ginger to reduce inflammation in arthritis.

Beverages

Rooibos Rose Iced Tea

This tea is delicious served hot or cold on ice. It has a flavor akin to black tea, only milder with rose-flavored undertones. Be sure to use organic dried rose petals as roses are normally sprayed with pesticides. Bulk herbs can be found at your local health food store or a local herb store.

10 cups water
¼ cup loose rooibos tea
¼ cup dried rose petals
2 tablespoons dried rose hips
raw honey
ice cubes

Bring the water to a boil. Place the dried herbs into an 8-cup Pyrex glass measuring cup, gallon glass jar, or large bowl. Pour the boiling water over the herbs. Let steep for about 20 minutes or until most of the herbs have fallen to the bottom of the container.

Carefully strain into a large glass pitcher using a small fine mesh strainer. Sweeten to taste with honey if desired. Let cool completely if serving over ice.

Yield: 10 cups

Warm Cranberry Orange Cider

I like to make this for Thanksgiving and Christmas with a dash of dark rum in each mug for the adults and a cinnamon stick in each child's mug. The spicy cinnamon-orange aromas will fill your house with lasting memories. Use less sweetener for a tarter flavor or more for a sweeter flavor.

4 cups orange juice
6 cups apple cider
one 8-ounce jar cranberry juice concentrate
¼ to ½ cup honey or coconut nectar
6 cinnamon sticks

Place all ingredients into an 8-quart stockpot. Cover and simmer for about one hour. When ready to serve, turn heat to low and place a ladle in the pot for serving.

Store any remaining cider in glass quart jars in the refrigerator for up to a week.

Yield: 11 cups

Pomegranate Chia Fresca

In the book, Born to Run, Christopher Mcdougall describes an energy drink made from water, chia seeds, citrus juice, and honey consumed by the Tarahumara, a tribe of natural superathletes in Mexico. Chia seeds are rich on omega-3 fatty acids, antioxidants, and protein. When consumed with other foods, they slow the absorption of sugars and starches into the bloodstream, thereby decreasing an insulin response. Serve this refreshing drink garnished with lime wedges on a hot afternoon or with a spicy meal.

2 cups pomegranate juice
3 to 4 tablespoons freshly squeezed lime juice
2 tablespoons whole chia seeds

Place all ingredients into a quart jar, cover, and shake. Let sit for 2 to 3 hours so the chia seeds can expand and form a gel. Chill before serving.

Store in the refrigerator for up to 5 days.

Yield: 4 small servings

Strawberry-Honey Lemonade

A glass of refreshing homemade strawberry lemonade in the summertime creates a memory that will last a lifetime. We love to go strawberry picking in June and bring home container after container of small organic strawberries so full of flavor you wouldn't dare want to cook with them. Fresh strawberries for breakfast, lunch, and dinner are always on the menu! This is one of our favorite ways to use them. Have your children make mint ice cubes by placing a few fresh spearmint leaves in each ice cube mold after adding the water, then freeze. These are especially fun to add to the lemonade.

2 to 3 cups fresh strawberries, hulled
5 cups water, divided
¼ cup honey
1 cup freshly squeezed lemon juice
liquid stevia to taste, if needed
fresh mint leaves, for garnish

Place strawberries, 1 cup of the water, and honey into a blender. Puree until smooth. Pour into a large pitcher and add the remaining 4 cups of water and the lemon juice. Stir with a long- handled spoon.

Taste, and adjust sweetness if necessary by adding up to ½ teaspoon of liquid stevia. Too much honey can throw off the flavor, which is why I increase the sweetness using stevia. Strawberries can be very sweet so you may not need any added stevia. Add more water if you would like a thinner lemonade.

Garnish each glass with a spring of fresh mint and a lemon wedge if desired.

Yield: About 8 cups

Nutrition Tip:

Chock-full of potent antioxidant chemicals, strawberries have been shown to lower the CRP (C-Reactive Protein) marker that is associated with increased heart attack risk. Consuming at least three servings a week can help decrease inflammation in your body. You may wonder, "Aren't strawberries high in sugar?", yet when consumed along with table sugar, strawberries have been shown to lessen sugar's negative effect on the body.

Citrus Spritzer

Our daughter will occasionally make us breakfast in bed—scrambled eggs, greens, and this spritzer. Serve it with a special occasion breakfast, brunch, or holiday meal. We've also made this recipe using blood oranges, which is quite delicious and a real treat. This recipe can easily be doubled or tripled as needed.

2 cups sparkling mineral water
2 cups freshly squeezed orange juice
2 tablespoons meyer lemon juice
fresh orange slices

Place the mineral water into a glass pitcher and then add the orange juice. Gently stir together and add a few orange slices, use blood orange slices for a beautiful presentation.

Serve within an hour.

Yield: About 4 cups

Ingredient Tip:

Use Valencia oranges for juicing as they contain more juice than other varieties of oranges. Meyer lemons are sweeter and more flavorful than regular lemons.

Ginger Lemon Soda

Icy cold ginger-lemon soda is most refreshing in the summertime but can also be used as a festive party drink around the holidays. Our children are especially fond of ginger so sometimes I add a bit more for their tastes. Any sugar will work here but I like to use coconut sugar for its low-glycemic properties.

3 tablespoons grated fresh ginger
½ cup coconut sugar
1 cup water
pinch sea salt
½ cup lemon juice
1 liter sparking water
liquid stevia, to taste

Optional Additions:
ice cubes
fresh mint leaves

Add the ginger, sugar, water, and salt to a small pot, cover and simmer for about 30 minutes.

Stir in lemon juice. Strain though a fine mesh strainer into a pitcher. Let cool completely then add the sparkling water, stir a little, then add liquid stevia drops to taste. The stevia will bring out the ginger and lemon flavors.

Add ice cubes and fresh mint leaves if desired. Serve immediately.

Yield: About 6 cups

Grape Soda

This natural, sugar-free grape soda is fun to serve at a child's birthday party or other gathering such as a baby or wedding shower. As we generally never have juice in the house, treats such as this recipe are reserved for special occasions. You can use any organic fruit juice in this recipe in place of the grape. For a party, make a double batch and place into a large bowl with a ladle. Float thin slices of oranges and limes to make a fruit punch! Have your children make raspberry or blackberry ice cubes by placing a berry in each ice cube mold and then filling with filtered water and freezing. You can float the berry ice cubes in the grape soda.

4 cups organic concord grape juice
1 liter sparkling mineral water

Mix ingredients together in a large pitcher. Serve immediately.

Yield: 8 cups

Nutrition Tip:

Organic unsweetened Concord grape juice is a rich source of the antioxidant flavonoids catechin, epicatechin, quercetin, and anthocyanins. A research article in the *American Journal of Clinical Nutrition* showed the consumption of Concord grape juice can decrease oxidative damage to proteins and lipids in the body.

Preserving The Harvest

I t has only been in the last 60 years or so that we have been able to buy any type of vegetable or fruit at any time of year. Historically, people ate what was available seasonally and preserved the rest. Our great-grandparents were very adept at pickling, canning, and dehydrating. Food wasn't wasted. These were basic survival skills that have been lost in recent generations, but are now making a comeback. Home food preservation not only saves you money, but it benefits your health and allows you and your family to connect with the wonderful foods that grow where you live.

We love to take our children out on berry picking adventures and then come home to make homemade honey-sweetened jam. By preserving food we are able to more fully connect with the rhythms of the seasons. We know that once the produce starts to become available in the spring that we must get busy. Our children know that the first salmonberry is a sure sign of summer and many more berries to come. Peaches represent the heat of the summer and apples come when summer begins to fade into autumn.

By preserving your own food you save on packaging and shipping—reducing the use of fossil fuels. Since the equipment and materials needed to store food are reusable, you'll produce much less waste that would otherwise end up in a landfill. Growing and preserving your own foods ensures that you have a wholesome, chemical-free food source that can feed your family.

Food Preservation Methods

As we're all aware, most produce is highly perishable. Many things work together in the decaying process. Since fresh produce has a high water content enzymes can begin to break it down and oxygen can react with it and cause spoilage. Also, bacteria, yeasts, and molds can grow and destroy fresh produce. Food can be preserved in a variety of ways to stop or slow this process of natural decay.

Canning
Canning food destroys enzymes, removes oxygen, and prevents the growth of harmful bacteria, yeasts, and molds from growing. Canning forms a tight vacuum seal, which keeps liquid in and air out. It is important to follow USDA canning guidelines in order to assure high-quality, safe home-canned food. For example, acidic food such as most fruits can be canned in a boiling water bath. Foods like squash and green beans need to be canned using a pressure canner. Because canning destroys the vitality of food we prefer to can only things like applesauce, jam, and tomato sauce. Freezing and dehydrating are our preferred

methods for long-term food storage. Canned food should be stored in a cool, dark place and used within a year.

Pickling

Pickling or brining is the process of preserving food by anaerobic fermentation, or lacto-fermentation. Salt is used to inhibit harmful microbes from growing while the lactic acid bacteria take over. Lactobacilli naturally present on the skins of vegetables begin to flourish by consuming the starches and sugars in the vegetables. They produce enough acid to inhibit harmful microbes from growing and properly preserve the food for many months. Pickling is thought to have begun over 4000 years ago in India using cucumbers. Cultures all over the world have been using lacto-fermentation to preserve food naturally. Unlike canning, pickling does not require the food and jars to be sterile. Some examples of naturally pickled foods include kim chi from Korea, the pickled radish in China, sauerkraut in Germany, and the famous cucumber dill pickle from North America. Naturally pickled food should be stored in a cool, dark place, such as a refrigerator or root cellar, where they will stay good for up to six months.

Vinegar is another way to pickle foods. Vinegar's high acidity inhibits harmful microbes such as botulism from growing in home-canned pickled vegetables. Be sure to use a vinegar with a 5% acidity or greater.

Dehydrating

Dehydrating food is probably the oldest method of food preservation known. There is evidence that since before recorded history people have been dehydrating meats, vegetables, fruits, and herbs to store and use at a later time. Microorganisms need moisture to grow and survive. Proper food dehydration removes 80 to 90 percent of the moisture so microbes are unable to function. Dehydrating is much easier and more effective if you are living in a warm, dry climate. If not, you will need a food dehydrator to assist in the process. Dehydrating at or below 118 degrees Fahrenheit keeps enzymes and nutrients intact retaining the food as a viable source of nutrition when fresh foods are unavailable. Store your dehydrated food in tightly sealed glass jars in a cool, dark place. We store our jars in the back of our pantry.

Freezing

Freezing is an ancient form of food preservation that originated in extreme northern latitudes. We use an upright deep freezer in our garage for food storage. Some foods can be frozen fresh such as berries, peaches, pears, peas, and onions, while others, such as corn, green beans, kale, carrots, and asparagus, need to be blanched for about 2 to 4 minutes before freezing.

I freeze whole Roma tomatoes in large containers, and then when I need a few cups of diced tomatoes for soup I take out two to three tomatoes and let them thaw on the counter for about 20 minutes and then dice them with a sharp knife. We freeze our berries, pitted cherries, halved peaches, and quartered pears in large reusable plastic containers. I don't like using plastic for anything but freezing. Plastic bags need to be thrown away once they have served their purpose but plastic containers can be used over and over again until they break at which point they can be recycled. We try to use our frozen foods within a year of freezing them. Usually in June most of our frozen produce has been used at which time we will defrost and clean the deep freezer to get ready for the next season's produce.

10 Tips for Preserving Food:

1. **Always start with fresh food** that has not begun to spoil.

2. **Use in-season produce** to capture the maximum amount of nutrients.

3. **Search out local, organic farms** that offer u-pick fruits and vegetables. You'll save money by picking your own and it is a fun activity to do with children that educates them about the seasons and how their food is grown.

4. **Follow USDA guidelines for canning** to prevent harmful organisms from growing such as botulism.

5. **Reduce, reuse, recycle.** Save glass containers from products you buy and use to store fermented vegetables or dehydrated fruits and vegetables.

6. **Place fermenting foods in a warm place where they can rest undisturbed.** I like to use the top of the refrigerator for this purpose.

7. **Using a large ceramic crock makes fermentation easy and reliable.** Plus, you'll be able to make larger batches at once, saving time.

8. **Consider purchasing an extra freezer.** You'll save money and reduce waste by freezing berries, cherries, peaches, corn, peas, squash puree, and local meats when they are in season.

9. **Consider investing in a food dehydrator** to preserve food you have grown or harvested.

10. **Be sure that your dehydrated foods are completely free of moisture** before storing them otherwise mold will begin to grow.

Four Thieves Vinegar

The legend of Four Thieves Vinegar dates back to the 1600's during the Black Plague in Europe. The story has it that a group of thieves were wandering through homes and businesses robbing the sick and dead. Four thieves were apprehended, but rather than punish them the judge offered them a deal. He offered to let them go if they gave him the secret of their resistance to the plague. Rather than be hung, they gave away their secret, a vinegar made from thyme, rosemary, sage, and lavender; herbs that offer powerful anti-viral, anti-bacterial, anti-fungal, and immune boosting chemicals. Preserved in vinegar they create the perfect medicine to drizzle over a plate full of summer greens or sip by the tablespoonful. I prefer to use either raw apple cider vinegar or raw coconut vinegar for this recipe, though white wine vinegar is typically used for its sweeter flavor. Although garlic was added to the mixture later, this basic infusion became famous and was used for hundreds of years across Europe. You can add a variety of herbs to the basic recipe. Try parsley, marjoram, mint, lemon balm, chives, and hyssop too. Whisk together a few tablespoons of your Four Thieves Vinegar with a few tablespoons extra virgin olive oil and a pinch or two of sea salt and drizzle over fresh salad greens. It can also be taken by the tablespoonful as a medicine for the common cold or flu.

1 quart jar
5 large sprigs fresh rosemary
5 large sprigs fresh thyme
5 large sprigs fresh sage
2 sprigs fresh lavender
4 to 5 cloves garlic, crushed
raw apple cider vinegar or coconut vinegar

Place the herbs and crushed garlic into a clean quart jar. Cover with vinegar leaving at least 2 inches of space from the top of the jar. Place the lid on the jar and tightly close. Let the vinegar infuse in a cool, dark place for 6 weeks.

After 6 weeks strain herbs and garlic out using a fine mesh strainer. Pour the strained vinegar into a clean glass jar or bottle. Label and date your vinegar. Store in your pantry or kitchen cabinet for up to a year.

Yield: About 1 quart

Black Currant Vinegar

We have a black currant bush in our garden that produces so many berries. Our children will pick the berries by the handfuls and bring them into the kitchen for me to deal with. We simply cannot eat them all right away. We like to toss them into our green smoothies, make strawberry-currant-honey jam, and make this nourishing vinegar. You can use this beautiful purple vinegar in salad dressings or eat it by the spoonful as daily medicine.

wide-mouthed quart jar
3 cups fresh black currants
raw coconut vinegar or white wine vinegar

Place the black currants into the jar and fill the jar with vinegar leaving about 2 inches from the top. Cover with a plastic lid and place into a kitchen cabinet or pantry. Let it sit for 6 to 12 weeks. A few times a week, gently shake the jar.

Then place a fine mesh strainer over a 4-cup liquid glass measure and pour the vinegar through it, mashing the berries in the strainer with the back of a spoon. Pour strained vinegar into another jar or glass bottle for storage. Vinegar will keep for a year in a cool, dark place.

Yield: About 3 cups

Nutrition Tip:

Studies indicate that anthocyanins, which create that dark purple color you see in black currants and other foods, show promising benefit as anti-oxidants, anti-inflammatories, and anti-microbials. As a result, they are being examined for their potential in combating cancers, neurodegenerative diseases (early stage cognitive decline and Alzheimers), eye diseases, and high blood pressure. The food industry is even considering using antioxidants from black currant extract as a preservative in processed meats.

Cayenne Hot Sauce

In the northwest hot peppers are grown in greenhouses because our summer temperatures are fairly mild. Hotter weather produces hotter peppers. Nonetheless, our farmer's markets are brimming with peppers of all kinds from late summer through early autumn. Making your own hot sauce takes very little time and is a wonderful way to preserve the harvest. I've kept bottles in the fridge through the winter. This hot sauce can also be canned in small jars using the water bath canning method. I use sweet Italian peppers to add sweetness and body without the addition of sugar—red bell peppers can also be used. Normally you would wear rubber gloves when cutting hot peppers, but I have designed the recipe in such a way that you don't need to. By only trimming the stems off and not cutting into the hot part of the pepper you won't need to wear gloves.

½ pound fresh cayenne peppers
3 sweet Italian peppers or red bell peppers
3 to 4 cloves garlic
2 teaspoons sea salt
1 ½ cups apple cider vinegar

Trim the stem end off of each cayenne pepper. If they are very large, cut them in half (leave the seeds in). Place into a 2 or 3-quart stainless steel pot. Cut the sweet peppers in half, remove the seeds and stem, and chop into large chunks. Place them into the pot along with the cayenne peppers. Add the remaining ingredients.

Cover the pot and simmer for 40 minutes. Transfer peppers and liquid to a blender; blend on high until completely pureed. I use a Vita-Mix to do this, if you use a regular blender you may need to strain the sauce through a fine mesh strainer to remove some of the seed chunks that didn't blend completely. Pour sauce back into pot and simmer again for 15 to 20 minutes.

Transfer to a glass jar and store in the refrigerator for up to 6 months. If you prefer to store some of the sauce for a longer period of time you may can the sauce in small, sterilized glass jars for 10 minutes in a boiling water bath.

Yield: About 1 ½ cups

Nutrition Tip:

Cultures who live in hot climates have been known to eat cayenne and other hot peppers to help combat the heat and regulate body temperature. Cayenne peppers are high in capsaicin, which helps to increase thermogenesis and fat burning. Many companies are now using capsaicin as an ingredient in weight loss supplements.

Beet Sauerkraut

My children call this "purple kraut." They absolutely love to help make this. The flavor is tangy like regular sauerkraut with earthy undertones from the beet and carrots. You might want to make a few jars at once while you are at it. I find we go through it so fast that it is easier to make more at once. Serve with a meat main dish or bean soup to make it more digestible. I also like to serve this over poached eggs for breakfast.

wide-mouthed quart jar
8 cups shredded cabbage (about 1 small head)
1 medium beet, peeled and shredded
2 large carrots, shredded
1 to 1 ½ tablespoons sea salt

To shred the cabbage I first remove the outer leaves and save one good-looking leaf for the top of the kraut. Then I cut the cabbage head into chunks. I use the slicing disk on my food processor to shred it. It is so easy and fast this way. Then measure out about 8 cups and place it into a large bowl.

Shred the beet and carrots and add them to the bowl. Sprinkle the sea salt over the top and toss the shredded veggies together. Then pound it all with a wooden mallet or other blunt object that won't break or damage the bowl—I use a wooden pestle. Keep pounding, this can take up to 10 minutes, until the veggies have released their juices. Then spoon the kraut into a clean quart jar. Firmly press it into the jar to push air bubbles out as you add it. I use the wooden pestle for this. Pack it all in there leaving about 2 inches of space from the top of the jar. Fold up the cabbage leaf and press it on top of the kraut. Use the pestle to firmly press it down so the juices rise above it. You want your kraut to stay below the juices to properly ferment.

Put a lid on the jar but don't tighten it all the way, this way there is room for extra gasses to release. Place the jar into a bowl or small Pyrex dish to catch any juices that leak out. Place in a warm spot. I like to place the jars on the top of my refrigerator. My kitchen is always the warmest spot in the house. Keep it out of direct sunlight though.

Let it ferment for 5 to 10 days, longer if your house is on the cooler side. Once it is done it should taste tangy and sour. Remove the large cabbage leaf on top of the jar, screw the lid back on and store in your refrigerator for up to 6 months.

Yield: 1 quart

Raw Sauerkraut

Raw sauerkraut originated in China over 2,000 years ago and eventually made its way to Europe where it became a cultural staple food, especially in Germany. Captain James Cook kept thousands of pounds of raw sauerkraut—which contains a good dose of vitamin C— aboard his ships to prevent scurvy among his crew during the long voyages. I like to keep a few crocks going at once so we always have an ample supply of sauerkraut around. Our children love the salty, crispy cabbage atop beans and quinoa for lunch or breakfast! This recipe uses a quart jar. Once you acquire a taste (and craving) for it, you might want to consider investing in a ceramic fermenting crock. This recipe requires about one medium head of green or red cabbage. I have measured it out in case you have different sized cabbage heads that need to be used.

wide-mouthed quart jar
10 to 12 cups shredded green or red cabbage
1 to 1 ½ tablespoons sea salt

To shred the cabbage I first remove the outer leaves and save one good-looking leaf for the top of the kraut. Then I cut the cabbage head into chunks. I use the slicing disk on my food processor to shred it. It is so easy and fast this way. Then measure out about 10 to 12 cups and place it into a large bowl.

Sprinkle the sea salt over the top and toss together. Then pound it all with a wooden mallet or other blunt object that won't break or damage the bowl—I use a wooden pestle. Keep pounding, this can take up to 10 minutes, until the cabbage has released its juices. Then spoon the kraut into a clean quart jar. Firmly press it into the jar to push air bubbles out as you add more. I use the wooden pestle for this. Pack it all in there leaving about 2 inches of space from the top of the jar. Fold up the cabbage leaf and press it on top of the kraut. Use the pestle to firmly press it down so the juices rise above it. You want your kraut to stay below the juices to properly ferment.

Put a lid on the jar but don't tighten it all the way, this way there is room for extra gasses to release. Place the jar into a bowl or small Pyrex dish to catch any juices that leak out. Place in a warm spot. I like to place the jars on the top of my refrigerator. My kitchen is always the warmest spot in the house. Keep it out of direct sunlight though.

Let it ferment for 5 to 10 days, or longer if your house is on the cooler side. I ferment sauerkraut in my ceramic crock for about 4 weeks in a cool place. Once it is done it should taste tangy and sour. If not, place the lid back on, and let it ferment for a few more days. Remove the large cabbage leaf on top of the jar, screw the lid back on and store in your refrigerator for up to 6 months.

Yield: 1 quart

Chili-Garlic Fermented Green Beans

This recipe uses lacto-fermentation to preserve raw green beans—no canning and subsequent loss of nutrients required! Usually it takes anywhere from 5 to 10 days to properly ferment, but can take as little as 3 days depending on the season and temperature in your home. Fermentation happens quickly in very warm weather! I've used small dried whole chilies, red chili flakes, and chopped fresh chilies. Use whatever you have on hand. Be sure to keep the liquid above the beans. Any beans, garlic, or chilies exposed to air could mold and spoil the whole batch!

1 wide-mouthed quart jar
3 to 4 cloves garlic, chopped
3 to 6 whole dried red chilies
½ to ¾ pound green beans, trimmed
2 cups purified water
1 ½ tablespoons sea salt
cabbage leaf

Clean a glass quart jar with hot water. Place the chopped garlic and red chilies at the bottom of the jar. Place all of the green beans in vertically (you may need more or less than a ½ pound). Pack them in tight. Placing them in this way prevents them from floating to the top and also keeps the garlic and chilies at the bottom. Make sure long green beans are cut in half so you have about 2 inches of space from the top of the jar.

Dissolve the sea salt in the water. Pour over the green beans. Add a touch more water if needed to submerge the beans completely. Press down a folded cabbage leaf on top of the beans. This will keep the beans submerged under the water. You can also place a small lid with a weight or boiled rock on top of it to keep the beans submerged. Cover the jar with a plastic lid and set somewhere in your kitchen out of reach of direct sunlight. I keep my ferments on top of my refrigerator.

After 3 days you should see little bubbles rising to the top. Use a fork to pull a bean out and taste it. It should be sour, salty, and crispy, if not let it ferment longer. Keep checking it until they are soured to your liking. For me, this is usually 5 to 7 days. Place the jar into the refrigerator where it will keep for up to 6 months.

Yield: 1 quart

Dilly Radishes

This recipe uses a method of preservation called lacto-fermentation. A salt brine is used to inhibit the growth of unfriendly microorganisms while letting the lactobacilli bacteria normally present on the vegetables flourish and grow. Eating fermented foods daily keeps our digestive system strong and healthy. Serve these tasty radishes with baked salmon and sautéed kale for balanced meal.

1 wide-mouthed quart jar
1 to 2 bunches radishes
¼ cup finely chopped fresh dill
3 cloves garlic, chopped
1 tablespoon red peppercorns
2 cups filtered water
1 to 1 ½ tablespoons sea salt

Rinse the radishes and trim off the ends. Cut into ¼-inch slices, set aside. Place the dill, garlic, and peppercorns at the bottom of the jar. Add enough radish slices to the jar leaving about one inch of space from the top of the jar.

In a small bowl or liquid glass measure, whisk together the filtered water and sea salt. Let it dissolve then pour over the radishes. Don't shake or stir the jar, you want to make sure the dill stays at the bottom, otherwise it can float to the top and mold during the fermentation process.

Press a folded cabbage leaf into the jar so the liquid rise above it and all of the radishes are submerged beneath it. If you need to, add a little extra brine. Cover the jar with a plastic lid and set it somewhere in your kitchen out of reach of direct sunlight. I keep my ferments on top of my refrigerator.

Let it sit for 5 to 10 days. Then remove the cabbage leaf and store in your refrigerator for up to 6 months.

Yield: 1 quart

Pickled Carrots and Cauliflower

This is one of our favorite fermentation recipes. We make a few jars of it c week. In some of the jars we add hot chili peppers and in others we simply add herbs and garlic so our children will eat them. If you grow cauliflower in your garden, this is a fabulous way to preserve it.

1 wide-mouthed quart jar
4 cloves garlic, chopped
1 teaspoon black peppercorns
4 sprigs fresh dill or tarragon
3 to 4 large carrots, finely chopped
2 to 3 cups finely chopped cauliflower
2 cups filtered water
1 to 1 ½ tablespoons sea salt

Place the peppercorns, garlic, and herbs at the bottom of the jar. Add layers of carrots and cauliflower to the jar leaving about one inch of space from the top.

In a small bowl or liquid glass measure, whisk together the filtered water and sea salt. Let it dissolve then pour it over the vegetables they are covered.

Press a folded cabbage leaf into the jar so the liquid rise above it and all of the radishes are submerged beneath it. If you need to, add a little extra water. Cover the jar with a plastic lid and set it somewhere in your kitchen out of reach of direct sunlight. I keep my ferments on top of my refrigerator.

Let it sit for 5 to 10 days. Taste it to see if it has soured (fermented) enough, if not, let it sit a few more days, checking and tasting it daily. Fermentation happens much faster in warmer temperatures so timing can vary widely. Then remove the cabbage leaf and store in your refrigerator for up to 6 months.

Yield: 1 quart

Raw Sour Dill Pickles

This recipe uses a form of fermentation called lacto-fermentation. This is one of the easiest ways to preserve some of the summer harvest. Lactobacilli bacteria normally present on the skins of cucumbers are allowed to grow in a salt brine creating an acidic, sour flavor that is not only tasty but also very beneficial for your gut. I prefer to use small to medium-sized pickling cucumbers. They can be found at your local Farmer's market in the summertime. I also buy them by the case from organic farms. Pickles made this way can be stored in your refrigerator for up to six months!

1 gallon glass jar or ceramic fermenting crock
4 pounds pickling cucumbers
2 to 3 bunches fresh flowering dill
¼ to ½ cup pickling spice
1 to 2 heads garlic, peeled and chopped
2 quarts filtered water
6 tablespoons sea salt
1 fresh grape leaf or sour cherry leaf (optional)

Rinse your gallon jar out with very hot water and set aside. Wash the cucumbers in water and rub them to remove the flowering part if still intact as well as any dirt or debris present. Set aside.

Place the dill, pickling spice, and garlic at the bottom of the jar. Add the pickles until they are a few inches from the top of the jar. In a pitcher, dissolve the salt in the water. Pour over the pickles. If you need more liquid, add a little less than 1 tablespoon of salt per cup of filtered water until the water covers the pickles. You can add a fresh grape leaf if desired: the tannins in the leaf help to keep the pickles crisp, though I never use one and my pickles are always very crispy.

Use another jar lid with a weight or boiled rock to keep the pickles beneath the brine. This is very important! Your pickles will begin to mold if they are exposed to air. This is also why I place the dill, spices, and garlic into the bottom of the jar first. You don't want them floating to the top. A small plastic Ziploc bag filled with water also works. Then cover the jar tightly with the lid and place in an undisturbed spot in your house away from direct sunlight to ferment.

Let them ferment for 1 to 2 weeks, depending on the temperature. If it is very warm in your house they may take less than a week. In the Pacific Northwest, without air conditioning, I let them ferment for close to 2 weeks, sometimes longer. The brine will get cloudy and this is what you want to see. You might find a little scum floating on the top of the brine, which you can just scoop out. Then cover and refrigerate for up to 6 months.

Yield: 1 gallon

Fresh Tomato Basil Marinara Sauce

This recipe is a great way to use up an abundant tomato harvest. Instead of removing the skins and seeds from all of the tomatoes, I simply puree them, making this one of the easiest sauce recipes imaginable! If you want to make a smaller batch you can cut this recipe into thirds. Use about 6 to 7 pounds of tomatoes and one large onion. I like to use a 12-quart or larger pot when making this sauce. This sauce can be frozen in quart jars or canned according to the USDA guidelines.

½ cup extra virgin olive oil
3 large onions, minced
1 whole head garlic, minced
20 pounds fresh tomatoes
½ cup red wine vinegar
2 to 4 tablespoons coconut sugar or honey
2 to 3 tablespoons Italian seasoning
2 tablespoons sea salt
2 to 3 cups packed fresh basil, chopped

Heat a 12-quart or larger stockpot over medium heat. Add the olive oil and then the minced onions and garlic. Sauté for about 10 minutes. Remove the stem-end of the tomatoes. Process some of them in a food processor, leaving them a little chunky. You can also blend the remaining tomatoes until smooth in a blender. Then begin to add the tomatoes to the pot of onions in batches as you puree them. Add the vinegar, sugar, Italian seasoning, and sea salt.

Cook, uncovered, for about 3 to 4 hours or until sauce has cooked down and thickened. Be sure to stir it on occasion and keep it on a rapid simmer. Keep cooking until sauce has thickened to your liking. Taste and add more salt if needed. Stir in the chopped basil and simmer a few minutes more. Pour sauce into clean wide-mouthed quart jars, leaving at least an inch of space from the top. Let cool completely and then place into your freezer without a lid. Once frozen, screw on a lid. For canning, you'll need to sterilize your jars and lids and follow the USDA guidelines for acidity and timing.

Yield: 5 to 6 quarts

Homemade Applesauce

Making your own applesauce is so easy and what better way is there to preserve the apple harvest? Applesauce is best made from sweet apples—you won't need to add any additional sweetener. Galas, Jonagold, Jonathon, Yellow Delicious, and Fuji are all great choices. Use one variety or a combination of a few. If you are not picking your own then buy "seconds" from a local organic farmer. Imperfect apples are cheaper and perfectly suited to be made into applesauce. The sauce can then be frozen or processed in a water bath canner and stored in your pantry for about 2 years.

10 pounds apples, washed
quart or pint jars
food mill

You can make applesauce two different ways. When I first began making my own sauce I didn't have any special equipment. So I peeled and cored all of my apples and canned them in my largest pot at the time, an 8-quart stockpot. Now I have a large canning pot and a food mill, which makes the process go much faster and smoother.

If you don't have a food mill then you will need to core, peel, and chop all of the apples. If you do own one, simply chop the apples—no need to peel or core them.

Add about an inch of water to a heavy-bottomed 8-quart stockpot. Then add the chopped apples. Cover the pot. Turn heat to medium-high. Once apples are boiling, stir, and turn to medium heat. As the apples cook they will release more water. Continue to cook for about 10 to 15 minutes or until apples are cooked through and soft, stirring occasionally.

Next, if you do not own a food mill, then you can put your cooked (and peeled) apples in a food processor or use a potato masher or large slotted spoon to mash up the apples into sauce. Otherwise put the apples through a food mill to remove the skins and seeds and make it into sauce.

Pour into clean, sterilized pint or quart jars to ¼ inch from the top. Wipe off any spills from the top of the jar. Cover with sterilized (boiled) lids. And then carefully, using a jar grabber, set into a pot of boiling water. Process for 15 minutes (pint jars) or 20 minutes (quart jars) at sea level. Add about 5 minutes for every 3000 feet above sea level. If you do not want to can the sauce then you can refrigerate what you will use within 2 weeks and freeze the rest.

Yield: 3 to 4 quarts

Variation:

Add fresh or frozen cranberries to the pot for a beautiful ruby-red sauce that is a little tart and tangy. You can also add pears, peaches, plums, or berries.

Homemade Pumpkin Puree

Making your own pumpkin puree is easy and tastes so much better than pumpkin from a can! You can cook any type of winter squash, but sugar pie pumpkins are by far our favorite. Sugar pie pumpkins can be found at your local health food store or Farmer's Market in autumn. Once you have made your puree you can freeze it to use throughout the year. If you want to can it, you'll need a pressure canner and need to follow guideline posted by the USDA.

one 3 to 4-pound sugar pie pumpkin

Preheat oven to 400 degrees F. Set out a large baking dish with a lid.

Place your pumpkin on a large cutting board and use a heavy-duty, sharp knife to cut it in half cross-wise. Use a large spoon to scoop out the seeds.

Place the seeds into bowl to sort out later and roast if desired. Roasted pumpkin seeds with sea salt and coconut oil are a favorite snack at our house!

Cut the halves into quarters and then eighths. Place the pumpkin pieces into a shallow baking dish, skin-side down, cover with a lid, and roast for about one hour.

Scoop the flesh out and place into a food processor fitted with the "s" blade and process until a smooth puree forms. Scoop the puree into glass jars or storage containers and freeze or refrigerate until ready to use. If you are using a very moist squash you may need to drain off excess water by placing the puree in a fine mesh strainer fitted over a bowl to catch excess water. Let it drain for one to two hours before storing.

Place into a glass jar or container, cover, and refrigerate for up to a week or freeze for a year.

Yield: About 4 cups

Strawberry Lime Jam

We built a three-tiered strawberry bed in our back yard years ago. In it we grow ever-bearing strawberries, or berries that grow from late spring through early October. Most of the harvest comes in during late June and July though. Our children love to run outside every morning and pick what is ripe. This jam recipe is fun to make with what is left from their morning forays in the garden. This jam will last up to two weeks in the refrigerator or for many months in the freezer.

1 pound fresh strawberries, hulled
¼ cup honey
1 tablespoon freshly squeezed lime juice
1 teaspoon lime zest
1 to 1 ½ tablespoons arrowroot powder

Place the hulled strawberries in a food processor fitted with the "s" blade. Pulse the berries until they are ground into a chunky puree.

In a small bowl, whisk together the honey, lime juice, lime zest, and arrowroot. Use more arrowroot if your berries are very juicy, less if they are on the firmer side.

Pour the strawberry puree into a 2-quart saucepan. Add the honey-lime juice mixture. Whisk together. Turn heat to high and bring mixture to a boil; immediately turn heat to medium and continue to simmer for 8 to 10 minutes, stirring frequently, until translucent, thickened, and reduced. The key is to keep stirring so the liquid reduces and forms a jam rather than a sauce.

Jam will remain slightly runny hot off the stove but will solidify once chilled. Pour into one pint-sized jar or two half-pint jars. Cool uncovered in the refrigerator until chilled. Once chilled, place a lid on the jar and store for up to two weeks.

Yield: 16 ounces or 1 pint

Variation:

You can make jam this way using any type of fresh fruit. Replace the lime juice with lemon juice and omit lime zest. Try blueberries, peaches, plums, or cherries. If using blackberries or raspberries there is no need to process them first in a food processor, they will mash on their own during cooking.

Vanilla Plum Butter

Italian plums are one of our favorite fruits to pick. Our children eat them like candy. I can't imagine a more perfect snack food. Once ripe, Italian plums spoil quickly. We like to cut them in half, remove the pits and dehydrate most of them, then freeze the rest. In the midst of freezing and dehydrating, I like to make a few batches of this fruit butter. Unripe apples, which are very high in pectin, help to naturally thicken the butter. There should be plenty of unripe apples available on the trees in your area when plums are in season. Serve plum butter over toast or as part of a nut butter sandwich.

4 cups pureed Italian plums
1 small unripe apple, cored
1 whole vanilla bean
1 cup coconut sugar or Sucanat

Pit the plums, then use your blender or Vita-Mix to blend the plums into a smooth puree. Keep adding plums until the 4-cup mark is reached. Then add the unripe apple pieces and whole vanilla bean; blend again until the apple and vanilla bean are completely pureed.

Pour mixture into a large, wide pot or deep skillet; bring to a boil. Add coconut sugar, whisk together, reduce heat, and simmer for about 10 to 20 minutes, uncovered. Be sure to stir it so it doesn't burn on the bottom. Cook until reduced and thickened. Once it cools it will thicken even more.

Fill sterilized jam jars to ¼-inch of the top. Cover with sterilized lids. Place into a boiling water bath canner for 10 minutes. Add 1 minute for every 1000 feet above sea level. If you do not want to can them, place the jars into the refrigerator where they will last for about 3 weeks. You can also freeze the cooled plum butter in small jars.

Yield: 4 cups or four 8-ounce jam jars

Sun Dried Tomatoes

Making true "sun-dried" tomatoes can be done in a very dry, hot climate in the summertime such as in parts of the southwest and west. Here in the Northwest it is far too moist to dry anything out in the open so we need use a food dehydrator. Roma tomatoes work best for this recipe because of their low moisture content. Dried tomatoes can be rehydrated with hot water to make tomato sauce or pizza sauce. They are great added to soups that will be pureed. I also use them to make savory crackers and biscuits.

10 pounds ripe Roma tomatoes
sea salt

You will need a food dehydrator with at least 5 trays. Cut the tomatoes in half and arrange them face up on each sheet so they are not touching each other. This provides enough airflow to properly dehydrate the tomatoes. Sprinkle them with a little sea salt.

Dehydrate for 12 to 48 hours at 130 degrees. Timing depends on size and moisture content of the tomatoes. They should feel leathery when done with no soft mushy spots anywhere on the piece. I check each piece as I place them into the jar. If some are underdone, simply leave those pieces to dehydrate a few hours longer.

Store in a tightly sealed glass jar for up to a year in a cool, dark place. We store our dehydrated fruit and vegetables in the back of our pantry.

Yield: 4 to 5 cups

Kale-Herb Seaweed Sprinkle

This is a good way to use up extra kale growing in your garden. We have so much sometimes we don't know what to do with it all and have to call in friends to take some of it away—of course, they don't mind at all! Dehydrating kale is a fantastic way to preserve it. Use this sprinkle over popcorn, soup, stew, mashed potatoes, steamed vegetables, grilled fish, or fresh salads.

1 bunch kale
2 to 4 tablespoons kelp granules
1 tablespoon dried dill
1 tablespoon dried rosemary

If your kale has any bugs on it you can wash them off and spin the leaves dry in a salad spinner. Then remove the thick inner rib that runs up each leaf. Then tear the kale into pieces. Place the pieces into about 3 to 4 racks of your food dehydrator and set the temperature to 118 degrees F. Dehydrate until dry and crispy, about 3 to 6 hours.

After the kale is fully dehydrated, place it into your food processor fitted with the "s" blade. Add the remaining ingredients and process until you have a finely ground powdery mixture. Carefully pour into a glass jar and close tightly with a lid. Store in a cool dark place for up to a year.

Yield: Approximately ½ cup

Variation:

Add any combination of dried herbs you have on hand. Dried thyme, chives, parsley, garlic powder, onions granules, or chili flakes would all work.

Nutrition Tip:

Kelp, like many sea vegetables, is a concentrated source of iodine, which is needed to produce the thyroid hormones, T3 and T4. Thyroid hormones are composed of a tyrosine amino acid attached to either three or four iodine molecules, so it is absolutely essential that we consume enough iodine in our diet to produce enough thyroid hormones. These hormones regulate our metabolism, which regulates our body temperature, body weight, and energy production. Did you know every single cell in the body has a receptor for thyroid hormones? People with food sensitivities often have elevated autoantibodies to their thyroid gland. If you have food sensitivities and low thyroid function, you might want to consider having your thyroid autoantibodies tested.

Appendix

Resources
and Recommendations

Alternative Sweeteners

Coconut Sugar
Essential Living Foods
www.essentiallivingfoods.com

Coconut Nectar
Coconut Secret
www.coconutsecret.com

Maple Syrup Grade B
Coombs
www.coombsfamilyfarms.com

Stevia
Sweet Leaf Liquid Stevia
www.sweetleaf.com

Oils

Organic Extra Virgin Olive Oil
Napa Valley Naturals
www.worldpantry.com

Virgin Coconut Oil
Nutiva
www.nutiva.com

Organic Palm Shortening
Spectrum
www.spectrumorganics.com

Gluten-Free Flours

Coconut Flour
Bob's Red Mill
www.bobsredmill.com

Blanched Almond flour
Lucy's Kitchen Shop
www.lucyskitchenshop.com

Organic Blanched Almond flour
Benefit Your Life
www.benefityourlife.com

Almond Meal
Bob's Red Mill
www.bobsredmill.com

Hazelnut Meal
Bob's Red Mill
www.bobsredmill.com

Organic GF Cornmeal
Arrowhead Mills
www.arrowheadmills.com

Gluten-Free Whole Grain Flours
Bob's Red Mill
www.bobsredmill.com

Organic Sorghum Flour
Buffalo Valley Grains
www.fieldsofgrain.com

Sprouted Gluten-Free Flours
To Your Health Sprouted Flour Co.
www.organicsproutedflour.net

Teff Flour
The Teff Company
www.teffco.com

Superfine Flours
Authentic Foods
www.authenticfoods.com

Arrowroot Powder
Bob's Red Mill
www.bobsredmill.com

Nut & Seed Butters

Raw Sprouted Nut and Seed Butters
Better Than Roasted
www.bluemountainorganics.com

Sunflower Seed Butter
Organic Sunbutter
www.sunbutter.com

Organic Almond Butter
Zinke Orchards
www.zinkeorchards.com

Organic Peanut Butter
Santa Cruz Organics
www.scojuice.com

Non-Dairy Milks

Coconut Milk
Native Forest Organic
www.edwardandsons.com

Meat

Pastured Meats
Tropical Traditions
www.tropicaltraditions.com

Whole Grains

Organic Gluten-Free Whole Grains
Bob's Red Mill
www.bobsredmill.com

Sea Vegetables

Organic Nori
Sound Sea Vegetables

Kombu, Hijiki, Arame
Eden Foods
www.edenfoods.com

Salts & Seasonings

Herbamare
A. Vogel
www.avogel.com

Sea Salt
Real Salt
www.realsalt.com

Coconut Aminos
Coconut Secret
www.coconutsecret.com

Wheat-Free Tamari
San-J
www.san-j.com

Food Buying

Bulk Natural Foods
Azure Standard
www.azurestandard.com

Food Buying Clubs
UNFI
www.unitedbuyingclubs.com

Farmer's Markets
Local Harvest
www.localharvest.com

Food Co-ops
Co-op Directory Service
www.coopdirectory.org

References

Introduction

CDC website for Autism Spectrum Disorders. Data and Statistics. Retrieved March 20, 2012, from http://www.cdc.gov/ncbddd/autism/index.html

Branum AM, Lukacs SL. (Oct 10, 2008). Food Allergy Among U.S. Children: Trends in Prevalence and Hospitalizations. NCHS Data Brief Number 10. Retrieved February 16, 2012, from http://www.cdc.gov/nchs/data/databriefs/db10.htm

CDC Diabetes Public Health Resource website. 2011 National Diabetes Fact Sheet. Retrieved on February 16, 2012, from http://www.cdc.gov/diabetes/pubs/factsheet11.htm

CDC Attention-Deficit/Hyperactivity Disorder (ADHD) website. Data and Statistics. Retrieved on February 16, 2012, from, http://www.cdc.gov/NCBDDD/adhd/data.html

Why Whole Foods?

Demmig-Adams B, Adams WW 3rd. Antioxidants in photosynthesis and human nutrition. Science. 2002 Dec 13;298(5601):2149-53. PMID: 12481128

Subbiah MT. Understanding the nutrigenomic definitions and concepts at the food-genome junction. OMICS. 2008 Dec;12(4):229-35. PMID: 18687041

Hanhineva K, Törrönen R, Bondia-Pons I, et al. Impact of dietary polyphenols on carbohydrate metabolism. Int J Mol Sci. 2010 Mar 31;11(4):1365-402. PMID: 20480025

Hardy TM, Tollefsbol TO. Epigenetic diet: impact on the epigenome and cancer. Epigenomics. 2011 Aug;3(4):503-18. PMID: 22022340

Javierre BM, Hernando H, Ballestar E. Environmental triggers and epigenetic deregulation in autoimmune disease. Discov Med. 2011 Dec;12(67):535-45. PMID: 22204770

Barbeau WE. What is the key environmental trigger in type 1 diabetes - Is it viruses, or wheat gluten, or both? Autoimmun Rev. 2012 May 22. [Epub ahead of print] PMID: 22633932

Masala S, Paccagnini D, Cossu D, et al. Antibodies recognizing Mycobacterium avium paratuberculosis epitopes cross-react with the beta-cell antigen ZnT8 in Sardinian type 1 diabetic patients. PLoS One. 2011;6(10):e26931. Epub 2011 Oct 27. PMID: 22046415

Abhilash M, Sauganth Paul MV, Varghese MV, et al. Long-term consumption of aspartame and brain antioxidant defense status. Drug Chem Toxicol. 2012 Mar 2. [Epub ahead of print] PMID: 22385158

Abdel-Salam OM, Salem NA, Hussein JS. Effect of aspartame on oxidative stress and monoamine neurotransmitter levels in lipopolysaccharide-treated mice. Neurotox Res. 2012 Apr;21(3):245-55. PMID: 21822758

Pisarik P, Kai D. Vestibulocochlear toxicity in a pair of siblings 15 years apart secondary to aspartame: two case reports. Cases J. 2009 Sep 15;2:9237. PMID: 20181217

Rommens CM, Shakya R, Heap M, et al. Tastier and healthier alternatives to French fries. J Food Sci. 2010 May;75(4):H109-15. PMID: 20546404

Roberts HJ. (Jan 7, 2004) Aspartame Disease: An FDA-Approved Epidemic. Mercola.com. Retrieved on January 11, 2012, from http://articles.mercola.com/sites/articles/archive/2004/01/07/aspartame-disease-part-two.aspx

Ellis WG. Uncured rice as a cause of Beriberi. Br Med J. 1909 Oct 2;2(2544):935. PMID: 20764688

Lanou AJ, Svenson B. Reduced cancer risk in vegetarians: an analysis of recent reports. Cancer Manag Res. 2010 Dec 20;3:1-8. PMID: 21407994

Crinnion WJ. Organic foods contain higher levels of certain nutrients, lower levels of pesticides, and may provide health benefits for the consumer. Altern Med Rev. 2010 Apr;15(1):4-12. Review. PMID: 20359265

Roberts EM, English PB, Grether JK, et al. Maternal residence near agricultural pesticide applications and autism spectrum disorders among children in the California Central Valley. Environ Health Perspect. 2007 Oct;115(10):1482-9. PMID: 17938740

Rauh V, Arunajadai S, Horton M, et al. Seven-year neurodevelopmental scores and prenatal exposure to chlorpyrifos, a common agricultural pesticide. Environ Health Perspect. 2011 Aug;119(8):1196-201. PMID: 21507777

Bouchard MF, Chevrier J, Harley KG, et al. Prenatal exposure to organophosphate pesticides and IQ in 7-year-old children. Environ Health Perspect. 2011 Aug;119(8):1189-95. PMID: 21507776

Engel SM, Wetmur J, Chen J, et al. Prenatal exposure to organophosphates, paraoxonase 1, and cognitive development in childhood. Environ Health Perspect. 2011 Aug;119(8):1182-8. PMID: 21507778

Eskenazi B, Rosas LG, Marks AR, et al. Pesticide toxicity and the developing brain. Basic Clin Pharmacol Toxicol. 2008 Feb;102(2):228-36. Pesticide toxicity and the developing brain. PMID: 18226078

Rosas LG, Eskenazi B. Pesticides and child neurodevelopment. Curr Opin Pediatr. 2008 Apr;20(2):191-7. PMID: 18332717

Why Gluten-Free?

Volta U, De Giorgio R. New understanding of gluten sensitivity. Nat Rev Gastroenterol Hepatol. 2012 Feb 28;9(5):295-9. PMID: 22371218

Di Sabatino A, Corazza GR. Nonceliac gluten sensitivity: sense or sensibility? Ann Intern Med. 2012 Feb 21;156(4):309-11. PMID: 22351716

Sapone A, Bai JC, Ciacci C, Dolinsek J, et al. Spectrum of gluten-related disorders: consensus on new nomenclature and classification. BMC Med. 2012 Feb 7;10:13. PMID: 22313950

Hollén E, Högberg L, Stenhammar L, et al. Antibodies to oat prolamines (avenins) in children with coeliac disease. Scand J Gastroenterol. 2003 Jul;38(7):742-6. PMID: 12889560

Drago S, El Asmar R, Di Pierro M, et al. Gliadin, zonulin and gut permeability: Effects on celiac and non-celiac intestinal mucosa and intestinal cell lines. Scand J Gastroenterol. 2006 Apr;41(4):408-19. PMID: 16635908

García-Manzanares A, Lucendo AJ. Nutritional and dietary aspects of celiac disease. Nutr Clin Pract. 2011 Apr;26(2):163-73. PMID: 21447770

Visser J, Rozing J, Sapone A, et al. Tight junctions, intestinal permeability, and autoimmunity: celiac disease and type 1 diabetes paradigms. Ann N Y Acad Sci. 2009 May;1165:195-205. PMID: 19538307

Malterre T. Digestive and nutritional considerations in celiac disease: could supplementation help? Altern Med Rev. 2009 Sep;14(3):247-57. PMID: 19803549

Rostami K, Steegers EA, Wong WY, et al. Coeliac disease and reproductive disorders: a neglected association. Eur J Obstet Gynecol Reprod Biol. 2001 Jun;96(2):146-9. PMID: 11384797

Hwang C, Ross V, Mahadevan U. Micronutrient deficiencies in inflammatory bowel disease: From A to zinc. Inflamm Bowel Dis. 2012 Apr 5. PMID: 22488830

Gimenez MS, Oliveros LB, Gomez NN. Nutritional deficiencies and phospholipid metabolism. Int J Mol Sci. 2011;12(4):2408-33. PMID: 21731449

Alvarez-Jubete L, Arendt EK, Gallagher E. Nutritive value and chemical composition of pseudocereals as gluten-free ingredients. Int J Food Sci Nutr. 2009;60 Suppl 4:240-57. PMID: 19462323

Why the Rise in Food Allergies and Sensitivities?

Gruzieva O, Bellander T, Eneroth K, et al. Traffic-related air pollution and development of allergic sensitization in children during the first 8 years of life. J Allergy Clin Immunol. 2012 Jan;129(1):240-6. Epub 2011 Nov 21. PMID: 22104609

Genuis SJ, Sears M, Schwalfenberg G, et al. Incorporating environmental health in clinical medicine. J Environ Public Health. 2012;2012:103041. Epub 2012 May 17. PMID: 22675371

Genuis SJ. What's out there making us sick? J Environ Public Health. 2012;2012:605137. Epub 2011 Oct 24. PMID: 22262979

Genuis SJ. Sensitivity-related illness: the escalating pandemic of allergy, food intolerance and chemical sensitivity. Sci Total Environ. 2010 Nov 15;408(24):6047-61. PMID:20920818

Uddin R, Huda NH. Arsenic poisoning in bangladesh. Oman Med J. 2011 May;26(3):207. PMID: 22043419

Daley CA, Abbott A, Doyle PS, et al. A review of fatty acid profiles and antioxidant content in grass-fed and grain-fed beef. Nutr J. 2010 Mar 10;9:10. Review. PMID: 20219103

Aljada A, Mohanty P, Ghanim H, et al. Increase in intranuclear nuclear factor kappaB and decrease in inhibitor kappaB in mononuclear cells after a mixed meal: evidence for a proinflammatory effect. Am J Clin Nutr. 2004 Apr;79(4):682-90. PMID: 15051615

Demmig-Adams B, Adams WW 3rd. Antioxidants in photosynthesis and human nutrition. Science. 2002 Dec 13;298(5601):2149-53. PMID: 12481128

Cotter PD, Stanton C, Ross RP, et al. The impact of antibiotics on the gut microbiota as revealed by high throughput DNA sequencing. Discov Med. 2012 Mar;13(70):193-9. PMID: 22463795

Pistiner M, Gold DR, Abdulkerim H, et al. Birth by cesarean section, allergic rhinitis, and allergic sensitization among children with a parental history of atopy. J Allergy Clin Immunol. 2008 Aug;122(2):274-9. PMID: 18571710

Turpin W, Humblot C, Thomas M, et al. Lactobacilli as multifaceted probiotics with poorly disclosed molecular mechanisms. Int J Food Microbiol. 2010 Oct 15;143(3):87-102. PMID: 20801536

Liu AH. Hygiene theory and allergy and asthma prevention. Paediatr Perinat Epidemiol. 2007 Nov;21 Suppl 3:2-7. PMID: 17935569

Aris A, Leblanc S. Maternal and fetal exposure to pesticides associated to genetically modified foods in Eastern Townships of Quebec, Canada. Reprod Toxicol. 2011 May;31(4):528-33. PMID: 21338670

de Vendômois JS, Roullier F, Cellier D, et al. A comparison of the effects of three GM corn varieties on mammalian health. Int J Biol Sci. 2009 Dec 10;5(7):706-26. PMID: 20011136

Dean, A., Armstron, J. (May 8, 2009). Genetically Modified Foods, American Academy of Environmental Medicine Position Paper. http://aaemonline.org/gmopost.html

7 Ways to Help your Child Thrive!

Peraza MA, Ayala-Fierro F, Barber DS, et al. Effects of micronutrients on metal toxicity. Environ Health Perspect. 1998 Feb;106 Suppl 1:203-16. PMID: 9539014

Binns HJ, Brumberg HL, Forman JA, et al. Chemical-management policy: prioritizing children's health. Pediatrics. 2011 May;127(5):983-90. PMID: 21518722

Johnston M, Landers S, Noble L, et al. Breastfeeding and the use of human milk. Pediatrics. 2012 Mar;129(3):e827-41. PMID: 22371471

Dufault R, Schnoll R, Lukiw WJ, et al. Mercury exposure, nutritional deficiencies and metabolic disruptions may affect learning in children. Behav Brain Funct. 2009 Oct 27;5:44. PMID: 19860886

Nourishing Your Growing Child

Dovey TM, Staples PA, Gibson EL, et al. Food neophobia and 'picky/fussy' eating in children: a review. Appetite. 2008 Mar-May;50(2-3):181-93. PMID: 17997196

Mennella JA, Jagnow CP, Beauchamp GK. Prenatal and postnatal flavor learning by human infants. Pediatrics. 2001 Jun;107(6):E88. PMID: 11389286

Varendi H, Porter RH, Winberg J. Attractiveness of amniotic fluid odor: evidence of prenatal olfactory learning? Acta Paediatr. 1996 Oct;85(10):1223-7. PMID: 8922088

Forestell CA, Mennella JA. Early determinants of fruit and vegetable acceptance. Pediatrics. 2007 Dec;120(6):1247-54. PMID: 18055673

Disantis KI, Collins BN, Fisher JO, et al. Do infants fed directly from the breast have improved appetite regulation and slower growth during early childhood compared with infants fed from a bottle? Int J Behav Nutr Phys Act. 2011 Aug 17;8:89. PMID: 21849028

Sevenhuysen GP, Holodinsky C, Dawes C. Development of salivary alpha-amylase in infants from birth to 5 months. Am J Clin Nutr. 1984 Apr;39(4):584-8. PMID: 6608871

Clifford SM, Bunker AM, Jacobsen JR, et al. Age and gender specific pediatric reference intervals for aldolase, amylase, ceruloplasmin, creatine kinase, pancreatic amylase, prealbumin, and uric acid. Clin Chim Acta. 2011 Apr 11;412(9-10):788-90. PMID: 21238443

Sawasdivorn S, Taeviriyakul S. Are infants exclusively breastfed up to 6 months of age at risk of anemia? J Med Assoc Thai. 2011 Aug;94 Suppl 3:S178-82. PMID: 22043773

Georgieff MK. Nutrition and the developing brain: nutrient priorities and measurement. Am J Clin Nutr. 2007 Feb;85(2):614S-620S. PMID: 17284765

Fiese BH, Schwartz M. Reclaiming The Family Table: Mealtimes and Child Health and Wellbeing. Social Policy Report. 2008. Vol 22, Number 4. Retrieved on April 24, 2011, from http://www.yaleruddcenter.org/resources/upload/docs/what/reports/ReclaimingFamilyTable.pdf

Pearson N, Biddle SJ, Gorely T. Family correlates of fruit and vegetable consumption in children and adolescents: a systematic review. Public Health Nutr. 2009 Feb;12(2):267-83. PMID: 18559129

Shibuya-Saruta H, Kasahara Y, Hashimoto Y. Human serum dipeptidyl peptidase IV (DPPIV) and its unique properties. J Clin Lab Anal. 1996;10(6):435-40. PMID: 8951616

Shattock P, Whiteley P. Biochemical aspects in autism spectrum disorders: updating the opioid-excess theory and presenting new opportunities for biomedical intervention. Expert Opin Ther Targets. 2002 Apr;6(2):175-83. PMID: 12223079

Grant EC.Developmental dyslexia and zinc deficiency. Lancet. 2004 Jul 17-23;364(9430):247-8. PMID: 15262100

Hambidge M. Human zinc deficiency. J Nutr. 2000 May;130(5S Suppl):1344S-9S. PMID: 10801941

Dórea JG. Zinc deficiency in nursing infants. J Am Coll Nutr. 2002 Apr;21(2):84-7. PMID: 11999547

Caulfield LE, Zavaleta N, Shankar AH, et al. Potential contribution of maternal zinc supplementation during pregnancy to maternal and child survival. Am J Clin Nutr. 1998 Aug;68(2 Suppl):499S-508S. PMID: 9701168

Wiklund I, Norman M, Uvnäs-Moberg K, et al. Epidural analgesia: breast-feeding success and related factors. Midwifery. 2009 Apr;25(2):e31-8. PMID: 17980469

Scott KD, Klaus PH, Klaus MH. The obstetrical and postpartum benefits of continuous support during childbirth. J Womens Health Gend Based Med. 1999 Dec;8(10):1257-64. PMID: 10643833

Johnston M, Landers S, Noble L, et al. Breastfeeding and the use of human milk. Pediatrics. 2012 Mar;129(3):e827-41. PMID: 22371471

Jantscher-Krenn E, Bode L. Human milk oligosaccharides and their potential benefits for the breast-fed neonate. Minerva Pediatr. 2012 Feb;64(1):83-99. PMID: 22350049

Gao Y, Zhang J, Wang C, et al. [Fatty acid composition of mature human milk in three regions of China]. Wei Sheng Yan Jiu. 2011 Nov;40(6):731-4. PMID: 22279667 [Article in Chinese]

Uriu-Adams JY, Keen CL. Zinc and reproduction: effects of zinc deficiency on prenatal and early postnatal development. Birth Defects Res B Dev Reprod Toxicol. 2010 Aug;89(4):313-25. PMID: 20803691

King JC. Determinants of maternal zinc status during pregnancy. Am J Clin Nutr. 2000 May;71(5 Suppl):1334S-43S. PMID: 10799411

Yasuda H, Yoshida K, Yasuda Y, et al. Infantile zinc deficiency: association with autism spectrum disorders. Sci Rep. 2011;1:129. Epub 2011 Nov 3. PMID 22355646

Grant EC. Developmental dyslexia and zinc deficiency. Lancet. 2004 Jul 17-23;364(9430):247-8. PMID: 15262100

Botero-López JE, Araya M, Parada A, et al. Micronutrient deficiencies in patients with typical and atypical celiac disease. J Pediatr Gastroenterol Nutr. 2011 Sep;53(3):265-70. PMID: 21865972

Holick MF. Vitamin D deficiency. N Engl J Med. 2007 Jul 19;357(3):266-81. PMID: 17634462

Thorne-Lyman A, Fawzi WW. Vitamin D During Pregnancy and Maternal, Neonatal and Infant Health Outcomes: A Systematic Review and Meta-analysis. Paediatr Perinat Epidemiol. 2012 Jul;26 Suppl 1:75-90. PMID: 22742603

Wei SQ, Audibert F, Hidiroglou N, et al. Longitudinal vitamin D status in pregnancy and the risk of pre-eclampsia. BJOG. 2012 Jun;119(7):832-9. PMID: 22462640

Hollis BW, Wagner CL. Vitamin D and Pregnancy: Skeletal Effects, Nonskeletal Effects, and Birth Outcomes. Calcif Tissue Int. 2012 May 24. [Epub ahead of print] PMID: 22623177

Hollis BW. Vitamin D requirement during pregnancy and lactation. J Bone Miner Res. 2007 Dec;22 Suppl 2:V39-44. PMID: 18290720

Cannell JJ, Vieth R, Willett W, et al. Cod liver oil, vitamin A toxicity, frequent respiratory infections, and the vitamin D deficiency epidemic. Ann Otol Rhinol Laryngol. 2008 Nov;117(11):864-70. PMID: 19102134

Vermeer C. Vitamin K: the effect on health beyond coagulation - an overview. Food Nutr Res. 2012;56. PMID: 22489224

Houston M. The role of magnesium in hypertension and cardiovascular disease. J Clin Hypertens (Greenwich). 2011 Nov;13(11):843-7. PMID: 22051430

Chacko SA, Sul J, Song Y, et al. Magnesium supplementation, metabolic and inflammatory markers, and global genomic and proteomic profiling: a randomized, double-blind, controlled, crossover trial in overweight individuals. Am J Clin Nutr. 2011 Feb;93(2):463-73. PMID: 21159786

Zhang Q, Ananth CV, Li Z, et al. Maternal anaemia and preterm birth: a prospective cohort study. Int J Epidemiol. 2009 Oct;38(5):1380-9. PMID: 19578127

Allen LH. Anemia and iron deficiency: effects on pregnancy outcome. Am J Clin Nutr. 2000 May;71(5 Suppl): 1280S-4S. PMID: 10799402

Scholl TO. Iron status during pregnancy: setting the stage for mother and infant. Am J Clin Nutr. 2005 May;81(5):1218S-1222S. PMID: 15883455

Skeaff SA. Iodine deficiency in pregnancy: the effect on neurodevelopment in the child. Nutrients. 2011 Feb;3(2):265-73. PMID: 22254096

Zimmermann MB. Iodine deficiency in pregnancy and the effects of maternal iodine supplementation on the offspring: a review. Am J Clin Nutr. 2009 Feb;89(2):668S-72S. PMID: 19088150

Vermiglio F, Lo Presti VP, Moleti M, et al. Attention deficit and hyperactivity disorders in the offspring of mothers exposed to mild-moderate iodine deficiency: a possible novel iodine deficiency disorder in developed countries. J Clin Endocrinol Metab. 2004 Dec;89(12):6054-60. PMID: 15579758

Higdon J. (2002). Updated by Drake VJ (2007). The OSU Linus Pauling Institute website. Micronutrient Information Center. Retrieved on January 19, 2012, from http://lpi.oregonstate.edu/infocenter/vitamins/fa/

Scholl TO, Johnson WG. Folic acid: influence on the outcome of pregnancy. Am J Clin Nutr. 2000 May;71(5 Suppl):1295S-303S. PMID: 10799405

Villamor E, Rifas-Shiman SL, Gillman MW, et al. Maternal intake of methyl-donor nutrients and child cognition at 3 years of age. Paediatr Perinat Epidemiol. 2012 Jul;26(4):328-35. PMID: 22686384

Untersmayr E, Bakos N, Schöll I, et al. Anti-ulcer drugs promote IgE formation toward dietary antigens in adult patients. FASEB J. 2005 Apr;19(6):656-8. Epub 2005 Jan 25. PMID: 15671152

Packing a Healthy Lunchbox

Turner L, Chaloupka FJ. Slow Progress in Changing the School Food Environment: Nationally Representative Results from Public and Private Elementary Schools. J Acad Nutr Diet. 2012 Jun 4. [Epub ahead of print] PMID: 22673797

McGray D. A revolution in school lunches. Getting kids to want to eat healthy food isn't easy. Serving wholesome fare at fast-food prices is even harder. How Revolution Foods is helping school cafeterias swear off frozen pizza and fries. Time. 2010 Apr 26;175(16):50-3. PMID: 20429247

References

Getting Started

Daley CA, Abbott A, Doyle PS, et al. A review of fatty acid profiles and antioxidant content in grass-fed and grain-fed beef. Nutr J. 2010 Mar 10;9:10. PMID: 20219103

Manning, R. (April/May 2009). The Amazing Benefits of Grass-fed Meat. Mother Earth News. Retrieved Dec 12, 2011, from http://www.motherearthnews.com/Sustainable-Farming/Grass-Fed-Meat-Benefits.aspx

Alterman, T. (Oct 15, 2008). Relish blog. Eggciting News!!! Mother Earth News. Retrieved on Nov 19, 2011, from http://www.motherearthnews.com/Relish/Pastured-Eggs-Vitamin-D-Content.aspx

Ebbeling CB, Swain JF, Feldman HA, et al. Effects of dietary composition on energy expenditure during weight-loss maintenance. JAMA. 2012 Jun 27;307(24):2627-34. PMID: 22735432

Datta N, Hayes MG, Deeth HC, et al. Significance of frictional heating for effects of high pressure homogenisation on milk. J Dairy Res. 2005 Nov;72(4):393-9. PMID: 16223453

Michalski MC, Januel C. Does homogenization affect the human health properties of cow's milk? Trends Food Sci Tech 2006 Aug;17(8):423-37.

Lee SJ, Sherbon JW. Chemical changes in bovine milk fat globule membrane caused by heat treatment and homogenization of whole milk. J Dairy Res. 2002 Nov;69(4):555-67. PMID: 12463693

Bhatnagar S, Aggarwal R. Lactose intolerance. BMJ. 2007 Jun 30;334(7608):1331-2. PMID: 17599979

Macdonald LE, Brett J, Kelton D, et al. A systematic review and meta-analysis of the effects of pasteurization on milk vitamins, and evidence for raw milk consumption and other health-related outcomes. J Food Prot. 2011 Nov;74(11):1814-32. PMID: 18588554

Roth-Walter F, Berin MC, Arnaboldi P, et al. Pasteurization of milk proteins promotes allergic sensitization by enhancing uptake through Peyer's patches. Allergy. 2008 Jul;63(7):882-90. PMID: 18588554

Gregory JF 3rd. Denaturation of the folacin-binding protein in pasteurized milk products. J Nutr. 1982 Jul;112(7):1329-38. PMID: 7097350

Haug A, Høstmark AT, Harstad OM. Bovine milk in human nutrition--a review. Lipids Health Dis. 2007 Sep 25;6:25. PMID: 17894873

Kilshaw PJ, Heppell LM, Ford JE. Effects of heat treatment of cow's milk and whey on the nutritional quality and antigenic properties. Arch Dis Child. 1982 Nov;57(11):842-7. PMID: 6983327

Perkin MR. Unpasteurized milk: health or hazard? Clin Exp Allergy. 2007 May;37(5):627-30. PMID: 17456210

Said HM, Ong DE, Shingleton JL. Intestinal uptake of retinol: enhancement by bovine milk beta-lactoglobulin. Am J Clin Nutr. 1989 Apr;49(4):690-4. PMID: 2929489

Shah NP. Effects of milk-derived bioactives: an overview. Br J Nutr. 2000 Nov;84 Suppl 1:S3-10. PMID: 11242440

Urbano G, López-Jurado M, Aranda P, et al. The role of phytic acid in legumes: antinutrient or beneficial function? J Physiol Biochem. 2000 Sep;56(3):283-94. PMID: 11198165

Ibrahim SS, Habiba RA, Shatta AA, et al. Effect of soaking, germination, cooking and fermentation on antinutritional factors in cowpeas. Nahrung. 2002 Apr;46(2):92-5. PMID: 12017999

Mensah P, Tomkins A. Household-level technologies to improve the availability and preparation of adequate and safe complementary foods. Food Nutr Bull. 2003 Mar;24(1):104-25. PMID: 12664529

Han JR, Deng B, Sun J, et al. Effects of dietary medium-chain triglyceride on weight loss and insulin sensitivity in a group of moderately overweight free-living type 2 diabetic Chinese subjects. Metabolism. 2007 Jul;56(7):985-91. PMID: 17570262

Kasai M, Nosaka N, Maki H, et al. Effect of dietary medium- and long-chain triacylglycerols (MLCT) on accumulation of body fat in healthy humans. Asia Pac J Clin Nutr. 2003;12(2):151-60. PMID: 12810404

St-Onge MP, Bosarge A. Weight-loss diet that includes consumption of medium-chain triacylglycerol oil leads to a greater rate of weight and fat mass loss than does olive oil. Am J Clin Nutr. 2008 Mar;87(3):621-6. PMID: 18326600

Smoothies

Lacombe A, Wu VC, White J, et al. The antimicrobial properties of the lowbush blueberry (Vaccinium angustifolium) fractional components against foodborne pathogens and the conservation of probiotic Lactobacillus rhamnosus. Food Microbiol. 2012 May;30(1):124-31. PMID: 22265292

Vendrame S, Guglielmetti S, Riso P, et al. Six-week consumption of a wild blueberry powder drink increases bifidobacteria in the human gut. J Agric Food Chem. 2011 Dec 28;59(24):12815-20. PMID: 22060186

Wang SY, Chen CT, Sciarappa W, et al. Fruit quality, antioxidant capacity, and flavonoid content of organically and conventionally grown blueberries. J Agric Food Chem. 2008 Jul 23;56(14):5788-94. PMID: 18590274

Lohachoompol V, Srzednicki G, Craske J. The Change of Total Anthocyanins in Blueberries and Their Antioxidant Effect After Drying and Freezing. J Biomed Biotechnol. 2004;2004(5):248-252. PMID: 15577185

Müller D, Schantz M, Richling E. High Performance Liquid Chromatography Analysis of Anthocyanins in Bilberries (Vaccinium myrtillus L.), Blueberries (Vaccinium corymbosum L.), and Corresponding Juices. J Food Sci. 2012 Apr;77(4):C340-5. PMID: 22394068

Dunjic BS, Svensson I, Axelson J, et al. Green banana protection of gastric mucosa against experimentally induced injuries in rats. A multicomponent mechanism?. Scand J Gastroenterol 1993 Oct;28(10):894-8. PMID: 8266018

Hills BA, Kirwood CA. Surfactant approach to the gastric mucosal barrier: Protection of rats by banana even when acidified. Gastroenterology 1989;97:294-303. 1 PMID: 2744353

Rabbani GH, Teka T, Saha SK, et al. Green banana and pectin improve small intestinal permeability and reduce fluid loss in Bangladeshi children with persistent diarrhea. Dig Dis Sci. 2004 Mar;49(3):475-84. PMID:15139502.

Thurnham DI, Northrop-Clewes CA, McCullough FS, et al. Innate immunity, gut integrity, and vitamin A in Gambian and Indian infants. J Infect Dis. 2000 Sep;182 Suppl 1:S23-8. PMID: 10944481

Krajka-Kuźniak V, Szaefer H, Ignatowicz E, et al. Beetroot juice protects against N-nitrosodiethylamine-induced liver injury in rats. Food Chem Toxicol. 2012 Jun;50(6):2027-33. PMID: 22465004

Jin F, Nieman DC, Sha W, et al. Supplementation of Milled Chia Seeds Increases Plasma ALA and EPA in Postmenopausal Women. Plant Foods Hum Nutr. 2012 Jun;67(2):105-10. PMID: 22538527

Kensler TW, Egner PA, Agyeman AS, et al. Keap1-Nrf2 Signaling: A Target for Cancer Prevention by Sulforaphane. Top Curr Chem. 2012 Jul 3. [Epub ahead of print] PMID: 22752583

McCann JC, Ames BN. Vitamin K, an example of triage theory: is micronutrient inadequacy linked to diseases of aging? Am J Clin Nutr. 2009 Oct;90(4):889-907. PMID: 19692494

Breakfast

de Castro JM. The time of day of food intake influences overall intake in humans.

J Nutr. 2004 Jan;134(1):104-11. PMID: 14704301

Keim NL, Van Loan MD, Horn WF, et al. Weight loss is greater with consumption of large morning meals and fat-free mass is preserved with large evening meals in women on a controlled weight reduction regimen. J Nutr. 1997 Jan;127(1):75-82. PMID: 9040548

USDA SR-21 Nutrient Data (2010). "Nutrition Facts for Seeds, chia seeds, dried" Nutrition Data. Retrieved Nov 11, 2010.

Sharafetdinov KhKh, Gapparov MM, Plotnikova OA, et al. [Influence of breads with use of barley, buckwheat and oat flours and barley flakes on postprandial glycaemia in patients with type 2 diabetes mellitus]. Vopr Pitan. 2009;78(4):40-6. PMID: 19999818 [Article in Russian]

Li SQ, Zhang QH. Advances in the development of functional foods from buckwheat. Crit Rev Food Sci Nutr. 2001 Sep;41(6):451-64. PMID: 11592684

Jensen HH, Batres-Marquez SP, Carriquiry A, et al. Choline in the diets of the US population: NHANES, 2003-2004. The FASEB Journal 2007;21:lb219.

Egli I, Davidsson L, Juillerat MA, et al. Phytic Acid Degradation in Complementary Foods Using Phytase Naturally Occurring in Whole Grain Cereals. J Food Sci 2003 June 68;5:1855-59

Fernandes AA, Novelli EL, Okoshi K, et al. Influence of rutin treatment on biochemical alterations in experimental diabetes. Biomed Pharmacother. 2010 Mar;64(3):214-9. PMID: 19932588

Li L, Seeram NP. Further investigation into maple syrup yields 3 new lignans, a new phenylpropanoid, and 26 other phytochemicals. J Agric Food Chem. 2011 Jul 27;59(14):7708-16. PMID: 21675726

Breads and Muffins

Kasim S, Moriarty KJ, Liston R. Nonresponsive celiac disease due to inhaled gluten. N Engl J Med. 2007 Jun 14;356(24):2548-9. PMID: 17568042

Vuksan V, Whitham D, Sievenpiper JL, et al. Supplementation of conventional therapy with the novel grain Salba (Salvia hispanica L.) improves major and emerging cardiovascular risk factors in type 2 diabetes: results of a randomized controlled trial. Diabetes Care. 2007 Nov;30(11):2804-10. PMID: 17686832

Skrabanja V, Liljeberg Elmstahl HG, Kreft I, et al. Nutritional properties of starch in buckwheat products: studies in vitro and in vivo. Agric Food Chem 2001 Jan;49(1):490-6. PMID: 11170616

Kawa JM, Taylor CG, Przybylski R. Buckwheat concentrate reduces serum glucose in streptozotocin-diabetic rats. J Agric Food Chem. 2003 Dec 3; 51(25): 7287-91. PMID: 14640572

Middleton E, Kandaswami C. Effects of flavonoids on immune and inflammatory cell functions. Biochem Pharmacol 1992;43(6):1167-1179. PMID: 1562270

Gabrovska D, Fiedlerova V, Holasova M et al. The nutritional evaluation of underutilized cereals and buckwheat. Food Nutr Bull 2002 Sep;23(3 Suppl):246-9. PMID: 12362805

Alvarez P, Alvarado C, Puerto M, et al. Improvement of leukocyte functions in prematurely aging mice after five weeks of diet supplementation with polyphenol-rich cereals. Nutrition. 2006 Sep;22(9):913-21. PMID: 16809023

Soups and Stews

Siebecker, A. (Feb/March 2005). Traditional Bone Broths in Modern Health and Disease. Townsend Letter for Doctors and Patients. Retrieved on Oct 18, 2011, from http://www.townsendletter.com/FebMarch2005/broth0205.htm

Klentrou P, Cieslak T, MacNeil M, et al. Effect of moderate exercise on salivary immunoglobulin A and infection risk in humans. Eur J Appl Physiol. 2002 Jun;87(2):153-8. PMID: 12070626

Gleeson M, McDonald WA, Pyne DB, et al. Salivary IgA levels and infection risk in elite swimmers. Med Sci Sports Exerc 1999, 31:67-73. PMID: 9927012

Jeong SC, Koyyalamudi SR, Pang G. Dietary intake of Agaricus bisporus white button mushroom accelerates salivary immunoglobulin A secretion in healthy volunteers. Nutrition. 2012 May;28(5):527-31. PMID: 22113068

Hernández-Salazar M, Osorio-Diaz P, Loarca-Piña G et al. In vitro fermentability and antioxidant capacity of the indigestible fraction of cooked black beans (Phaseolus vulgaris L.), lentils (Lens culinaris L.) and chickpeas (Cicer arietinum L.). J Sci Food Agric. 2010 Jul;90(9):1417-22. 2010. PMID: 20549791

Environmental Working Group. (March 2007). EWG Research. A Survey of Bisphenol A in U.S. Canned Foods. Retrieved on Nov 11, 2011, from http://www.ewg.org/reports/bisphenola

Salads and Vegetables

Chainy GB, Manna SK, Chaturvedi MM, et al. Anethole blocks both early and late cellular responses transduced by tumor necrosis factor: effect on NF-kappaB, AP-1, JNK, MAPKK and apoptosis. Oncogene 2000 Jun 8;19(25):2943-50. 2000. PMID:12930.

Lu QY, Zhang Y, Wang Y, et al. California Hass Avocado: Profiling of Carotenoids, Tocopherol, Fatty Acid, and Fat Content During Maturation and From Different Growing Areas. J Agric Food Chem. 2009; 57.10408-13. PMID: 19813713

USDA Agricultural Research Service. (Modified April 8, 2005). Phytonutrient FAQ's. Retrieved on Sept 22,

2011, from http://www.ars.usda.gov/aboutus/docs.htm?docid=4142

Morrow, M., Morrow, R. (Aug 11, 2010) California Avocado Commission. California Avocado Aommission Spreads the Word on Avocado Nutrition. Retreived on Nov 9, 2011, from http://www.avocado.org/california-avocado-commission-spreads-the-word-on-avocado-nutrition/

Aga M, Iwaki K, Ueda Y, et al. Preventive effect of Coriandrum sativum (Chinese parsley) on localized lead deposition in ICR mice. J Ethnopharmacol. 2001 Oct;77(2-3):203-8. PMID: 11535365

Zava TT, Zava DT. Assessment of Japanese iodine intake based on seaweed consumption in Japan: A literature-based analysis. Thyroid Res. 2011 Oct 5;4:14. PMID: 21975053

D'Orazio N, Gemello E, Gammone MA, et al. Fucoxantin: a treasure from the sea. Mar Drugs. 2012 Mar;10(3):604-16. PMID 22611357

Thompson CA, Habermann TM, Wang AH, et al. Antioxidant intake from fruits, vegetables and other sources and risk of non-Hodgkin's lymphoma: the Iowa Women's Health Study. Int J Cancer. 2010 Feb 15;126(4):992-1003. PMID: 19685491

Kijlstra A, Tian Y, Kelly ER, et al. Lutein: More than just a filter for blue light. Prog Retin Eye Res. 2012 Jul;31(4):303-15. PMID: 22465791

Morris MC, Evans DA, Tangney CC, et al. Associations of vegetable and fruit consumption with age-related cognitive change. Neurology. 2006 Oct 24;67(8):1370-6. PMID: 17060562

Park WT, Kim JK, Park S, et al. Metabolic Profiling of Glucosinolates, Anthocyanins, Carotenoids, and Other Secondary Metabolites in Kohlrabi (Brassica oleracea var. gongylodes).J Agric Food Chem. 2012 Jun 28. [Epub ahead of print] PMID: 22742768

Dinkova-Kostova AT. Chemoprotection Against Cancer by Isothiocyanates: A Focus on the Animal Models and the Protective Mechanisms. Top Curr Chem. 2012 Jul 3. [Epub ahead of print] PMID: 22752581

Ryan E, Galvin K, O'Connor TP, et al. Fatty acid profile, tocopherol, squalene and phytosterol content of brazil, pecan, pine, pistachio and cashew nuts. Int J Food Sci Nutr. 2006 May-Jun;57(3-4):219-28. PMID: 17127473

Sikora E, Bodziarczyk I. Composition and antioxidant activity of kale (Brassica oleracea L. var. acephala) raw and cooked. Acta Sci Pol Technol Aliment. 2012 Jul 1;11(3):239-48. PMID: 22744944

Keck AS, Finley JW. Cruciferous vegetables: cancer protective mechanisms of glucosinolate hydrolysis products and selenium. Integr Cancer Ther. 2004 Mar;3(1):5-12.

Whole Grains

Hurrell RF, Reddy MB, Juillerat MA, et al. Degradation of phytic acid in cereal porridges improves iron absorption by human subjects. Am J Clin Nutr. 2003 May;77(5):1213-9. PMID: 12716674

Famularo G, De Simone C, Pandey V, et al. Probiotic lactobacilli: an innovative tool to correct the malabsorption syndrome of vegetarians? Med Hypotheses. 2005;65(6):1132-5. Epub 2005 Aug 10. PMID: 16095846

Vucenik I, Shamsuddin AM. Cancer inhibition by inositol hexaphosphate (IP6) and inositol: from laboratory to clinic. J Nutr. 2003 Nov;133(11 Suppl 1):3778S-3784S. PMID: 14608114

Zhang H, Onning G, Oste R, et al. Improved iron bioavailability in an oat-based beverage: the combined effect of citric acid addition, dephytinization and iron supplementation. Eur J Nutr. 2007 Mar;46(2):95-102. PMID: 17225920

Vega-Gálvez A, Miranda M, Vergara J, et al. Nutrition facts and functional potential of quinoa (Chenopodium quinoa willd.), an ancient Andean grain: a review. J Sci Food Agric. 2010 Dec;90(15):2541-7. PMID: 20814881

Brown Rice is Recommended for Breast Cancer. (n.d.). FoodforBreastCancer.com. Retrieval on Feb 20, 2012, from http://foodforbreastcancer.com/foods/brown-rice

Jackson BP, Taylor VF, Karagas MR, et al. Arsenic, organic foods, and brown rice syrup. Environ Health Perspect. 2012 May;120(5):623-6. PMID: 22336149

Cebrian D, Tapia A, Real A, et al. Inositol hexaphosphate: a potential chelating agent for uranium. Radiat Prot Dosimetry. 2007;127(1-4):477-9. PMID: 17627956

Greiner R, Konietzny U, Jany K-D. Phytate - an undesirable constituent of plant-based foods? Journal für Ernährungsmedizin 2006; 8 (3): 18-28

Pallauf J, Rimbach G. Nutritional significance of phytic acid and phytase. Arch Tierernähr. 1997;50(4):301-19. PMID: 9345595

Guallar-Castillón P, Rodríguez-Artalejo F, Tormo MJ, et al. Major dietary patterns and risk of coronary heart disease in middle-aged persons from a Mediterranean country: the EPIC-Spain cohort study. Nutr Metab Cardiovasc Dis. 2012 Mar;22(3):192-9. PMID: 20708394

Thacher TD, Aliu O, Griffin IJ, et al. Meals and dephytinization affect calcium and zinc absorption in Nigerian children with rickets. J Nutr. 2009 May;139(5):926-32. PMID: 19321589

Fretham SJ, Carlson ES, Georgieff MK. The role of iron in learning and memory. Adv Nutr. 2011 Mar;2(2):112-21. PMID: 22332040

Jonnalagadda SS, Harnack L, Liu RH, et al. Putting the Whole Grain Puzzle Together: Health Benefits Associated with Whole Grains—Summary of American Society for Nutrition 2010 Satellite Symposium. J Nutr. 2011 May; 141(5): 1011S–1022S. PMID: 21451131

Topping DL, Clifton PM. Short-chain fatty acids and human colonic function: roles of resistant starch and nonstarch polysaccharides. Physiol Rev. 2001 Jul;81(3):1031-64. PMID: 11427691

Main Meals

Hernández-Ramírez RU, Galván-Portillo MV, Ward MH, et al. Dietary intake of polyphenols, nitrate and nitrite and gastric cancer risk in Mexico City. Int J Cancer. 2009 Sep 15;125(6):1424-30. PMID: 19449378

Kumar V, Sinha AK, Makkar HP, et al. Dietary roles of non-starch polysachharides in human nutrition: a review. Crit Rev Food Sci Nutr. 2012 Oct;52(10):899-935. PMID: 22747080

Riso P, Klimis-Zacas D, Del Bo' C, et al. Effect of a wild blueberry (Vaccinium angustifolium) drink intervention on markers of oxidative stress, inflammation and endothelial function in humans with cardiovascular risk factors. Eur J Nutr. 2012 Jun 26. [Epub ahead of print] PMID: 22733001

Wedick NM, Pan A, Cassidy A, et al. Dietary flavonoid intakes and risk of type 2 diabetes in US men and women. Am J Clin Nutr. 2012 Apr;95(4):925-33. PMID: 22357723

Rhone M, Basu A. Phytochemicals and age-related eye diseases. Nutr Rev. 2008 Aug;66(8):465-72. PMID: 18667008

Hurrell RF, Juillerat MA, Reddy MB, et al. Soy protein, phytate, and iron absorption in humans. Am J Clin Nutr. 1992 Sep;56(3):573-8. PMID: 1503071

Aithal BK, Kumar MR, Rao BN, et al. Juglone, a naphthoquinone from walnut, exerts cytotoxic and genotoxic effects against cultured melanoma tumor cells. Cell Biol Int. 2009 Oct;33(10):1039-49. PMID: 19555758

Vinson JA, Cai Y. Nuts, especially walnuts, have both antioxidant quantity and efficacy and exhibit significant potential health benefits. Food Funct. 2012 Feb;3(2):134-40. PMID: 22187094

Urwin HJ, Miles EA, Noakes PS, et al. Salmon Consumption during Pregnancy Alters Fatty Acid Composition and Secretory IgA Concentration in Human Breast Milk. J Nutr. 2012 Jun 27. [Epub ahead of print] PMID: 22739373

Kiecolt-Glaser JK, Belury MA, Porter K, et al. Depressive Symptoms, omega-6:omega-3 Fatty Acids, and Inflammation in Older Adults. Psychosom Med. 2007 Apr;69(3):217-24. PMID:17401057

Mazza M, Pomponi M, Janiri L, et al. Omega-3 fatty acids and antioxidants in neurological and psychiatric diseases: an overview. Prog Neuropsychopharmacol Biol Psychiatry. 2007 Jan 30;31(1):12-26. PMID:16938373

Chua B, Flood V, Rochtchina E, Wang JJ, et al. Dietary fatty acids and the 5-year incidence of age-related maculopathy. Arch Ophthalmol. 2006 Jul;124(7):981-6. PMID:16832023

Seddon JM, George S, Rosner B. Cigarette smoking, fish consumption, omega-3 fatty acid intake, and associations with age-related macular degeneration: the US Twin Study of Age-Related Macular Degeneration. Arch Ophthalmol. 2006 Jul;124(7):995-1001. PMID:16832023.

Erkkila A, Lichtenstein A, Mozaffarian D, et al. Fish intake is associated with a reduced progression of coronary artery atherosclerosis in postmenopausal women with coronary artery disease. Am J Clin Nutr , Sept. 2004; (80(3):626-32. PMID:15321802

Harris WS, Pottala JV, Sands SA, et al. Comparison of the effects of fish and fish-oil capsules on the n 3 fatty acid content of blood cells and plasma phospholipids. Am J Clin Nutr. 2007 Dec;86(6):1621-5. PMID:18065578.

Caturla N, Funes L, Pérez-Fons L, et al. A randomized, double-blinded, placebo-controlled study of the effect of a combination of lemon verbena extract and fish oil omega-3 fatty acid on joint management. J Altern Complement Med. 2011 Nov;17(11):1051-63. PMID: 22087615

Harris WS, Pottala JV, Sands SA, et al. Comparison of the effects of fish and fish-oil capsules on the n 3 fatty acid content of blood cells and plasma phospholipids. Am J Clin Nutr. 2007 Dec;86(6):1621-5. PMID 18065578

Karimi R, Fitzgerald TP, Fisher NS. A Quantitative Synthesis of Mercury in Commercial Seafood and Implications for Exposure in the U.S. Environ Health Perspect. 2012 Jun 25. [Epub ahead of print] PMID: 22732656

Bernhoft RA. Mercury toxicity and treatment: a review of the literature. J Environ Public Health. 2012;2012:460508. Epub 2011 Dec 22. PMID: 22235210

Lasky T, Sun W, Kadry A,et al. Mean total arsenic concentrations in chicken 1989-2000 and estimated exposures for consumers of chicken. Environ Health Perspect. 2004 Jan;112(1):18-21. PMID: 14698925

Silbergeld EK, Nachman K. The environmental and public health risks associated with arsenical use in animal feeds. Ann N Y Acad Sci. 2008 Oct;1140:346-57. PMID: 18991934

Harris, G., Grady, D. (June 8, 2011). Pfizer Suspends Sales of Chicken Drug With Arsenic. NewYorkTimes.com. Retrieved on March 16, 2012, from http://www.nytimes.com/2011/06/09/business/09arsenic.html?_r=3

Cima G. Drug's sale halted over arsenic concerns. J Am Vet Med Assoc. 2011 Aug 1;239(3):290-1. PMID: 21916049

Wallinga, D. (April 2006) Playing Chicken: Avoiding Arsenic in Your Meat. Institute for Agriculture and Trade Policy. Retrieved on March 16, 2012, from http://www.iatp.org/files/421_2_80529.pdf

Vahter ME. Interactions between arsenic-induced toxicity and nutrition in early life. J Nutr. 2007 Dec;137(12):2798-804. PMID: 18029502

Reviewed by Seidu, L. (May 12, 2012) Allergies and Sulfite Sensitivity. WebMD.com. Retrieved on May 24, 2012, from http://www.webmd.com/allergies/guide/sulfite-sensitivity

Pauling L. Orthomolecular psychiatry. Varying the concentrations of substances normally present in the human body may control mental disease. Science. 1968 Apr 19;160(3825):265-71. PMID: 5641253

Kumar N. Acute and subacute encephalopathies: deficiency states (nutritional). Semin Neurol. 2011 Apr;31(2):169-83. PMID: 21590622

Le Floc'h N, Otten W, Merlot E. Tryptophan metabolism, from nutrition to potential therapeutic applications. Amino Acids. 2011 Nov;41(5):1195-205. PMID: 20872026

Daley CA, Abbott A, Doyle PS, et al. A review of fatty acid profiles and antioxidant content in grass-fed and grain-fed beef. Nutr J. 2010 Mar 10;9:10. PMID: 20219103

Manning, R. (April/May 2009) The Amazing Benefits of Grass-Fed Meat. MotherEarthNews.com. Retrieved on Nov 16, 2011, from http://www.motherearthnews.com/Sustainable-Farming/Grass-Fed-Meat-Benefits.aspx

Dressings, Dips, and Sauces

Victor L. Fulgoni, III, Mark L Dreher, et al. Avocado consumption is associated with better nutrient intake and better health indices in U.S. adults (19+ years): NHANES 2001–2006 FASEB J. April 2010;24 (Meeting Abstract Supplement)lb350

Dailey OD Jr, Wang X, Chen F, et al. Anticancer activity of branched-chain derivatives of oleic acid. Anticancer Res. 2011 Oct;31(10):3165-9. PMID: 21965723

Pauwels EK. The protective effect of the Mediterranean diet: focus on cancer and cardiovascular risk. Med Princ Pract. 2011;20(2):103-11. PMID: 21252562

Ashton OB, Wong M, McGhie TK, et al. Pigments in avocado tissue and oil. J Agric Food Chem. 2006 Dec 27;54(26):10151-8. PMID: 17177553

Kontogianni MD, Panagiotakos DB, Chrysohoou C, et al. The impact of olive oil consumption pattern on the risk of acute coronary syndromes: The CARDIO2000 case-control study. Clin Cardiol. 2007 Mar;30(3):125-9. PMID: 17385704

Masella R, Varì R, D'Archivio M, et al. Extra virgin olive oil biophenols inhibit cell-mediated oxidation of LDL by increasing the mRNA transcription of glutathione-related enzymes. J Nutr. 2004 Apr;134(4):785-91. PMID: 15051826

Covas MI, Nyyssönen K, Poulsen HE, et al. The effect of polyphenols in olive oil on heart disease risk factors: a randomized trial. Ann Intern Med. 2006 Sep 5;145(5):333-41. PMID: 16954359

Ruano J, Lopez-Miranda J, Fuentes F, et al. Phenolic content of virgin olive oil improves ischemic reactive hyperemia in hypercholesterolemic patients. J Am Coll Cardiol. 2005 Nov 15;46(10):1864-8. PMID: 16286173

Wraps and Rolls

Whfoods.com. (n.d.). Pumpkin Seeds. In-depth Nutrient Analysis. Retrieved on January 23, 2012, from http://www.whfoods.com/genpage.php?tname=nutrientprofile&dbid=117

Trumbo P, Yates AA, Schlicker S, et al. Dietary reference intakes: vitamin A, vitamin K, arsenic, boron, chromium, copper, iodine, iron, manganese, molybdenum, nickel, silicon, vanadium, and zinc. J Am Diet Assoc. 2001 Mar;101(3):294-301. PMID: 11269606

Baquer NZ, Sinclair M, Kunjara S, et al. Regulation of glucose utilization and lipogenesis in adipose tissue of diabetic and fat fed animals: effects of insulin and manganese. J Biosci. 2003 Mar;28(2):215-21. PMID: 12711814

Snacks and Treats

Zhang Y. Allyl isothiocyanate as a cancer chemopreventive phytochemical. Mol Nutr Food Res. 2010 Jan;54(1):127-35. PMID: 19960458

Dinkova-Kostova AT. Chemoprotection Against Cancer by Isothiocyanates: A Focus on the Animal Models and the Protective Mechanisms. Top Curr Chem. 2012 Jul 3. [Epub ahead of print] PMID: 22752581

Mauskop A, Varughese J. Why all migraine patients should be treated with magnesium. J Neural Transm. 2012 May;119(5):575-9. PMID: 22426836

Cunha AR, Umbelino B, Correia ML, et al. Magnesium and vascular changes in hypertension. Int J Hypertens. 2012;2012:754250. Epub 2012 Feb 29. PMID: 22518291

USDA. National Nutrient Database for Standard Reference Release 24. (March 30, 2012) Nutrient Data for 12036, Seeds, Sunflower Seed Kernels, Dried. Retrieved on April 16, 2012, from http://ndb.nal.usda.gov/ndb/foods/show/3688

Tucker JM, Townsend DM. Alpha-tocopherol: roles in prevention and therapy of human disease. Biomed Pharmacother. 2005 Aug;59(7):380-7. PMID: 16081238

Wiser J, Alexis NE, Jiang Q, et al. In vivo gamma-tocopherol supplementation decreases systemic oxidative stress and cytokine responses of human monocytes in normal and asthmatic subjects. Free Radic Biol Med. 2008 Jul 1;45(1):40-9. PMID: 18405673

Lee DH, Iwanski GB, Thoennissen NH. Cucurbitacin: ancient compound shedding new light on cancer treatment. ScientificWorldJournal. 2010 Mar 5;10:413-8. PMID: 20209387

Milder IE, Arts IC, van de Putte B, et al. Lignan contents of Dutch plant foods: a database including lariciresinol, pinoresinol, secoisolariciresinol and matairesinol. Br J Nutr. 2005 Mar;93(3):393-402. PMID: 15877880

Ríos JL, Recio MC, Escandell JM, et al. Inhibition of transcription factors by plant-derived compounds and their implications in inflammation and cancer. Curr Pharm Des. 2009;15(11):1212-37. PMID: 19355962

Thoennissen NH, Iwanski GB, Doan NB, et al. Cucurbitacin B induces apoptosis by inhibition of the JAK/STAT pathway and potentiates antiproliferative effects of gemcitabine on pancreatic cancer cells. Cancer Res. 2009 Jul 15;69(14):5876-84. PMID: 19605406

Desserts

Taubs, G. (April 13, 2011). Is Sugar Toxic. NewYorkTimes.com. Retrieved on Dec 14, 2011, from http://www.nytimes.com/2011/04/17/magazine/mag-17Sugar-t.html?pagewanted=all

Cassileth B. Lycium (Lycium barbarum). Oncology (Williston Park). 2010 Dec;24(14):1353. PMID: 21294484

Potterat O. Goji (Lycium barbarum and L. chinense): Phytochemistry, pharmacology and safety in the perspective of traditional uses and recent popularity. Planta Med. 2010 Jan;76(1):7-19. Epub 2009 Oct 20. PMID: 19844860

Gross PM, Zhang R, Zhang X. (2006). Wolfberry: Nature's Bounty of Nutrition and Health. BookSurge Publishing. ISBN 978-1-4196-2048-5

Victor L. Fulgoni, III, Mark L Dreher, et al. Avocado consumption is associated with better nutrient intake and better health indices in U.S. adults (19+ years): NHANES 2001–2006 FASEB J. April 2010;24 (Meeting Abstract Supplement)lb350

Dailey OD Jr, Wang X, Chen F, et al. Anticancer activity of branched-chain derivatives of oleic acid. Anticancer Res. 2011 Oct;31(10):3165-9. PMID: 21965723

Ashton OB, Wong M, McGhie TK, et al. Pigments in avocado tissue and oil. J Agric Food Chem. 2006 Dec 27;54(26):10151-8. PMID: 17177553

Baldwin EA, Bai J, Plotto A, et al. Effect of extraction method on quality of orange juice: hand-squeezed, commercial-fresh squeezed and processed. J Sci Food Agric. 2012 Aug 15;92(10):2029-42. PMID: 22290491

Josse AR, Kendall CW, Augustin LS, et al. Almonds and postprandial glycemia--a dose-response study. Metabolism. 2007 Mar;56(3):400-4. 2007. PMID:17292730

Beverages

Fung TT, Malik V, Rexrode KM, et al. Sweetened beverage consumption and risk of coronary heart disease in women. Am J Clin Nutr. 2009 Apr;89(4):1037-42. PMID: 19211821

de Koning L, Malik VS, Rimm EB, et al. Sugar-sweetened and artificially sweetened beverage consumption and risk of type 2 diabetes in men. Am J Clin Nutr. 2011 Jun;93(6):1321-7. PMID: 21430119

Fowler SP, Williams K, Resendez RG, et al. Fueling the obesity epidemic? Artificially sweetened beverage use and long-term weight gain. Obesity (Silver Spring). 2008 Aug;16(8):1894-900. PMID: 18535548

Bellisle F, Drewnowski A. Intense sweeteners, energy intake and the control of body weight. Eur J Clin Nutr. 2007 Jun;61(6):691-700. PMID: 17299484

Hadisaputro S, Djokomoeljanto RR, Judiono, et al. The effects of oral plain kefir supplementation on proinflammatory cytokine properties of the hyperglycemia wistar rats induced by streptozotocin. Acta Med Indones. 2012 Apr;44(2):100-4. PMID: 22745139

Grice EA, Segre JA. The Human Microbiome: Our Second Genome. Annu Rev Genomics Hum Genet. 2012 Jun 6. [Epub ahead of print] PMID: 22703178

House JD, Neufeld J, Leson G. Evaluating the quality of protein from hemp seed (Cannabis sativa L.) products through the use of the protein digestibility-corrected amino acid score method. J Agric Food Chem. 2010 Nov 24;58(22):11801-7. PMID: 20977230

Matthan NR, Dillard A, Lecker JL, Effects of dietary palmitoleic acid on plasma lipoprotein profile and aortic cholesterol accumulation are similar to those of other unsaturated fatty acids in the F1B golden Syrian hamster. J Nutr. 2009 Feb;139(2):215-21. Erratum in: J Nutr. 2009 Apr;139(4):793. J Nutr. 2010 Feb;140(2):419. PMID: 19106316

Griel AE, Cao Y, Bagshaw DD, et al. A macadamia nut-rich diet reduces total and LDL-cholesterol in mildly hypercholesterolemic men and women. J Nutr. 2008 Apr;138(4):761-7. PMID: 18356332

Borrelli F, Capasso R, Aviello G, et al. Effectiveness and safety of ginger in the treatment of pregnancy-induced nausea and vomiting. Obstet Gynecol. 2005 Apr;105(4):849-56. 2005. PMID: 16135602

Srivastava KC, Mustafa T. Ginger (Zingiber officinale) in rheumatism and musculoskeletal disorders. Med Hypotheses. 1992 Dec;39(4):342-8. PMID: 1494322

Srivastava KC, Mustafa T.Ginger (Zingiber officinale) and rheumatic disorders. Med Hypotheses. 1989 May;29(1):25-8.PMID: 2501634

Törrönen R, Sarkkinen E, Tapola N, et al. Berries modify the postprandial plasma glucose response to sucrose in healthy subjects. Br J Nutr. 2010 Apr;103(8):1094-7. PMID: 19930765

Sesso HD, Gaziano JM, Jenkins DJ, et al. Strawberry intake, lipids, C-reactive protein, and the risk of cardiovascular disease in women. J Am Coll Nutr. 2007 Aug;26(4):303-10. PMID: 17906180

O'Byrne DJ, Devaraj S, Grundy SM, et al. Comparison of the antioxidant effects of Concord grape juice flavonoids alpha-tocopherol on markers of oxidative stress in healthy adults. Am J Clin Nutr. 2002 Dec;76(6):1367-74. PMID: 12450905

Preserving the Harvest

USDA Complete Guide to Home Canning, 2009 revision. National Center for Home Food Preservation website. Retrieved on January 10, 2012, from http://nchfp.uga.edu/publications/publications_usda.html

Four Theives Vinegar. (Last Modification May 11, 2012) Wikipedia.org. Retrieved on October 16, 2011, from http://en.wikipedia.org/wiki/Four_Thieves_Vinegar

Gopalan A, Reuben SC, Ahmed S, et al. The health benefits of blackcurrants. Food Funct. 2012 Jun 6. [Epub ahead of print] PMID: 22673662

Yoshioka M, St-Pierre S, Drapeau V, et al. Effects of red pepper on appetite and energy intake. Br J Nutr. 1999 Aug;82(2):115-23. PMID: 10743483

Yoshioka M, St-Pierre S, Suzuki M, et al. Effects of red pepper added to high-fat and high-carbohydrate meals on energy metabolism and substrate utilization in Japanese women. Br J Nutr. 1998 Dec;80(6):503-10. PMID: 10211048

Zava TT, Zava DT. Assessment of Japanese iodine intake based on seaweed consumption in Japan: A literature-based analysis. Thyroid Res. 2011 Oct 5;4:14. PMID: 21975053

Index

Index

Index

Index

Index

Index

Index

Index